Surprise!
You may be reading the wrong way!

It's true: In keeping with the original Japanese comic format, this book reads from right to left—so action, sound effects, and word balloons are completely reversed. This preserves the orientation of the original artwork—plus, it's fun! Check out the diagram shown here to get the hang of things, and then turn to the other side of the book to get started!

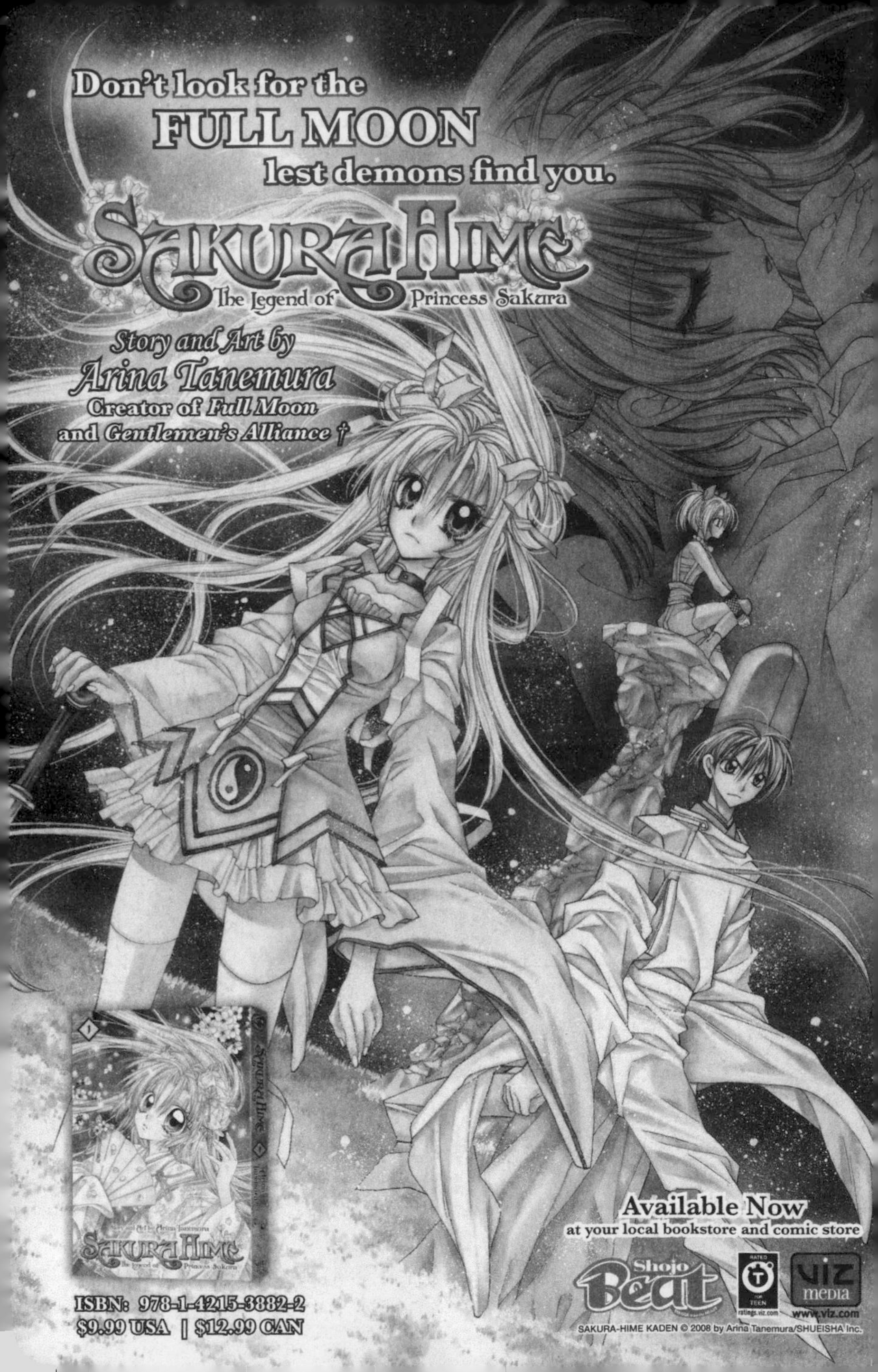
Don't look for the
FULL MOON
lest demons find you.
SAKURA HIME
The Legend of Princess Sakura
Story and Art by
Arina Tanemura
Creator of Full Moon
and Gentlemen's Alliance †
SAKURA HIME
The Legend of Princess Sakura
ISBN: 978-1-4215-3882-2
$9.99 USA | $12.99 CAN
Available Now
at your local bookstore and comic store
Shojo Beat
RATED T TEEN
ratings.viz.com
VIZ media
www.viz.com
SAKURA-HIME KADEN © 2008 by Arina Tanemura/SHUEISHA Inc.

A Devil and Her Love Song

Story & Art by
Miyoshi Tomori

Volume 4

A Devil and Her Love Song

Volume 4
CONTENTS

The devil makes me LOVELY!!!

STORY THUS FAR

Popular Hana Ibuki returns to school after being out sick, and she finds her classmates rebelling against the new girl, Maria. Maria is struggling to lead the class in the upcoming choral competition, so Hana decides to take over and unite the class. Hana also starts plotting to isolate Maria while making herself look good. However, Maria's determination and the growing bond between Maria, Meguro and Yusuke cause Hana's feelings to waver…

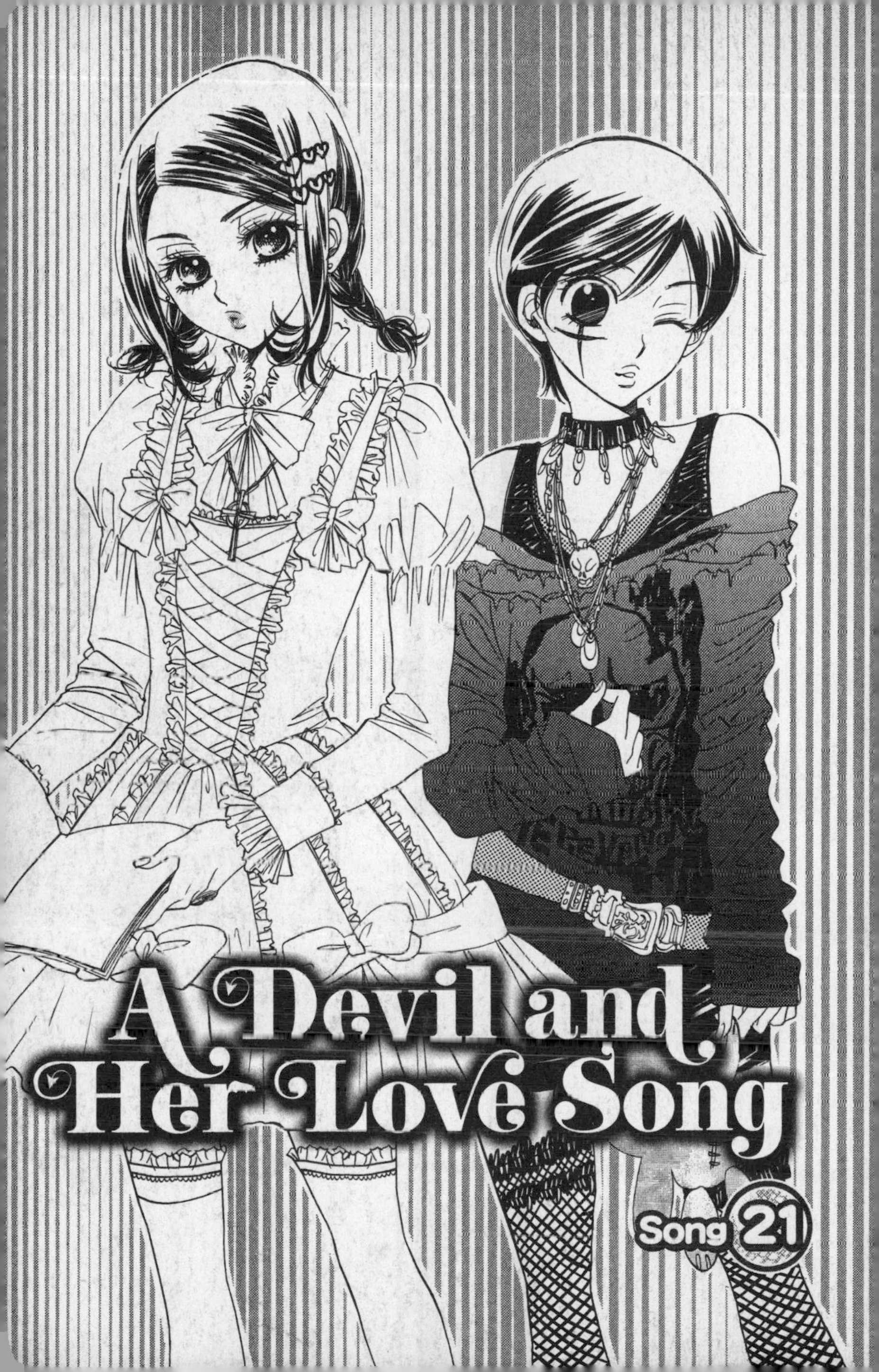
A Devil and
Her Love Song
Song 21

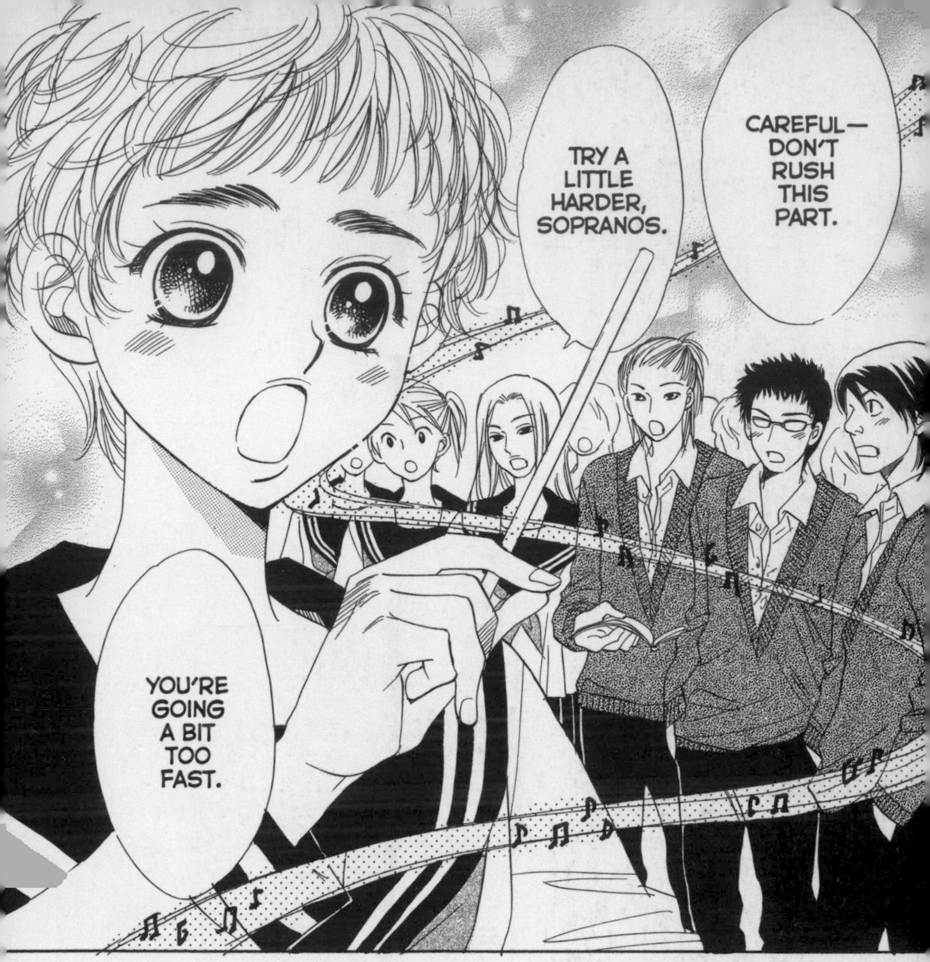
CAREFUL—DON'T RUSH THIS PART.
TRY A LITTLE HARDER, SOPRANOS.
YOU'RE GOING A BIT TOO FAST.

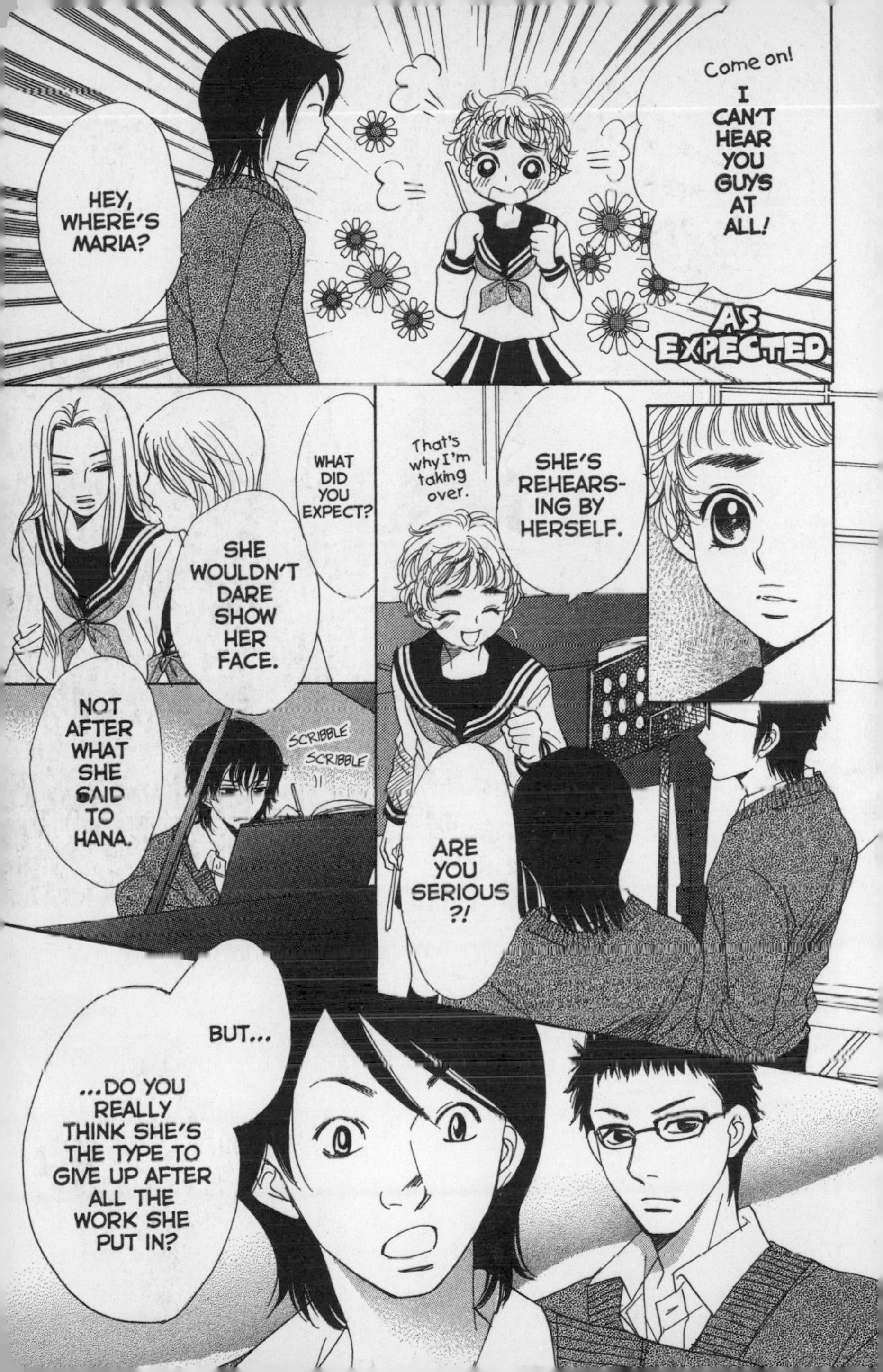

Come on!
I CAN'T HEAR YOU GUYS AT ALL!
AS EXPECTED
HEY, WHERE'S MARIA?
SHE'S REHEARS-ING BY HERSELF.
That's why I'm taking over.
ARE YOU SERIOUS?!
WHAT DID YOU EXPECT?
SHE WOULDN'T DARE SHOW HER FACE.
NOT AFTER WHAT SHE SAID TO HANA.
SCRIBBLE
SCRIBBLE
BUT...
...DO YOU REALLY THINK SHE'S THE TYPE TO GIVE UP AFTER ALL THE WORK SHE PUT IN?

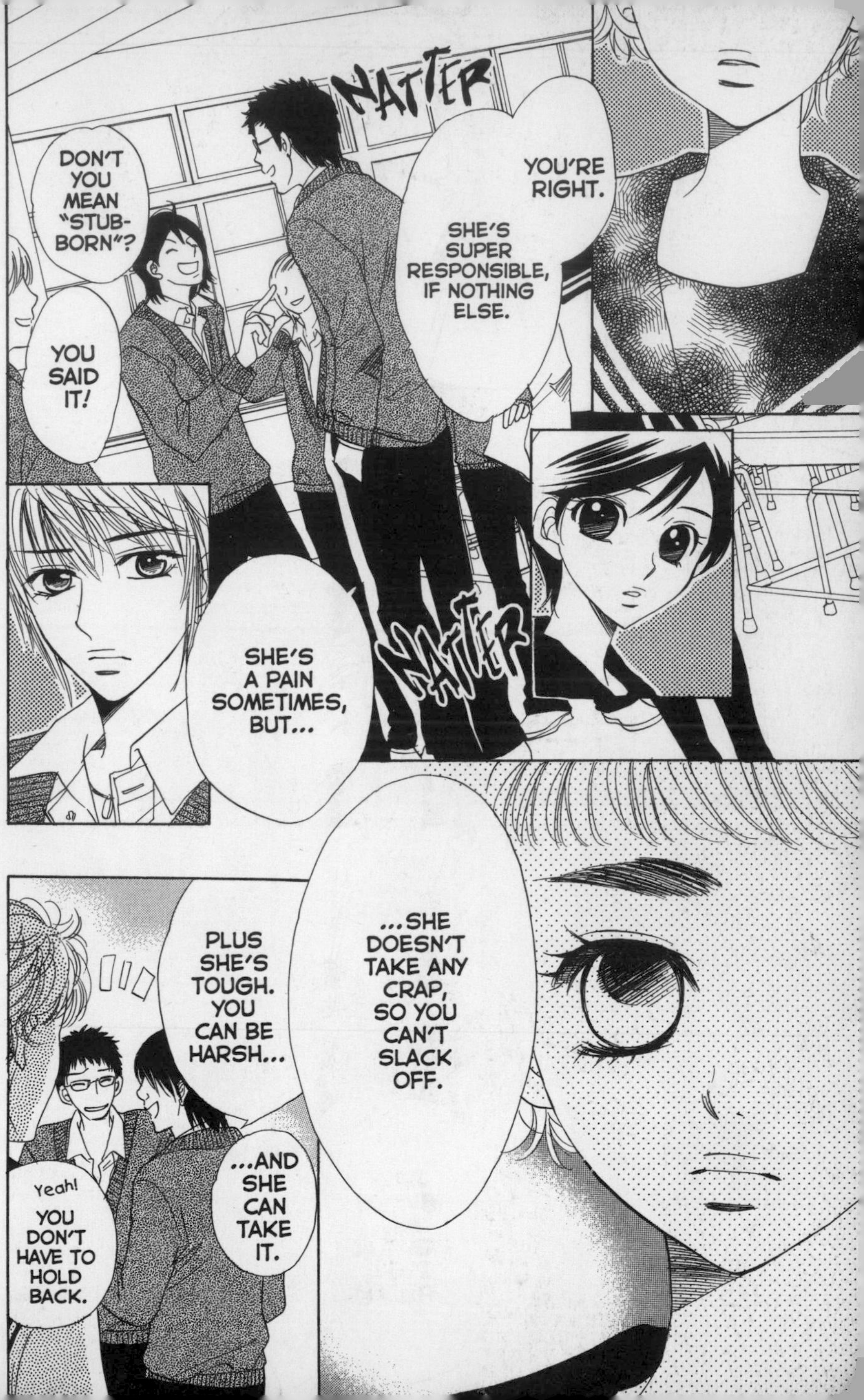
NATTER
YOU'RE RIGHT.
SHE'S SUPER RESPONSIBLE, IF NOTHING ELSE.
DON'T YOU MEAN "STUBBORN"?
YOU SAID IT!
NATTER
SHE'S A PAIN SOMETIMES, BUT...
...SHE DOESN'T TAKE ANY CRAP, SO YOU CAN'T SLACK OFF.
PLUS SHE'S TOUGH. YOU CAN BE HARSH...
...AND SHE CAN TAKE IT.
Yeah!
YOU DON'T HAVE TO HOLD BACK.

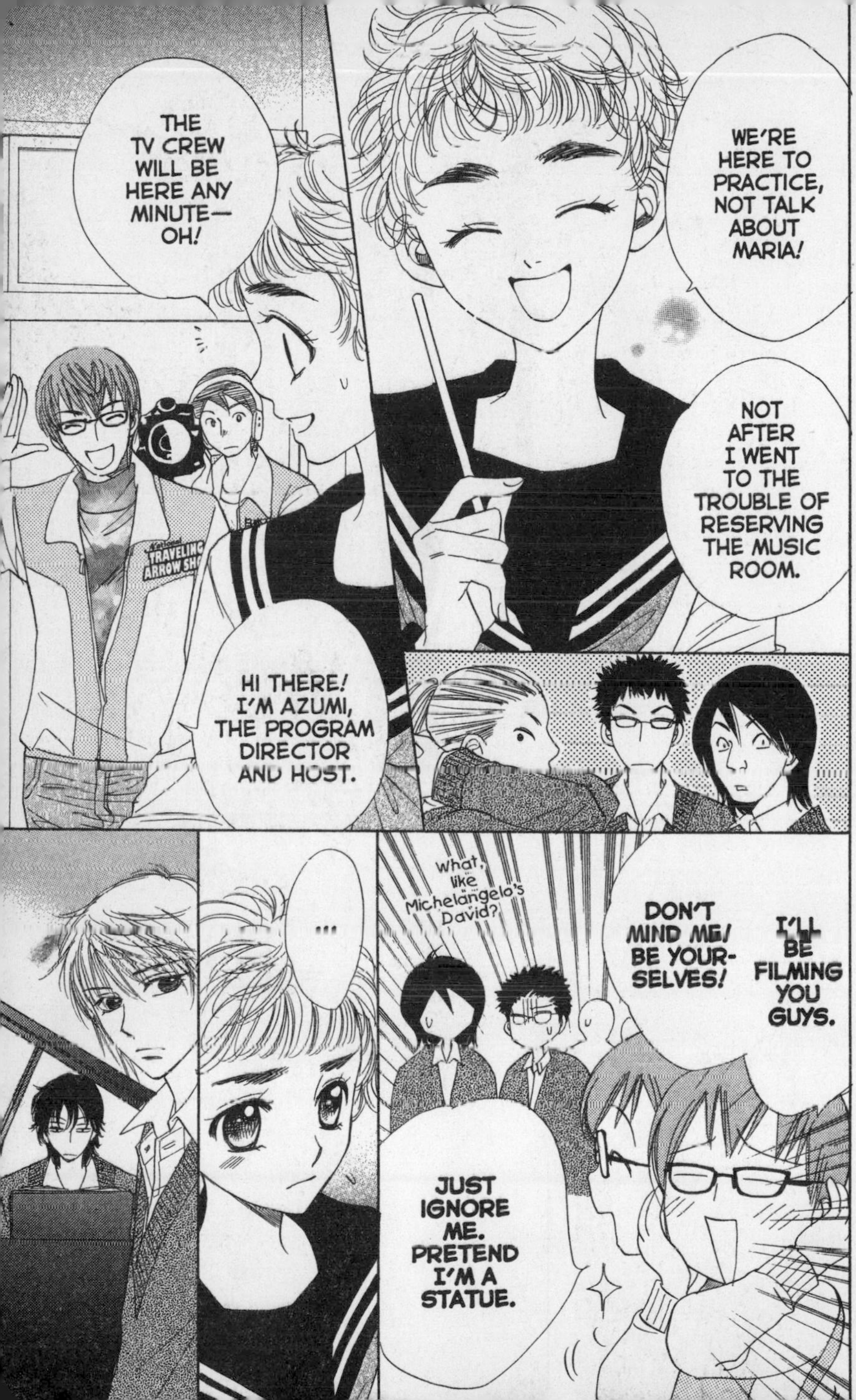

WE'RE HERE TO PRACTICE, NOT TALK ABOUT MARIA!
NOT AFTER I WENT TO THE TROUBLE OF RESERVING THE MUSIC ROOM.
THE TV CREW WILL BE HERE ANY MINUTE—OH!
HI THERE! I'M AZUMI, THE PROGRAM DIRECTOR AND HOST.
DON'T MIND ME! BE YOURSELVES!
I'LL BE FILMING YOU GUYS.
JUST IGNORE ME. PRETEND I'M A STATUE.
What, like Michelangelo's David?
...

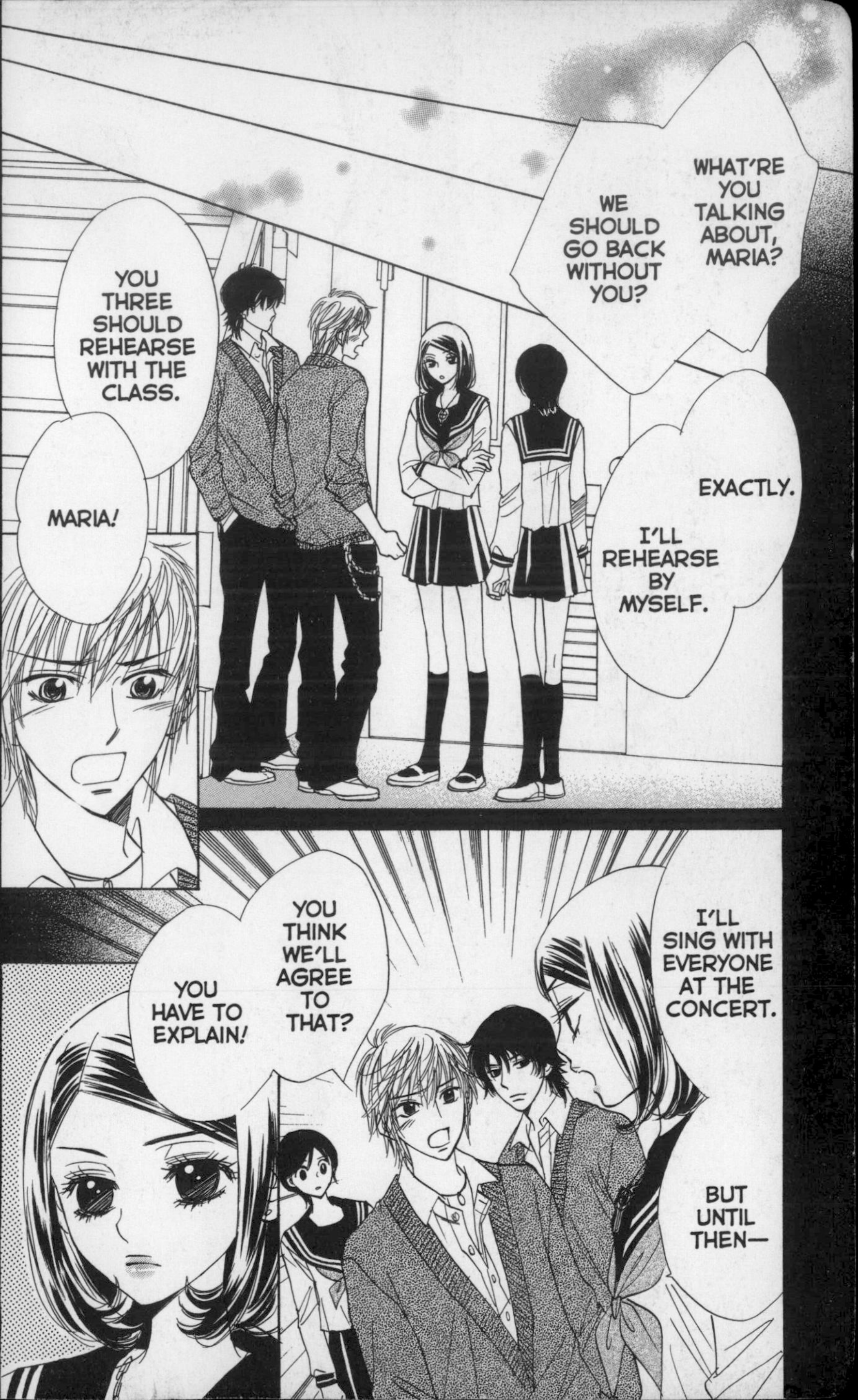
WHAT'RE YOU TALKING ABOUT, MARIA?
WE SHOULD GO BACK WITHOUT YOU?
EXACTLY.
I'LL REHEARSE BY MYSELF.
YOU THREE SHOULD REHEARSE WITH THE CLASS.
MARIA!
I'LL SING WITH EVERYONE AT THE CONCERT.
BUT UNTIL THEN—
YOU THINK WE'LL AGREE TO THAT?
YOU HAVE TO EXPLAIN!

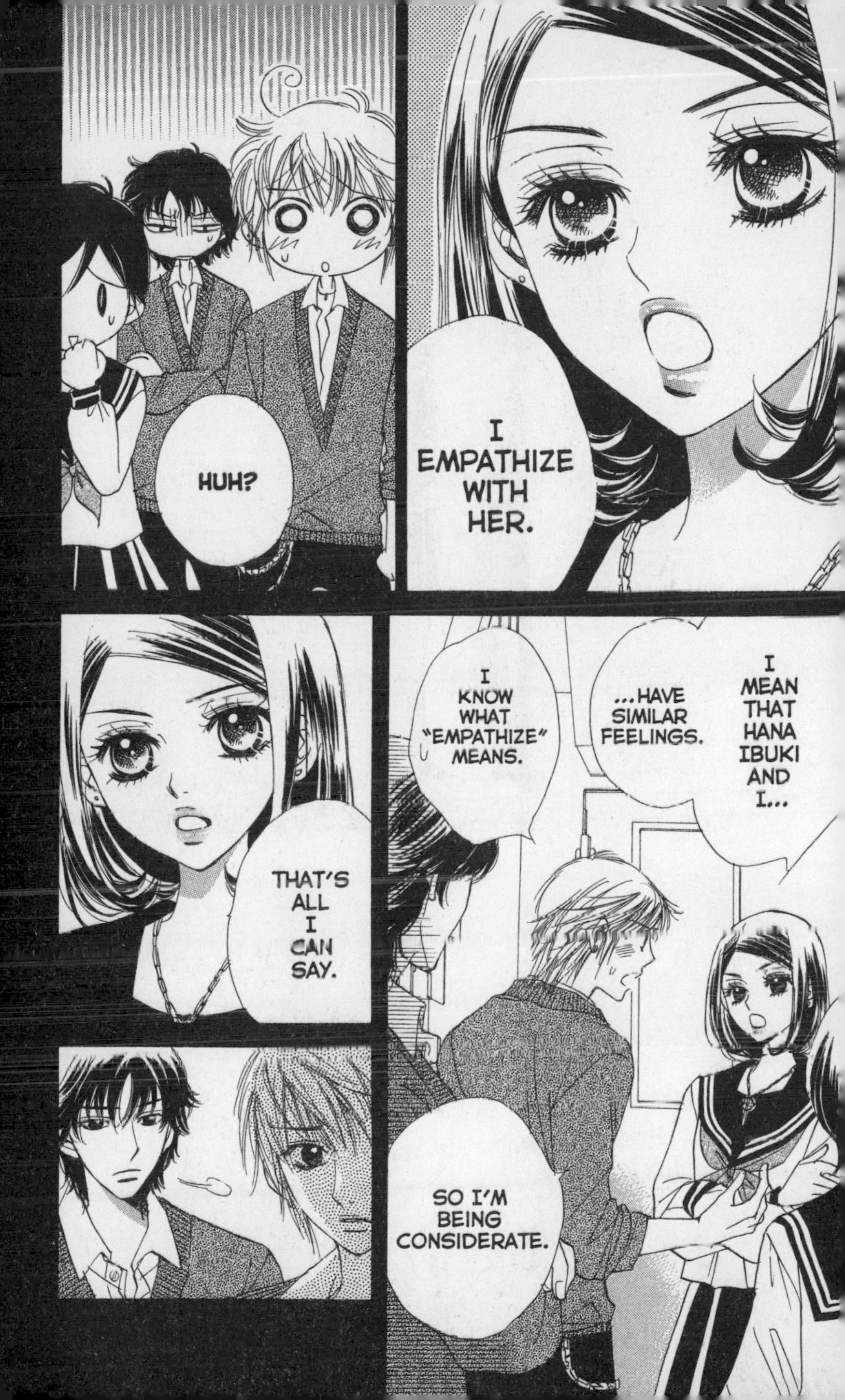
I EMPATHIZE WITH HER.
HUH?
I MEAN THAT HANA IBUKI AND I...
...HAVE SIMILAR FEELINGS.
I KNOW WHAT "EMPATHIZE" MEANS.
SO I'M BEING CONSIDERATE.
THAT'S ALL I CAN SAY.

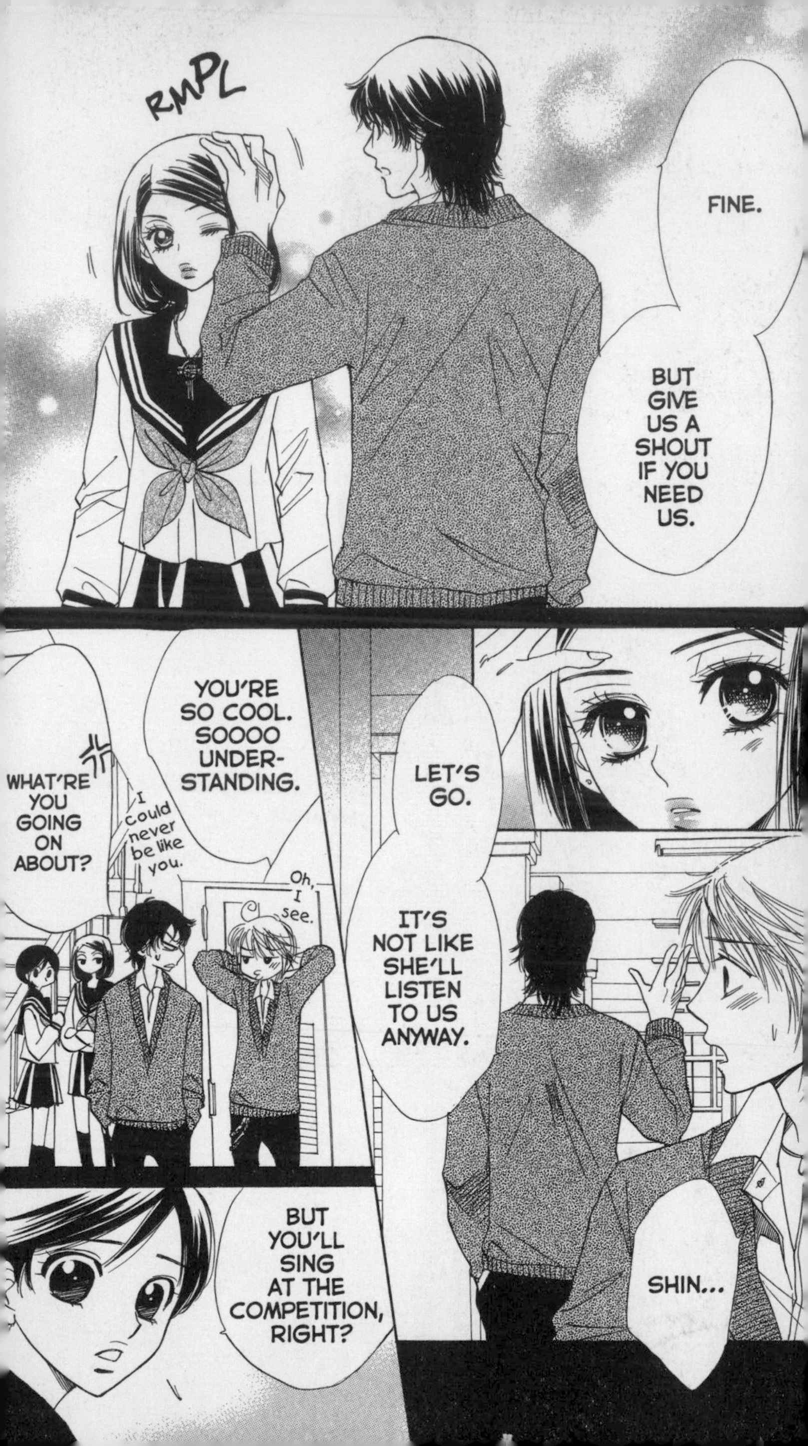
FINE.
BUT GIVE US A SHOUT IF YOU NEED US.
RMPL
LET'S GO.
IT'S NOT LIKE SHE'LL LISTEN TO US ANYWAY.
SHIN...
YOU'RE SO COOL. SOOOO UNDER-STANDING.
I could never be like you.
WHAT'RE YOU GOING ON ABOUT?
Oh, I see.
BUT YOU'LL SING AT THE COMPETITION, RIGHT?

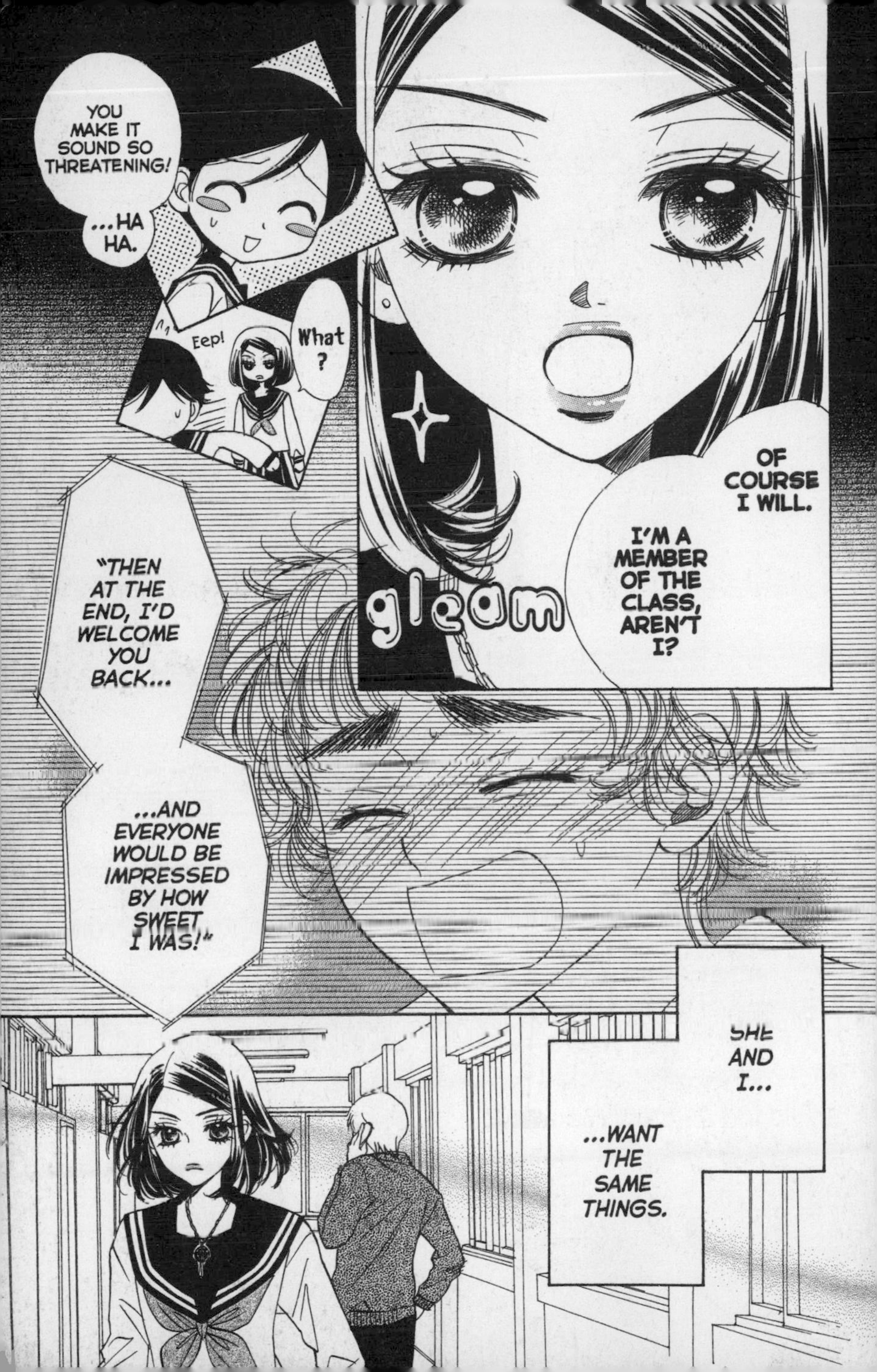
OF COURSE I WILL.
I'M A MEMBER OF THE CLASS, AREN'T I?
gleam
YOU MAKE IT SOUND SO THREATENING!
...HA HA.
What?
Eep!
"THEN AT THE END, I'D WELCOME YOU BACK...
...AND EVERYONE WOULD BE IMPRESSED BY HOW SWEET I WAS!"
SHE AND I...
...WANT THE SAME THINGS.

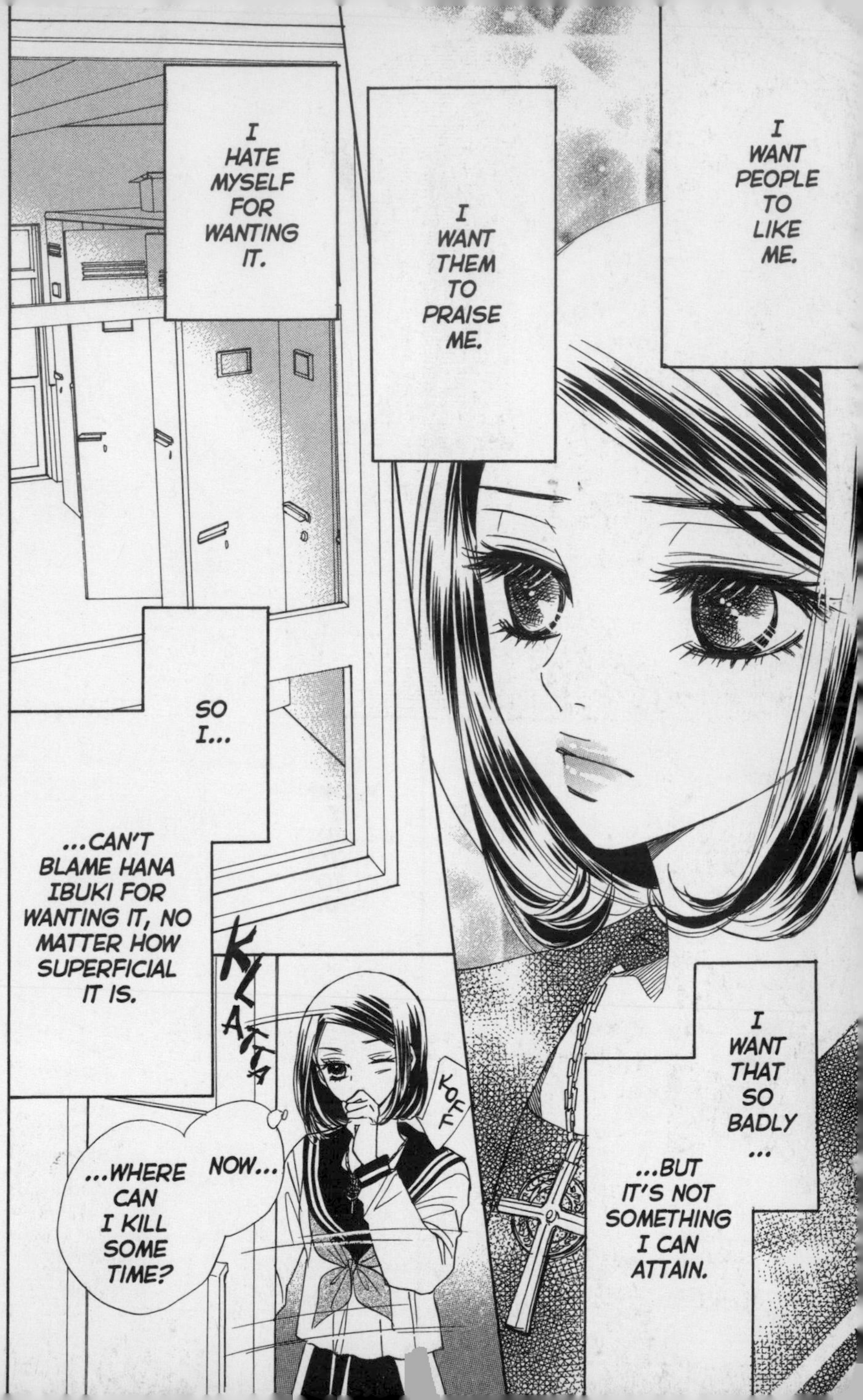
I WANT PEOPLE TO LIKE ME.
I WANT THEM TO PRAISE ME.
I HATE MYSELF FOR WANTING IT.
I WANT THAT SO BADLY ...
...BUT IT'S NOT SOMETHING I CAN ATTAIN.
SO I...
...CAN'T BLAME HANA IBUKI FOR WANTING IT, NO MATTER HOW SUPERFICIAL IT IS.
KLATTA
KOFF
NOW...
...WHERE CAN I KILL SOME TIME?

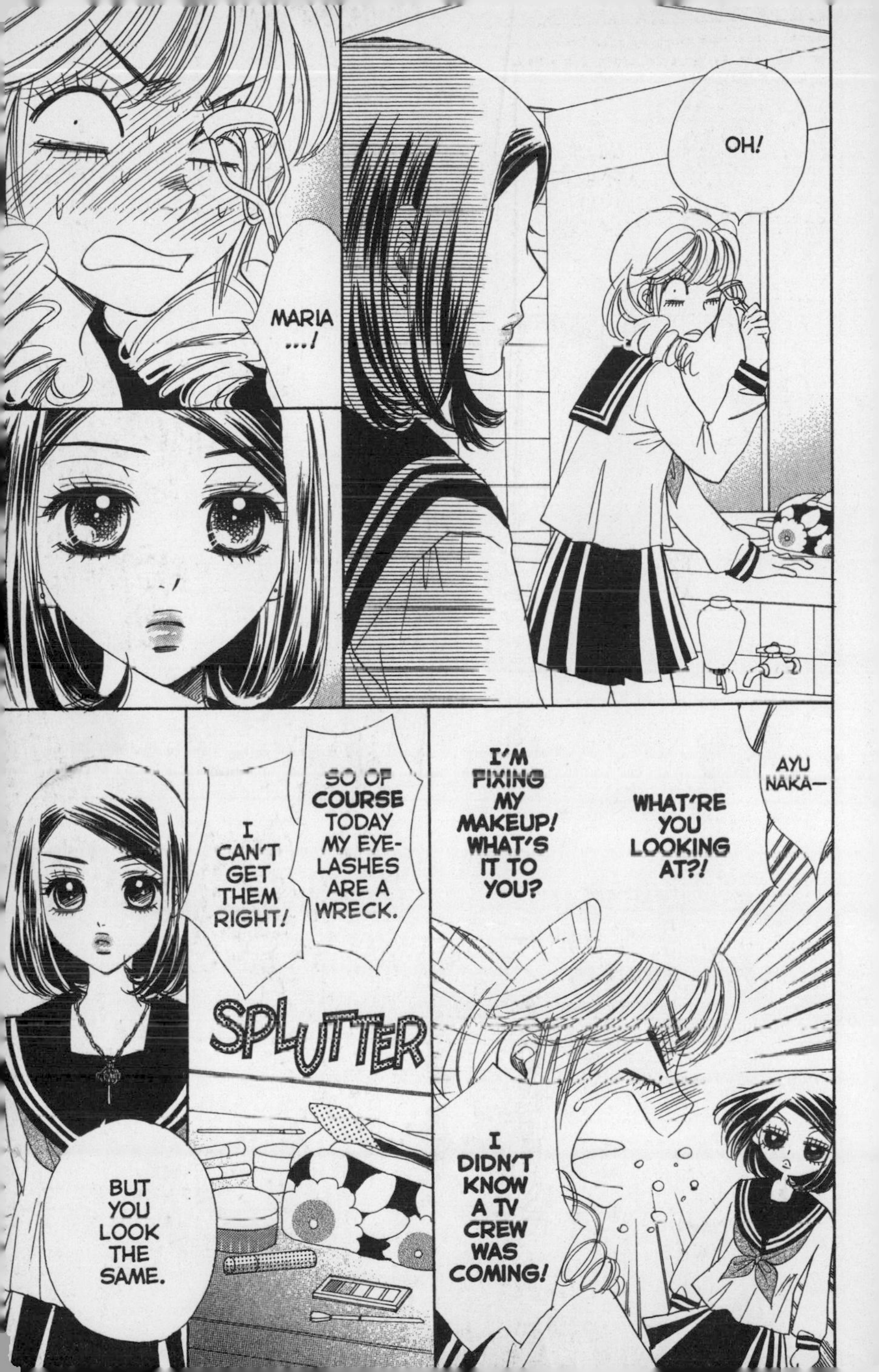
OH!
MARIA ...!
AYU NAKA—
WHAT'RE YOU LOOKING AT?!
I'M FIXING MY MAKEUP! WHAT'S IT TO YOU?
I DIDN'T KNOW A TV CREW WAS COMING!
SO OF COURSE TODAY MY EYE-LASHES ARE A WRECK.
I CAN'T GET THEM RIGHT!
SPLUTTER
BUT YOU LOOK THE SAME.

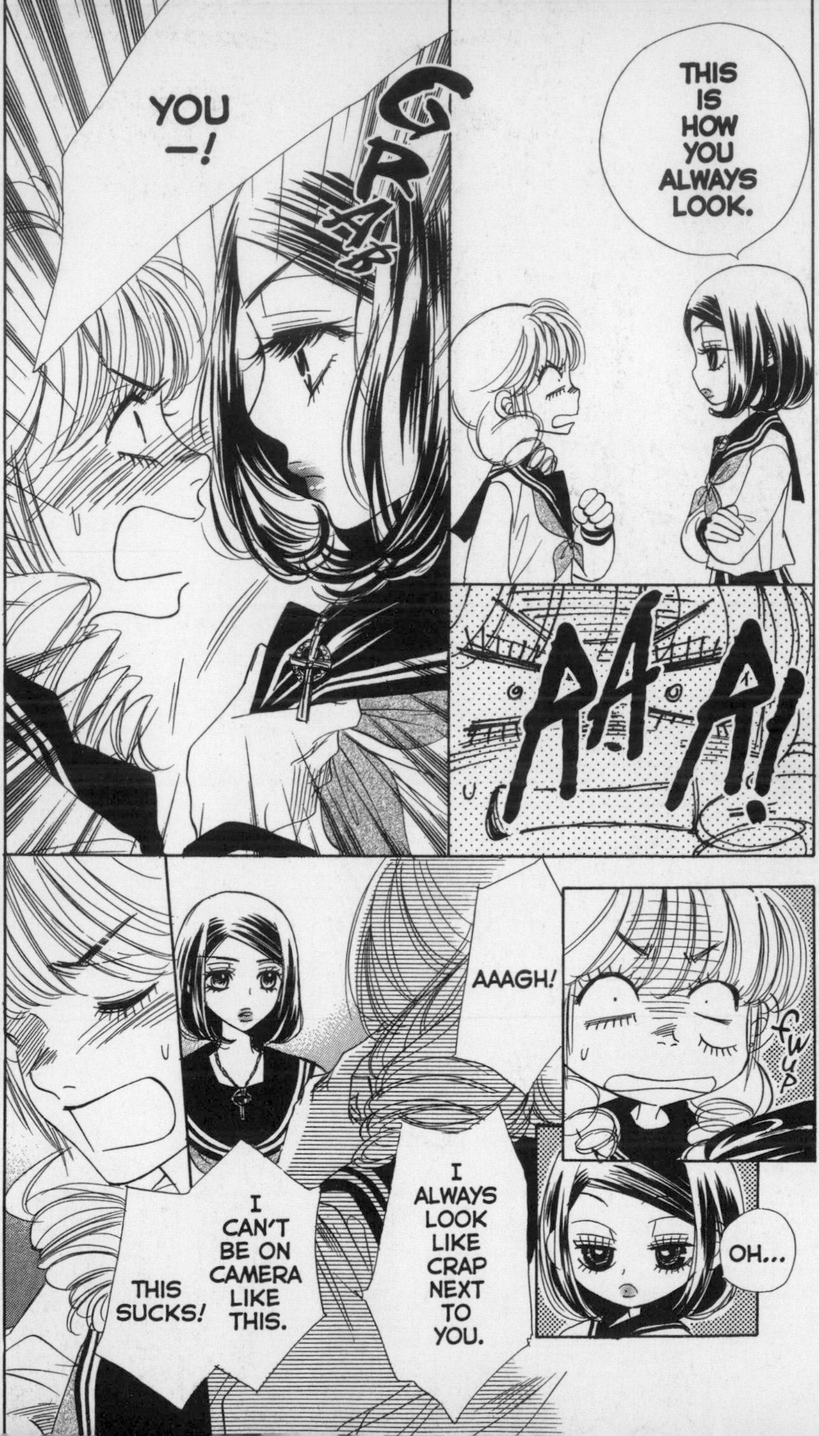
THIS IS HOW YOU ALWAYS LOOK.
RARI!
YOU—!
GRAB
AAAGH!
FWUP
OH...
I ALWAYS LOOK LIKE CRAP NEXT TO YOU.
I CAN'T BE ON CAMERA LIKE THIS.
THIS SUCKS!

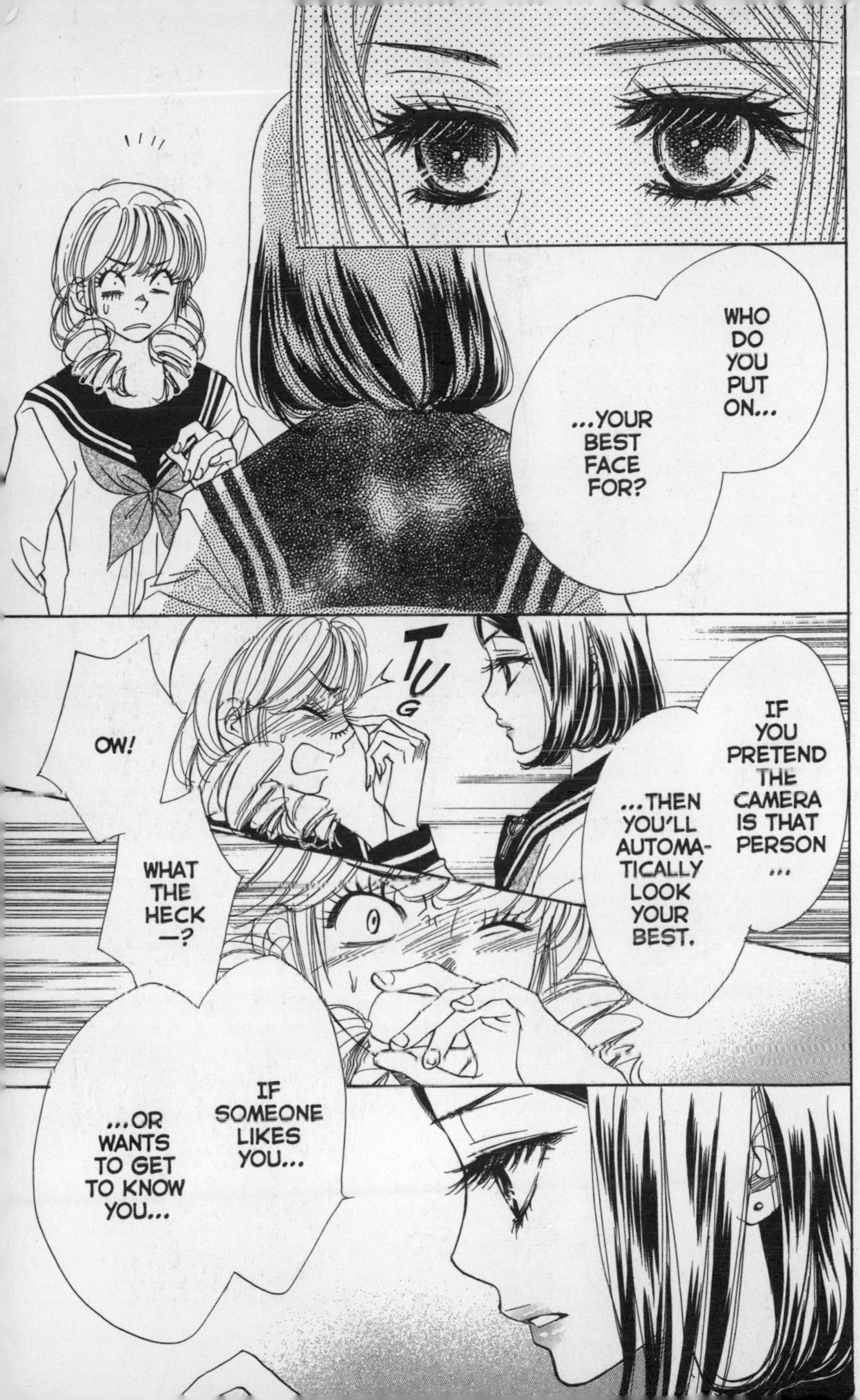
WHO DO YOU PUT ON...
...YOUR BEST FACE FOR?
IF YOU PRETEND THE CAMERA IS THAT PERSON...
...THEN YOU'LL AUTOMATICALLY LOOK YOUR BEST.
TUG
OW!
WHAT THE HECK—?
IF SOMEONE LIKES YOU...
...OR WANTS TO GET TO KNOW YOU...

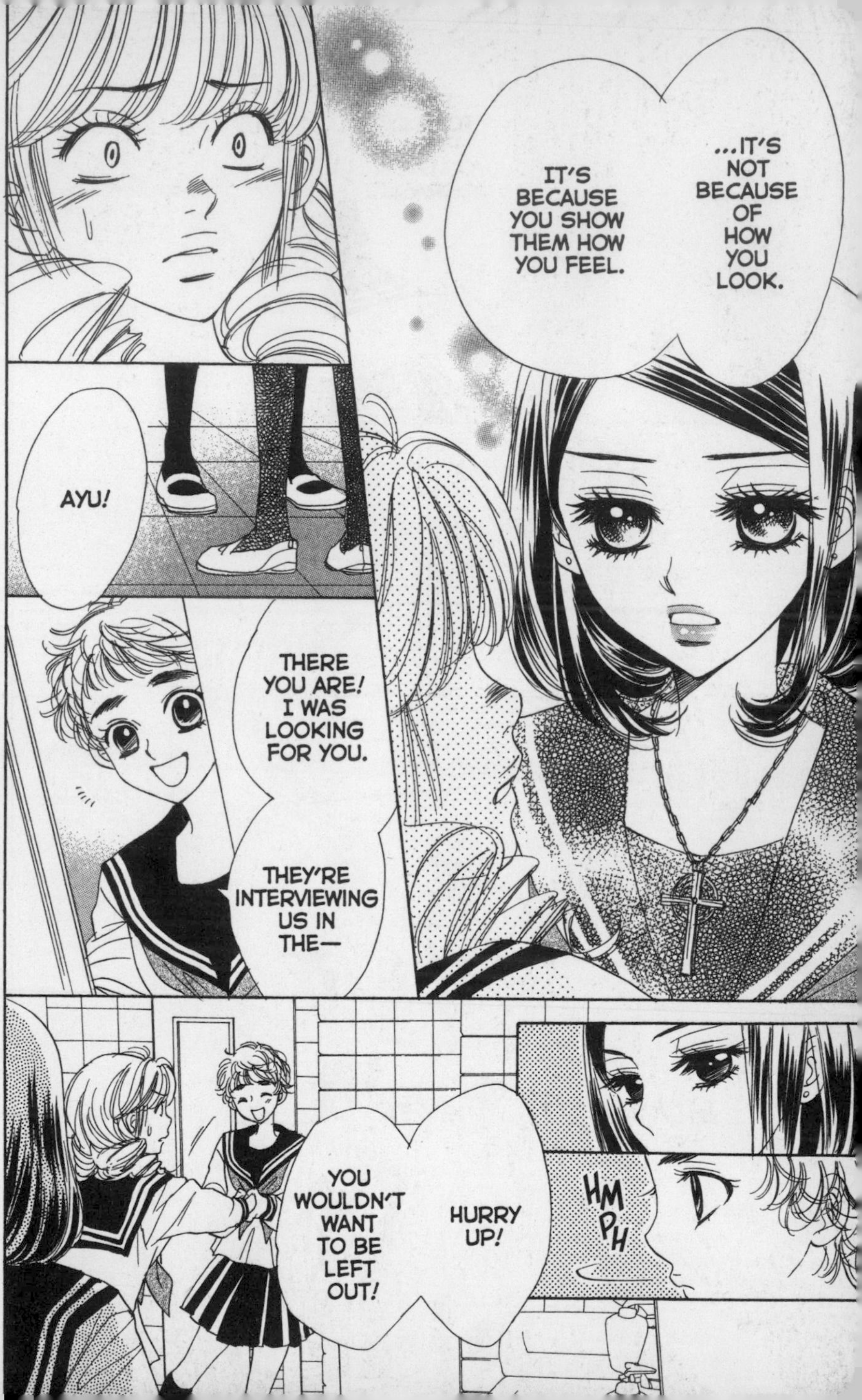
...IT'S NOT BECAUSE OF HOW YOU LOOK.
IT'S BECAUSE YOU SHOW THEM HOW YOU FEEL.
AYU!
THERE YOU ARE! I WAS LOOKING FOR YOU.
THEY'RE INTERVIEWING US IN THE—
HMPH
HURRY UP!
YOU WOULDN'T WANT TO BE LEFT OUT!

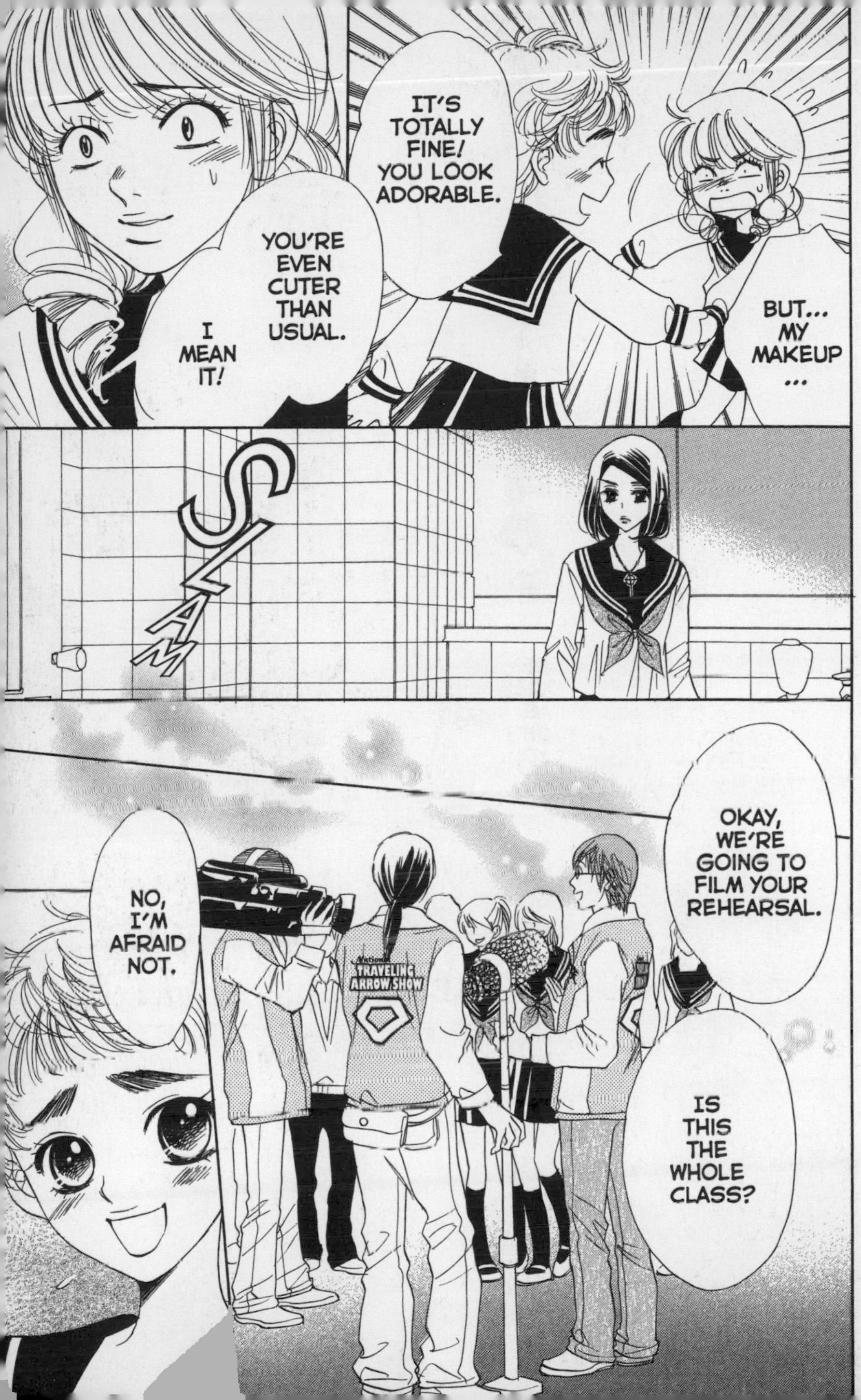
BUT... MY MAKEUP ...
IT'S TOTALLY FINE! YOU LOOK ADORABLE.
YOU'RE EVEN CUTER THAN USUAL.
I MEAN IT!
SLAM
OKAY, WE'RE GOING TO FILM YOUR REHEARSAL.
IS THIS THE WHOLE CLASS?
NO, I'M AFRAID NOT.
TRAVELING ARROW SHOW

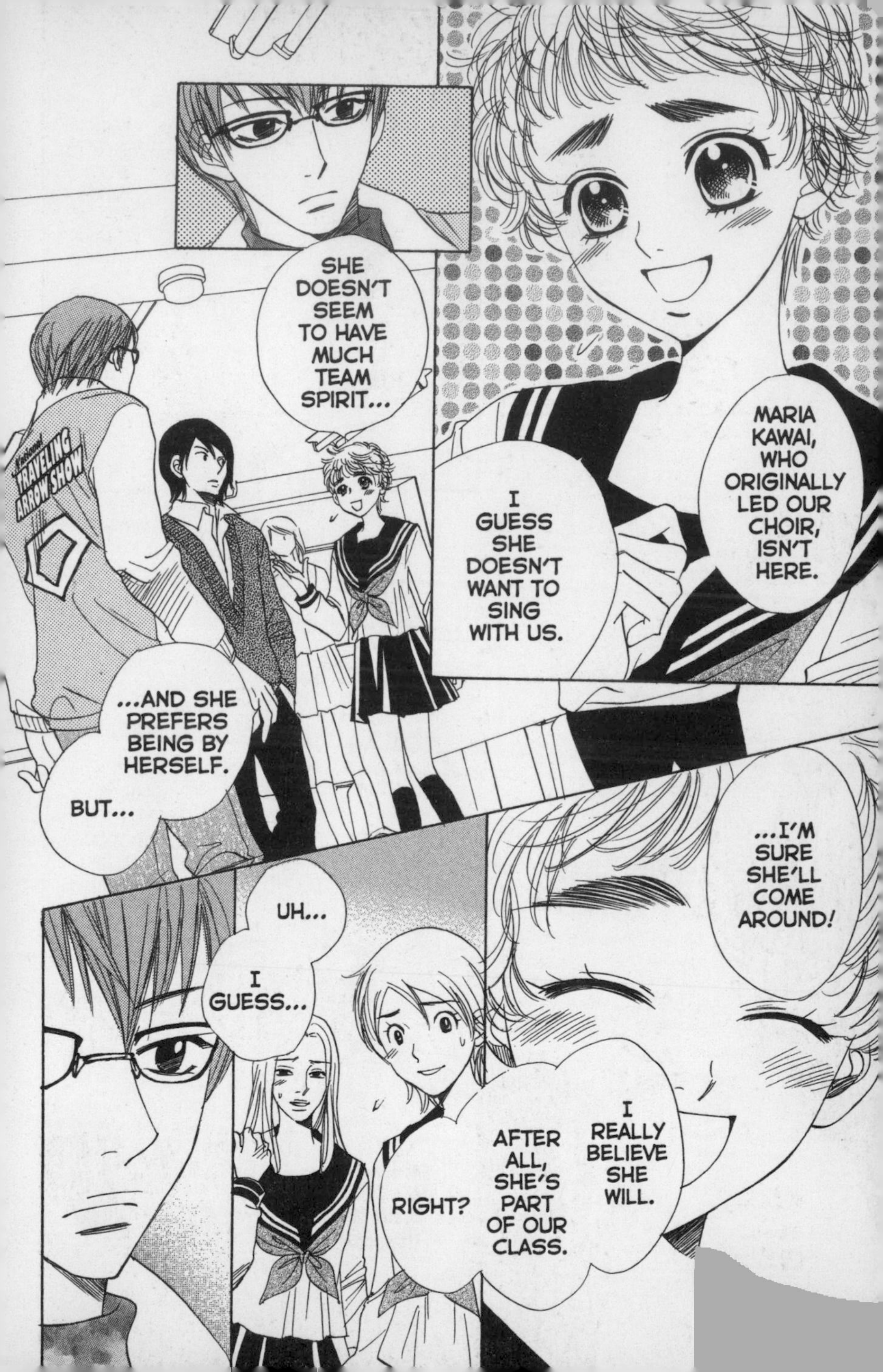
MARIA KAWAI, WHO ORIGINALLY LED OUR CHOIR, ISN'T HERE.
I GUESS SHE DOESN'T WANT TO SING WITH US.
SHE DOESN'T SEEM TO HAVE MUCH TEAM SPIRIT...
TRAVELING ARROW SHOW
...AND SHE PREFERS BEING BY HERSELF.
BUT...
...I'M SURE SHE'LL COME AROUND!
I REALLY BELIEVE SHE WILL.
AFTER ALL, SHE'S PART OF OUR CLASS.
RIGHT?
UH...
I GUESS...

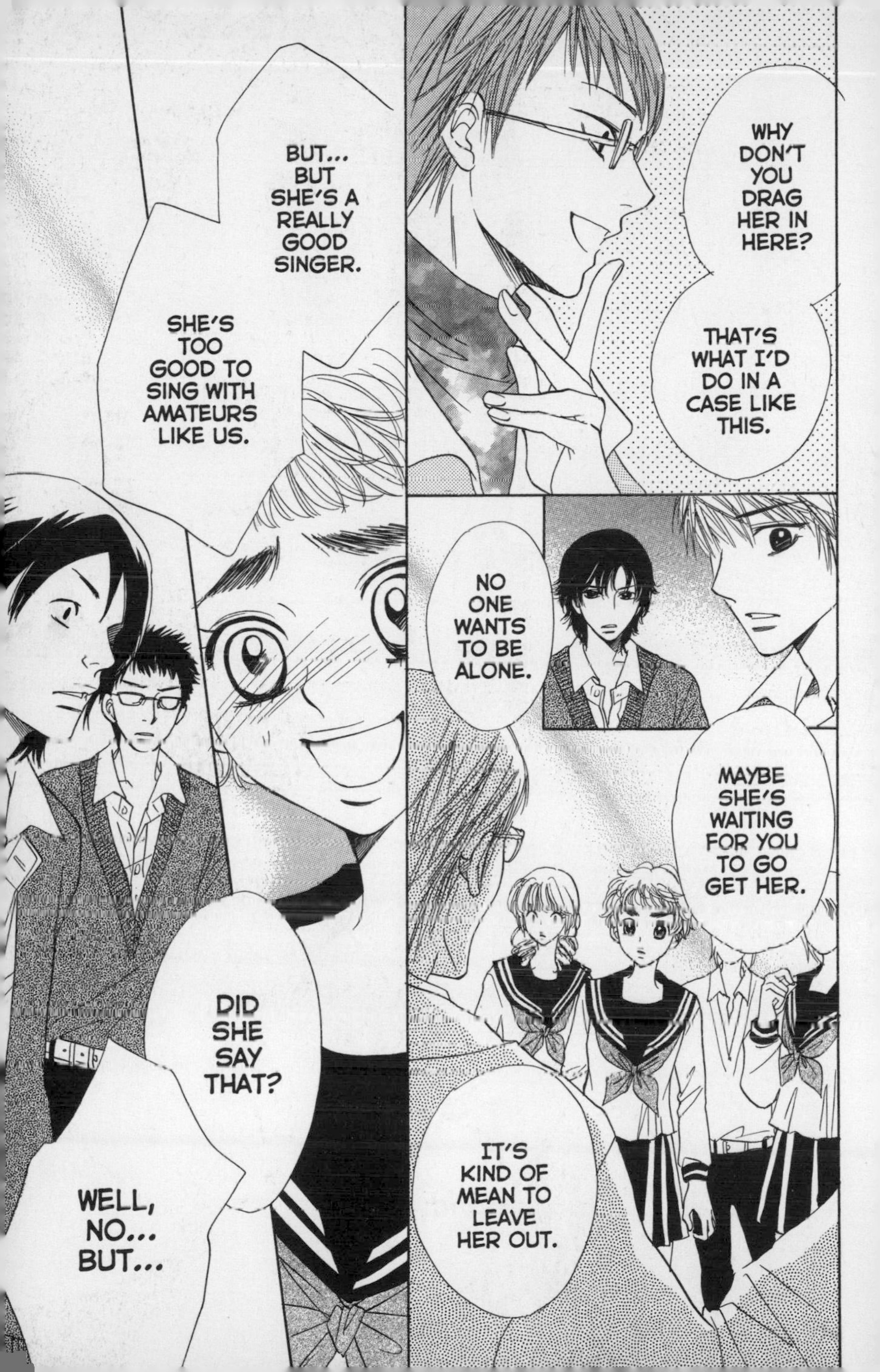
WHY DON'T YOU DRAG HER IN HERE?
THAT'S WHAT I'D DO IN A CASE LIKE THIS.
NO ONE WANTS TO BE ALONE.
MAYBE SHE'S WAITING FOR YOU TO GO GET HER.
IT'S KIND OF MEAN TO LEAVE HER OUT.
BUT... BUT SHE'S A REALLY GOOD SINGER.
SHE'S TOO GOOD TO SING WITH AMATEURS LIKE US.
DID SHE SAY THAT?
WELL, NO... BUT...

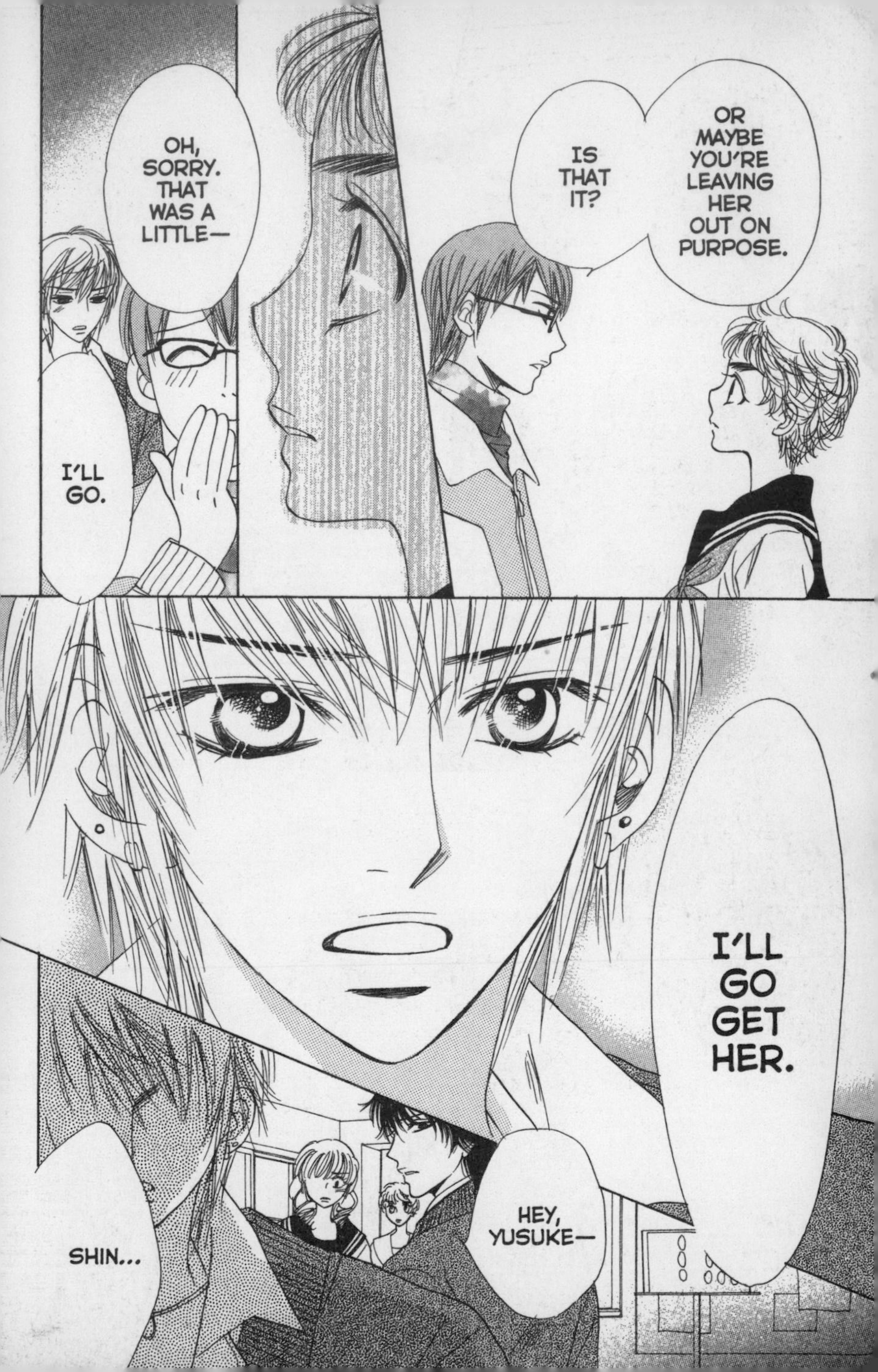
OR MAYBE YOU'RE LEAVING HER OUT ON PURPOSE.
IS THAT IT?
OH, SORRY. THAT WAS A LITTLE—
I'LL GO.
I'LL GO GET HER.
HEY, YUSUKE—
SHIN...

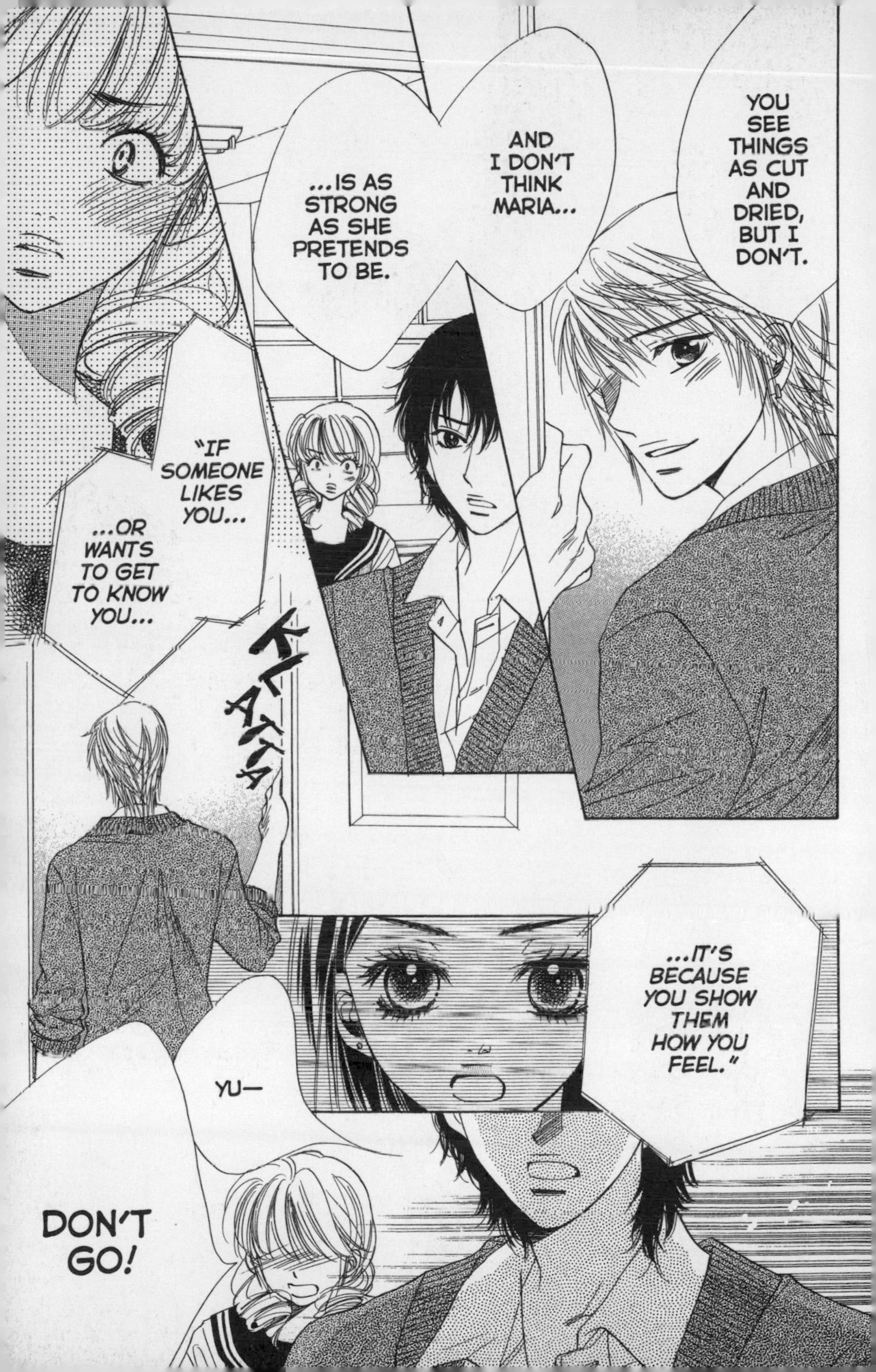
YOU SEE THINGS AS CUT AND DRIED, BUT I DON'T.
AND I DON'T THINK MARIA...
...IS AS STRONG AS SHE PRETENDS TO BE.
"IF SOMEONE LIKES YOU...
...OR WANTS TO GET TO KNOW YOU...
KLATTA
...IT'S BECAUSE YOU SHOW THEM HOW YOU FEEL."
YU—
DON'T GO!

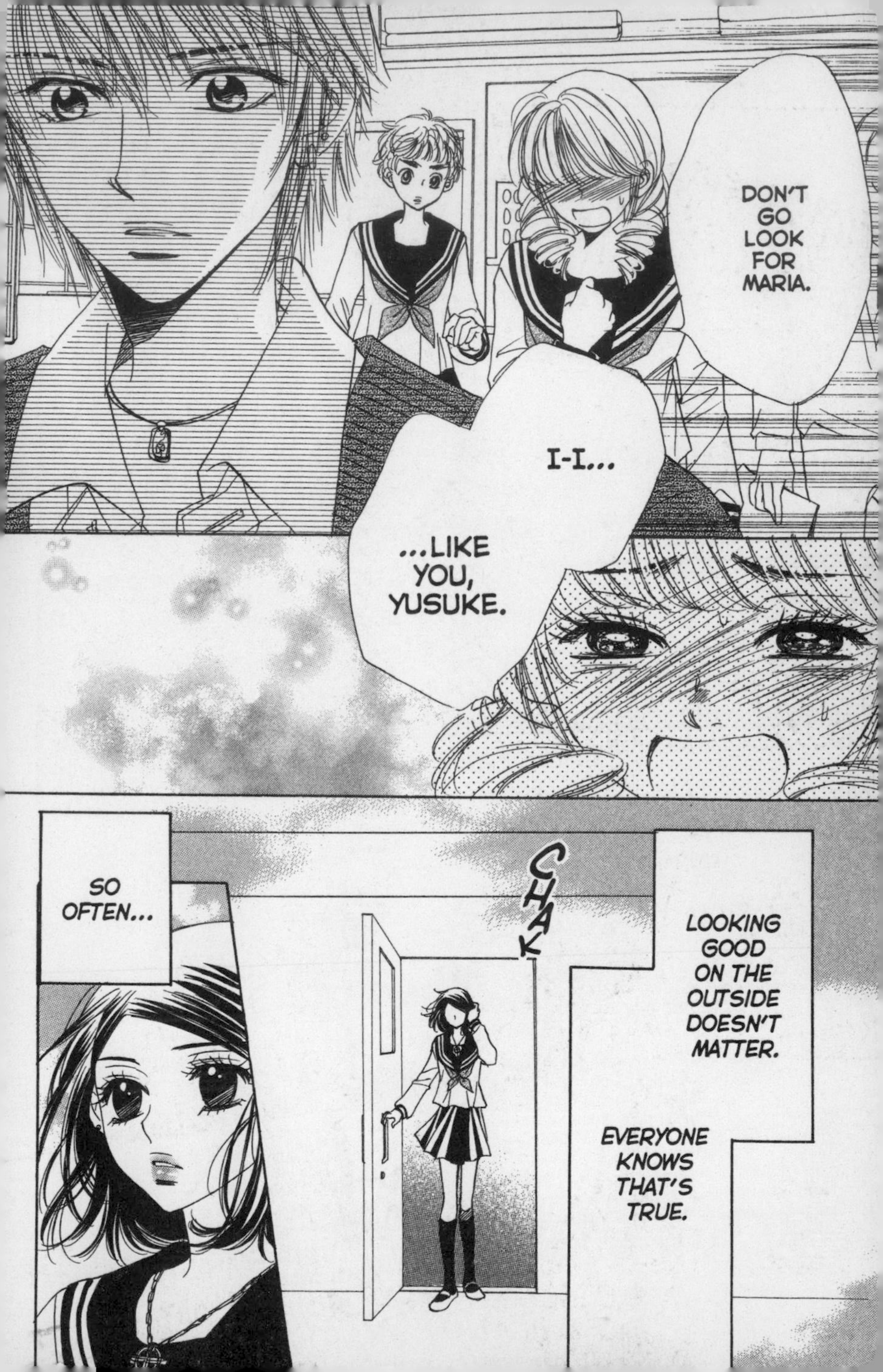
DON'T GO LOOK FOR MARIA.
I-I...
...LIKE YOU, YUSUKE.
LOOKING GOOD ON THE OUTSIDE DOESN'T MATTER.
EVERYONE KNOWS THAT'S TRUE.
CHAK
SO OFTEN...

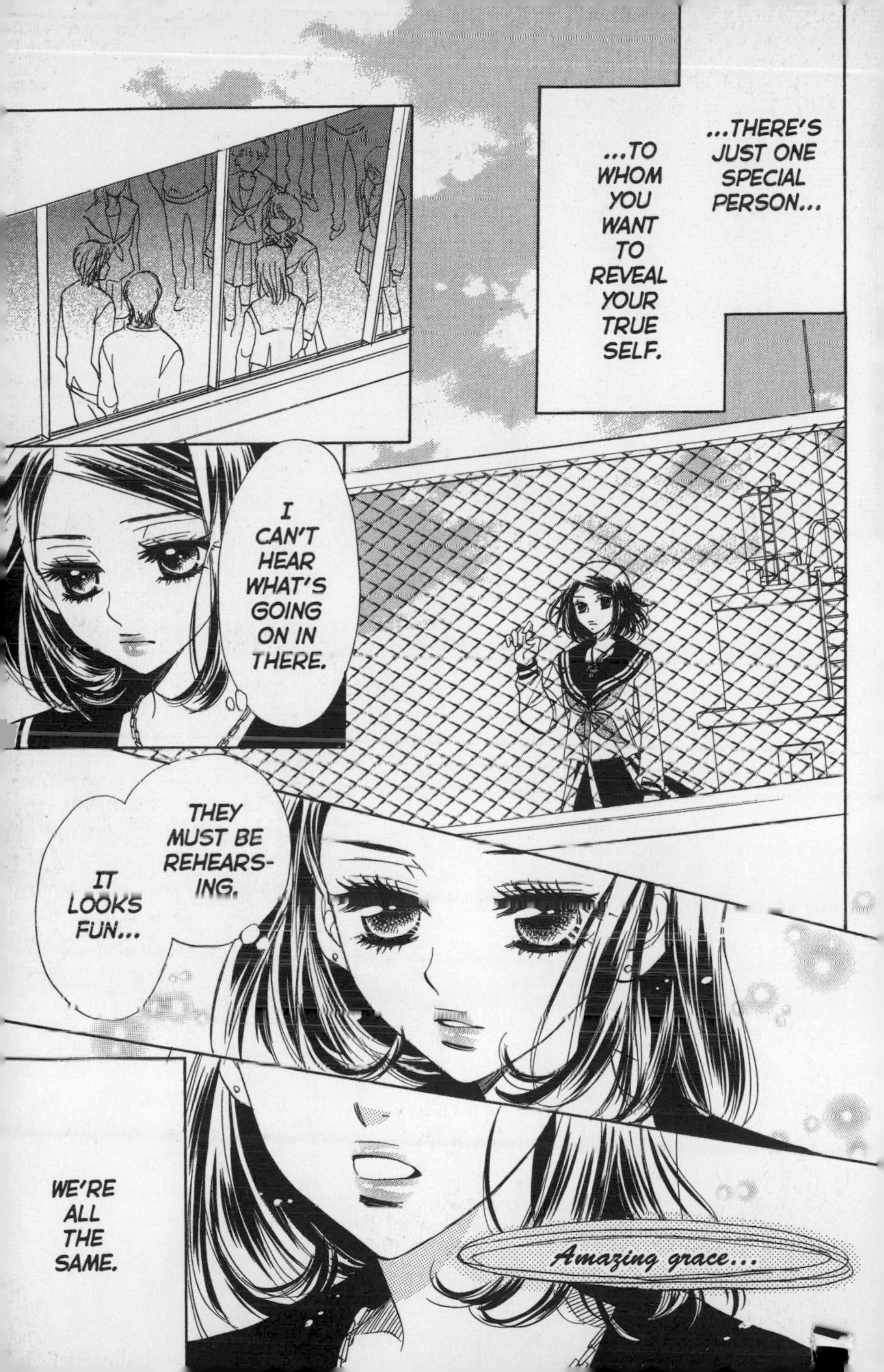
...THERE'S JUST ONE SPECIAL PERSON...
...TO WHOM YOU WANT TO REVEAL YOUR TRUE SELF.
I CAN'T HEAR WHAT'S GOING ON IN THERE.
THEY MUST BE REHEARSING.
IT LOOKS FUN...
Amazing grace...
WE'RE ALL THE SAME.

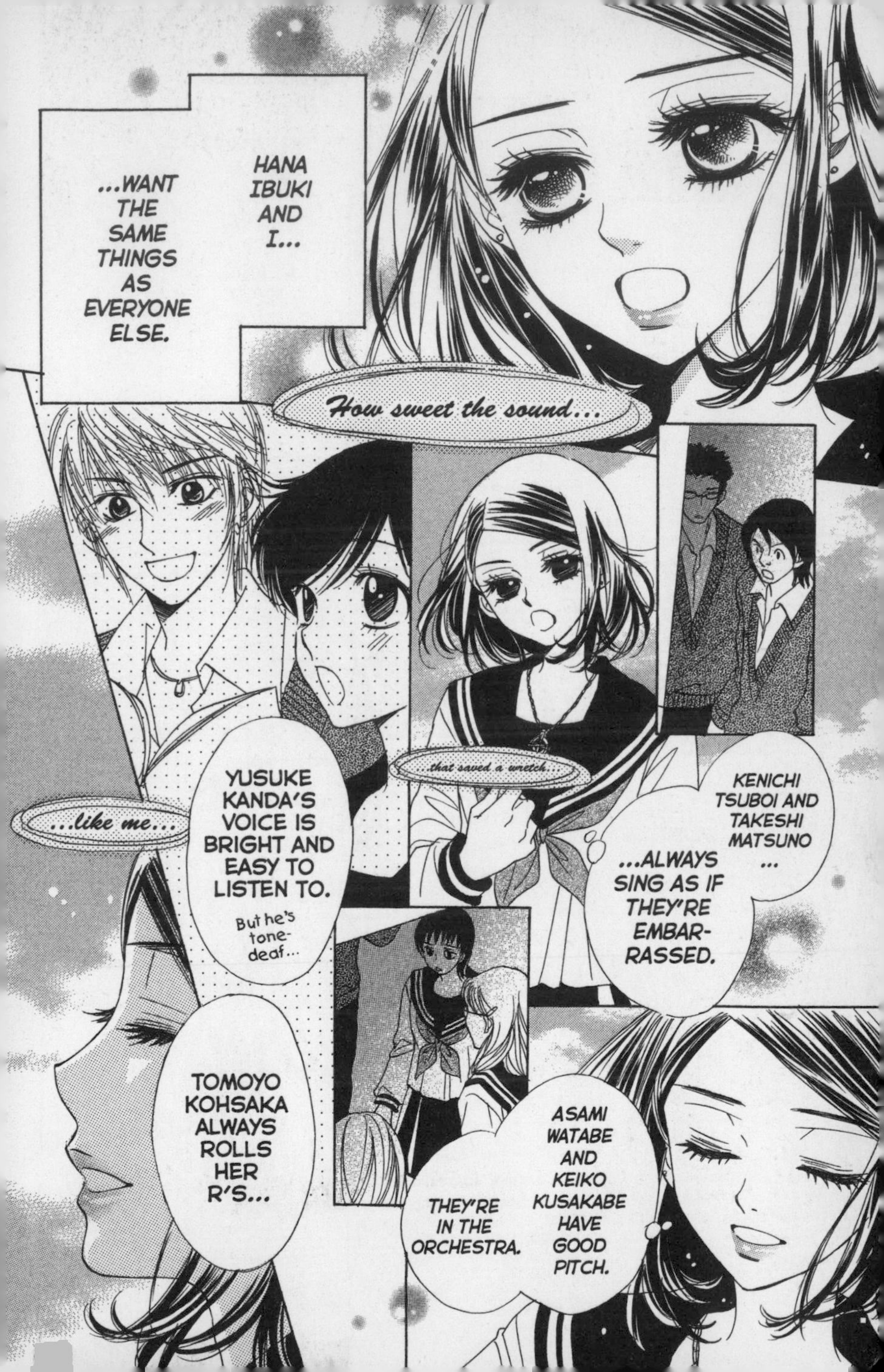
HANA IBUKI AND I...
...WANT THE SAME THINGS AS EVERYONE ELSE.
How sweet the sound...
KENICHI TSUBOI AND TAKESHI MATSUNO...
...ALWAYS SING AS IF THEY'RE EMBARRASSED.
...that saved a wretch...
...like me...
YUSUKE KANDA'S VOICE IS BRIGHT AND EASY TO LISTEN TO.
But he's tone-deaf...
ASAMI WATABE AND KEIKO KUSAKABE HAVE GOOD PITCH.
THEY'RE IN THE ORCHESTRA.
TOMOYO KOHSAKA ALWAYS ROLLS HER R'S...

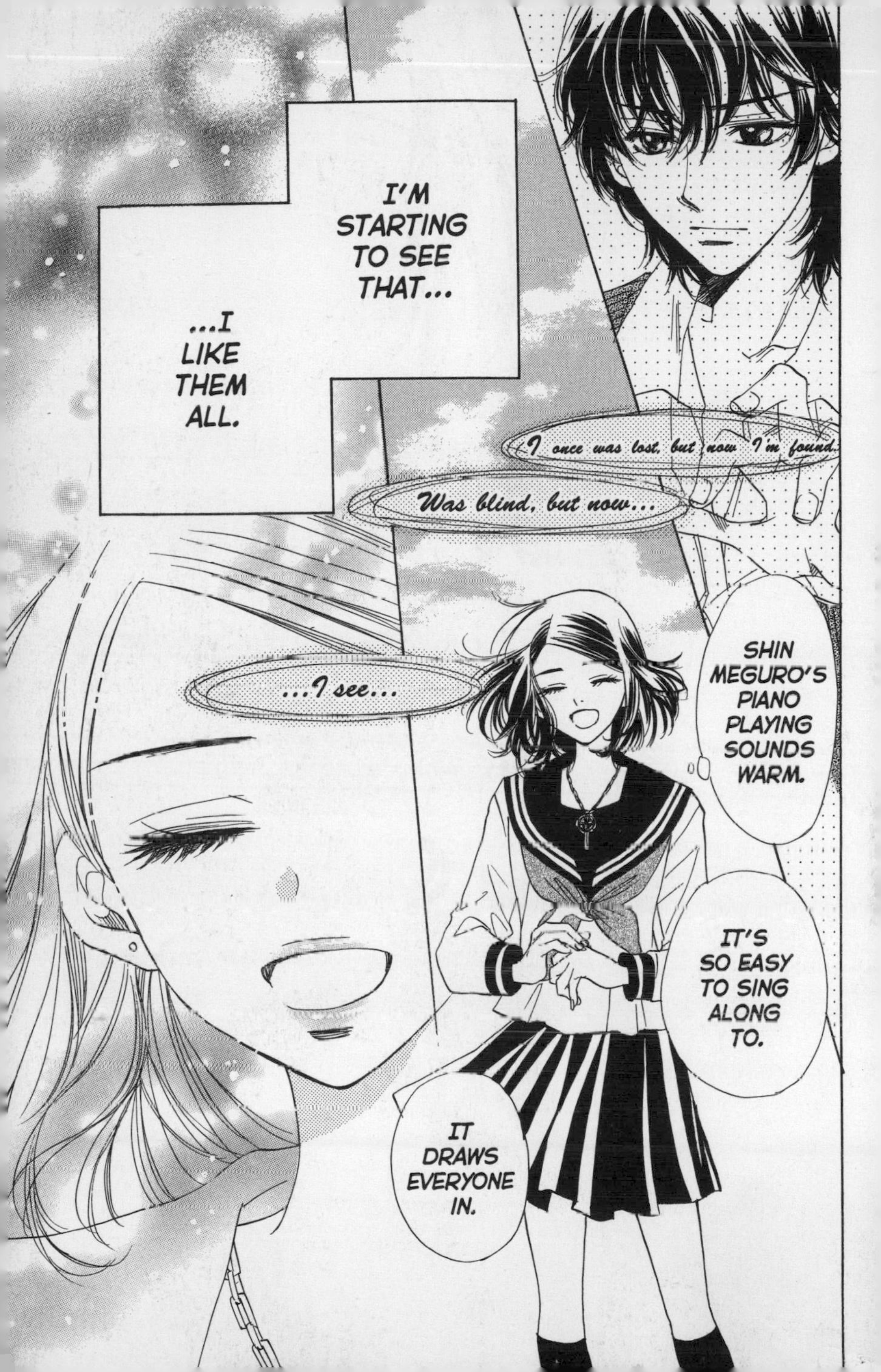
I once was lost, but now I'm found.
I'M STARTING TO SEE THAT...
...I LIKE THEM ALL.
Was blind, but now...
...I see...
SHIN MEGURO'S PIANO PLAYING SOUNDS WARM.
IT'S SO EASY TO SING ALONG TO.
IT DRAWS EVERYONE IN.

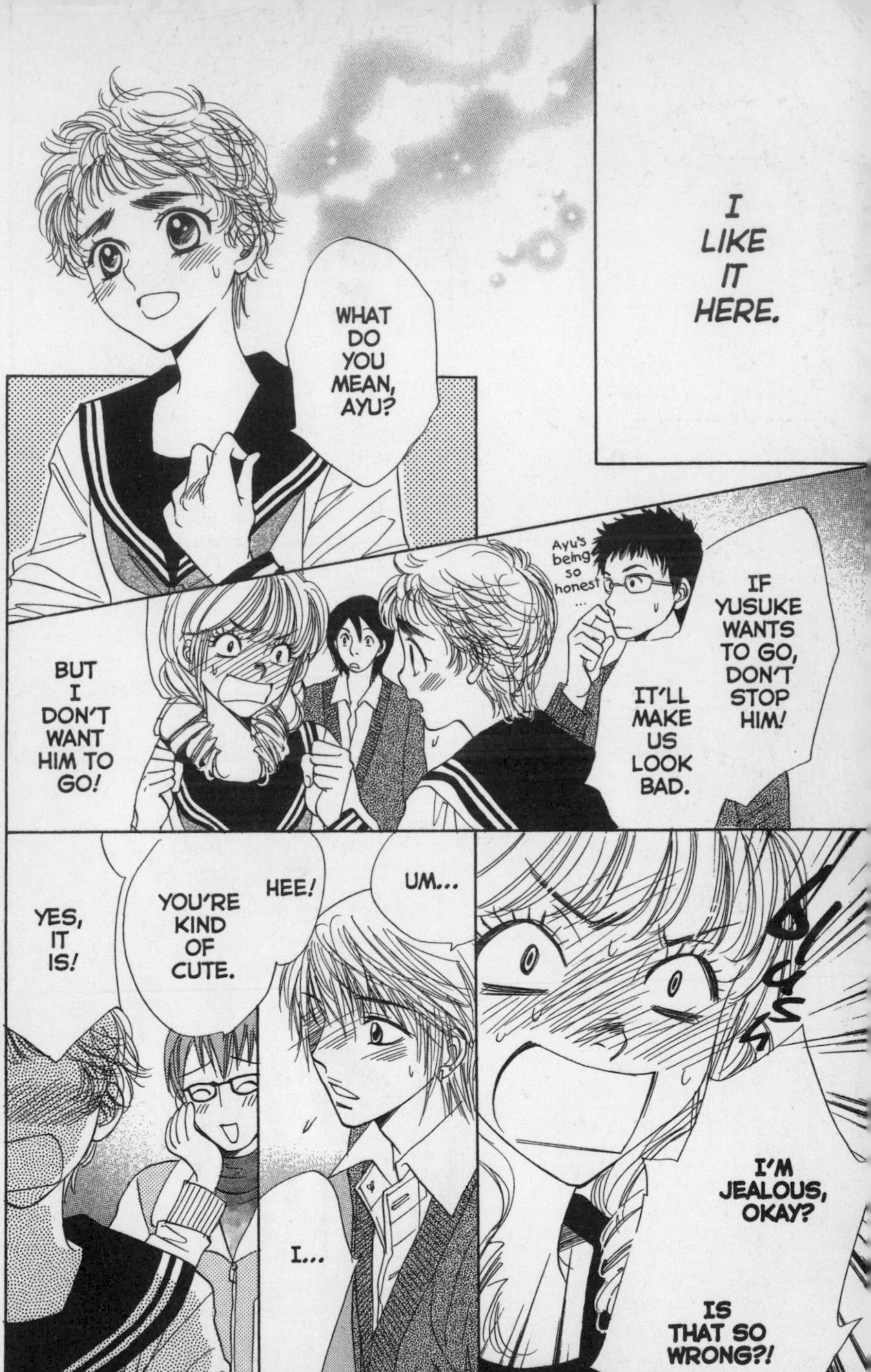
I LIKE IT HERE.
WHAT DO YOU MEAN, AYU?
IF YUSUKE WANTS TO GO, DON'T STOP HIM!
IT'LL MAKE US LOOK BAD.
Ayu's being so honest...
BUT I DON'T WANT HIM TO GO!
I'M JEALOUS, OKAY?
IS THAT SO WRONG?!
UM...
I...
HEE!
YOU'RE KIND OF CUTE.
YES, IT IS!

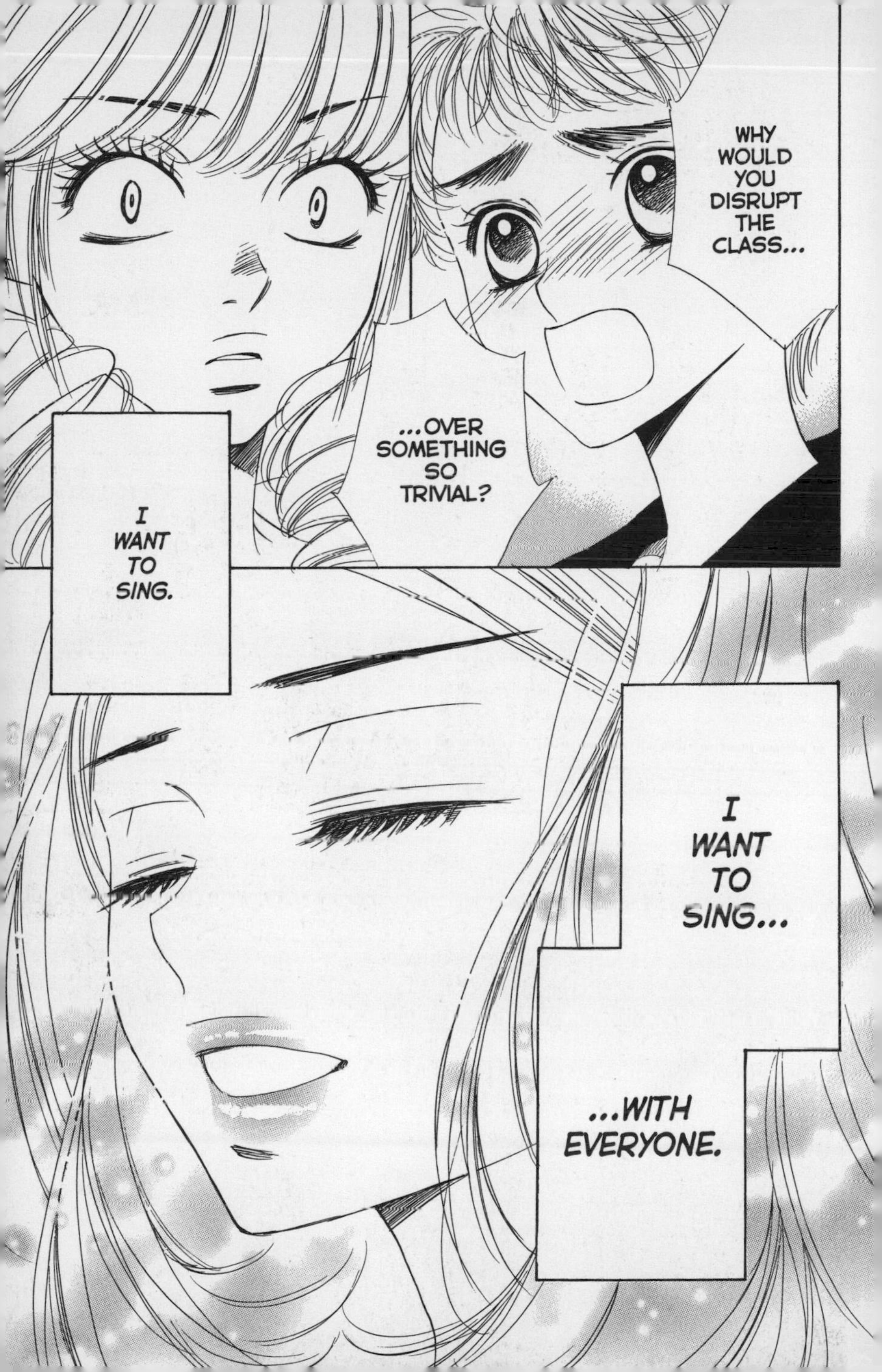
WHY WOULD YOU DISRUPT THE CLASS...
...OVER SOMETHING SO TRIVIAL?
I WANT TO SING.
I WANT TO SING...
...WITH EVERYONE.

A Devil and
Her Love Song

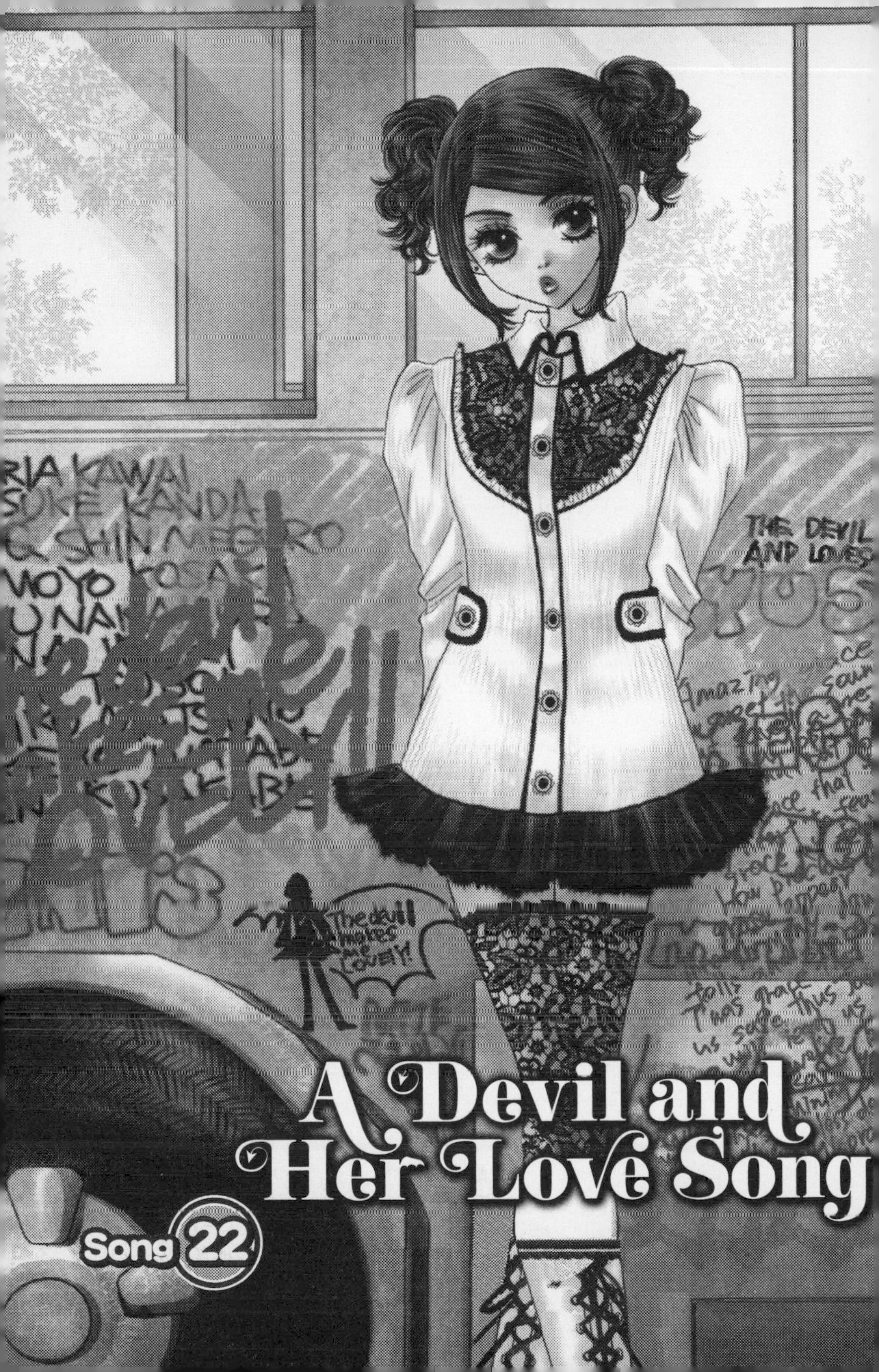
A Devil and Her Love Song
Song 22
THE DEVIL AND LOVES
The devil makes me LOVELY!

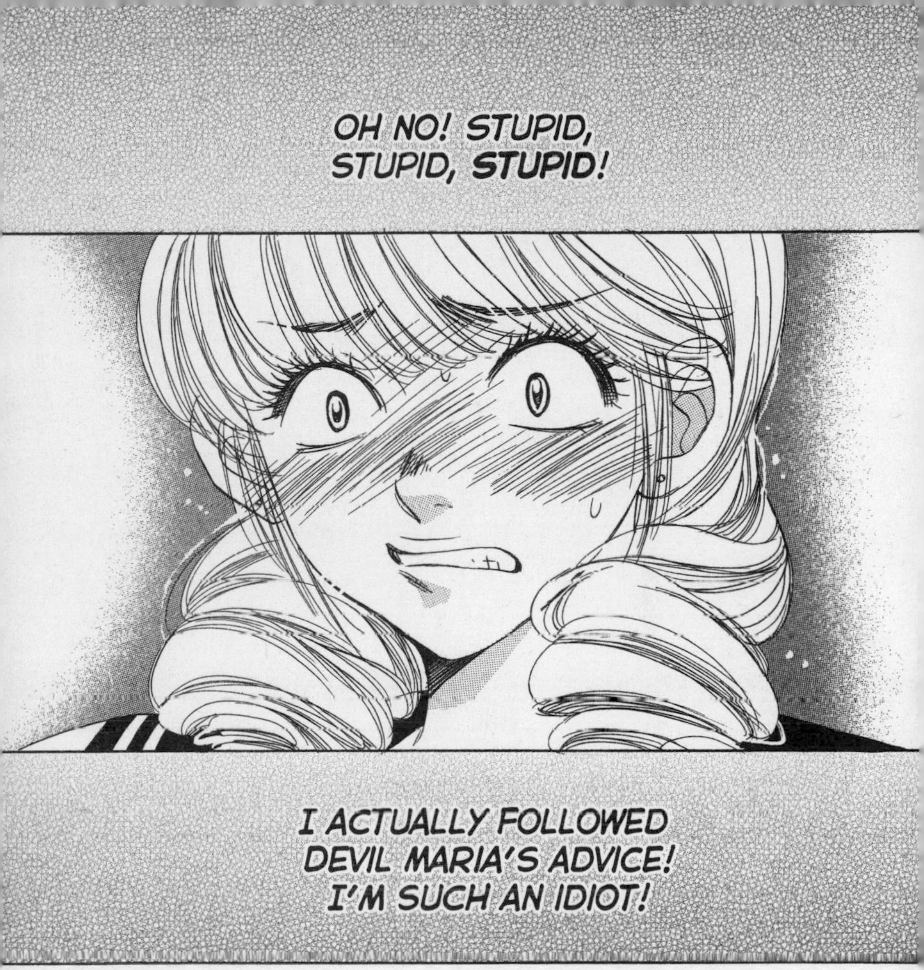
OH NO! STUPID, STUPID, STUPID!
I ACTUALLY FOLLOWED DEVIL MARIA'S ADVICE! I'M SUCH AN IDIOT!

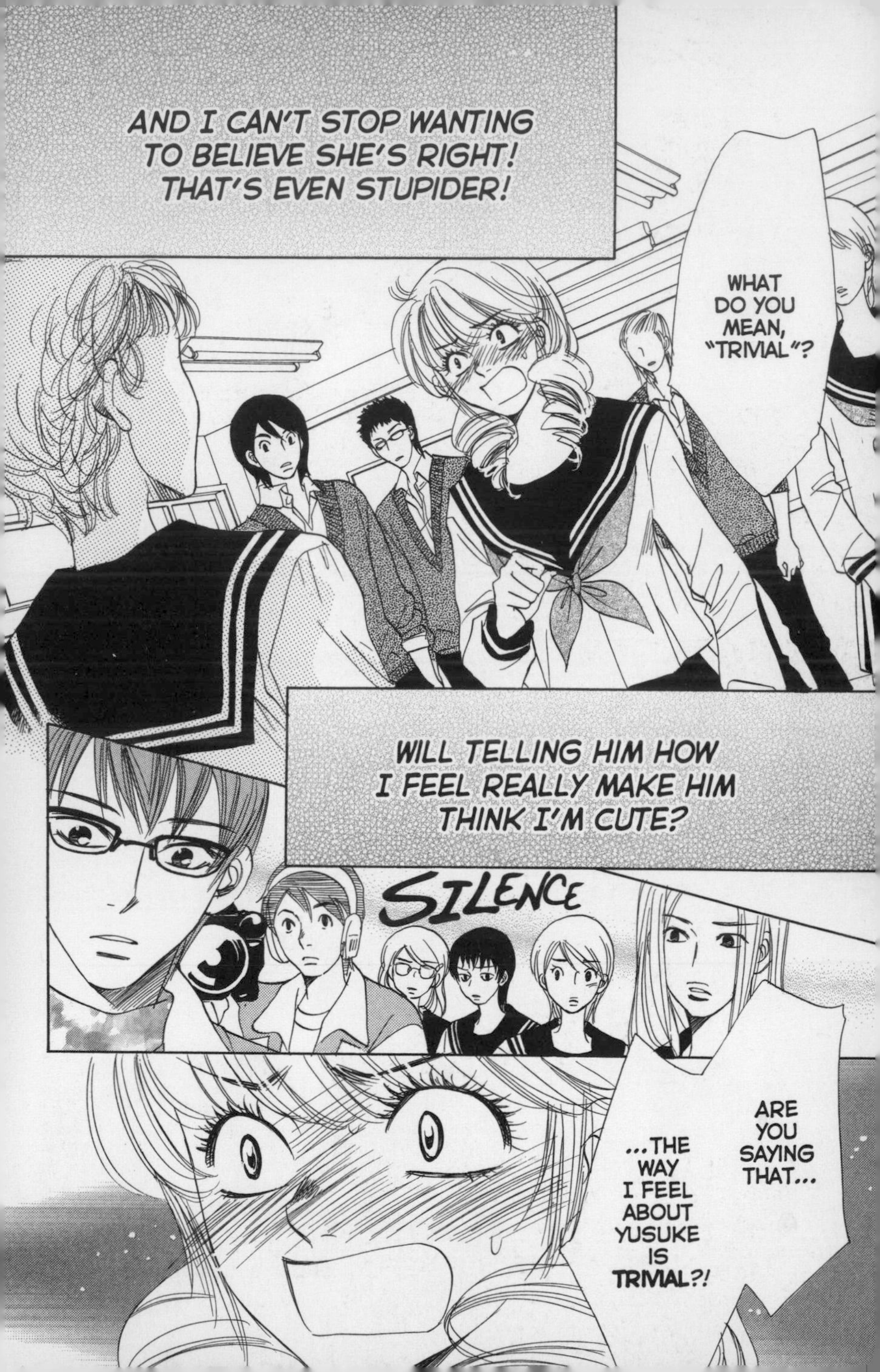
AND I CAN'T STOP WANTING TO BELIEVE SHE'S RIGHT! THAT'S EVEN STUPIDER!
WHAT DO YOU MEAN, "TRIVIAL"?
WILL TELLING HIM HOW I FEEL REALLY MAKE HIM THINK I'M CUTE?
SILENCE
ARE YOU SAYING THAT...
...THE WAY I FEEL ABOUT YUSUKE IS TRIVIAL?!

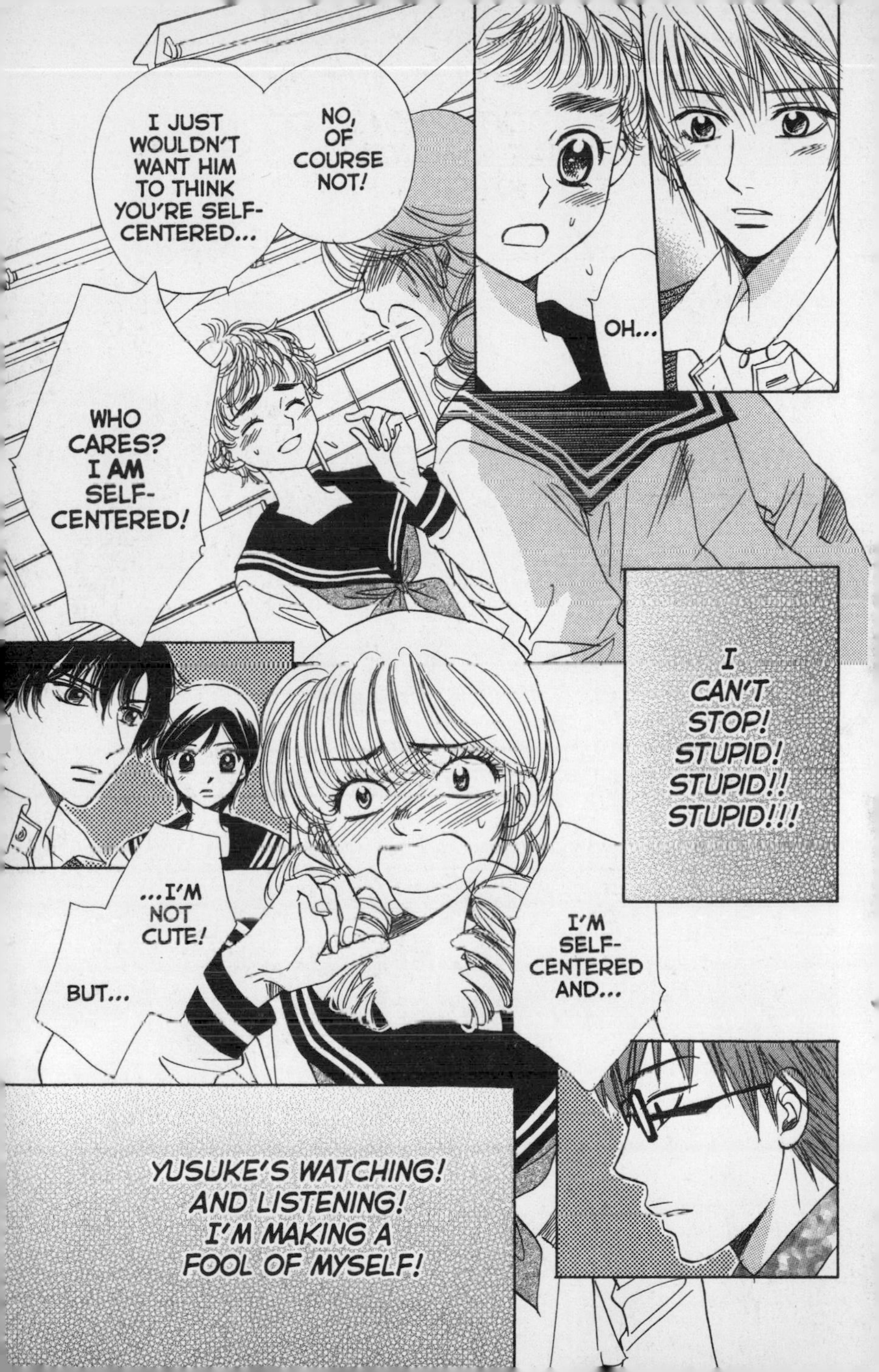
OH...
NO, OF COURSE NOT!
I JUST WOULDN'T WANT HIM TO THINK YOU'RE SELF-CENTERED...
WHO CARES? I AM SELF-CENTERED!
I CAN'T STOP! STUPID! STUPID!! STUPID!!!
I'M SELF-CENTERED AND...
...I'M NOT CUTE!
BUT...
YUSUKE'S WATCHING! AND LISTENING! I'M MAKING A FOOL OF MYSELF!

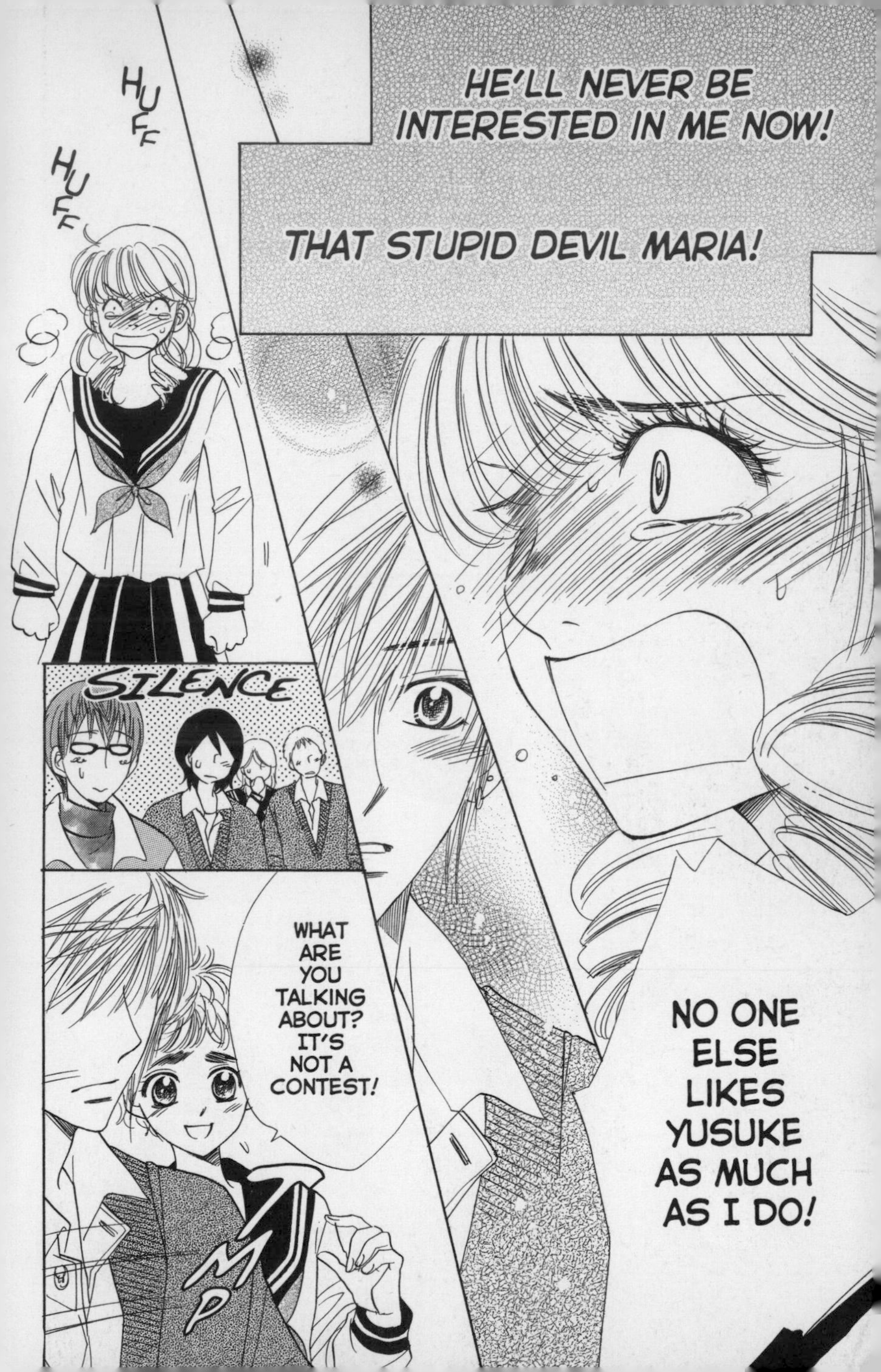
HE'LL NEVER BE INTERESTED IN ME NOW!
THAT STUPID DEVIL MARIA!
NO ONE ELSE LIKES YUSUKE AS MUCH AS I DO!
HUFF HUFF
SILENCE
WHAT ARE YOU TALKING ABOUT? IT'S NOT A CONTEST!
MP

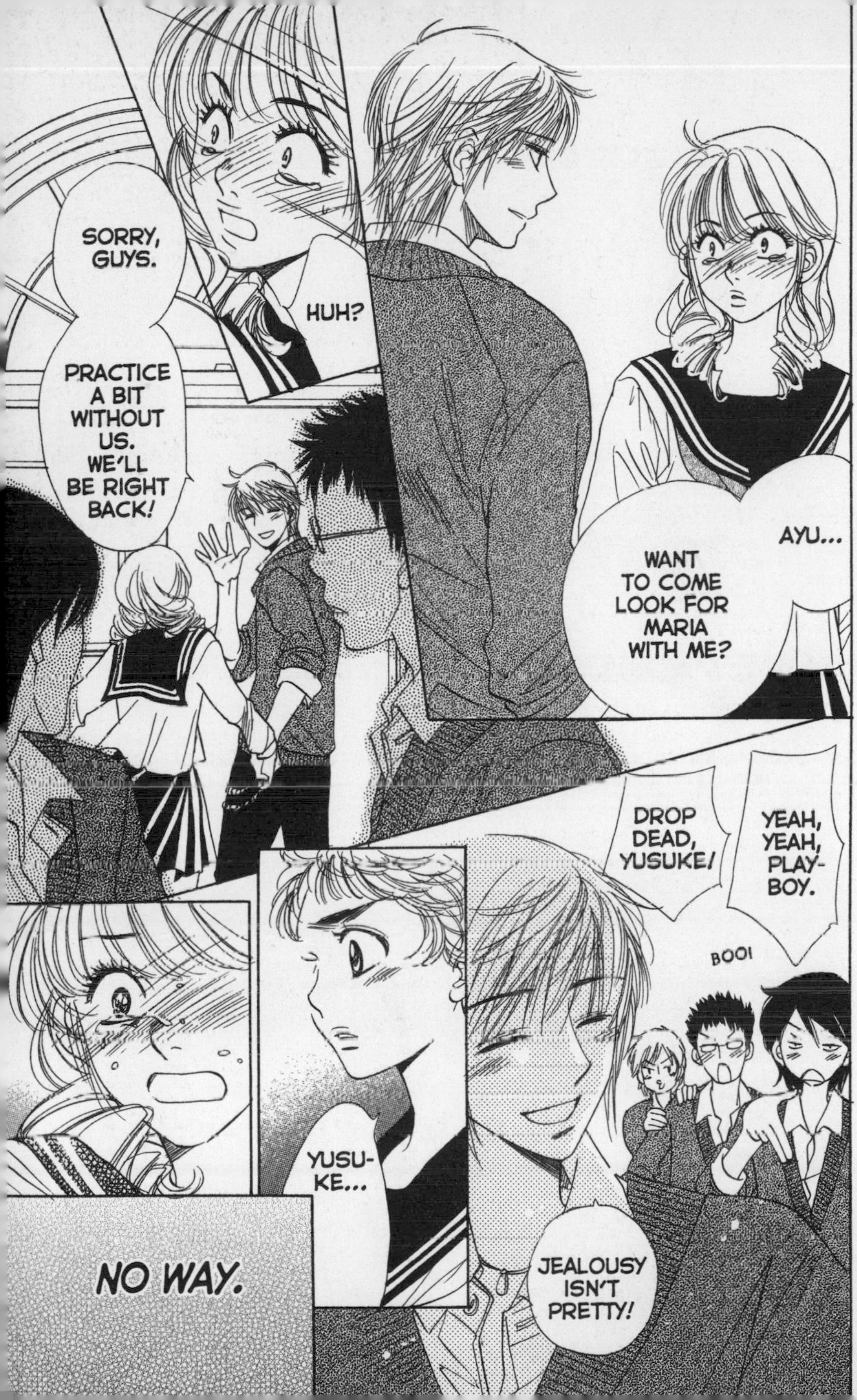
AYU...
WANT TO COME LOOK FOR MARIA WITH ME?
HUH?
SORRY, GUYS.
PRACTICE A BIT WITHOUT US. WE'LL BE RIGHT BACK!
YEAH, YEAH, PLAY-BOY.
DROP DEAD, YUSUKE!
BOO!
JEALOUSY ISN'T PRETTY!
YUSU-KE...
NO WAY.

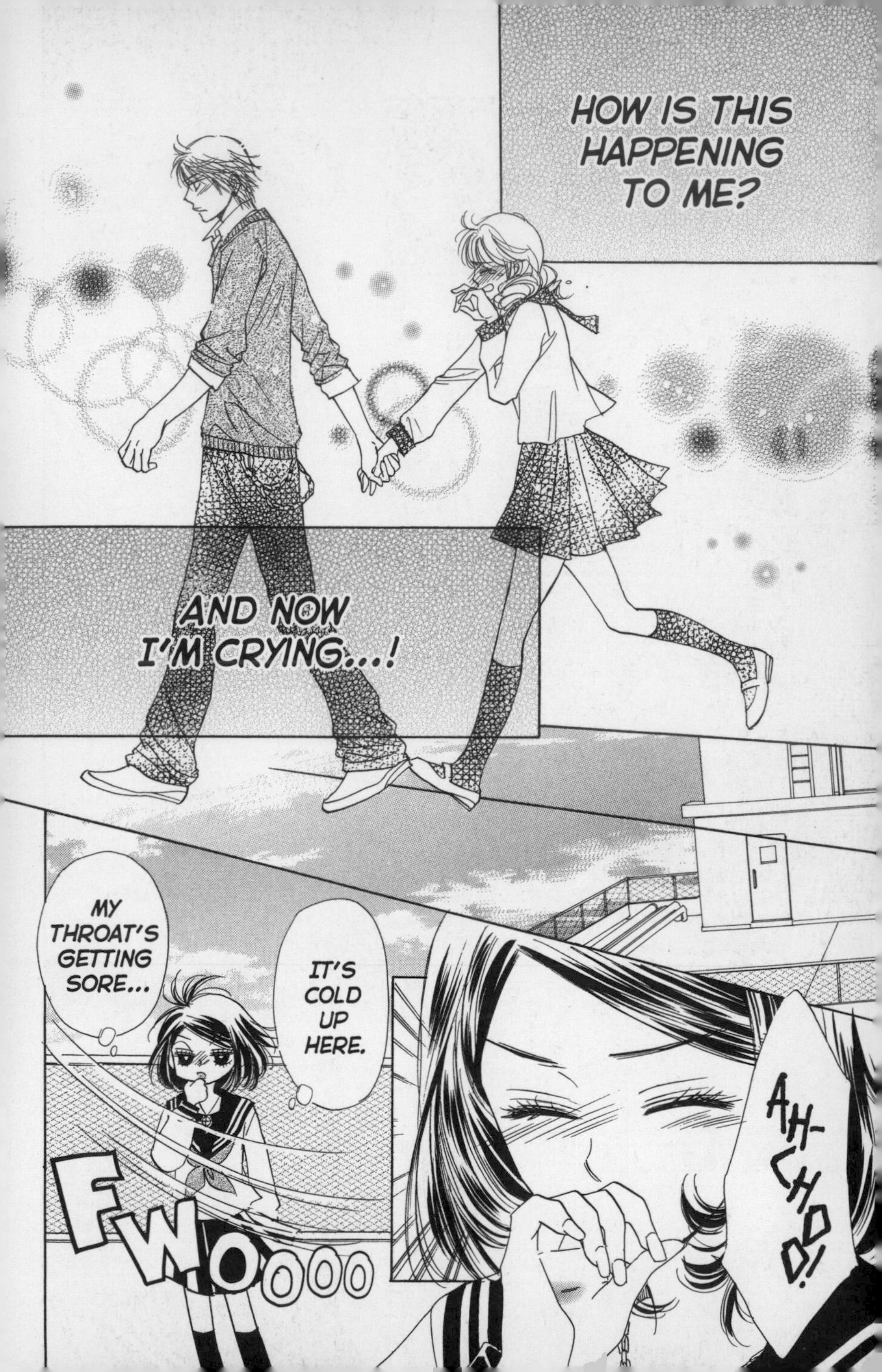
HOW IS THIS HAPPENING TO ME?
AND NOW I'M CRYING...!
AH-CHOO!
IT'S COLD UP HERE.
MY THROAT'S GETTING SORE...
FWOOOO

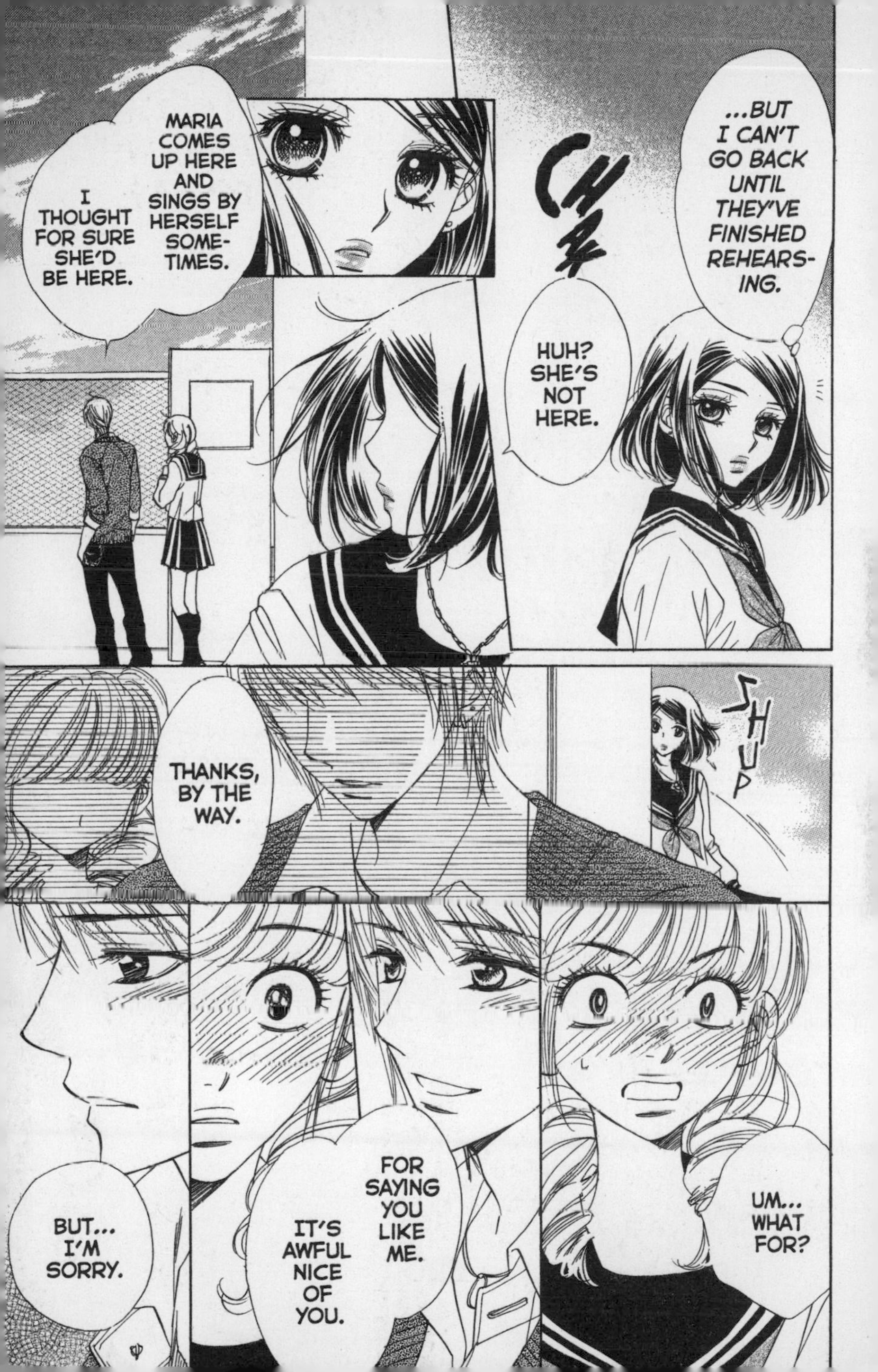
...BUT I CAN'T GO BACK UNTIL THEY'VE FINISHED REHEARS-ING.
CHA
HUH? SHE'S NOT HERE.
MARIA COMES UP HERE AND SINGS BY HERSELF SOME-TIMES.
I THOUGHT FOR SURE SHE'D BE HERE.
SHUP
THANKS, BY THE WAY.
UM... WHAT FOR?
FOR SAYING YOU LIKE ME.
IT'S AWFUL NICE OF YOU.
BUT... I'M SORRY.

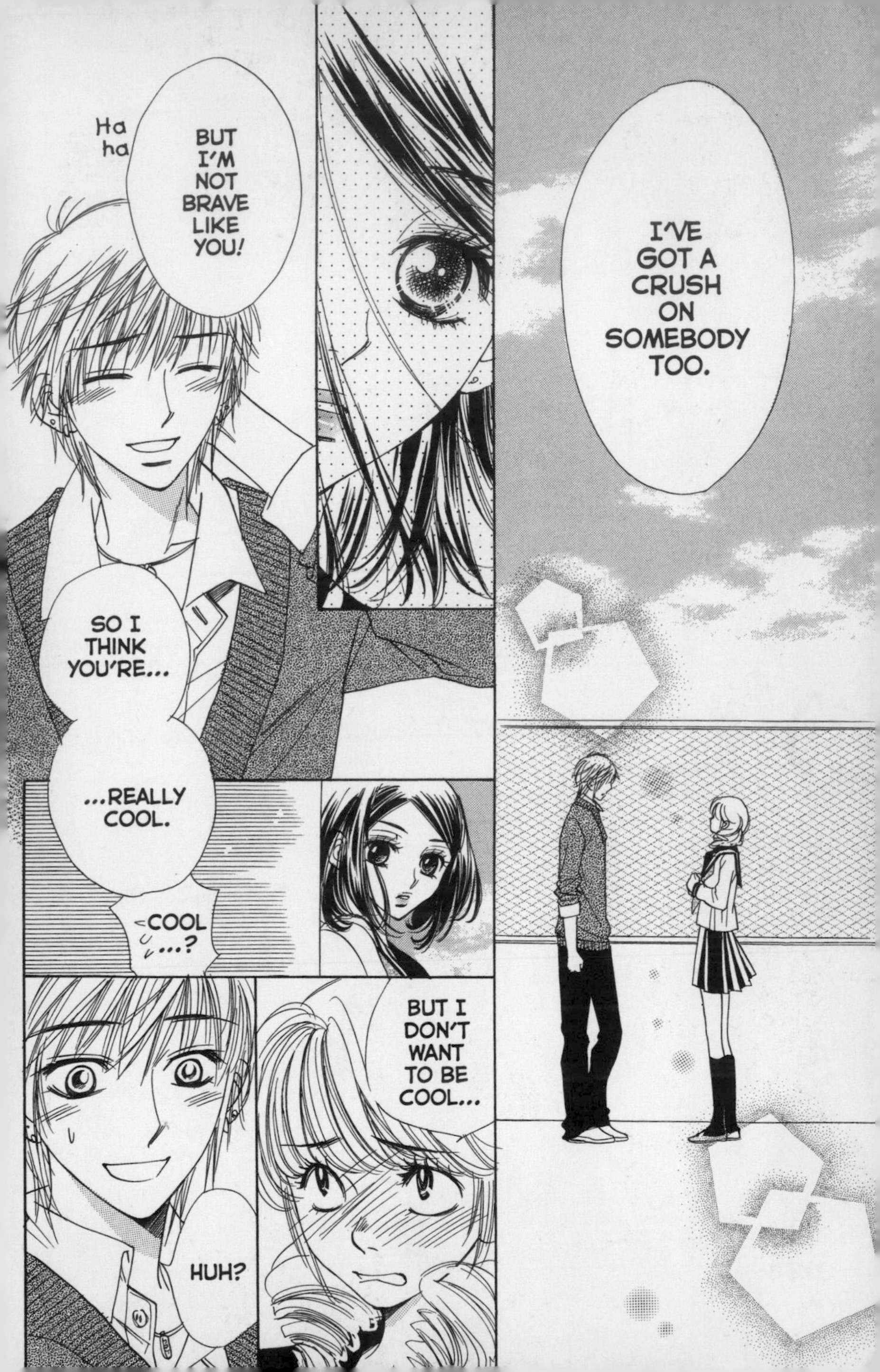
I'VE GOT A CRUSH ON SOMEBODY TOO.
BUT I'M NOT BRAVE LIKE YOU!
Ha ha
SO I THINK YOU'RE...
...REALLY COOL.
COOL...?
BUT I DON'T WANT TO BE COOL...
HUH?

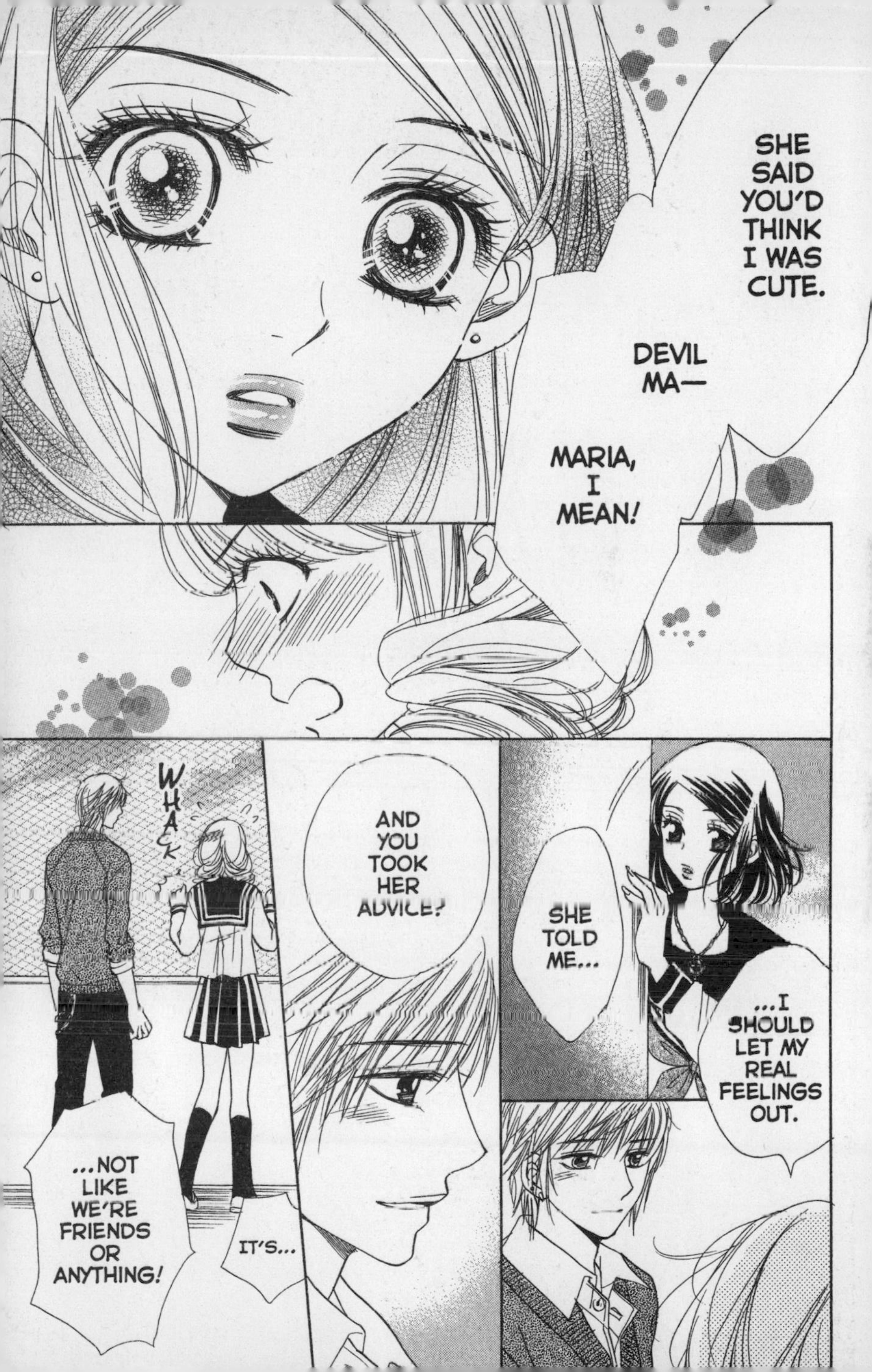
SHE SAID YOU'D THINK I WAS CUTE.
DEVIL MA—
MARIA, I MEAN!
SHE TOLD ME...
...I SHOULD LET MY REAL FEELINGS OUT.
AND YOU TOOK HER ADVICE?
IT'S...
WHACK
...NOT LIKE WE'RE FRIENDS OR ANYTHING!

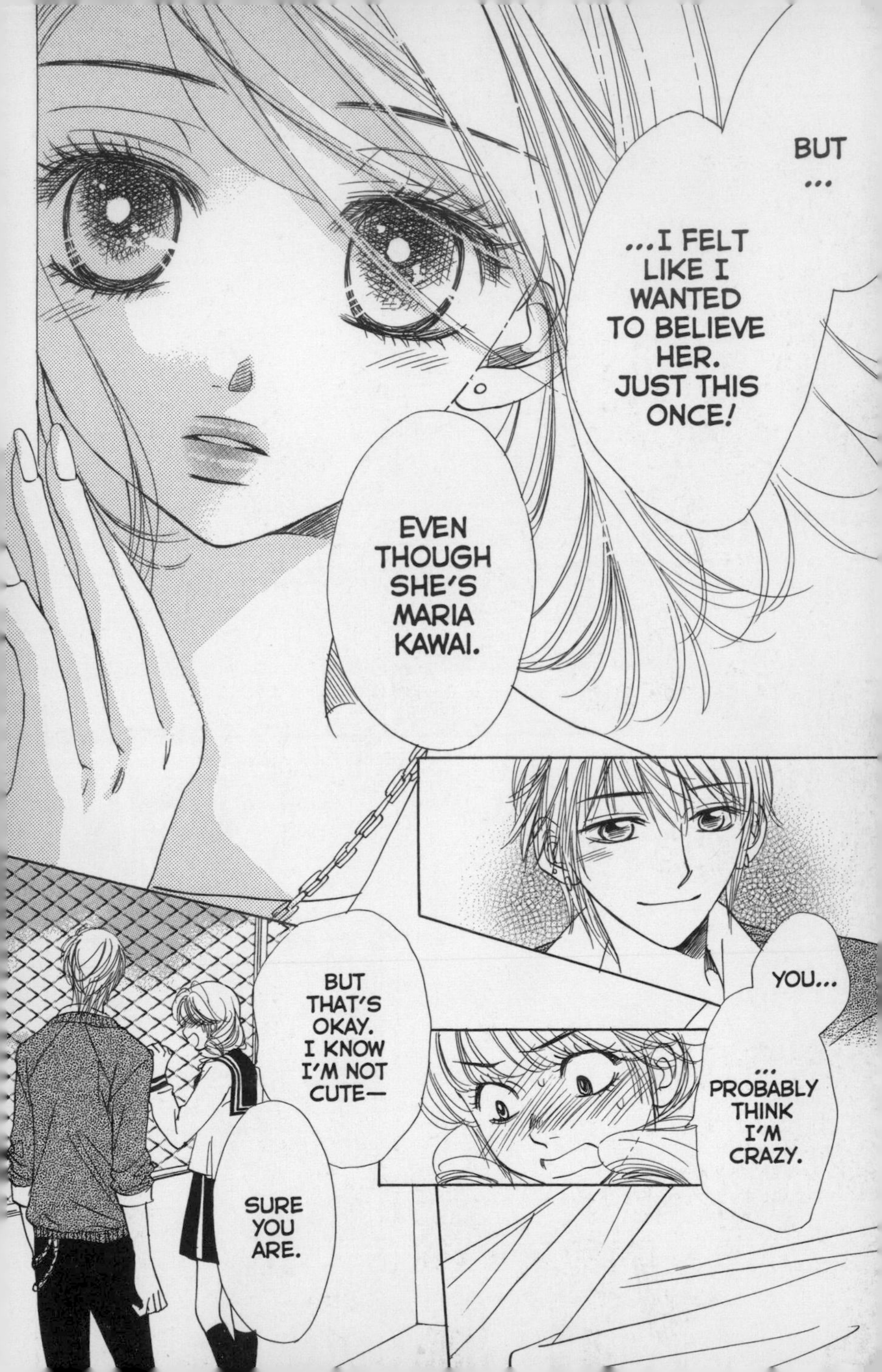
BUT ...
...I FELT LIKE I WANTED TO BELIEVE HER. JUST THIS ONCE!
EVEN THOUGH SHE'S MARIA KAWAI.
YOU...
...PROBABLY THINK I'M CRAZY.
BUT THAT'S OKAY. I KNOW I'M NOT CUTE—
SURE YOU ARE.

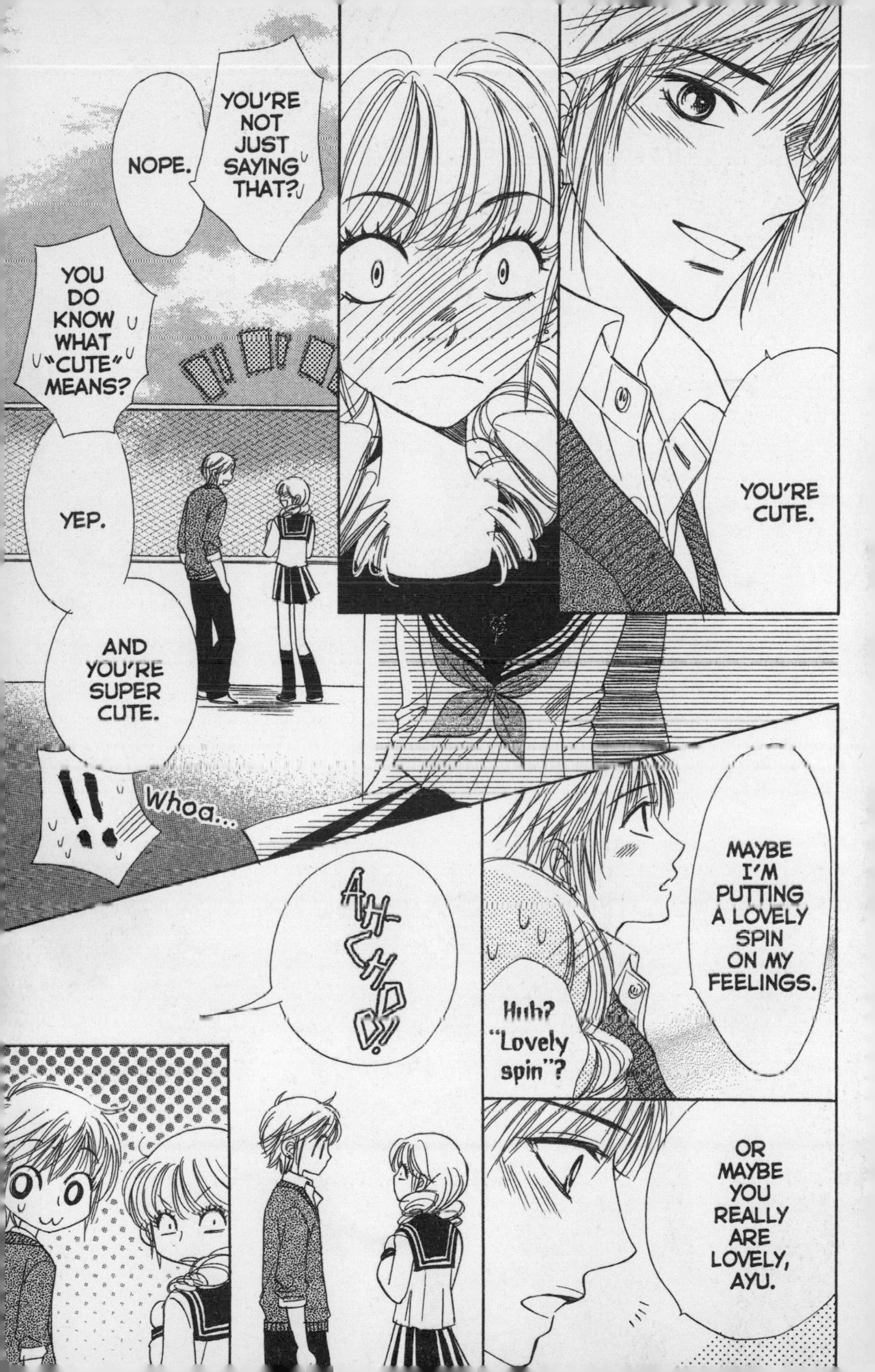
YOU'RE CUTE.
YOU'RE NOT JUST SAYING THAT?
NOPE.
YOU DO KNOW WHAT "CUTE" MEANS?
YEP.
AND YOU'RE SUPER CUTE.
!!
Whoa...
MAYBE I'M PUTTING A LOVELY SPIN ON MY FEELINGS.
Huh? "Lovely spin"?
AH-CHOO!
OR MAYBE YOU REALLY ARE LOVELY, AYU.

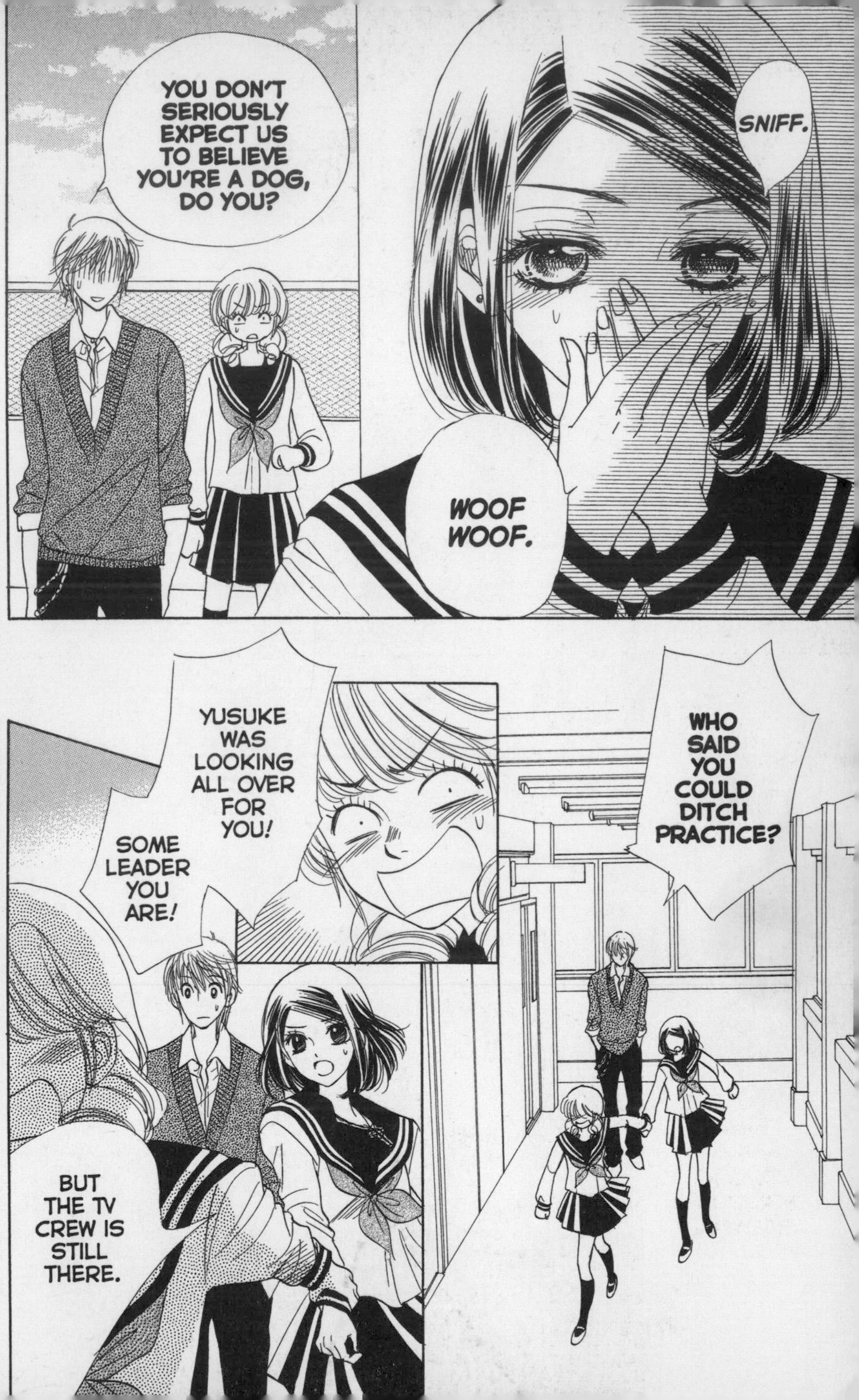
SNIFF.
WOOF WOOF.
YOU DON'T SERIOUSLY EXPECT US TO BELIEVE YOU'RE A DOG, DO YOU?
WHO SAID YOU COULD DITCH PRACTICE?
YUSUKE WAS LOOKING ALL OVER FOR YOU!
SOME LEADER YOU ARE!
BUT THE TV CREW IS STILL THERE.

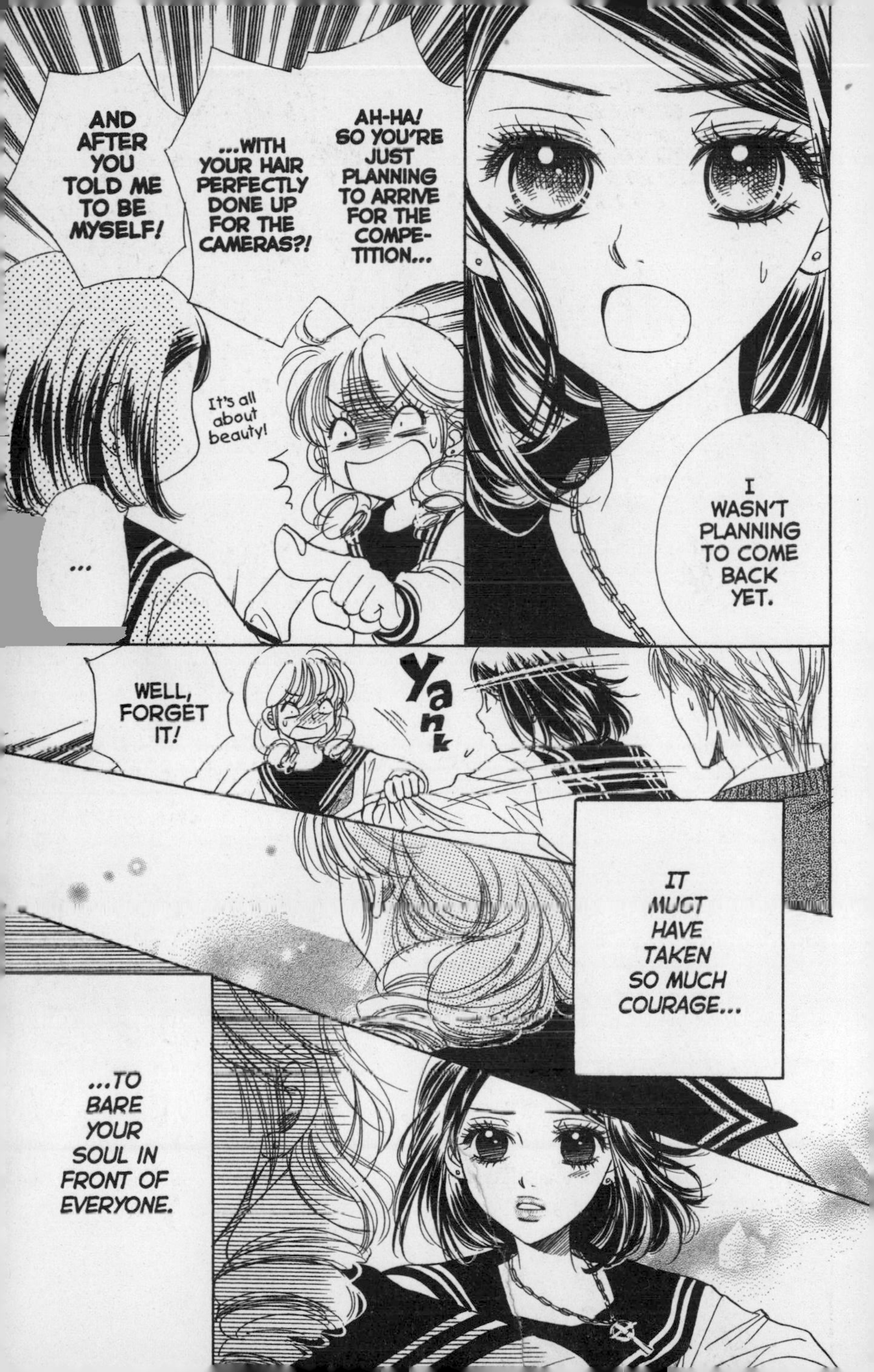
I WASN'T PLANNING TO COME BACK YET.
AH-HA! SO YOU'RE JUST PLANNING TO ARRIVE FOR THE COMPETITION...
...WITH YOUR HAIR PERFECTLY DONE UP FOR THE CAMERAS?!
AND AFTER YOU TOLD ME TO BE MYSELF!
It's all about beauty!
...
Yank
WELL, FORGET IT!
IT MUST HAVE TAKEN SO MUCH COURAGE...
...TO BARE YOUR SOUL IN FRONT OF EVERYONE.

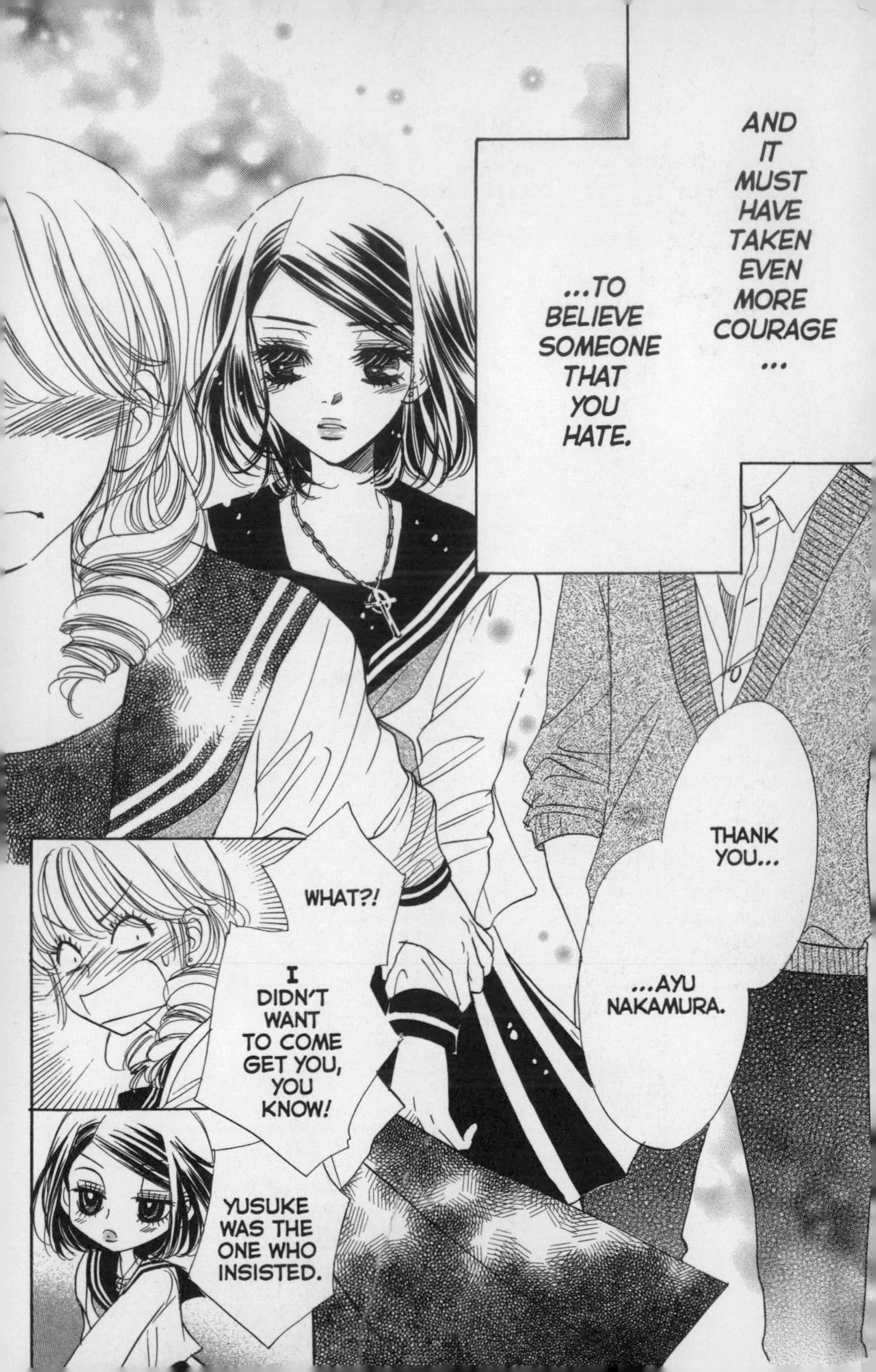
AND IT MUST HAVE TAKEN EVEN MORE COURAGE...
...TO BELIEVE SOMEONE THAT YOU HATE.
THANK YOU...
...AYU NAKAMURA.
WHAT?!
I DIDN'T WANT TO COME GET YOU, YOU KNOW!
YUSUKE WAS THE ONE WHO INSISTED.

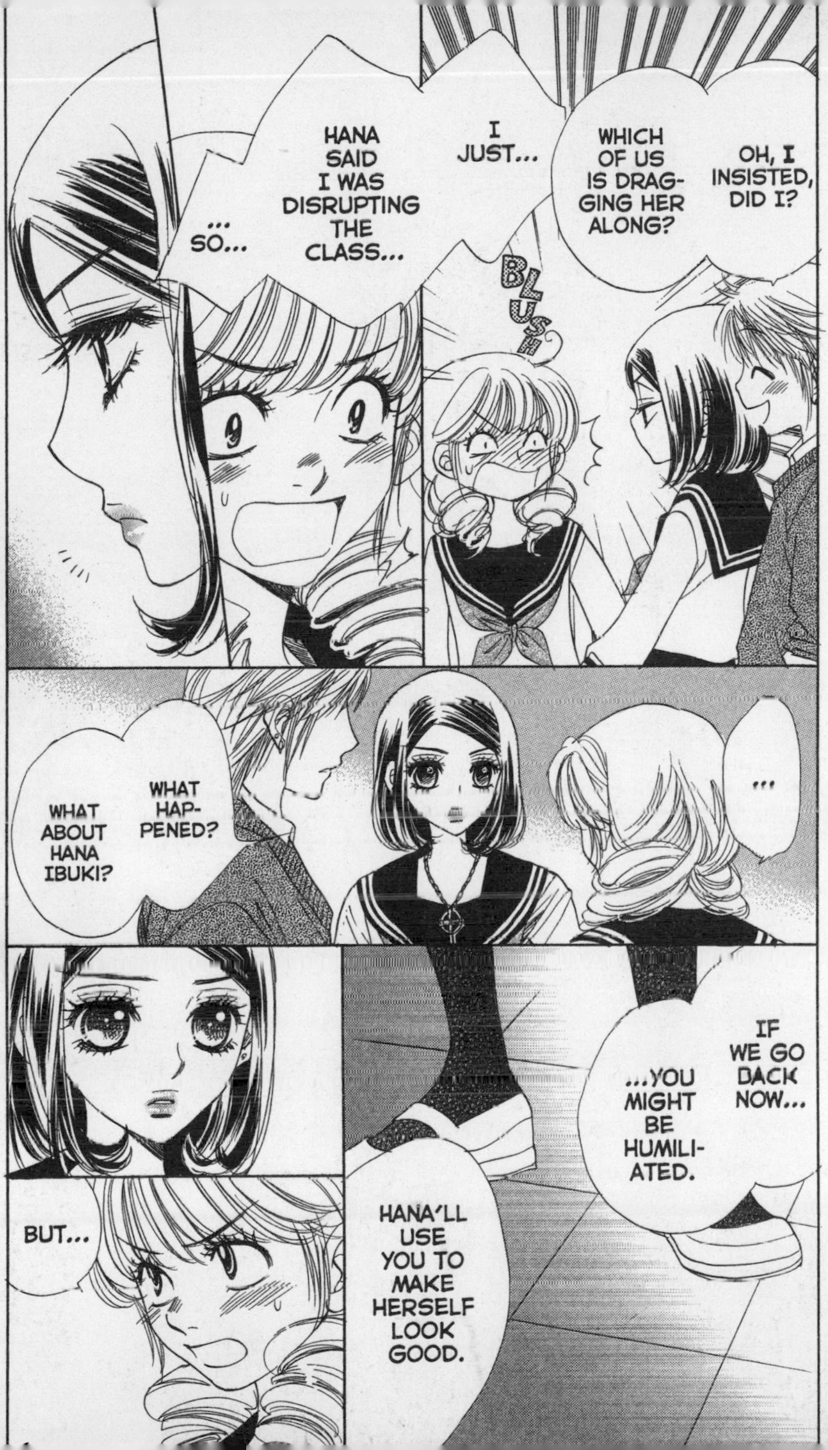
OH, I INSISTED, DID I?
WHICH OF US IS DRAG-GING HER ALONG?
BLUSH
I JUST...
HANA SAID I WAS DISRUPTING THE CLASS...
... SO...
...
WHAT HAP-PENED?
WHAT ABOUT HANA IBUKI?
IF WE GO BACK NOW...
...YOU MIGHT BE HUMILI-ATED.
HANA'LL USE YOU TO MAKE HERSELF LOOK GOOD.
BUT...

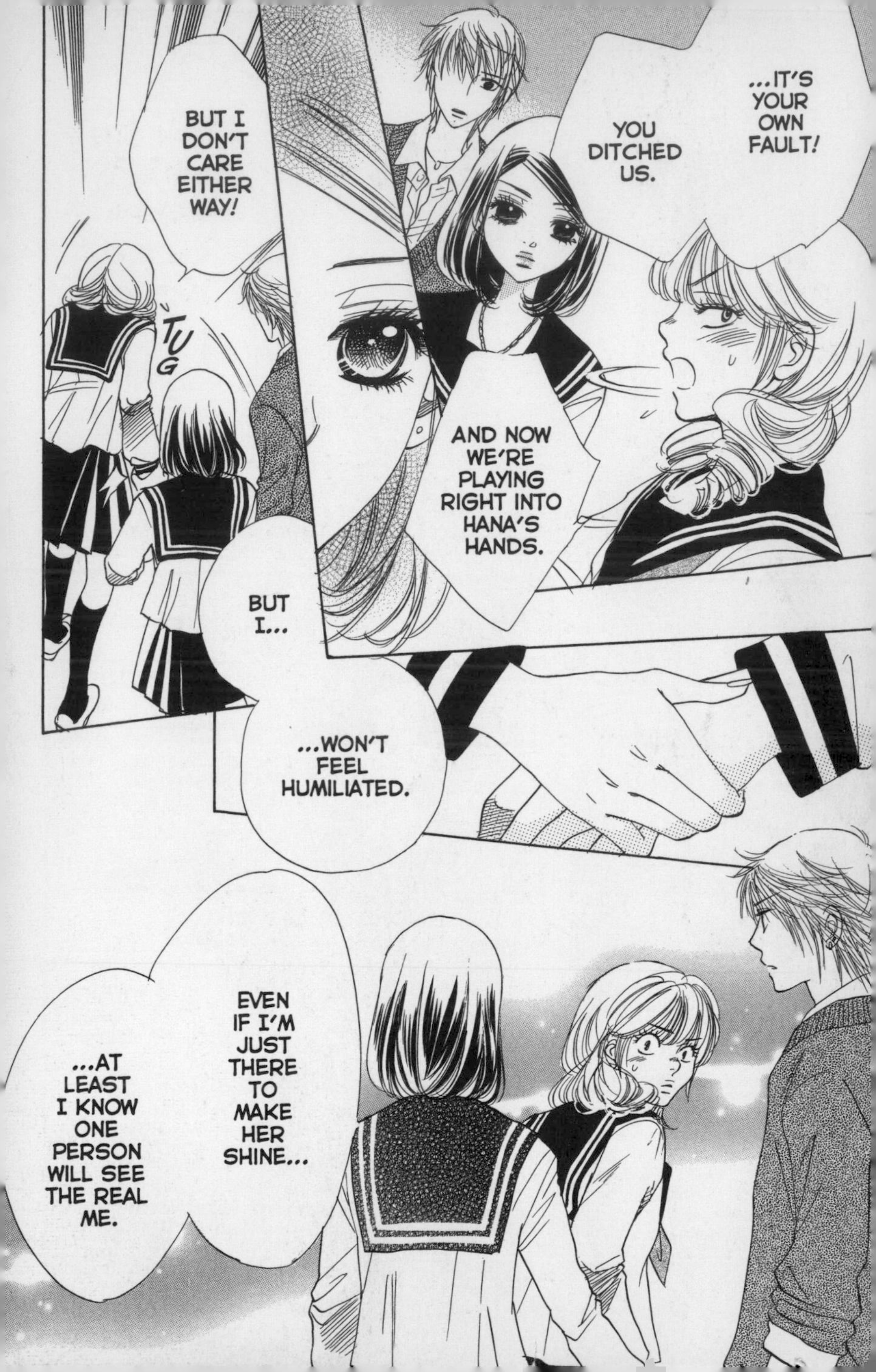
...IT'S YOUR OWN FAULT!
YOU DITCHED US.
AND NOW WE'RE PLAYING RIGHT INTO HANA'S HANDS.
BUT I DON'T CARE EITHER WAY!
TUG
BUT I...
...WON'T FEEL HUMILIATED.
EVEN IF I'M JUST THERE TO MAKE HER SHINE...
...AT LEAST I KNOW ONE PERSON WILL SEE THE REAL ME.

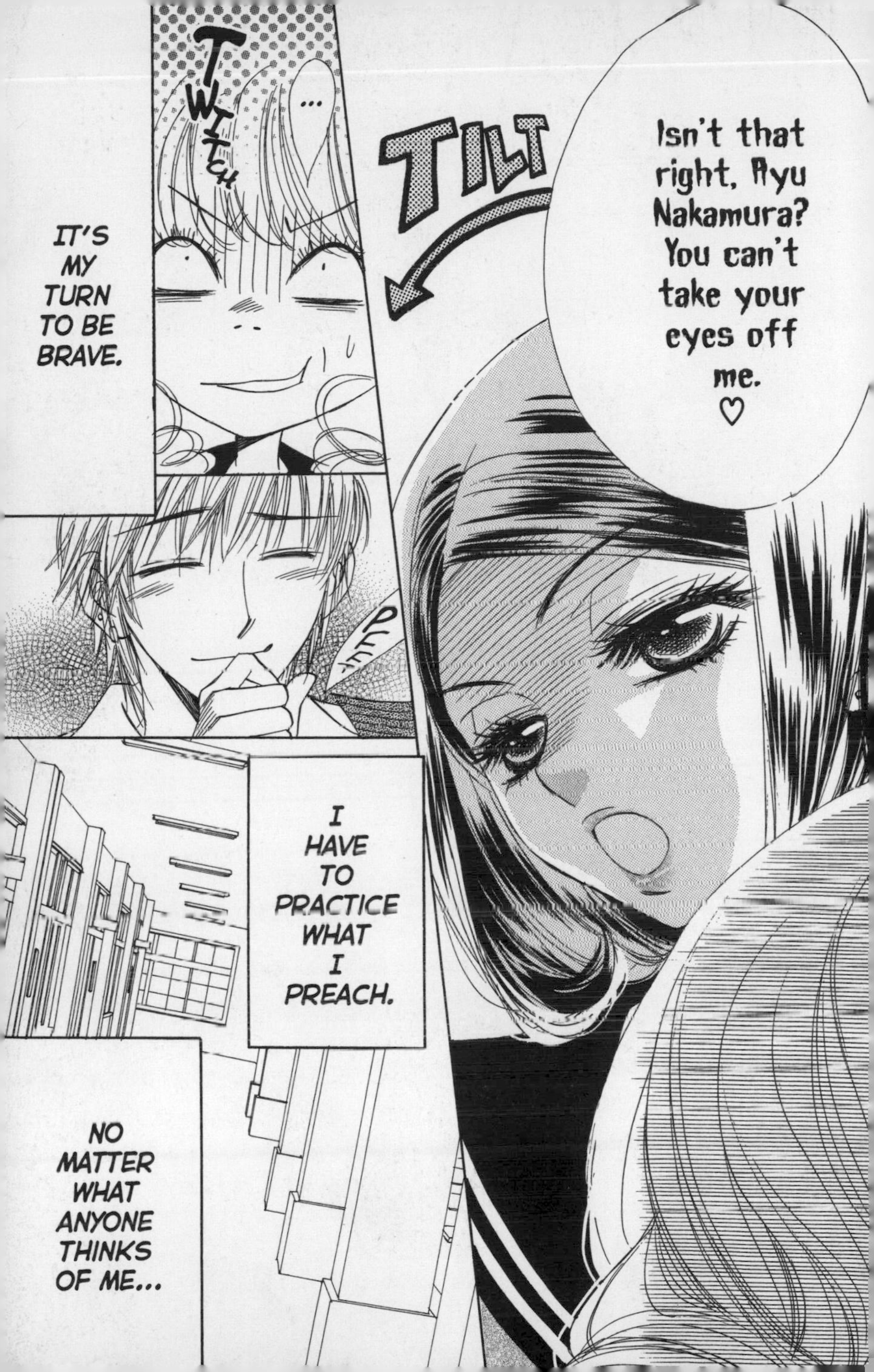
Isn't that right, Ayu Nakamura? You can't take your eyes off me. ♡
TILT
TWITCH
...
IT'S MY TURN TO BE BRAVE.
I HAVE TO PRACTICE WHAT I PREACH.
NO MATTER WHAT ANYONE THINKS OF ME...

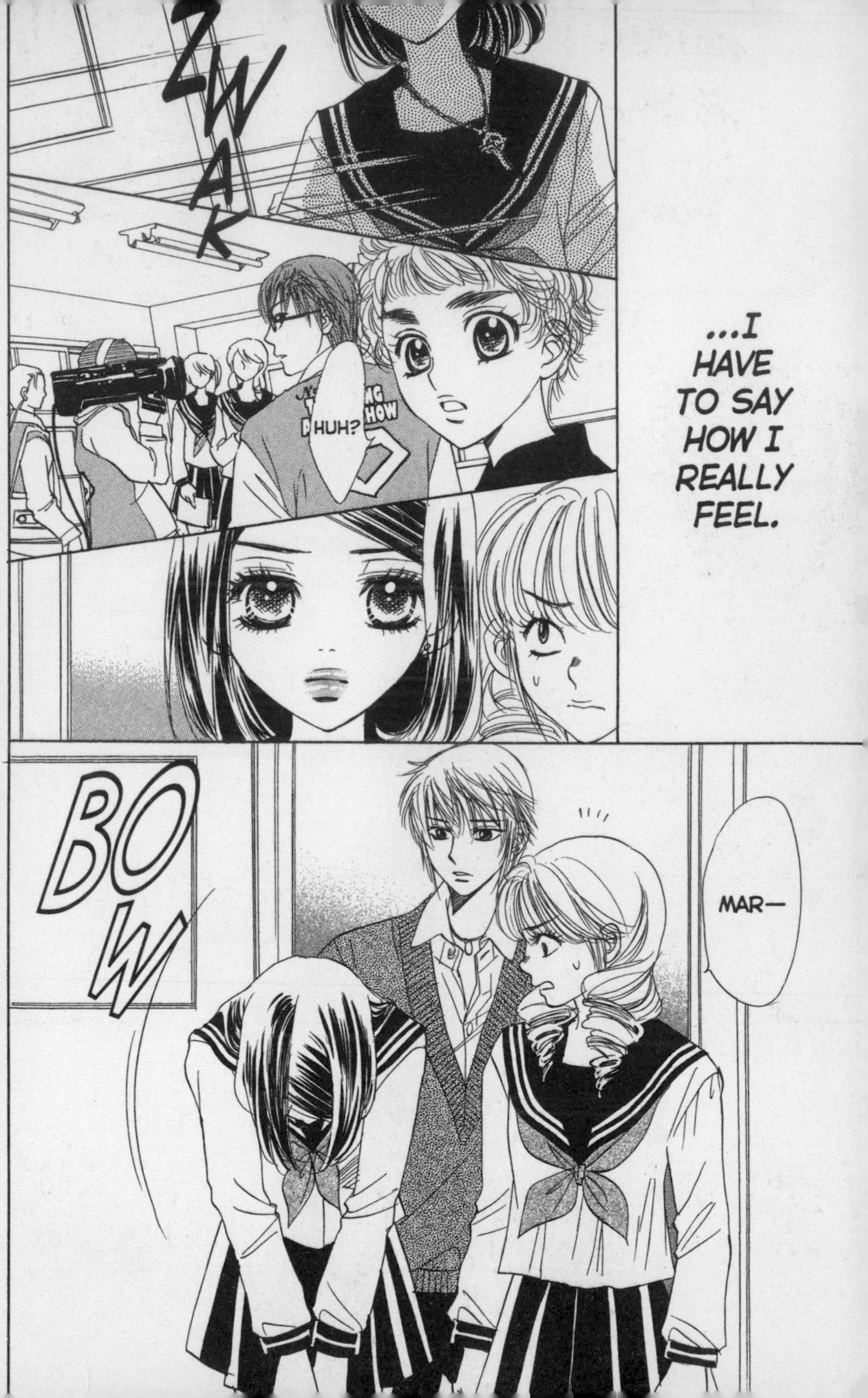
ZWAK
HUH?
...I HAVE TO SAY HOW I REALLY FEEL.
MAR—
BOW

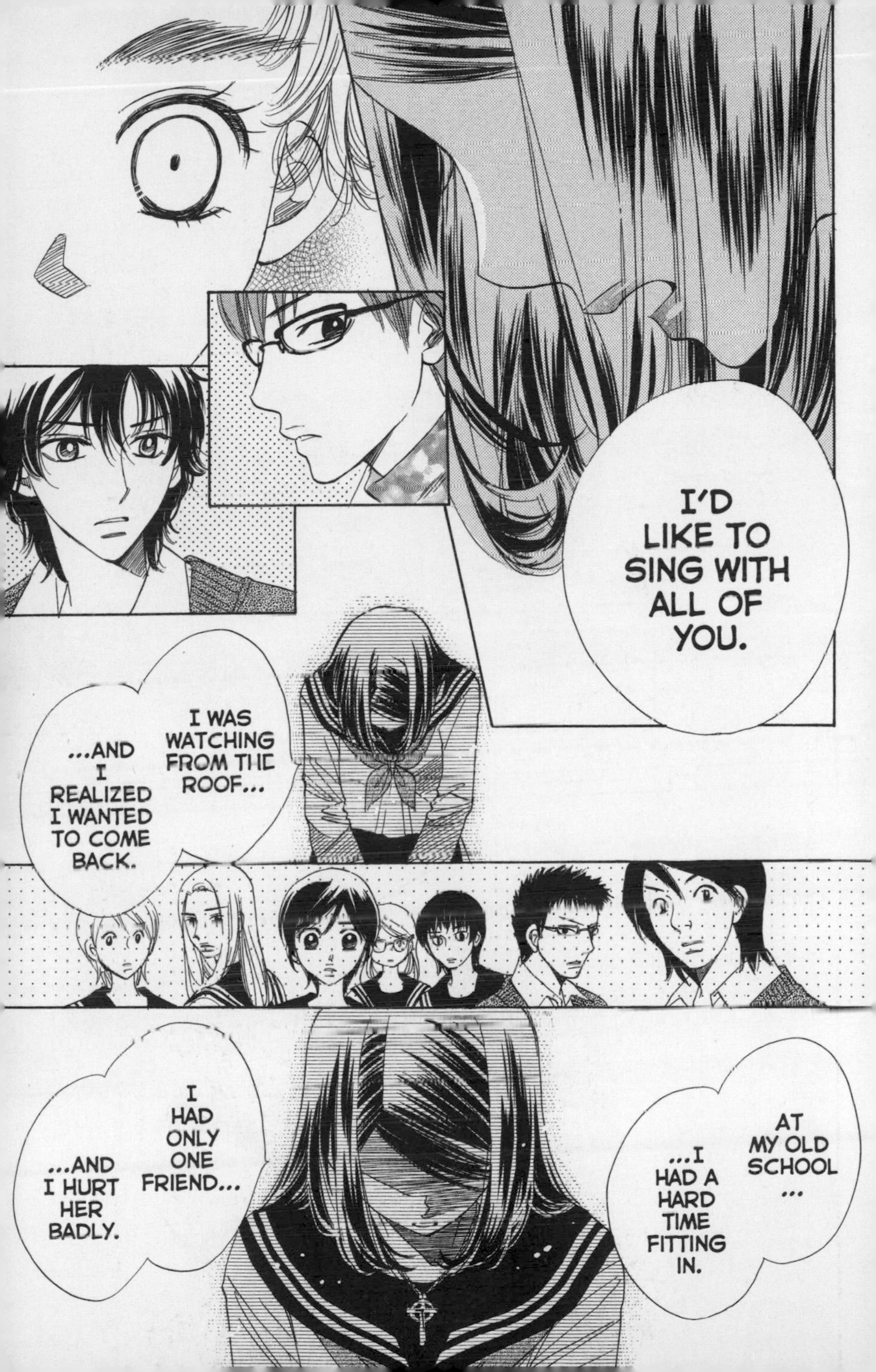
I'D LIKE TO SING WITH ALL OF YOU.
I WAS WATCHING FROM THE ROOF...
...AND I REALIZED I WANTED TO COME BACK.
AT MY OLD SCHOOL...
...I HAD A HARD TIME FITTING IN.
I HAD ONLY ONE FRIEND...
...AND I HURT HER BADLY.

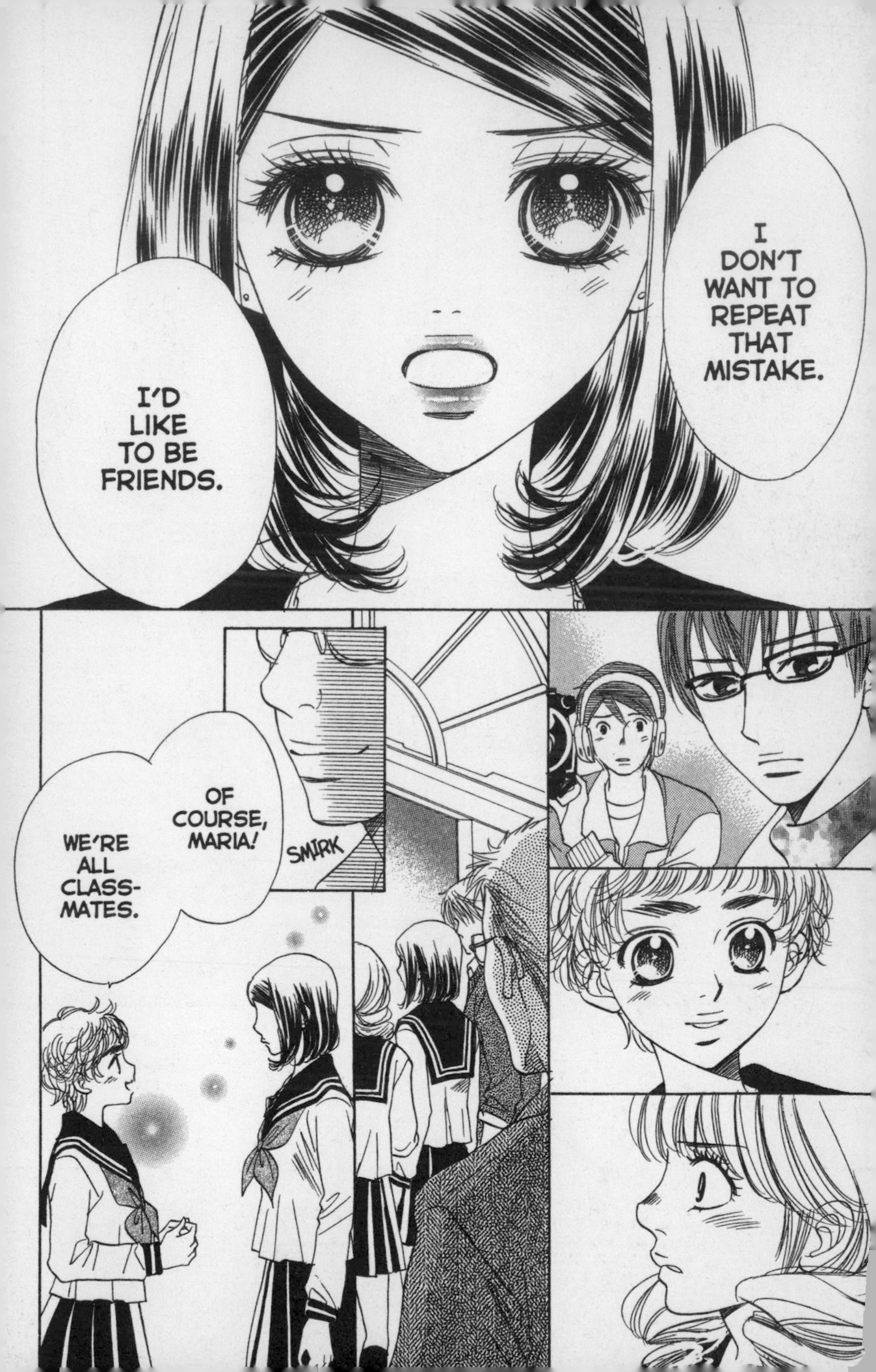
I DON'T WANT TO REPEAT THAT MISTAKE.
I'D LIKE TO BE FRIENDS.
OF COURSE, MARIA!
SMIRK
WE'RE ALL CLASS-MATES.

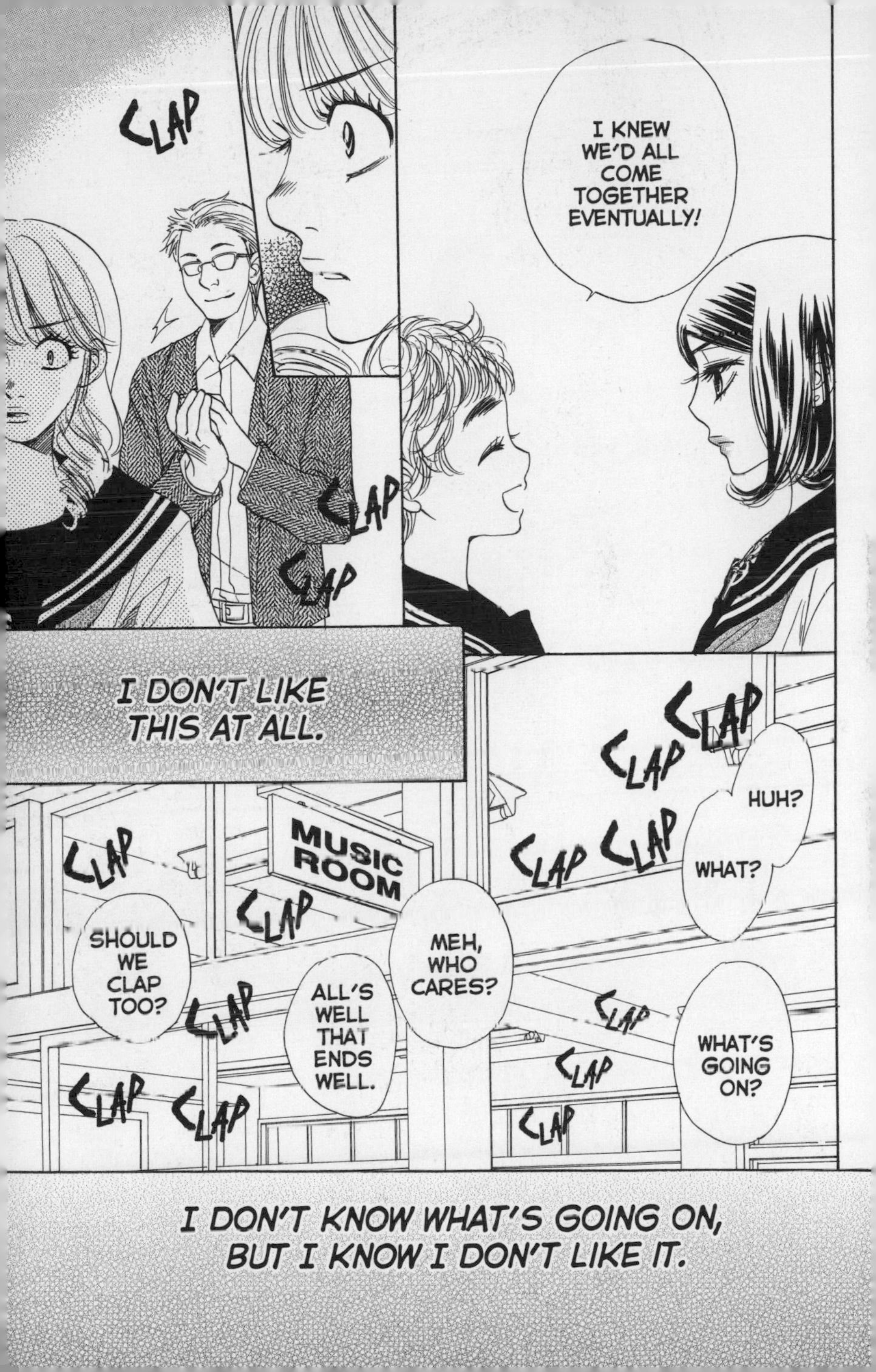
I KNEW WE'D ALL COME TOGETHER EVENTUALLY!
CLAP
CLAP
CLAP
I DON'T LIKE THIS AT ALL.
CLAP
CLAP
HUH?
WHAT?
CLAP
CLAP
WHAT'S GOING ON?
CLAP
CLAP
CLAP
MUSIC ROOM
MEH, WHO CARES?
ALL'S WELL THAT ENDS WELL.
CLAP
CLAP
CLAP
SHOULD WE CLAP TOO?
CLAP
CLAP
I DON'T KNOW WHAT'S GOING ON, BUT I KNOW I DON'T LIKE IT.

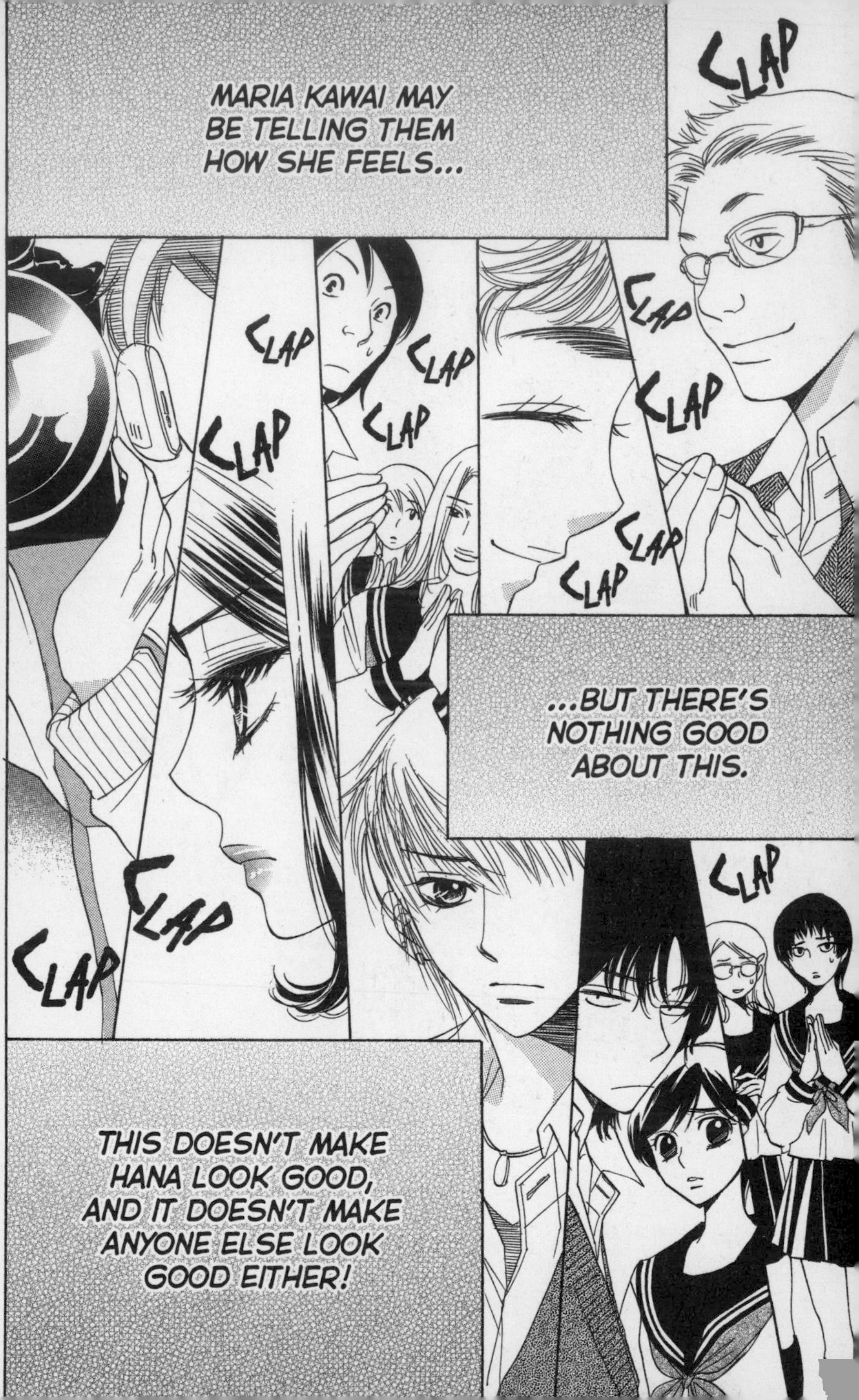
CLAP
MARIA KAWAI MAY BE TELLING THEM HOW SHE FEELS...
CLAP
CLAP
CLAP
CLAP
CLAP
CLAP
CLAP
CLAP
CLAP
CLAP
...BUT THERE'S NOTHING GOOD ABOUT THIS.
CLAP
THIS DOESN'T MAKE HANA LOOK GOOD, AND IT DOESN'T MAKE ANYONE ELSE LOOK GOOD EITHER!

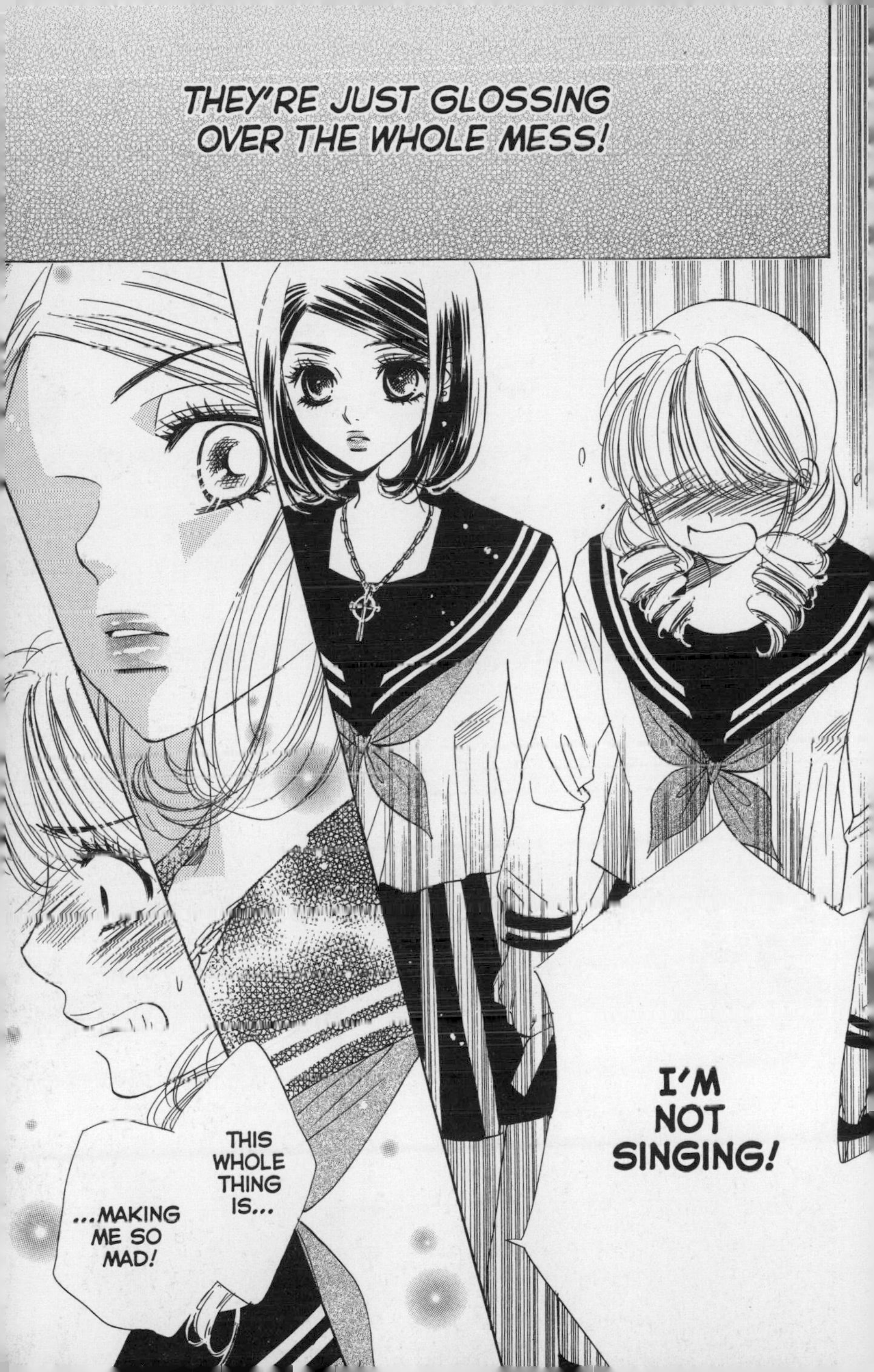
THEY'RE JUST GLOSSING OVER THE WHOLE MESS!
I'M NOT SINGING!
THIS WHOLE THING IS...
...MAKING ME SO MAD!

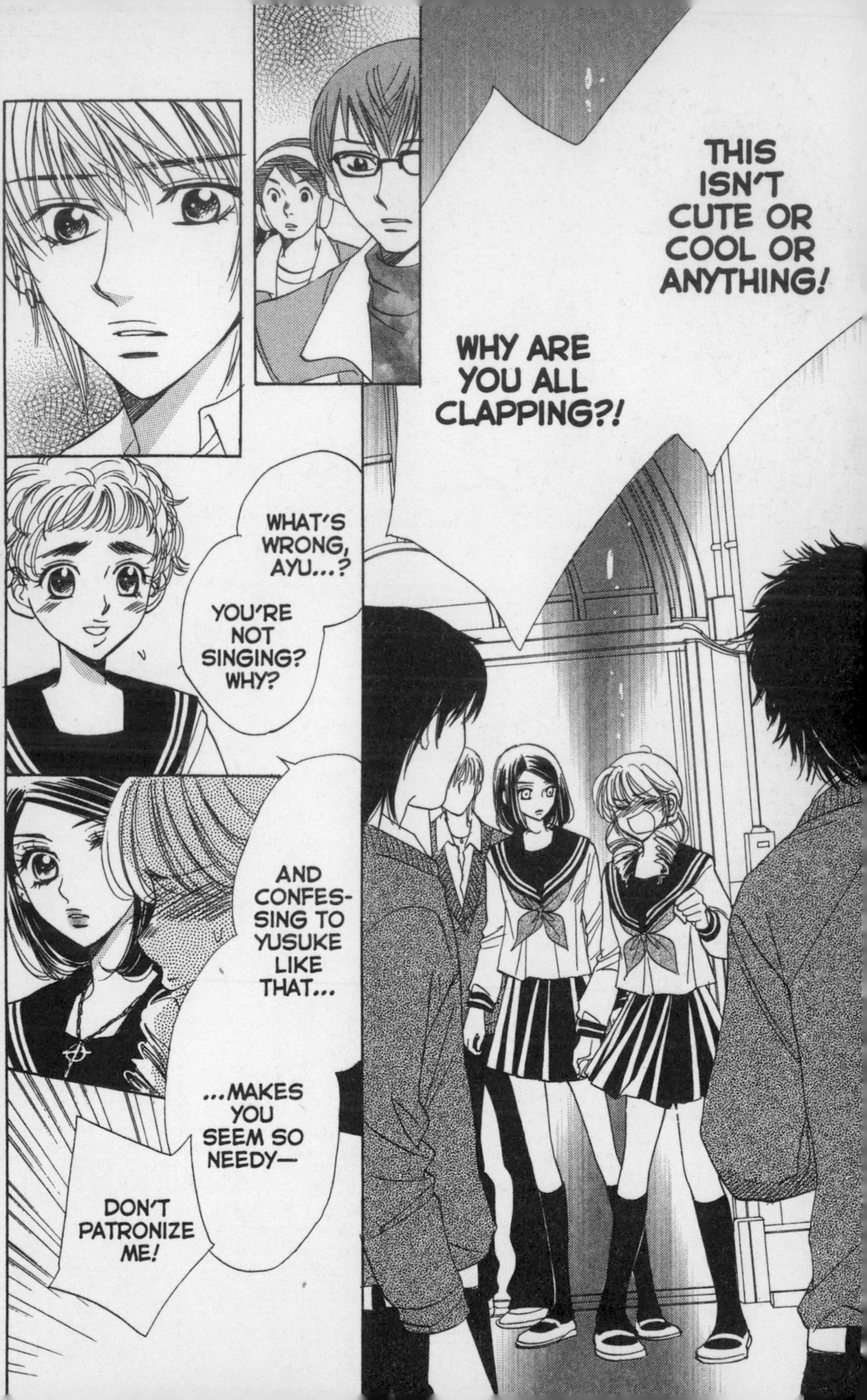
THIS ISN'T CUTE OR COOL OR ANYTHING!
WHY ARE YOU ALL CLAPPING?!
WHAT'S WRONG, AYU...?
YOU'RE NOT SINGING? WHY?
AND CONFES-SING TO YUSUKE LIKE THAT...
...MAKES YOU SEEM SO NEEDY—
DON'T PATRONIZE ME!

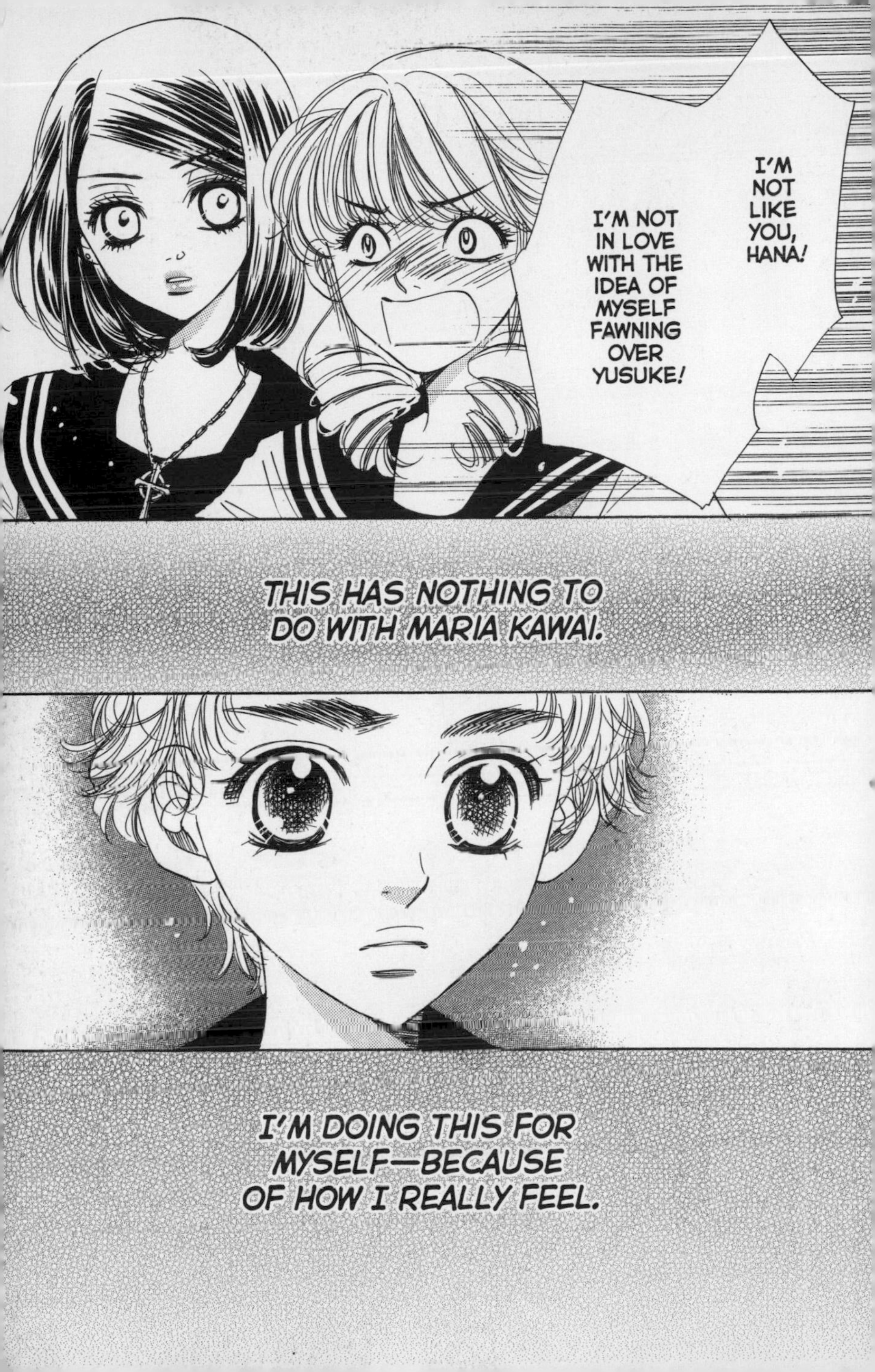
I'M NOT LIKE YOU, HANA!
I'M NOT IN LOVE WITH THE IDEA OF MYSELF FAWNING OVER YUSUKE!
THIS HAS NOTHING TO DO WITH MARIA KAWAI.
I'M DOING THIS FOR MYSELF—BECAUSE OF HOW I REALLY FEEL.

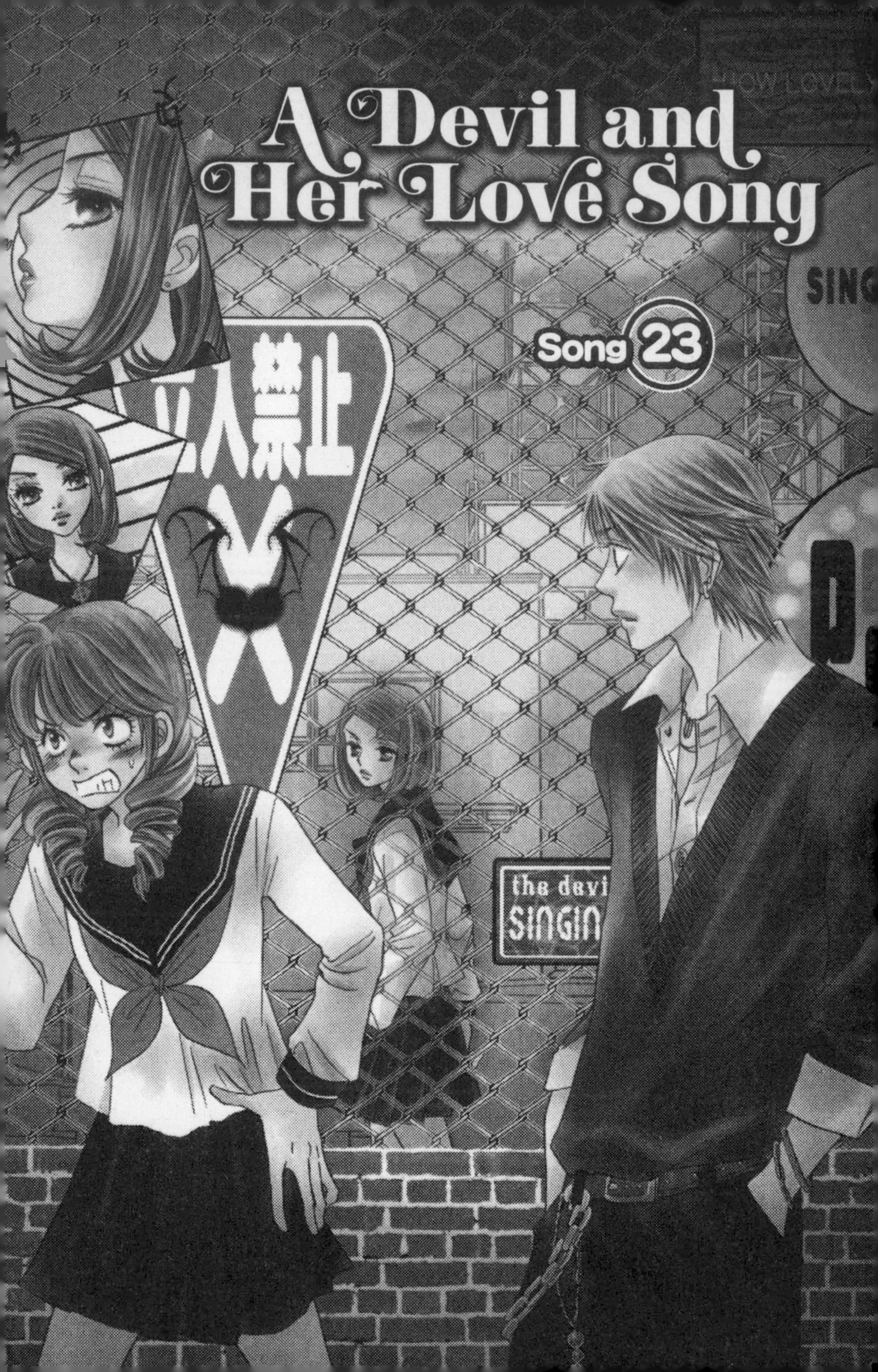
A Devil and Her Love Song
Song 23

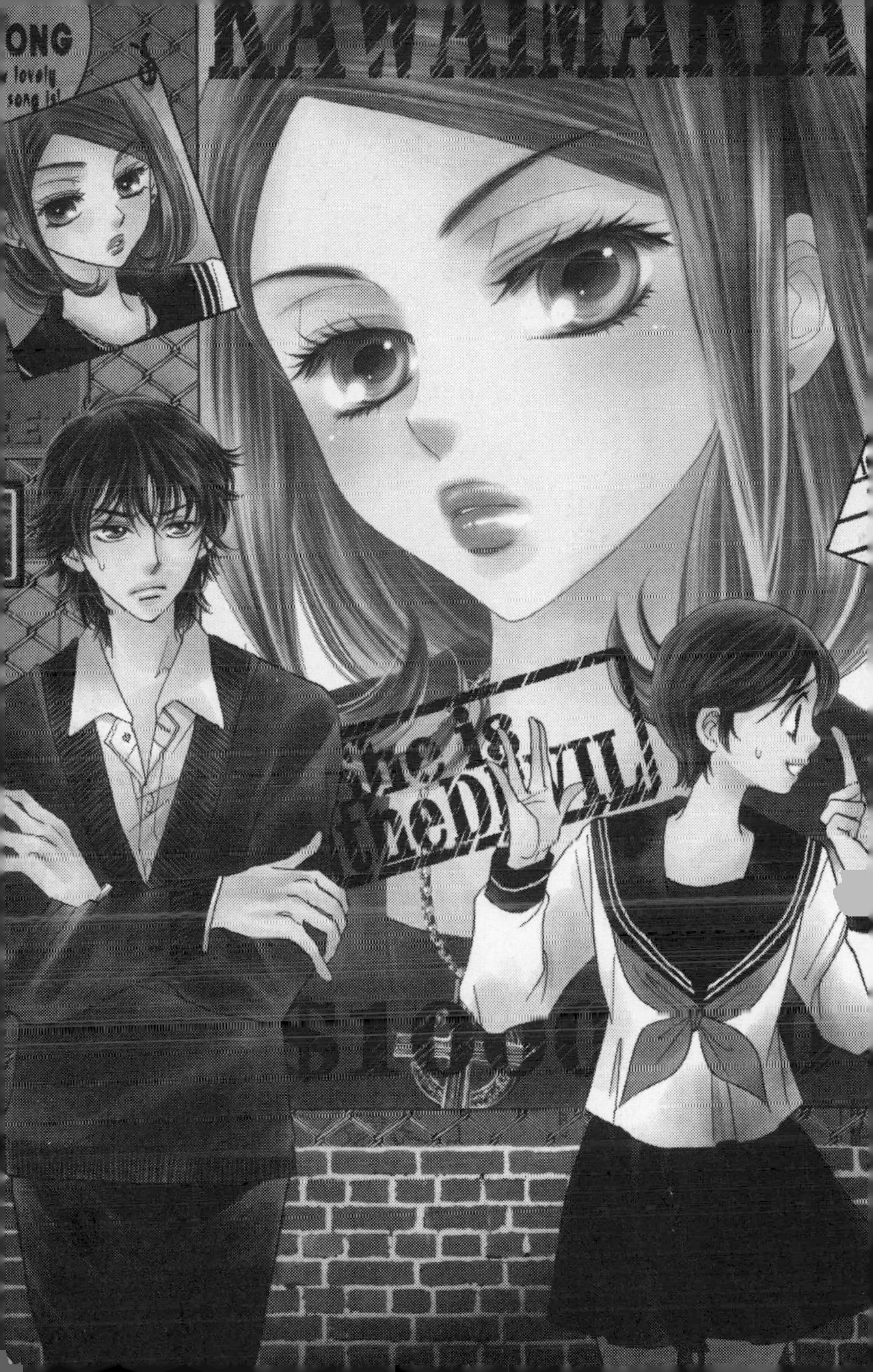
ONG
lovely
song is!

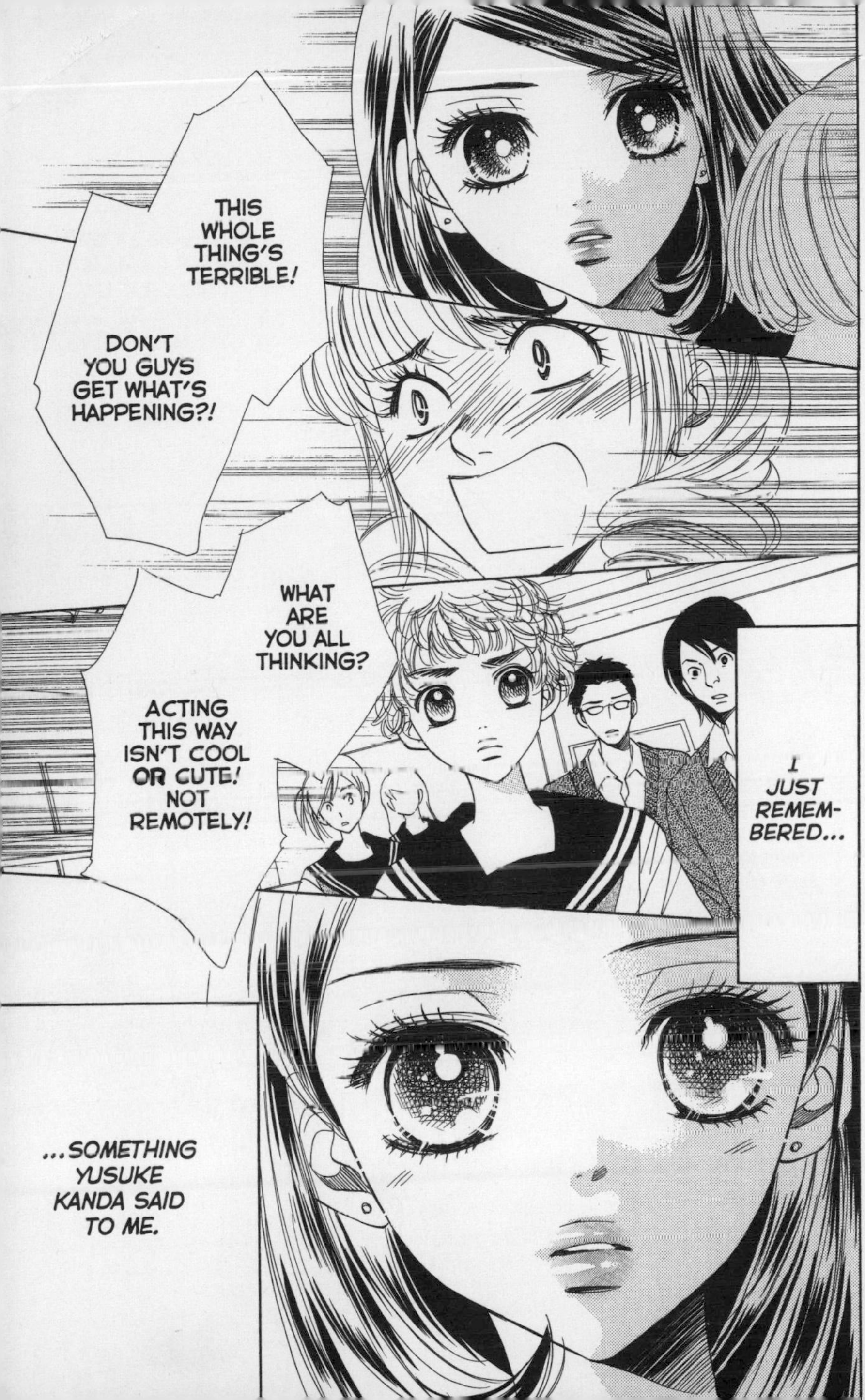
THIS WHOLE THING'S TERRIBLE!
DON'T YOU GUYS GET WHAT'S HAPPENING?!
WHAT ARE YOU ALL THINKING?
ACTING THIS WAY ISN'T COOL OR CUTE! NOT REMOTELY!
I JUST REMEMBERED...
...SOMETHING YUSUKE KANDA SAID TO ME.

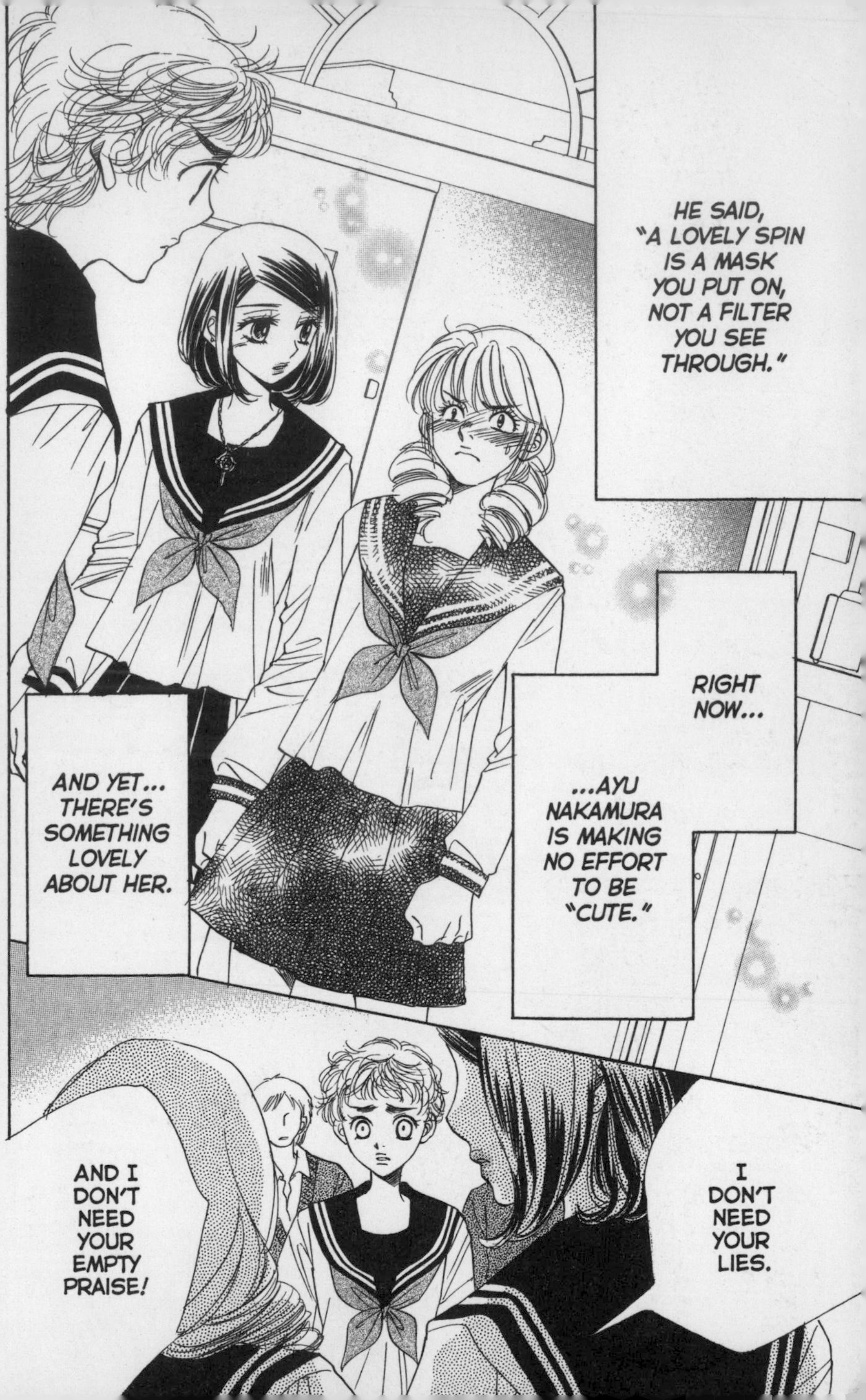
HE SAID, "A LOVELY SPIN IS A MASK YOU PUT ON, NOT A FILTER YOU SEE THROUGH."
RIGHT NOW...
...AYU NAKAMURA IS MAKING NO EFFORT TO BE "CUTE."
AND YET... THERE'S SOMETHING LOVELY ABOUT HER.
I DON'T NEED YOUR LIES.
AND I DON'T NEED YOUR EMPTY PRAISE!

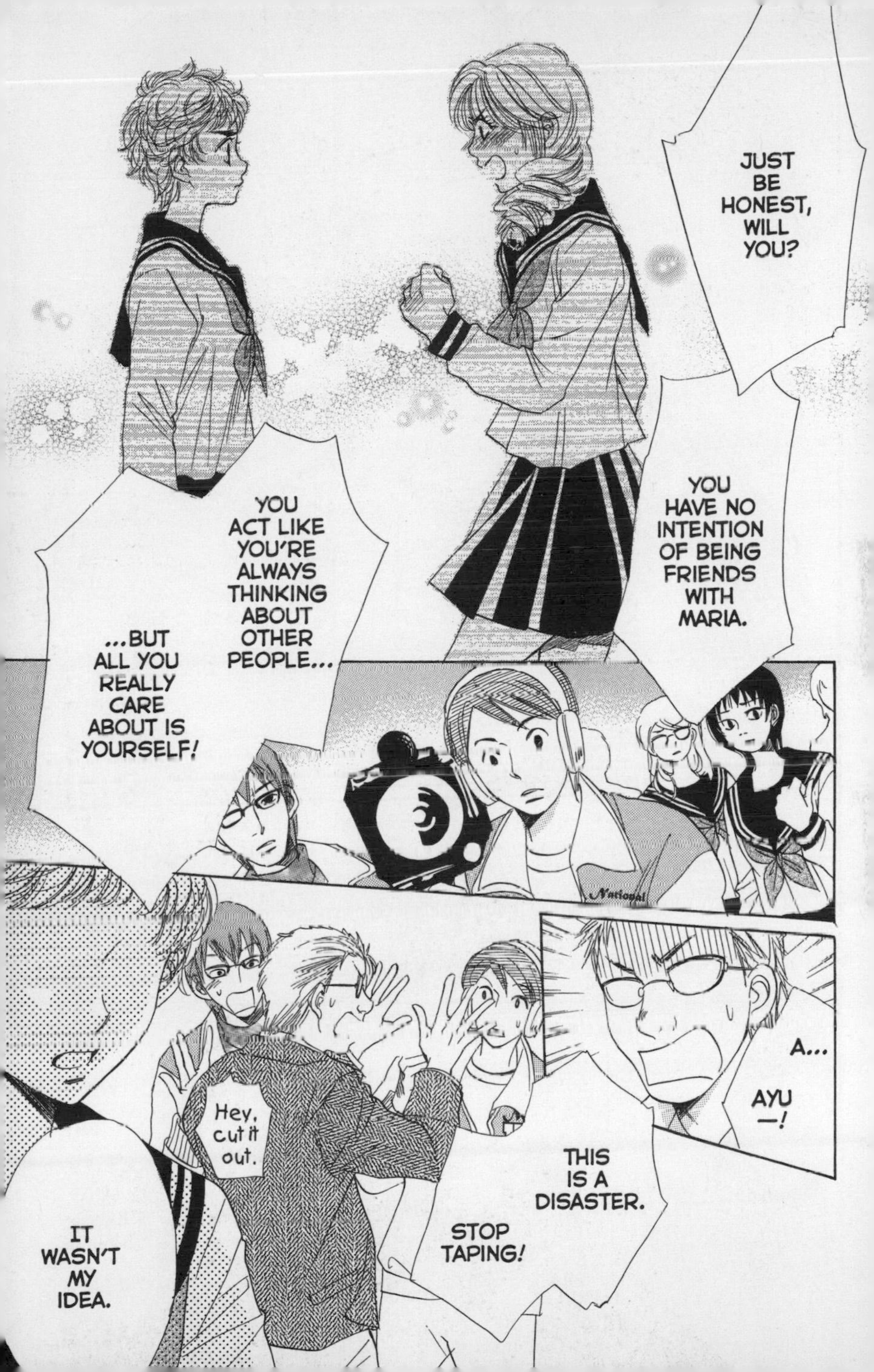
JUST BE HONEST, WILL YOU?
YOU HAVE NO INTENTION OF BEING FRIENDS WITH MARIA.
YOU ACT LIKE YOU'RE ALWAYS THINKING ABOUT OTHER PEOPLE...
...BUT ALL YOU REALLY CARE ABOUT IS YOURSELF!
A...
AYU—!
THIS IS A DISASTER.
STOP TAPING!
Hey, cut it out.
IT WASN'T MY IDEA.

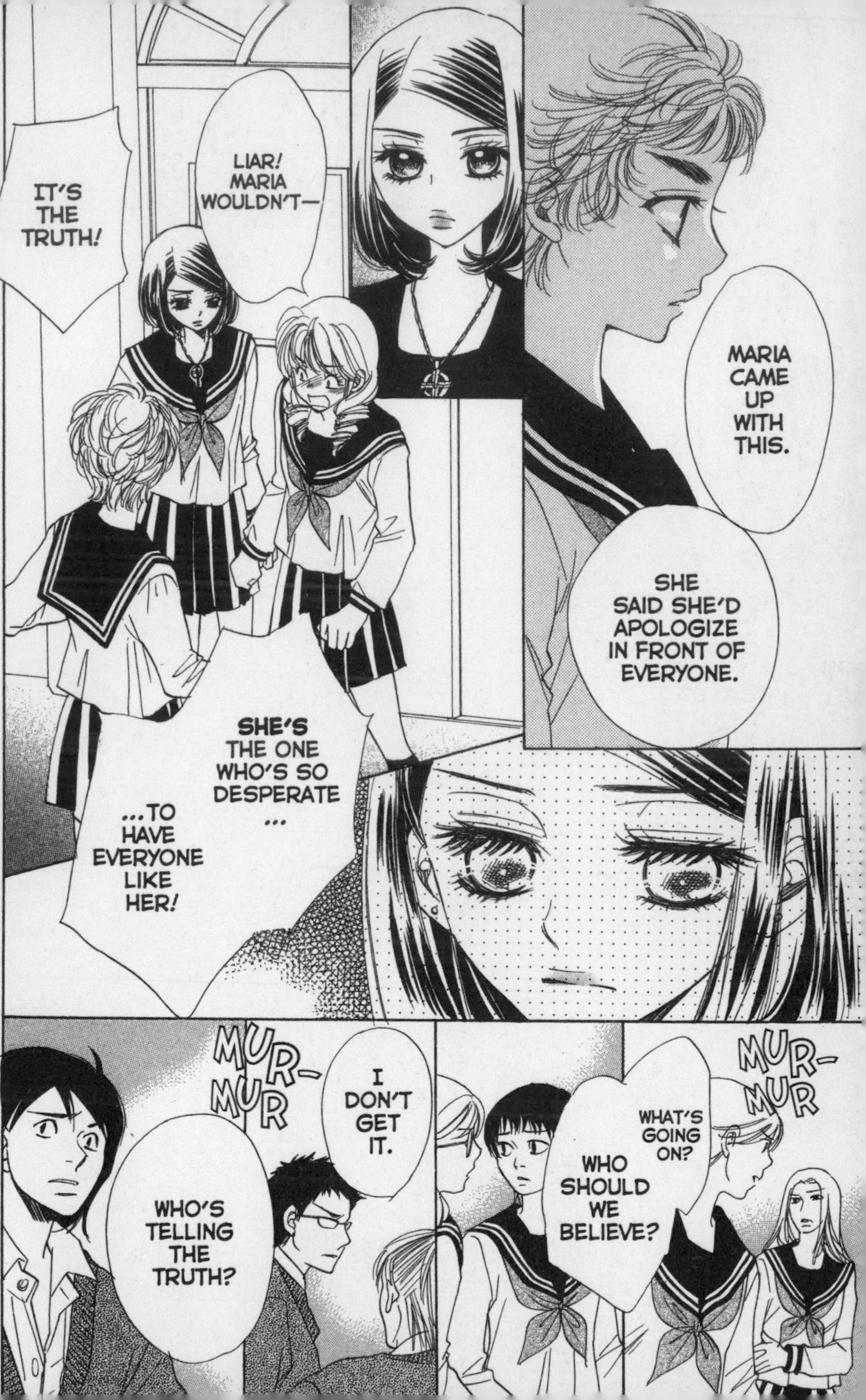
MARIA CAME UP WITH THIS.
SHE SAID SHE'D APOLOGIZE IN FRONT OF EVERYONE.
LIAR! MARIA WOULDN'T—
IT'S THE TRUTH!
SHE'S THE ONE WHO'S SO DESPERATE...
...TO HAVE EVERYONE LIKE HER!
MUR-MUR
WHAT'S GOING ON?
WHO SHOULD WE BELIEVE?
MUR-MUR
I DON'T GET IT.
WHO'S TELLING THE TRUTH?

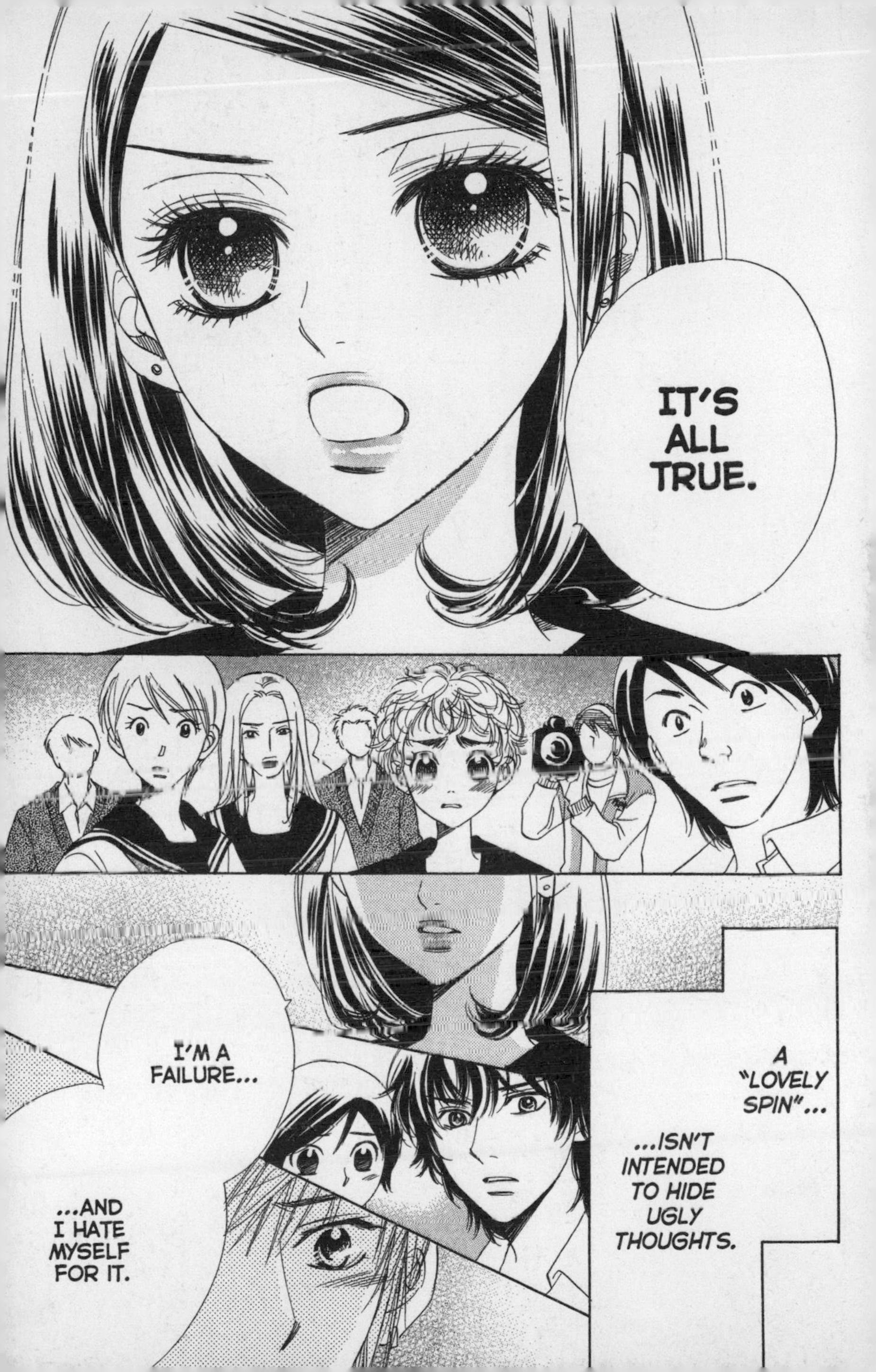
IT'S ALL TRUE.
A "LOVELY SPIN"...
...ISN'T INTENDED TO HIDE UGLY THOUGHTS.
I'M A FAILURE...
...AND I HATE MYSELF FOR IT.

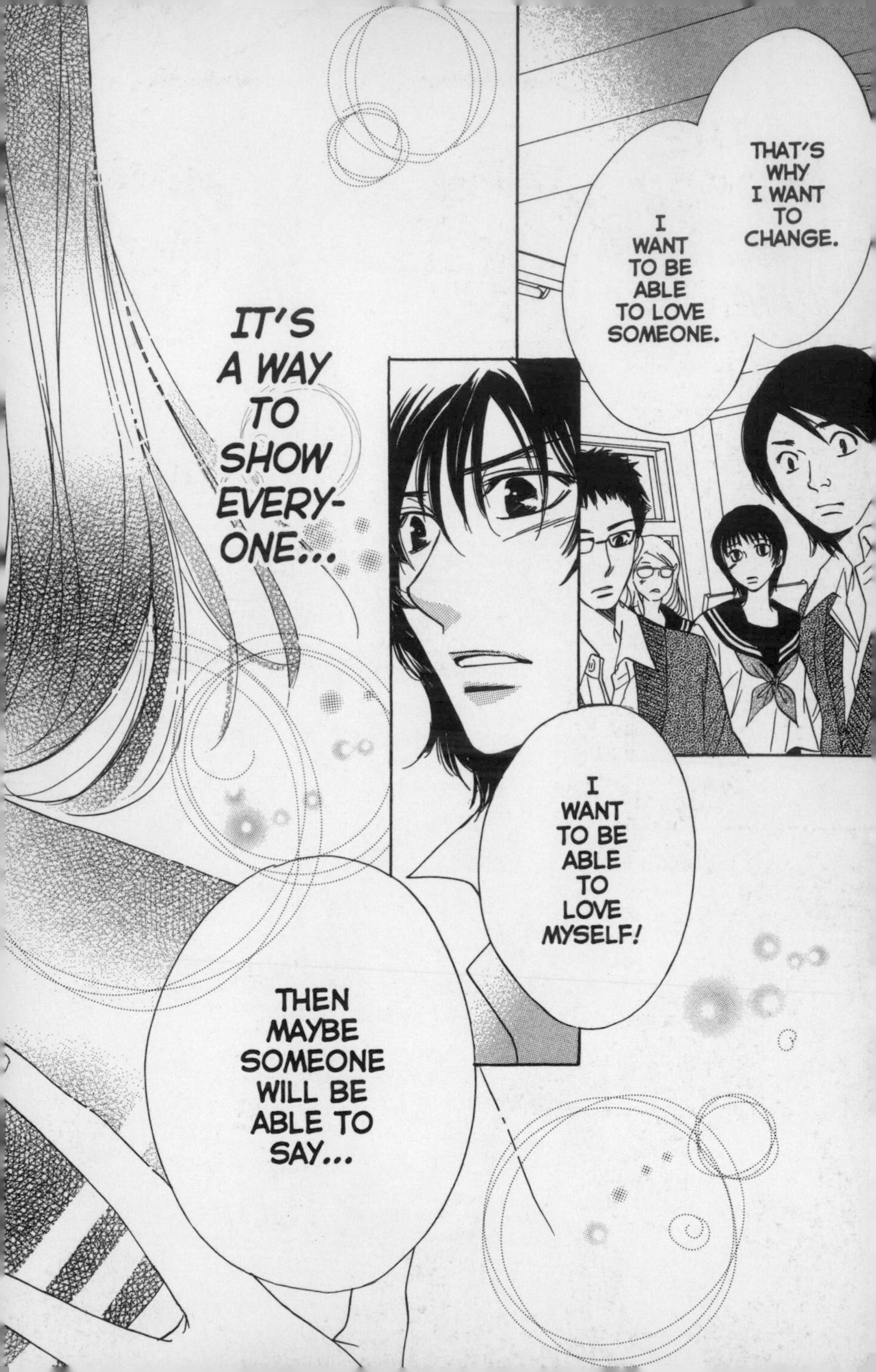
THAT'S WHY I WANT TO CHANGE.
I WANT TO BE ABLE TO LOVE SOMEONE.
I WANT TO BE ABLE TO LOVE MYSELF!
IT'S A WAY TO SHOW EVERYONE...
THEN MAYBE SOMEONE WILL BE ABLE TO SAY...

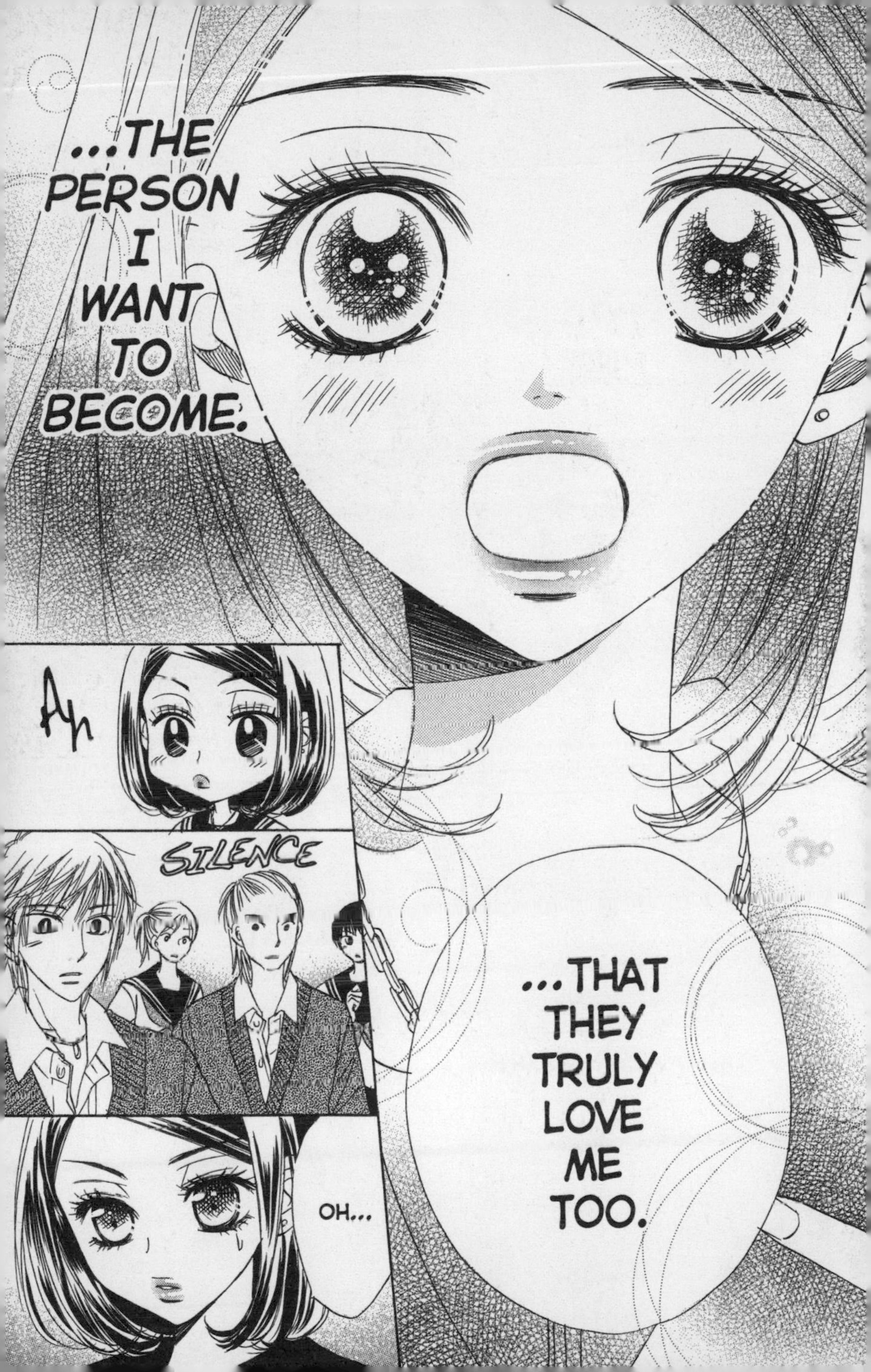
...THE PERSON I WANT TO BECOME.
...THAT THEY TRULY LOVE ME TOO.
Ah
SILENCE
OH...

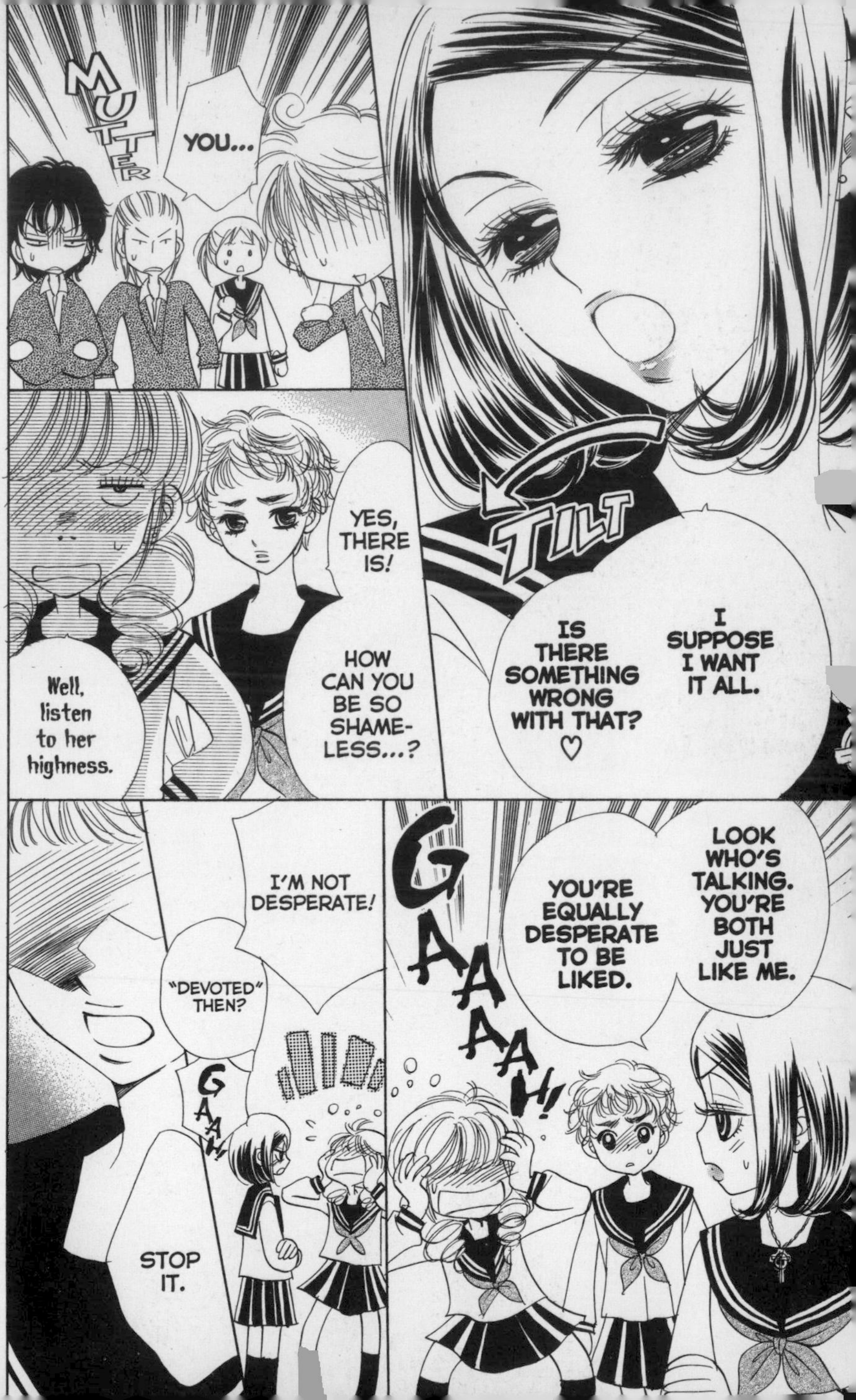
TILT
I SUPPOSE I WANT IT ALL.
IS THERE SOMETHING WRONG WITH THAT? ♡
MUTTER
YOU...
YES, THERE IS!
HOW CAN YOU BE SO SHAME-LESS...?
Well, listen to her highness.
LOOK WHO'S TALKING. YOU'RE BOTH JUST LIKE ME.
YOU'RE EQUALLY DESPERATE TO BE LIKED.
GAAAAH!
I'M NOT DESPERATE!
"DEVOTED" THEN?
GAAH!
STOP IT.

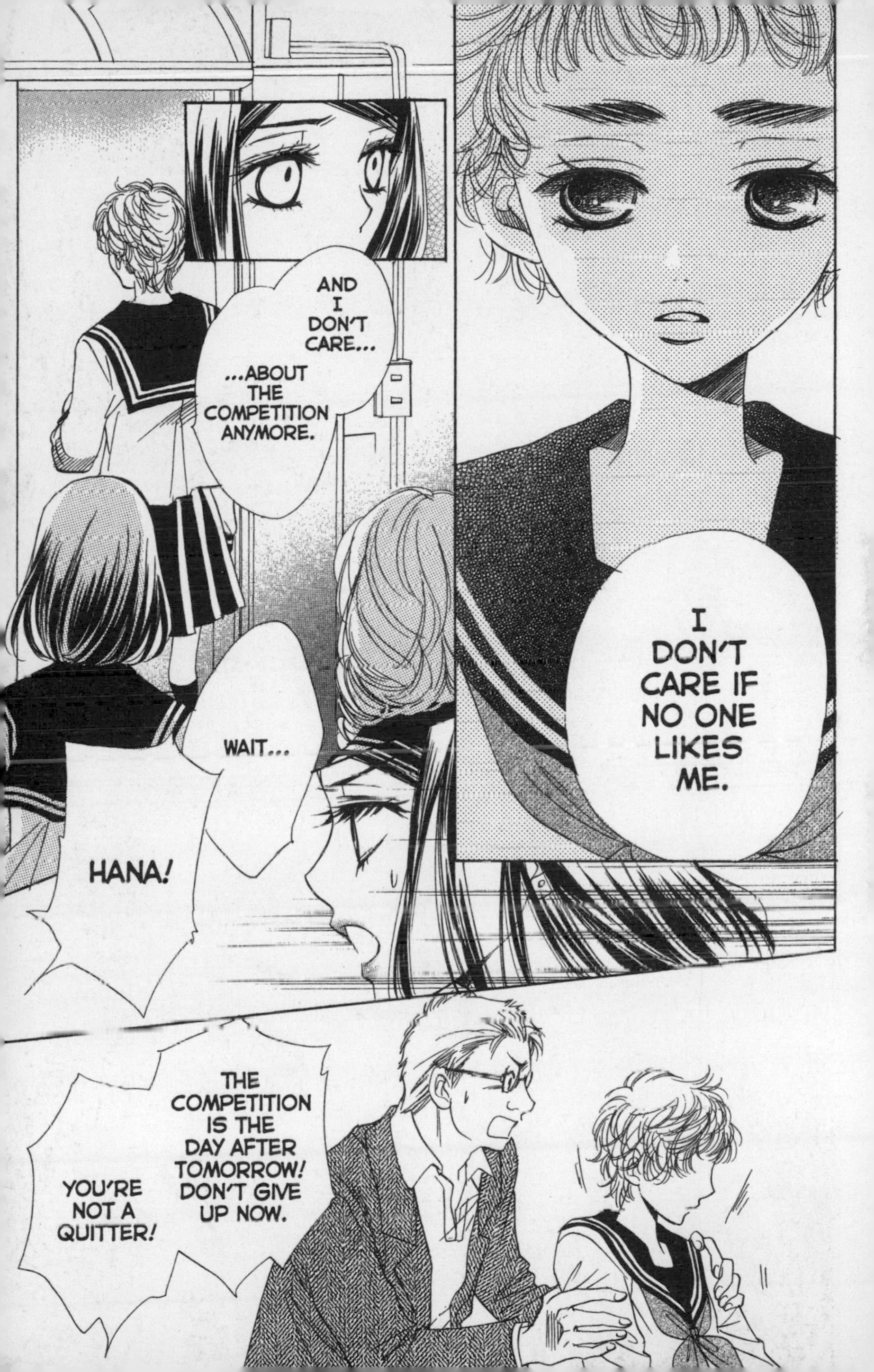
I DON'T CARE IF NO ONE LIKES ME.
AND I DON'T CARE...
...ABOUT THE COMPETITION ANYMORE.
WAIT...
HANA!
THE COMPETITION IS THE DAY AFTER TOMORROW! DON'T GIVE UP NOW.
YOU'RE NOT A QUITTER!

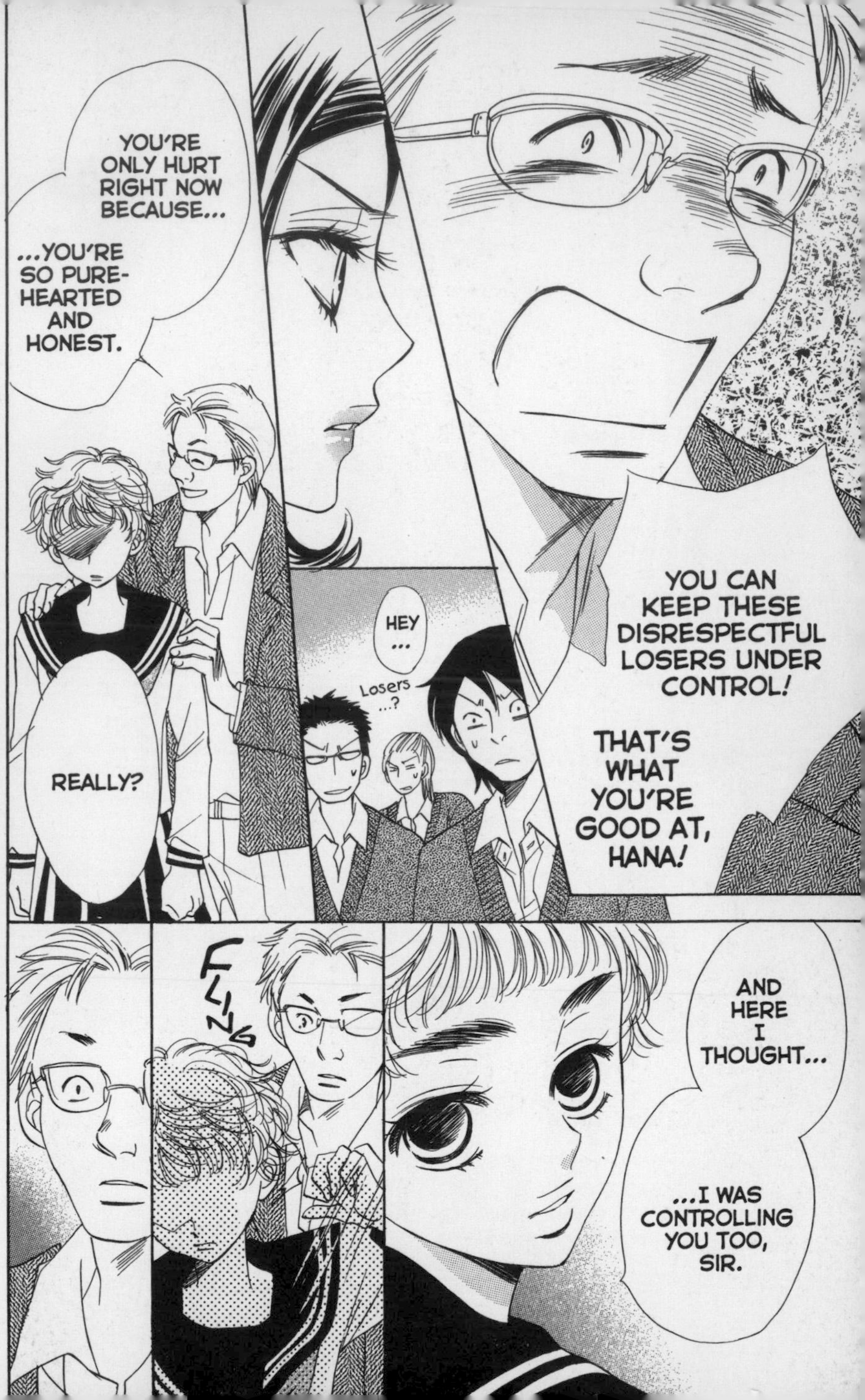
YOU CAN KEEP THESE DISRESPECTFUL LOSERS UNDER CONTROL!
THAT'S WHAT YOU'RE GOOD AT, HANA!
HEY ...
Losers ...?
YOU'RE ONLY HURT RIGHT NOW BECAUSE...
...YOU'RE SO PURE-HEARTED AND HONEST.
REALLY?
AND HERE I THOUGHT...
...I WAS CONTROLLING YOU TOO, SIR.
FLING

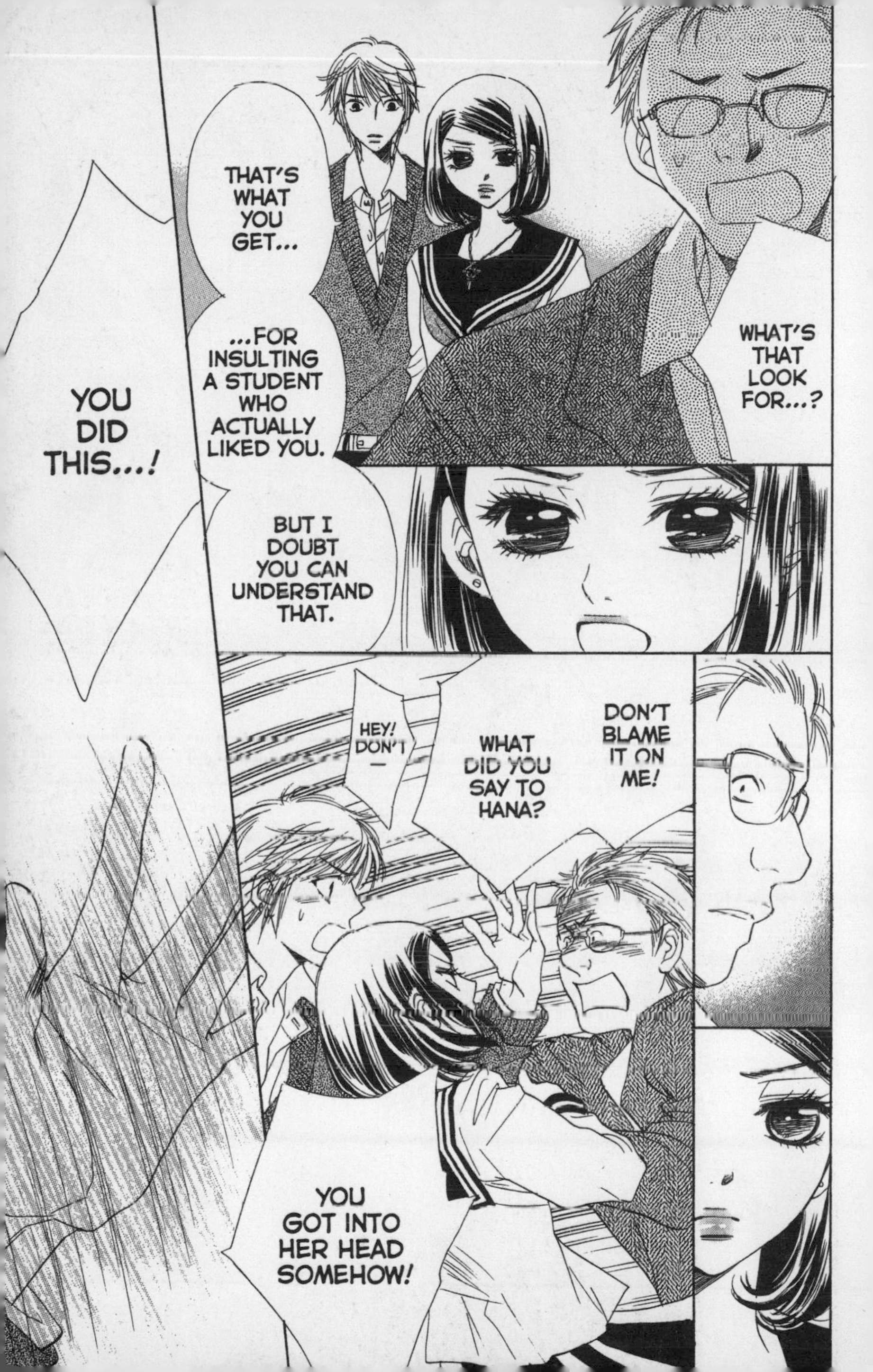
WHAT'S THAT LOOK FOR...?
THAT'S WHAT YOU GET...
...FOR INSULTING A STUDENT WHO ACTUALLY LIKED YOU.
BUT I DOUBT YOU CAN UNDERSTAND THAT.
DON'T BLAME IT ON ME!
WHAT DID YOU SAY TO HANA?
HEY! DON'T—
YOU GOT INTO HER HEAD SOMEHOW!
YOU DID THIS...!

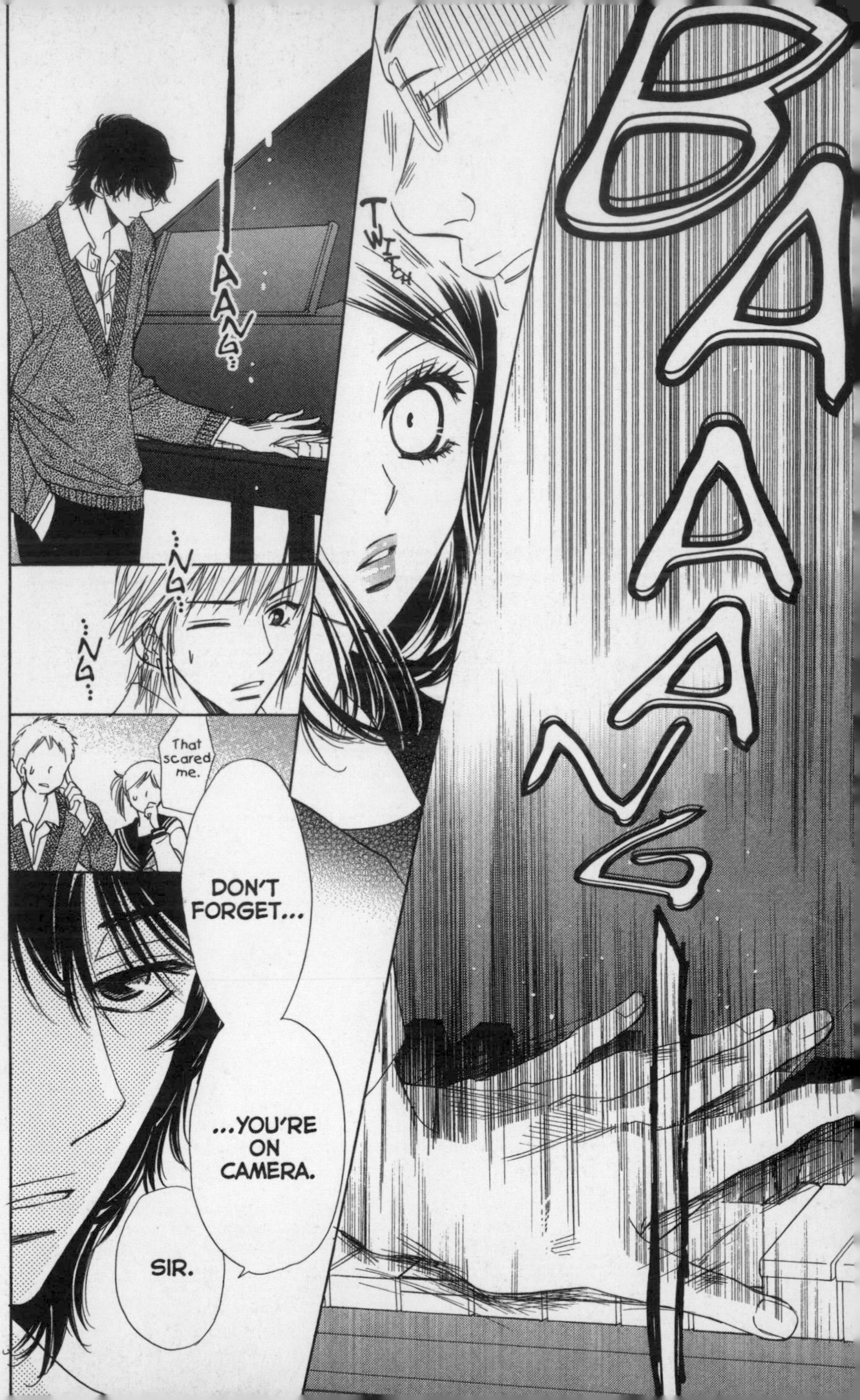
BAAANG
TWITCH
AAANG...
...NG...
...NG...
That scared me.
DON'T FORGET...
...YOU'RE ON CAMERA.
SIR.

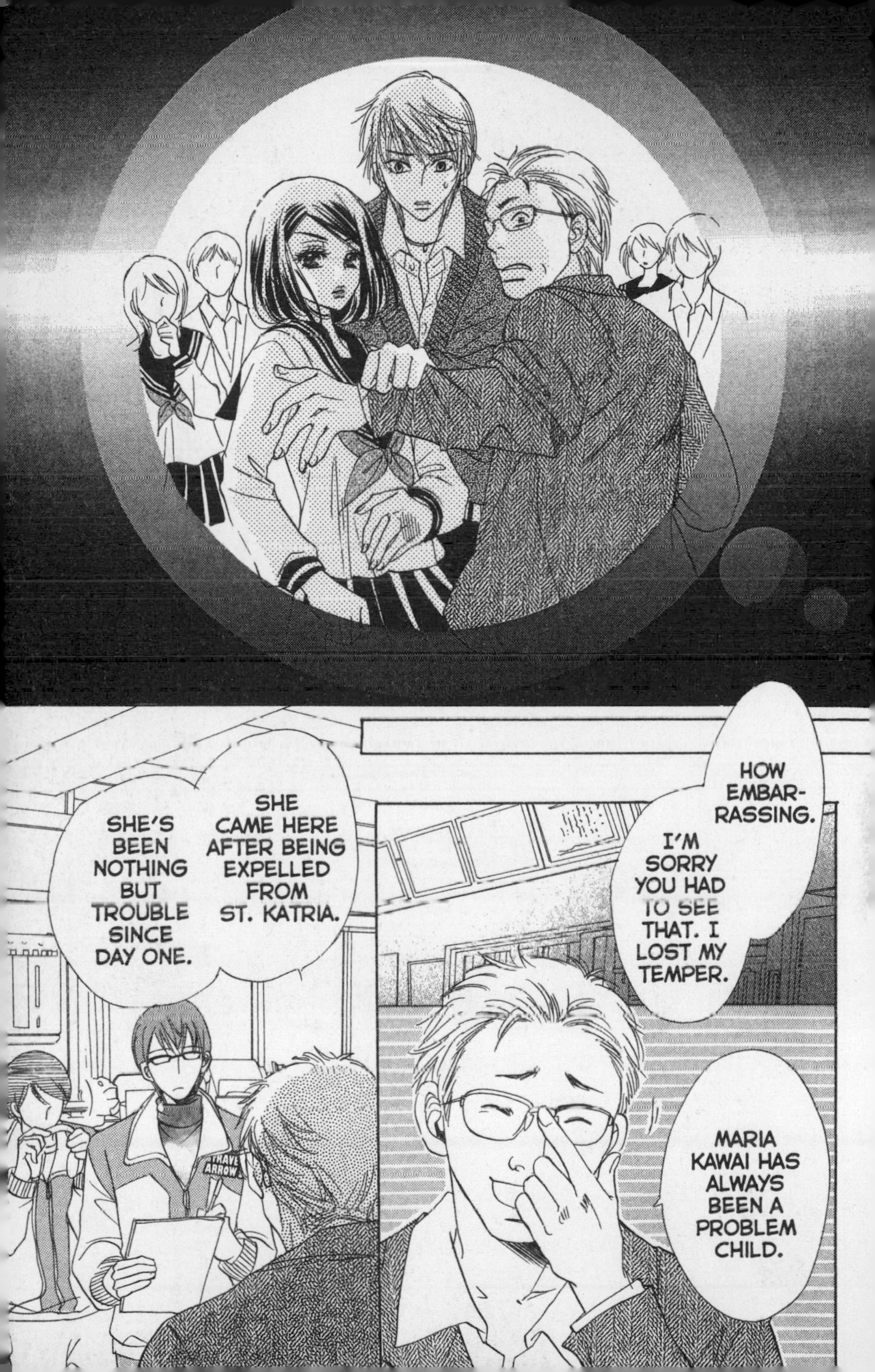
HOW EMBARRASSING.
I'M SORRY YOU HAD TO SEE THAT. I LOST MY TEMPER.
MARIA KAWAI HAS ALWAYS BEEN A PROBLEM CHILD.
SHE CAME HERE AFTER BEING EXPELLED FROM ST. KATRIA.
SHE'S BEEN NOTHING BUT TROUBLE SINCE DAY ONE.

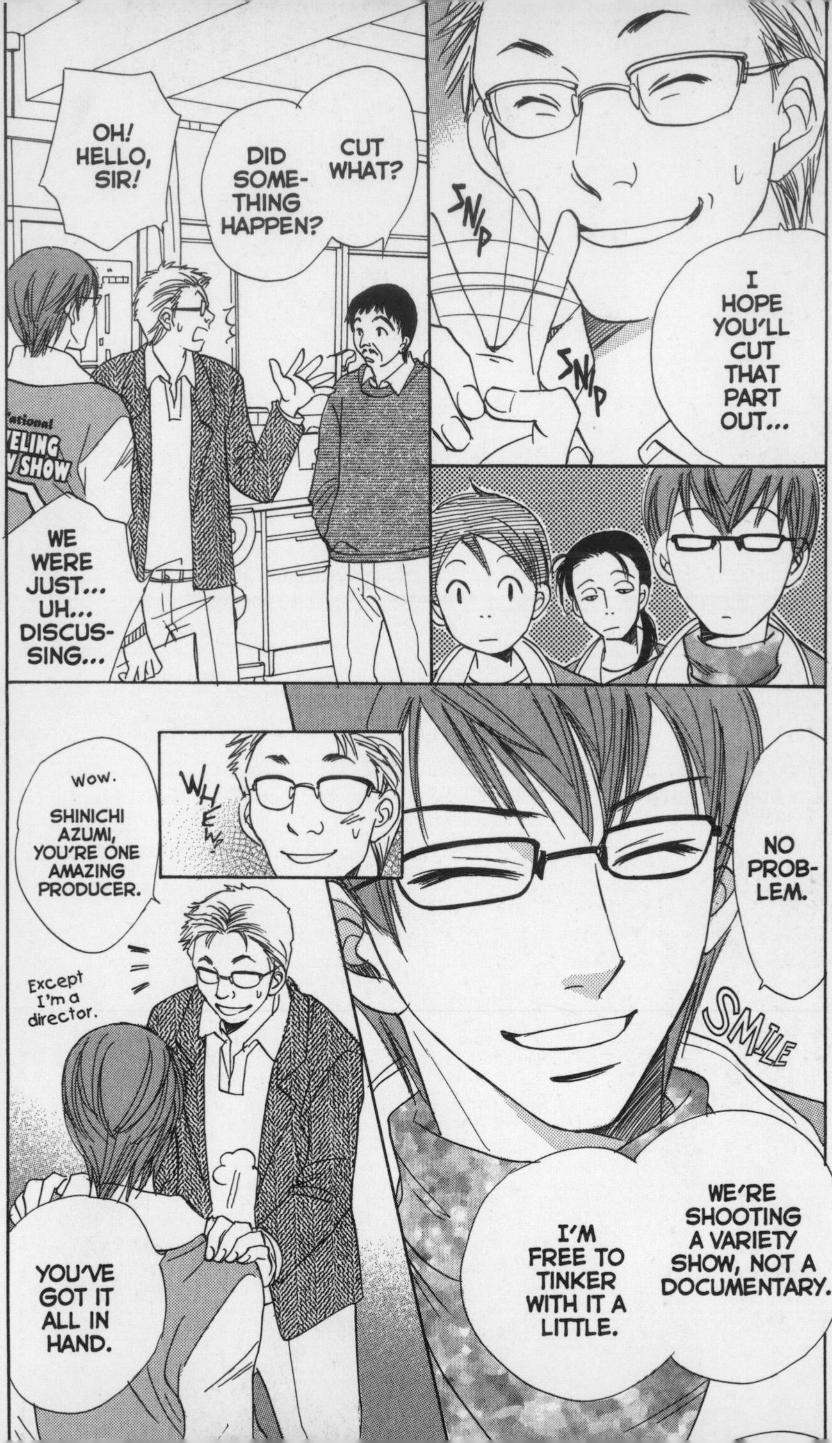
SNIP
SNIP
I HOPE YOU'LL CUT THAT PART OUT...
CUT WHAT?
DID SOME-THING HAPPEN?
OH! HELLO, SIR!
WE WERE JUST... UH... DISCUS-SING...
NO PROB-LEM.
SMILE
WE'RE SHOOTING A VARIETY SHOW, NOT A DOCUMENTARY.
I'M FREE TO TINKER WITH IT A LITTLE.
WHEW
Wow.
SHINICHI AZUMI, YOU'RE ONE AMAZING PRODUCER.
Except I'm a director.
YOU'VE GOT IT ALL IN HAND.

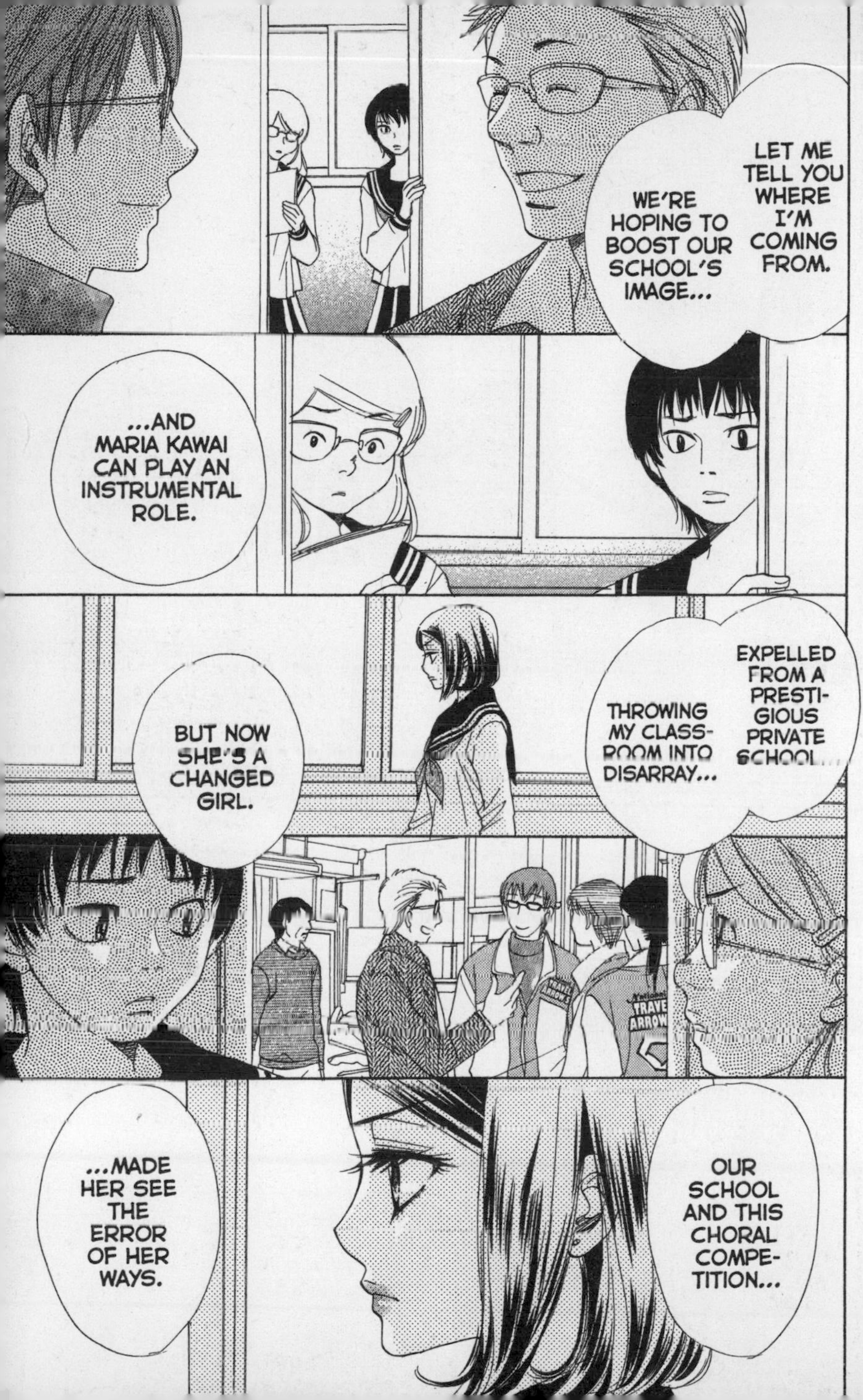
LET ME TELL YOU WHERE I'M COMING FROM.
WE'RE HOPING TO BOOST OUR SCHOOL'S IMAGE...
...AND MARIA KAWAI CAN PLAY AN INSTRUMENTAL ROLE.
EXPELLED FROM A PRESTIGIOUS PRIVATE SCHOOL...
THROWING MY CLASSROOM INTO DISARRAY...
BUT NOW SHE'S A CHANGED GIRL.
OUR SCHOOL AND THIS CHORAL COMPETITION...
...MADE HER SEE THE ERROR OF HER WAYS.

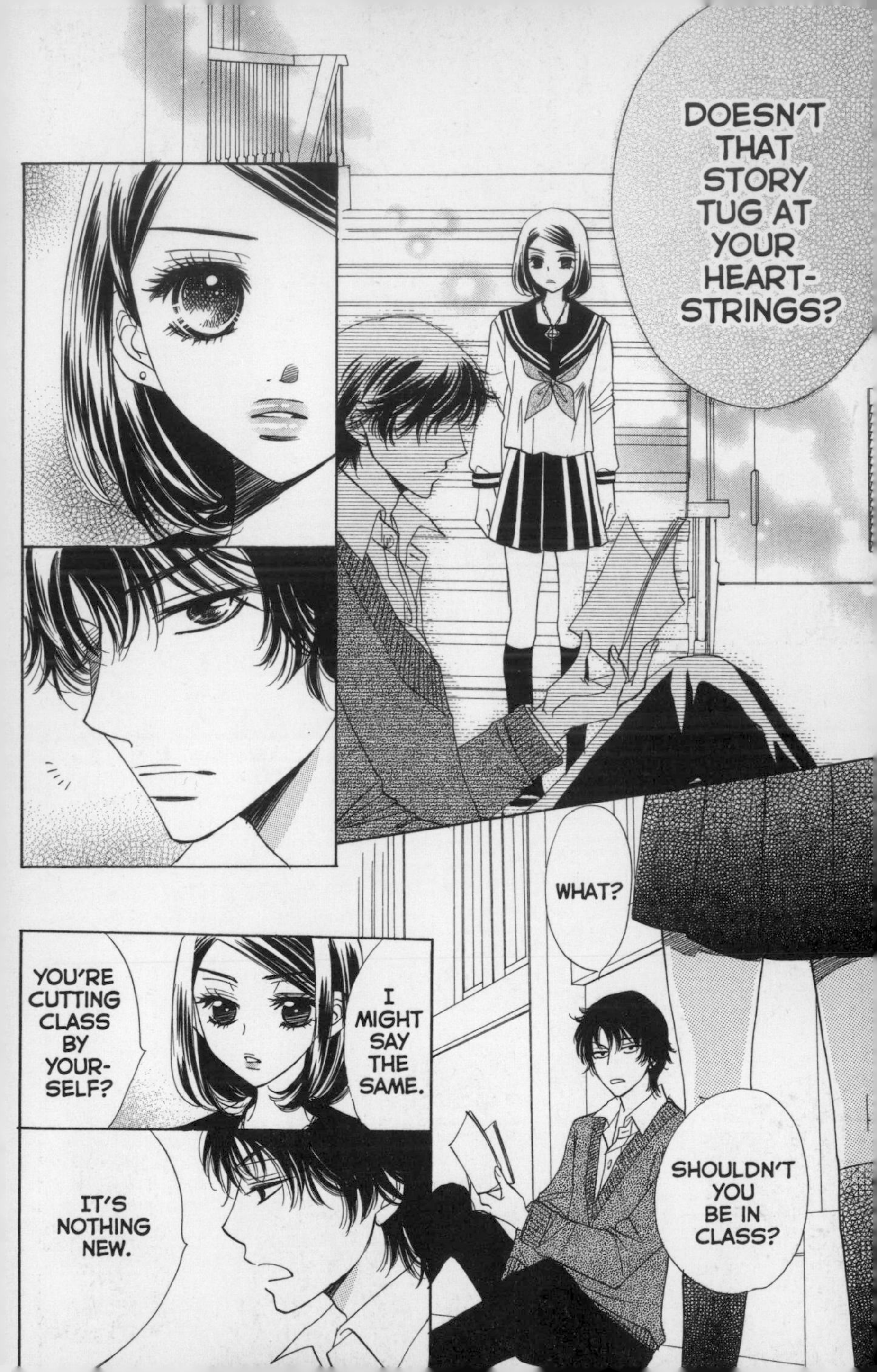
DOESN'T THAT STORY TUG AT YOUR HEART-STRINGS?
WHAT?
SHOULDN'T YOU BE IN CLASS?
I MIGHT SAY THE SAME.
YOU'RE CUTTING CLASS BY YOUR-SELF?
IT'S NOTHING NEW.

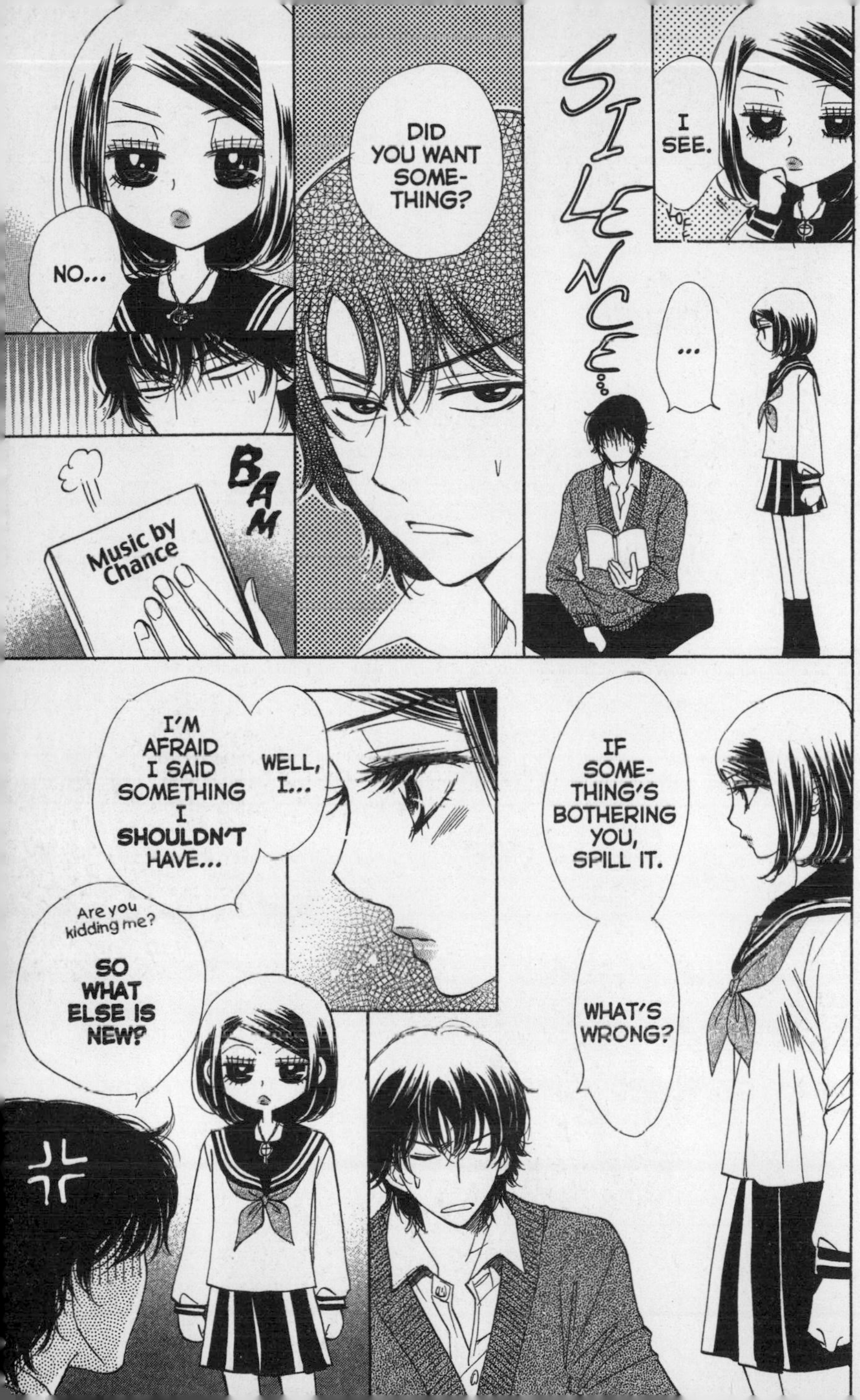
I SEE.
SILENCE...
...
DID YOU WANT SOMETHING?
NO...
BAM
Music by Chance
IF SOMETHING'S BOTHERING YOU, SPILL IT.
WHAT'S WRONG?
WELL, I...
I'M AFRAID I SAID SOMETHING I SHOULDN'T HAVE...
Are you kidding me?
SO WHAT ELSE IS NEW?

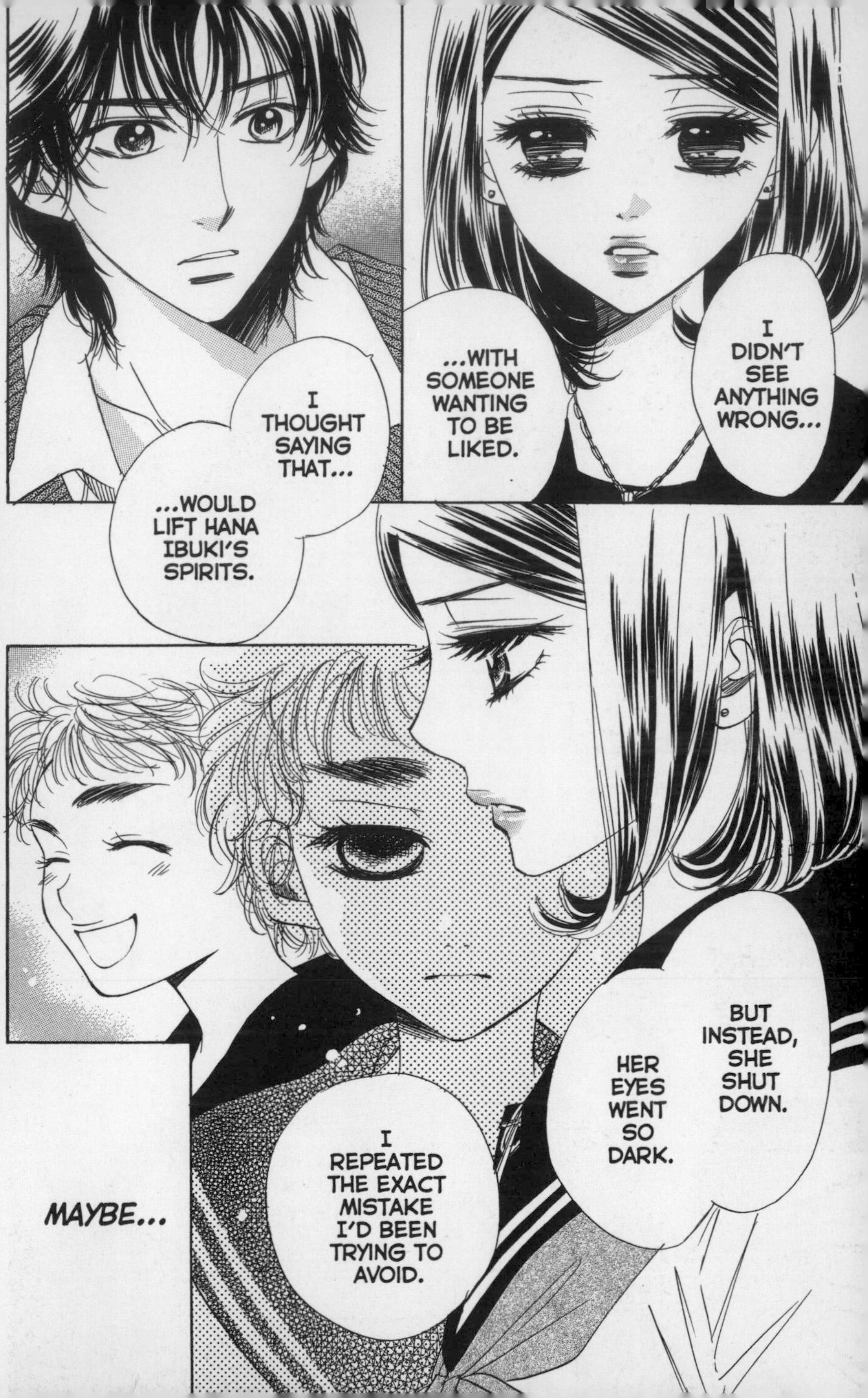
I DIDN'T SEE ANYTHING WRONG...
...WITH SOMEONE WANTING TO BE LIKED.
I THOUGHT SAYING THAT...
...WOULD LIFT HANA IBUKI'S SPIRITS.
BUT INSTEAD, SHE SHUT DOWN.
HER EYES WENT SO DARK.
I REPEATED THE EXACT MISTAKE I'D BEEN TRYING TO AVOID.
MAYBE...

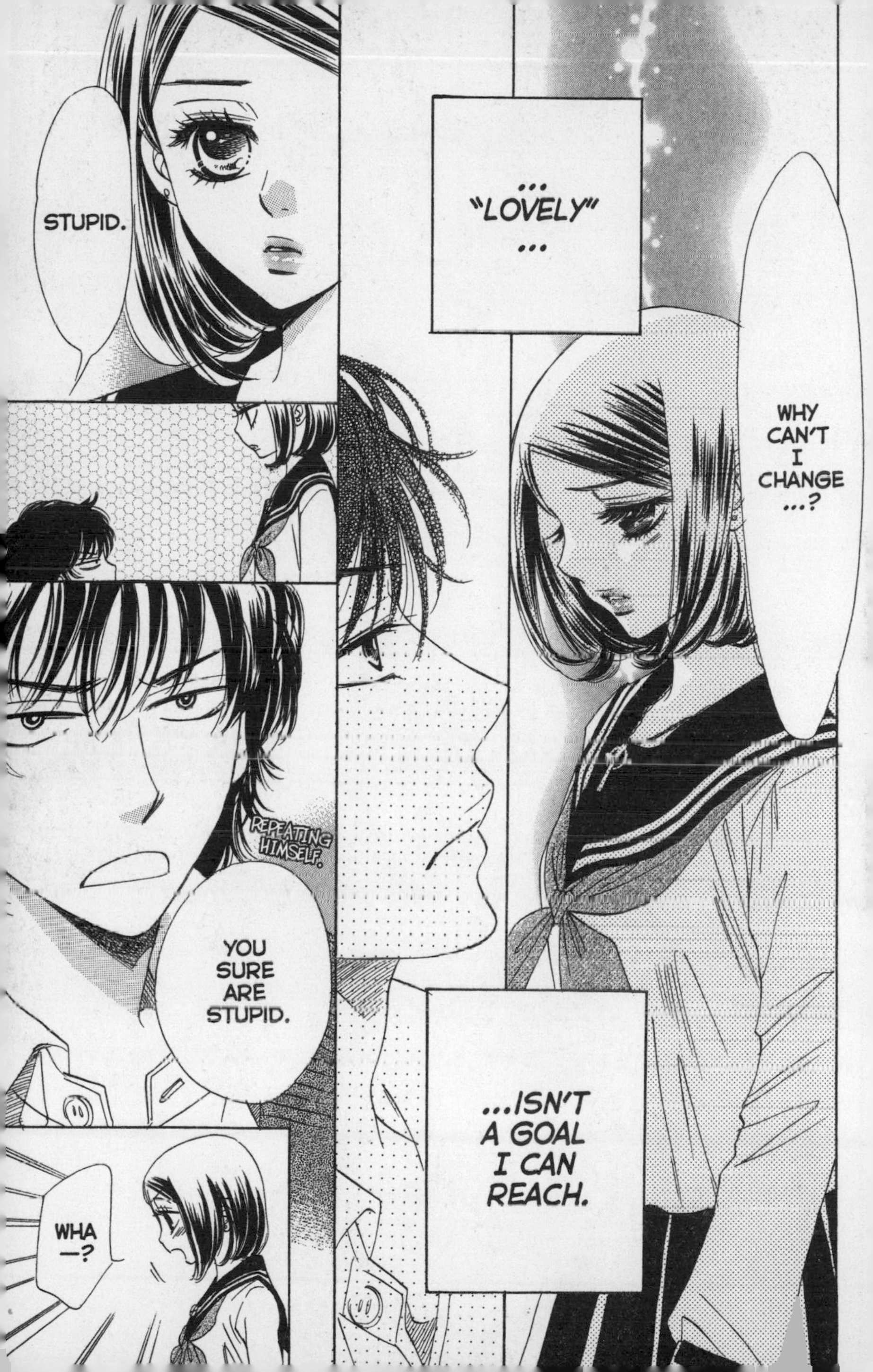

... "LOVELY" ...
WHY CAN'T I CHANGE ...?
...ISN'T A GOAL I CAN REACH.
STUPID.
REPEATING HIMSELF.
YOU SURE ARE STUPID.
WHA —?

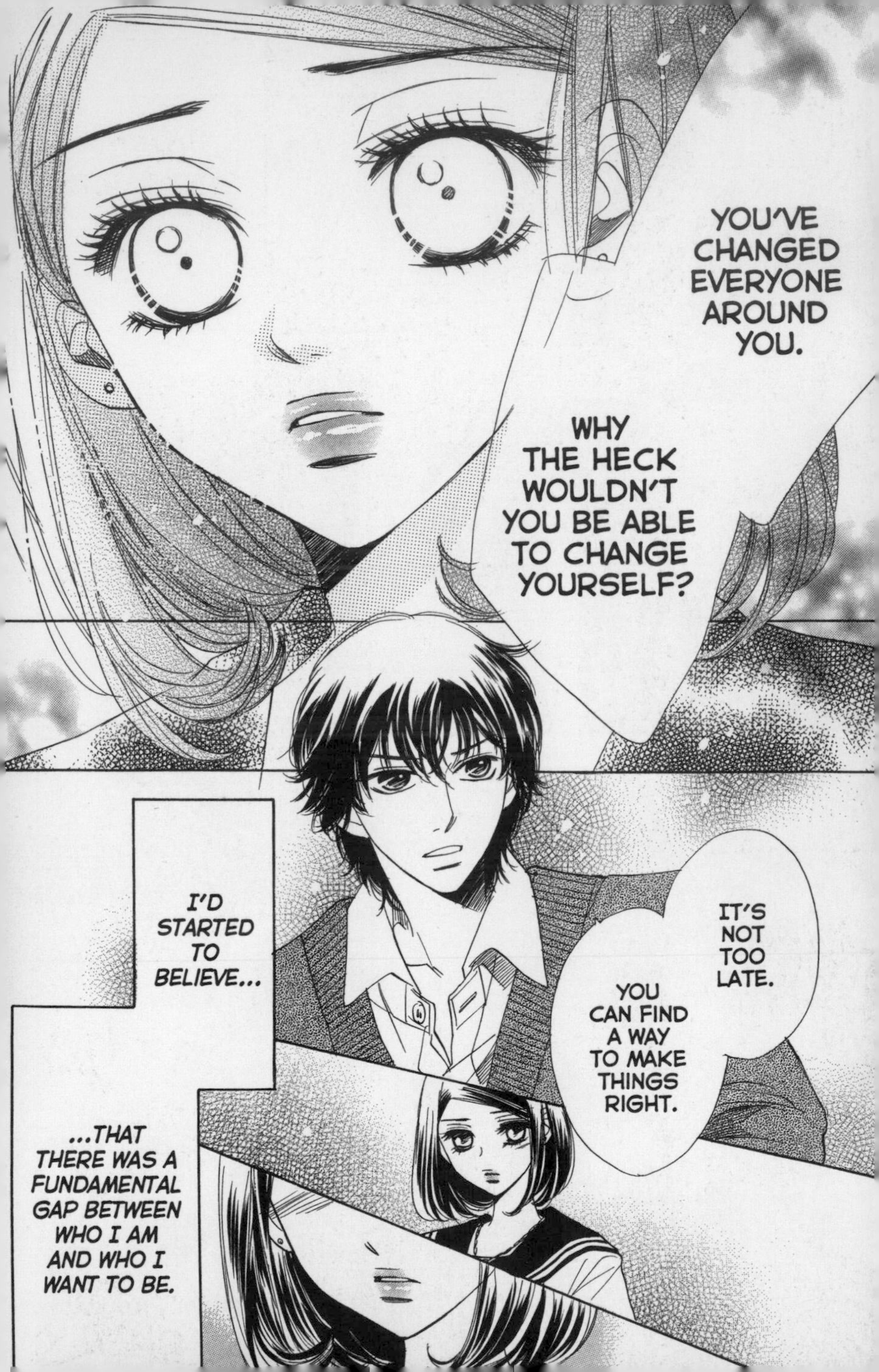
YOU'VE CHANGED EVERYONE AROUND YOU.
WHY THE HECK WOULDN'T YOU BE ABLE TO CHANGE YOURSELF?
IT'S NOT TOO LATE.
YOU CAN FIND A WAY TO MAKE THINGS RIGHT.
I'D STARTED TO BELIEVE...
...THAT THERE WAS A FUNDAMENTAL GAP BETWEEN WHO I AM AND WHO I WANT TO BE.

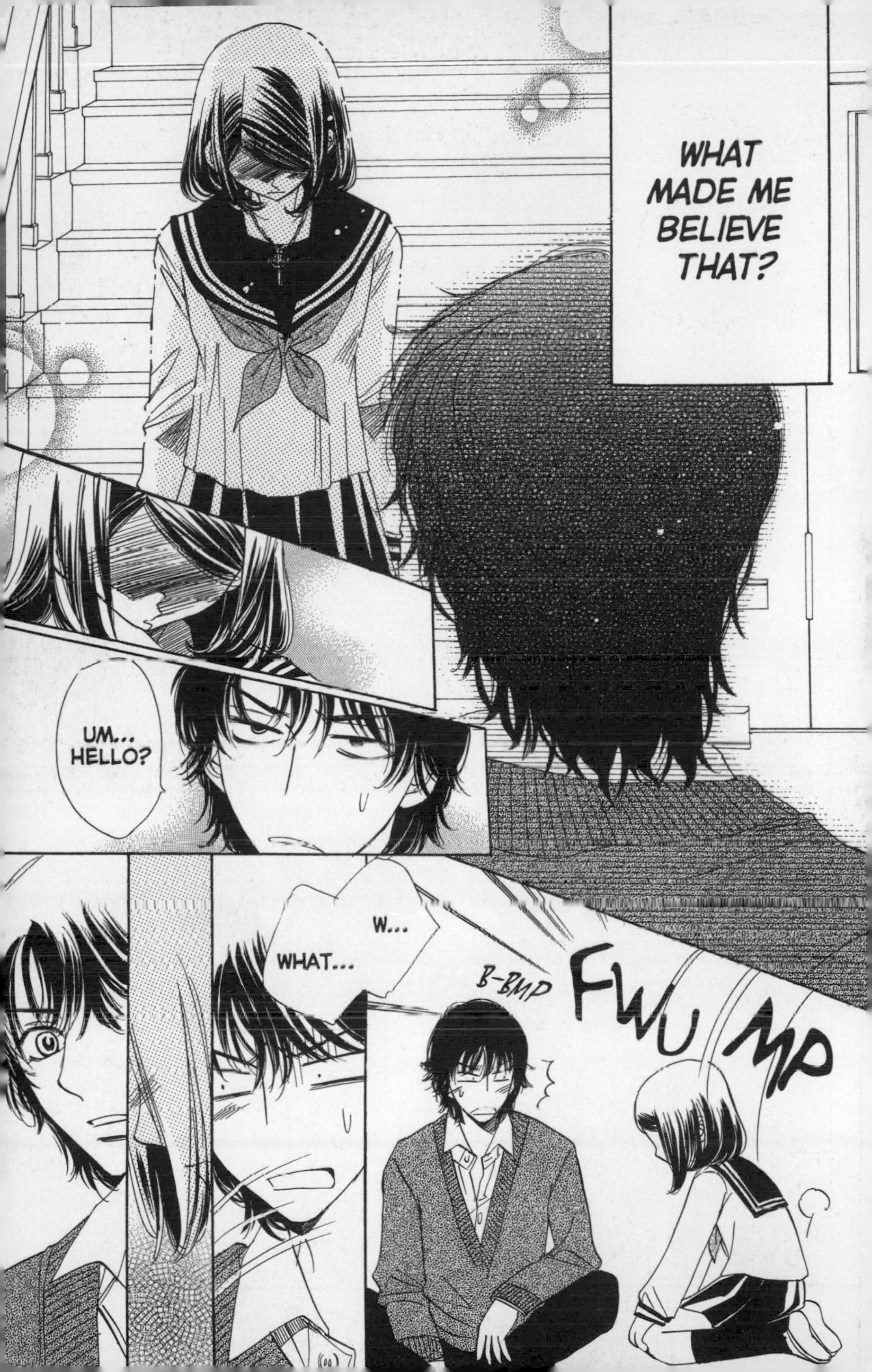
WHAT MADE ME BELIEVE THAT?
UM... HELLO?
FWUMP
B-BMP
W... WHAT...

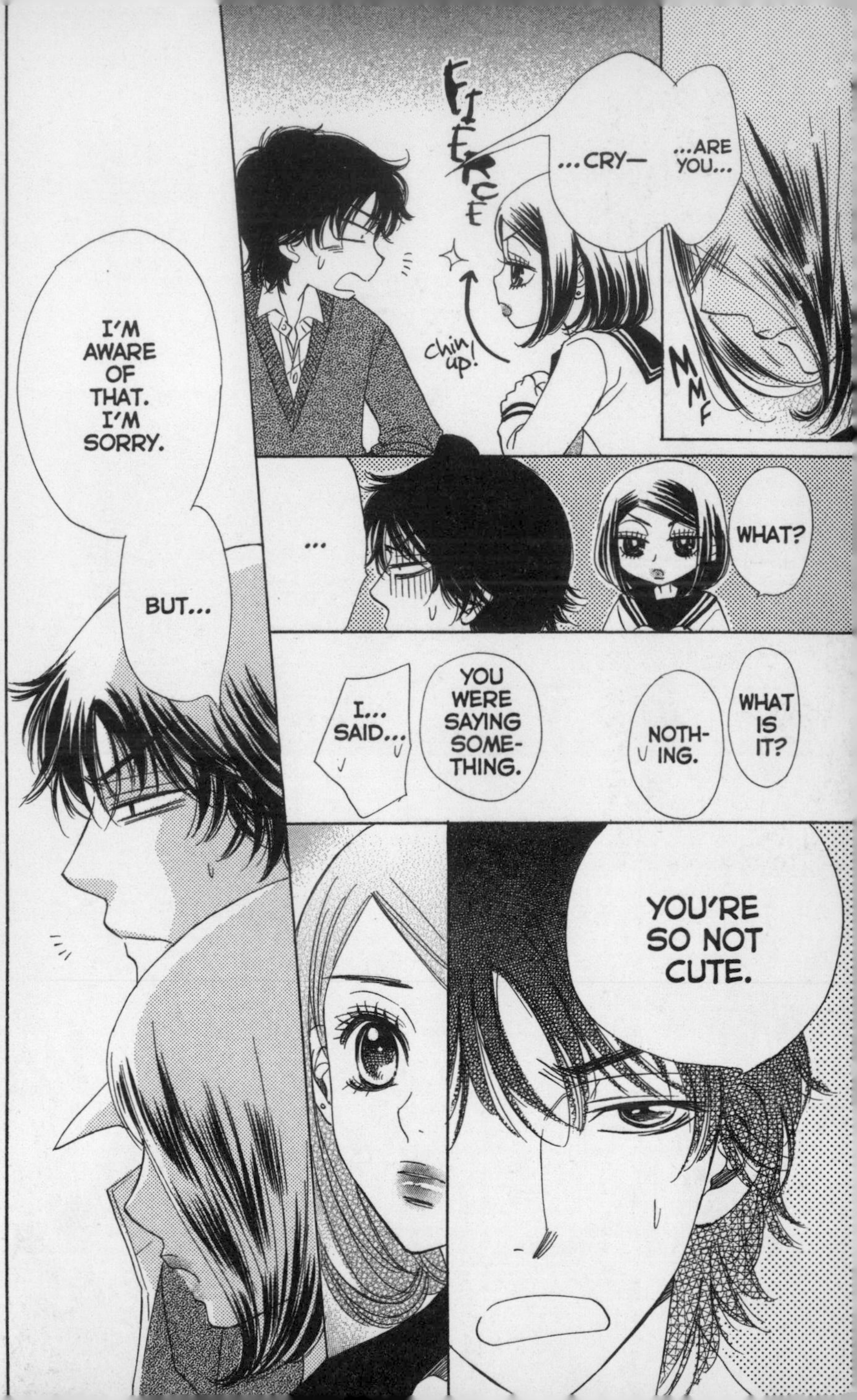
MMF
...ARE YOU...
...CRY—
FIERCE
Chin up!
WHAT?
...
WHAT IS IT?
NOTHING.
YOU WERE SAYING SOMETHING.
I... SAID...
YOU'RE SO NOT CUTE.
I'M AWARE OF THAT. I'M SORRY.
BUT...

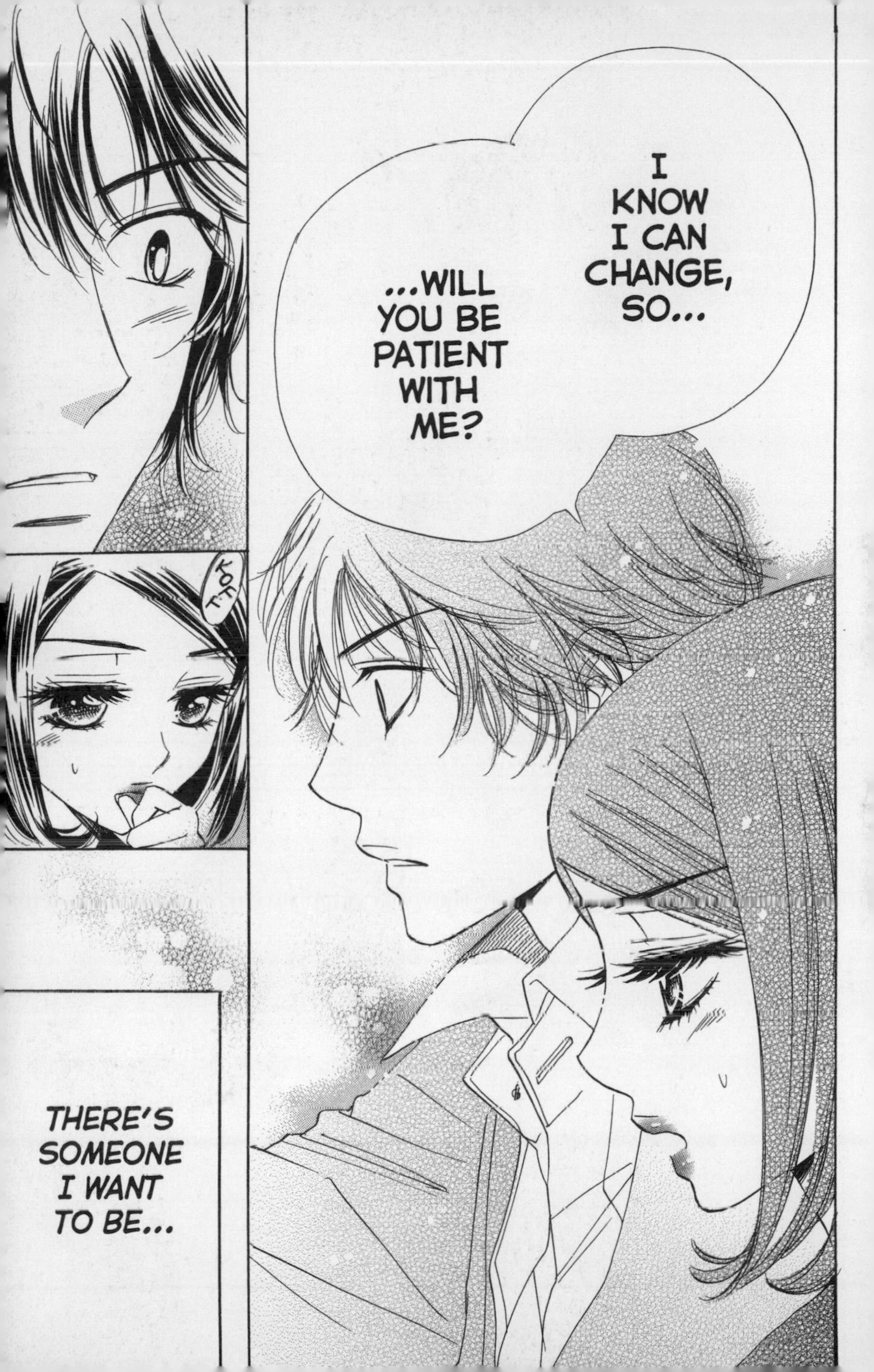
I KNOW I CAN CHANGE, SO...
...WILL YOU BE PATIENT WITH ME?
KOTT
THERE'S SOMEONE I WANT TO BE...

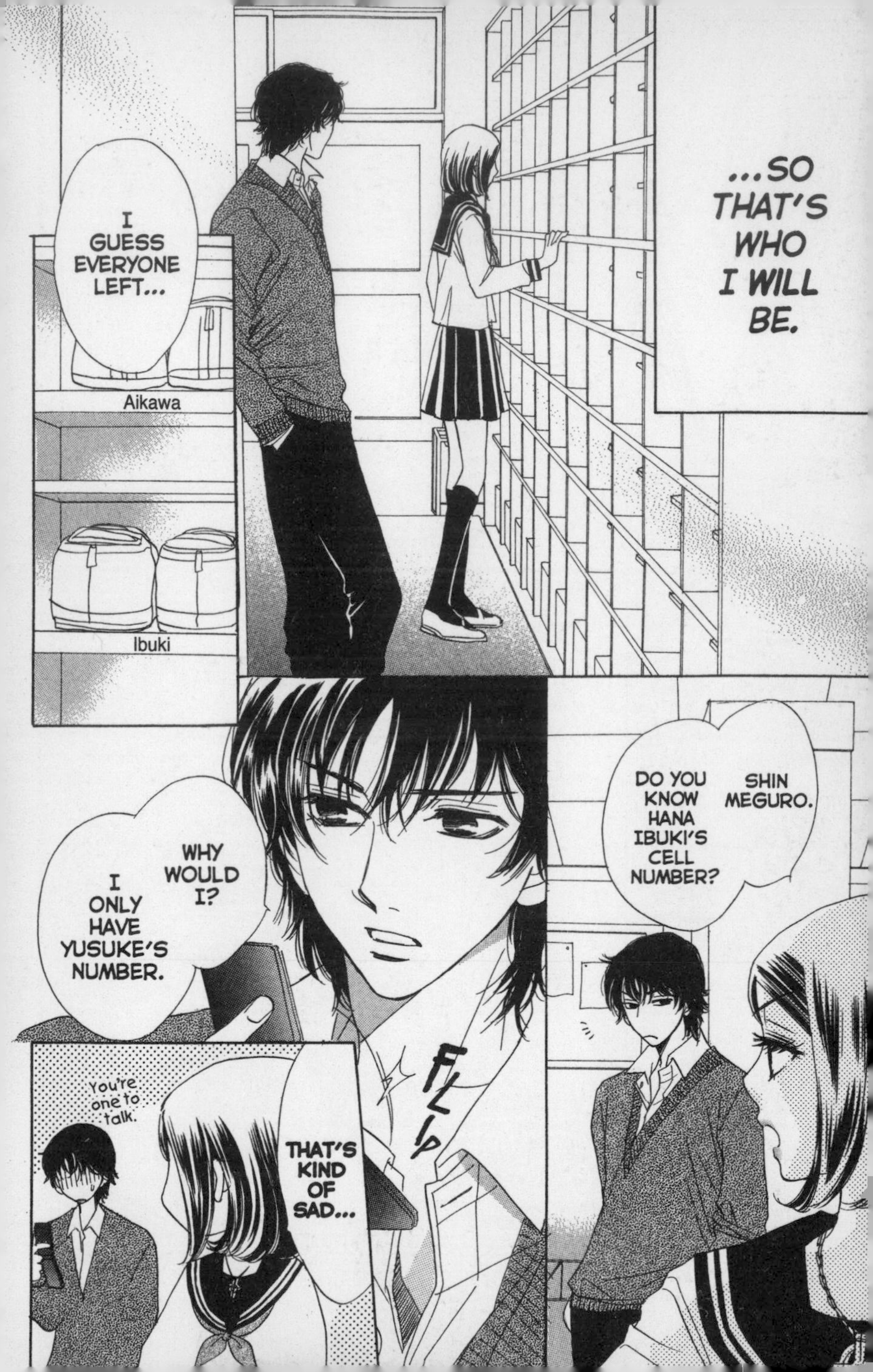
...SO THAT'S WHO I WILL BE.
I GUESS EVERYONE LEFT...
Aikawa
Ibuki
SHIN MEGURO.
DO YOU KNOW HANA IBUKI'S CELL NUMBER?
WHY WOULD I?
I ONLY HAVE YUSUKE'S NUMBER.
FLIP
THAT'S KIND OF SAD...
You're one to talk.

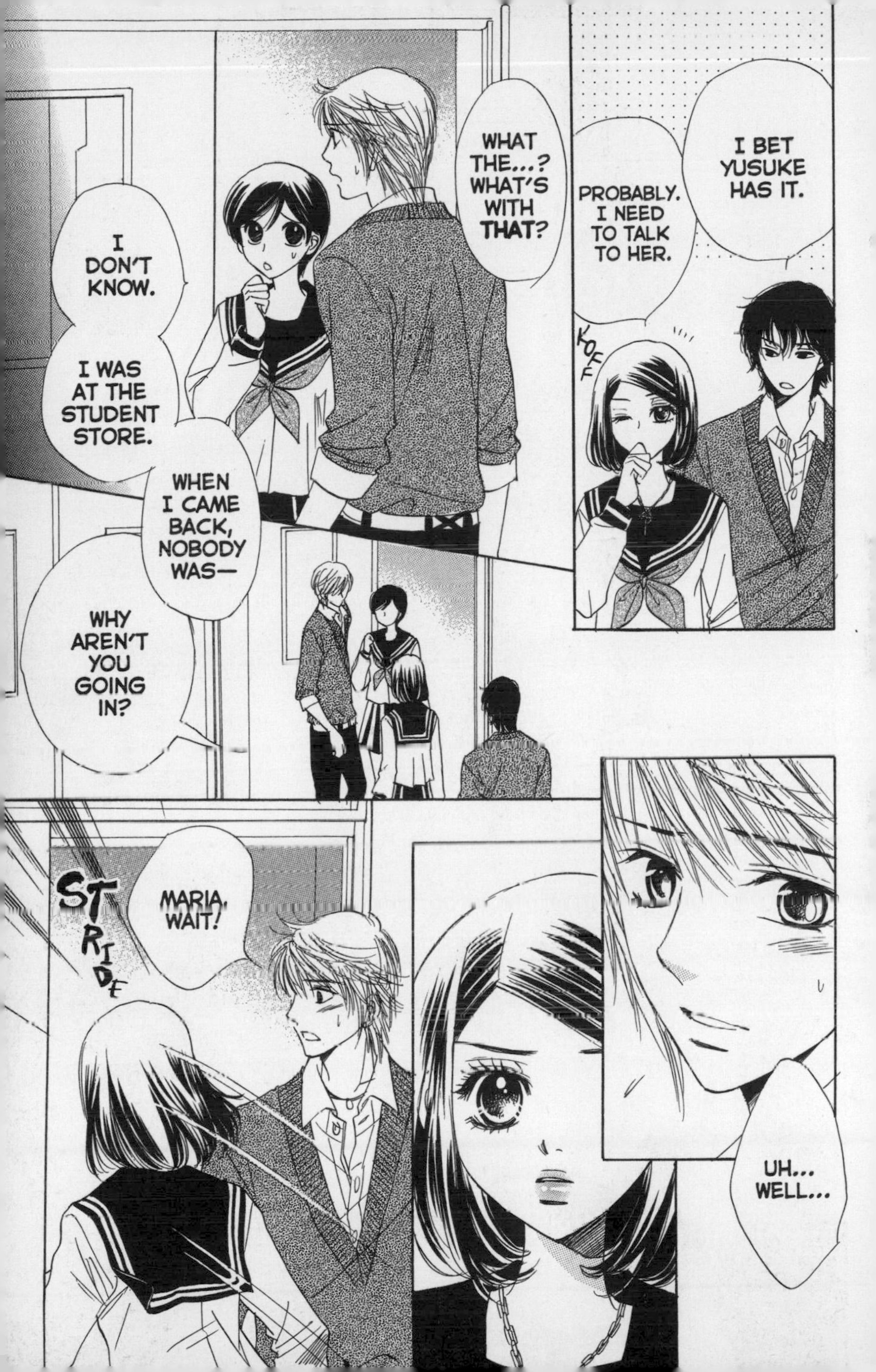
I BET YUSUKE HAS IT.
PROBABLY. I NEED TO TALK TO HER.
KOFF
WHAT THE...? WHAT'S WITH THAT?
I DON'T KNOW.
I WAS AT THE STUDENT STORE.
WHEN I CAME BACK, NOBODY WAS—
WHY AREN'T YOU GOING IN?
UH... WELL...
MARIA, WAIT!
STRIDE

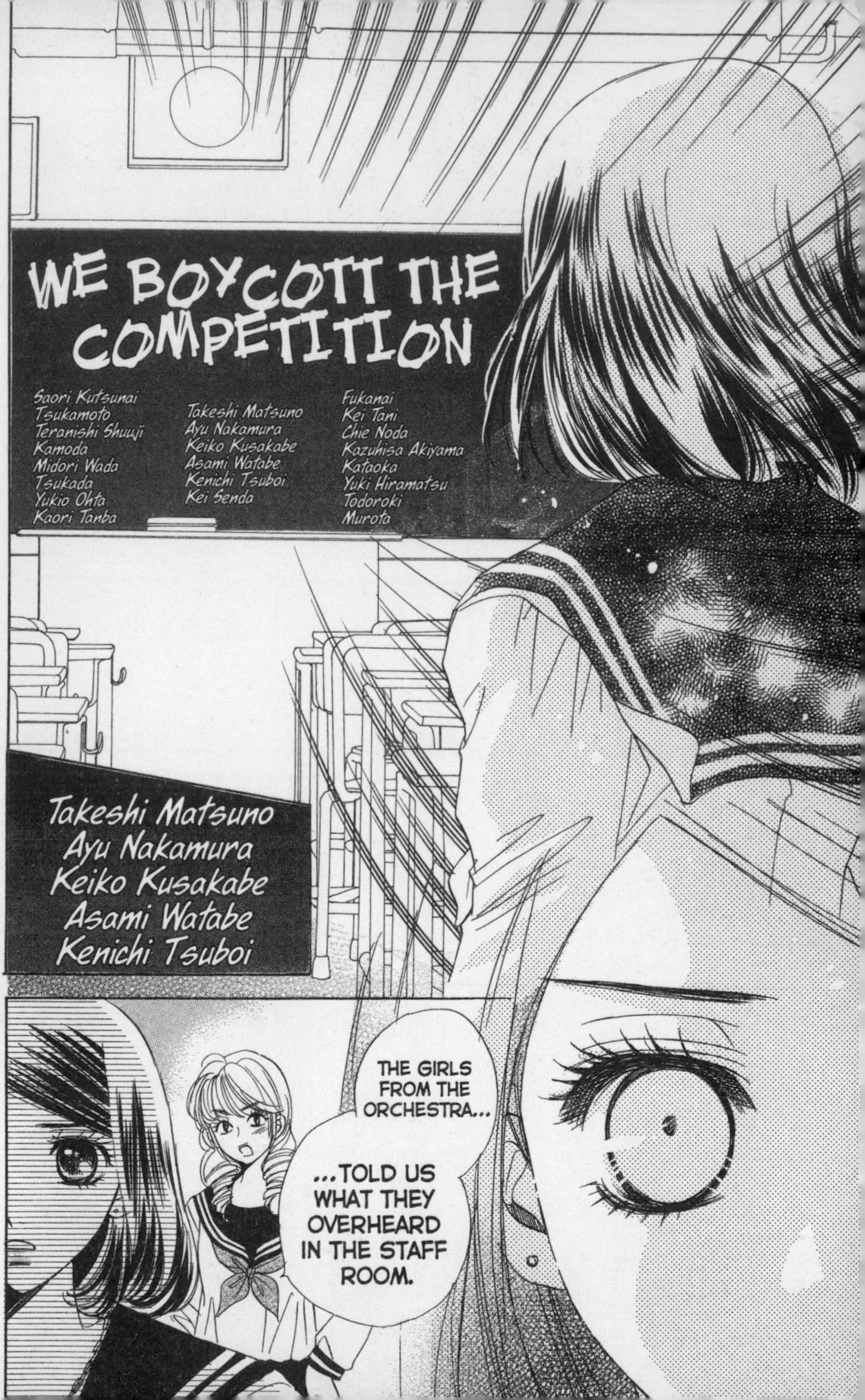
WE BOYCOTT THE COMPETITION
Saori Kutsunai
Tsukamoto
Teranishi Shuuji
Kamoda
Midori Wada
Tsukada
Yukio Ohta
Kaori Tanba
Takeshi Matsuno
Ayu Nakamura
Keiko Kusakabe
Asami Watabe
Kenichi Tsuboi
Kei Senda
Fukanai
Kei Tani
Chie Noda
Kazuhisa Akiyama
Kataoka
Yuki Hiramatsu
Todoroki
Murota
Takeshi Matsuno
Ayu Nakamura
Keiko Kusakabe
Asami Watabe
Kenichi Tsuboi
THE GIRLS FROM THE ORCHESTRA...
...TOLD US WHAT THEY OVERHEARD IN THE STAFF ROOM.

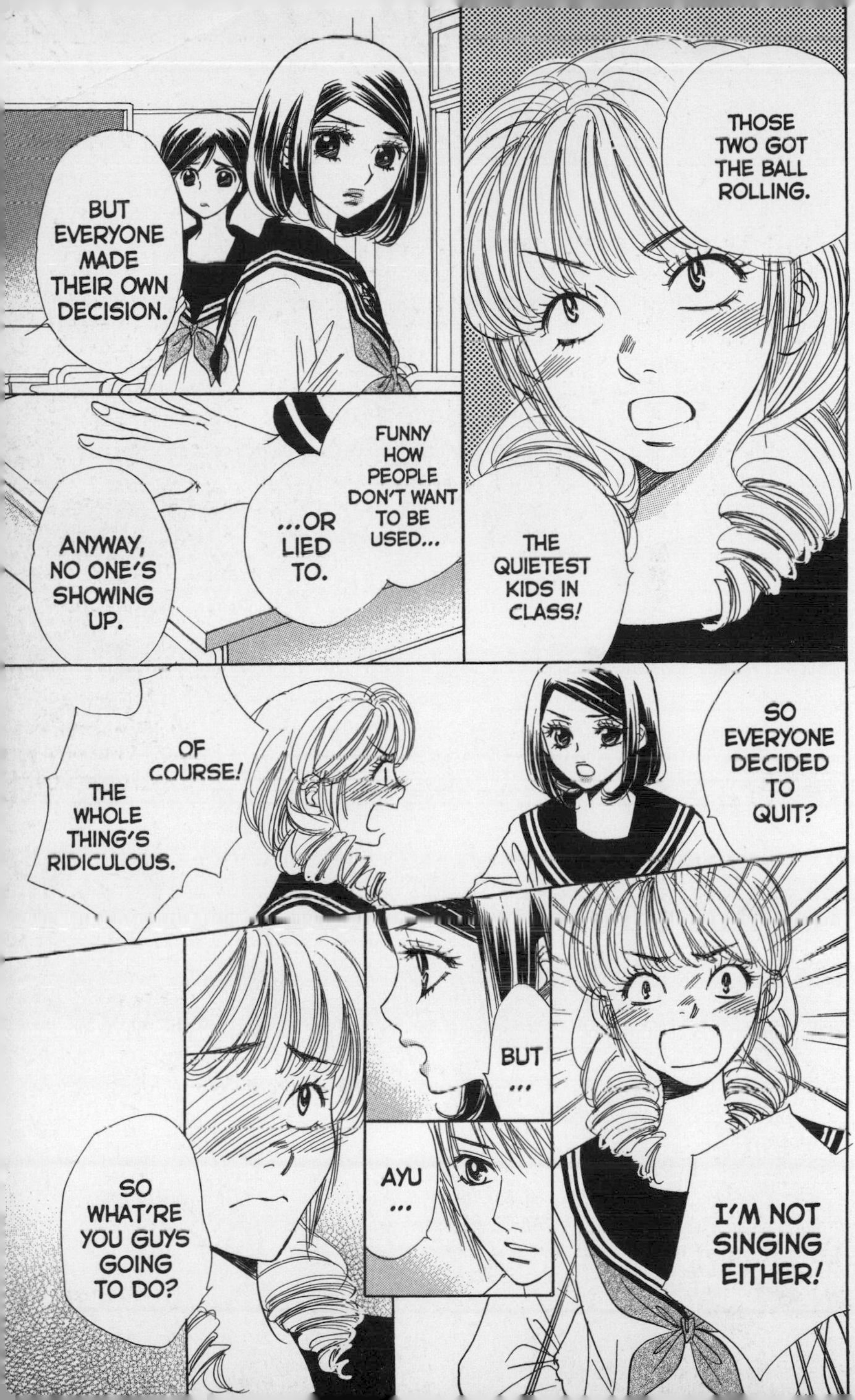
THOSE TWO GOT THE BALL ROLLING.
THE QUIETEST KIDS IN CLASS!
BUT EVERYONE MADE THEIR OWN DECISION.
FUNNY HOW PEOPLE DON'T WANT TO BE USED...
...OR LIED TO.
ANYWAY, NO ONE'S SHOWING UP.
SO EVERYONE DECIDED TO QUIT?
OF COURSE!
THE WHOLE THING'S RIDICULOUS.
I'M NOT SINGING EITHER!
BUT ...
AYU ...
SO WHAT'RE YOU GUYS GOING TO DO?

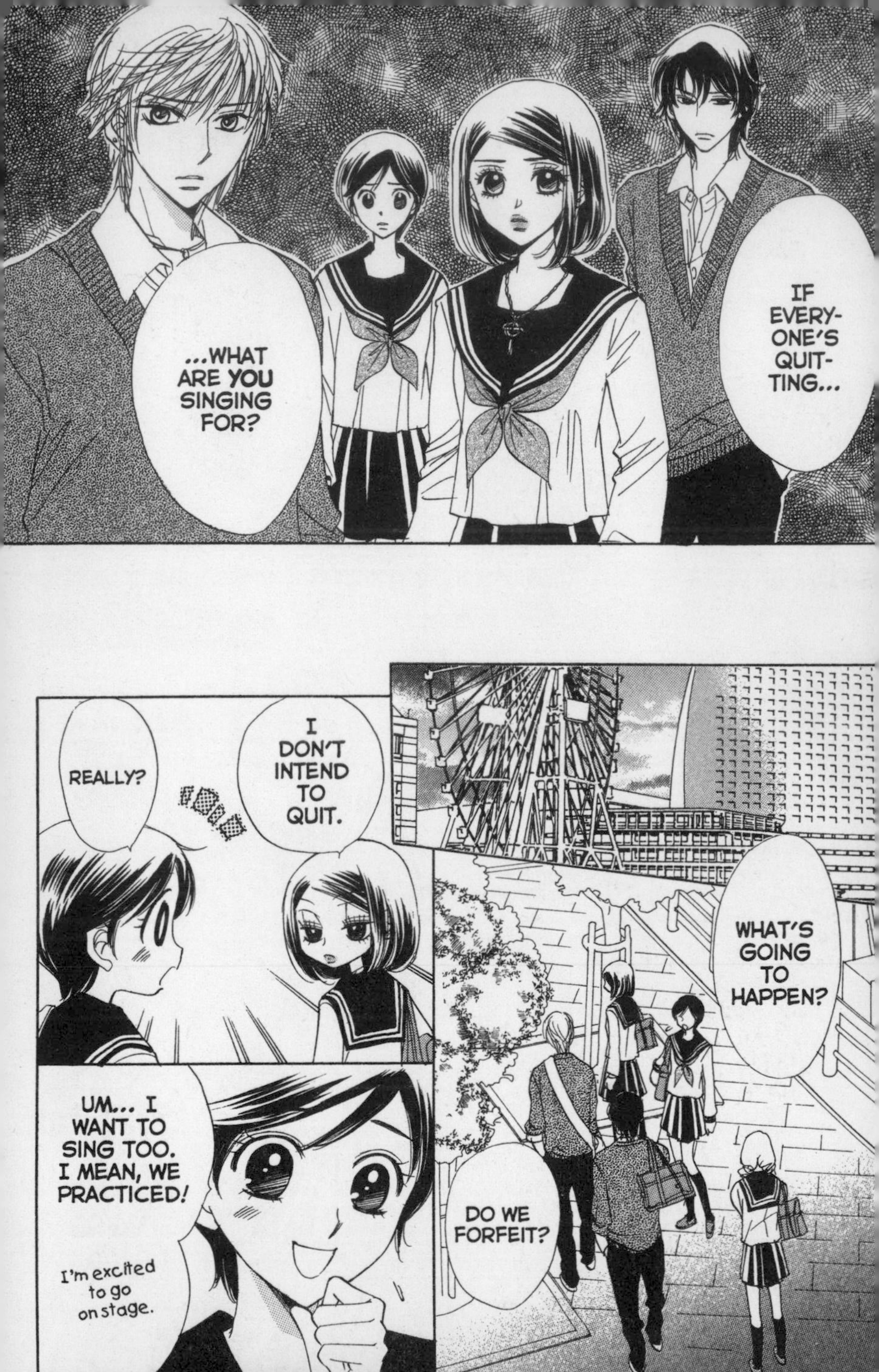
IF EVERYONE'S QUITTING...
...WHAT ARE YOU SINGING FOR?
WHAT'S GOING TO HAPPEN?
DO WE FORFEIT?
I DON'T INTEND TO QUIT.
REALLY?
UM... I WANT TO SING TOO. I MEAN, WE PRACTICED!
I'm excited to go on stage.

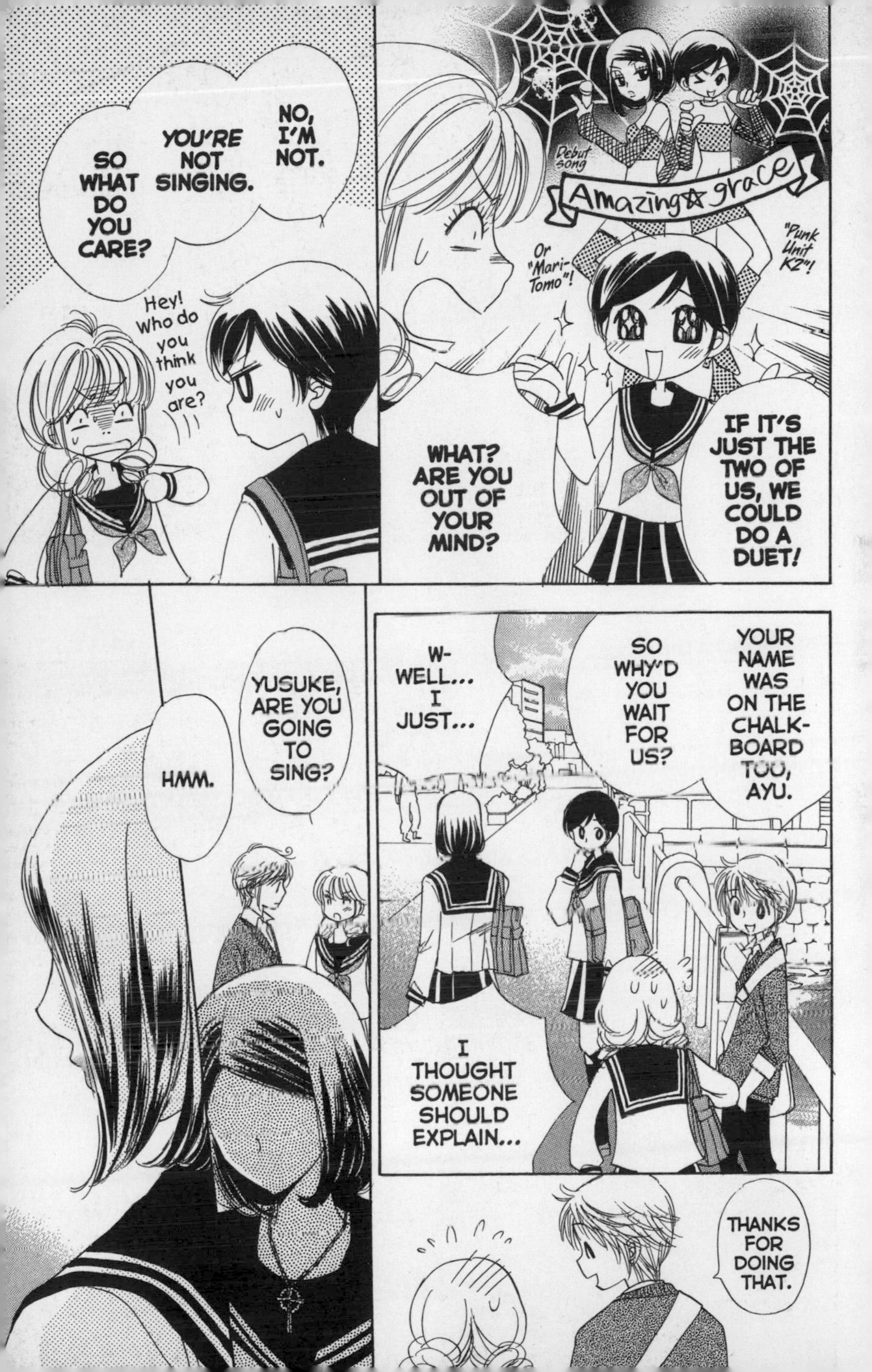
Debut song
Amazing☆grace
"Punk Unit KZ"!
Or "Mari-Tomo"!
IF IT'S JUST THE TWO OF US, WE COULD DO A DUET!
WHAT? ARE YOU OUT OF YOUR MIND?
NO, I'M NOT.
YOU'RE NOT SINGING.
SO WHAT DO YOU CARE?
Hey! Who do you think you are?
YOUR NAME WAS ON THE CHALKBOARD TOO, AYU.
SO WHY'D YOU WAIT FOR US?
W-WELL... I JUST...
I THOUGHT SOMEONE SHOULD EXPLAIN...
THANKS FOR DOING THAT.
YUSUKE, ARE YOU GOING TO SING?
HMM.

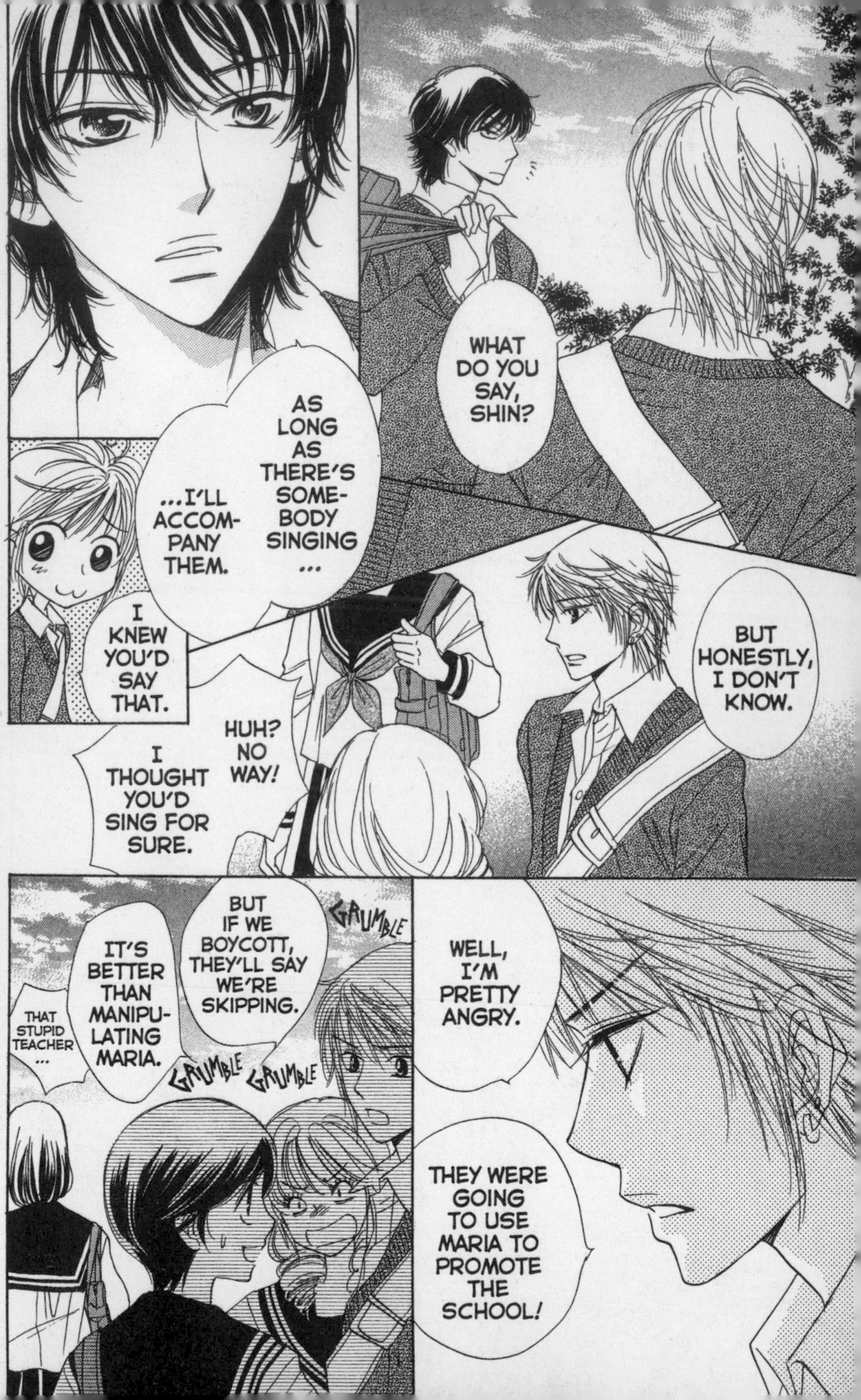
WHAT DO YOU SAY, SHIN?
AS LONG AS THERE'S SOME-BODY SINGING...
...I'LL ACCOM-PANY THEM.
I KNEW YOU'D SAY THAT.
BUT HONESTLY, I DON'T KNOW.
HUH? NO WAY!
I THOUGHT YOU'D SING FOR SURE.
WELL, I'M PRETTY ANGRY.
THEY WERE GOING TO USE MARIA TO PROMOTE THE SCHOOL!
GRUMBLE
BUT IF WE BOYCOTT, THEY'LL SAY WE'RE SKIPPING.
IT'S BETTER THAN MANIPU-LATING MARIA.
THAT STUPID TEACHER...
GRUMBLE GRUMBLE

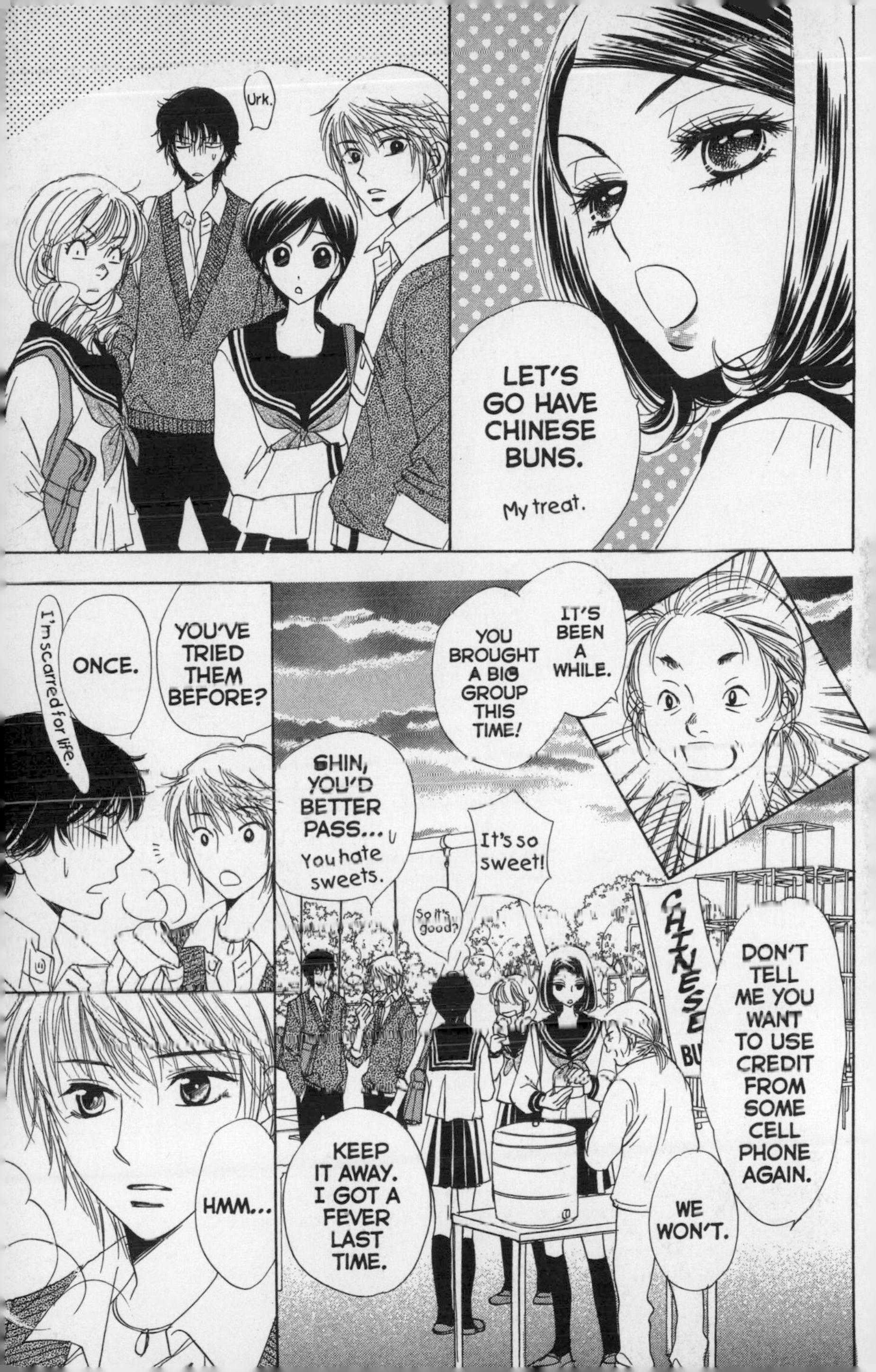
LET'S GO HAVE CHINESE BUNS.
My treat.
Urk.
IT'S BEEN A WHILE.
YOU BROUGHT A BIG GROUP THIS TIME!
DON'T TELL ME YOU WANT TO USE CREDIT FROM SOME CELL PHONE AGAIN.
WE WON'T.
CHINESE BU
It's so sweet!
So it's good?
SHIN, YOU'D BETTER PASS...
You hate sweets.
KEEP IT AWAY. I GOT A FEVER LAST TIME.
YOU'VE TRIED THEM BEFORE?
ONCE.
I'm scarred for life.
HMM...

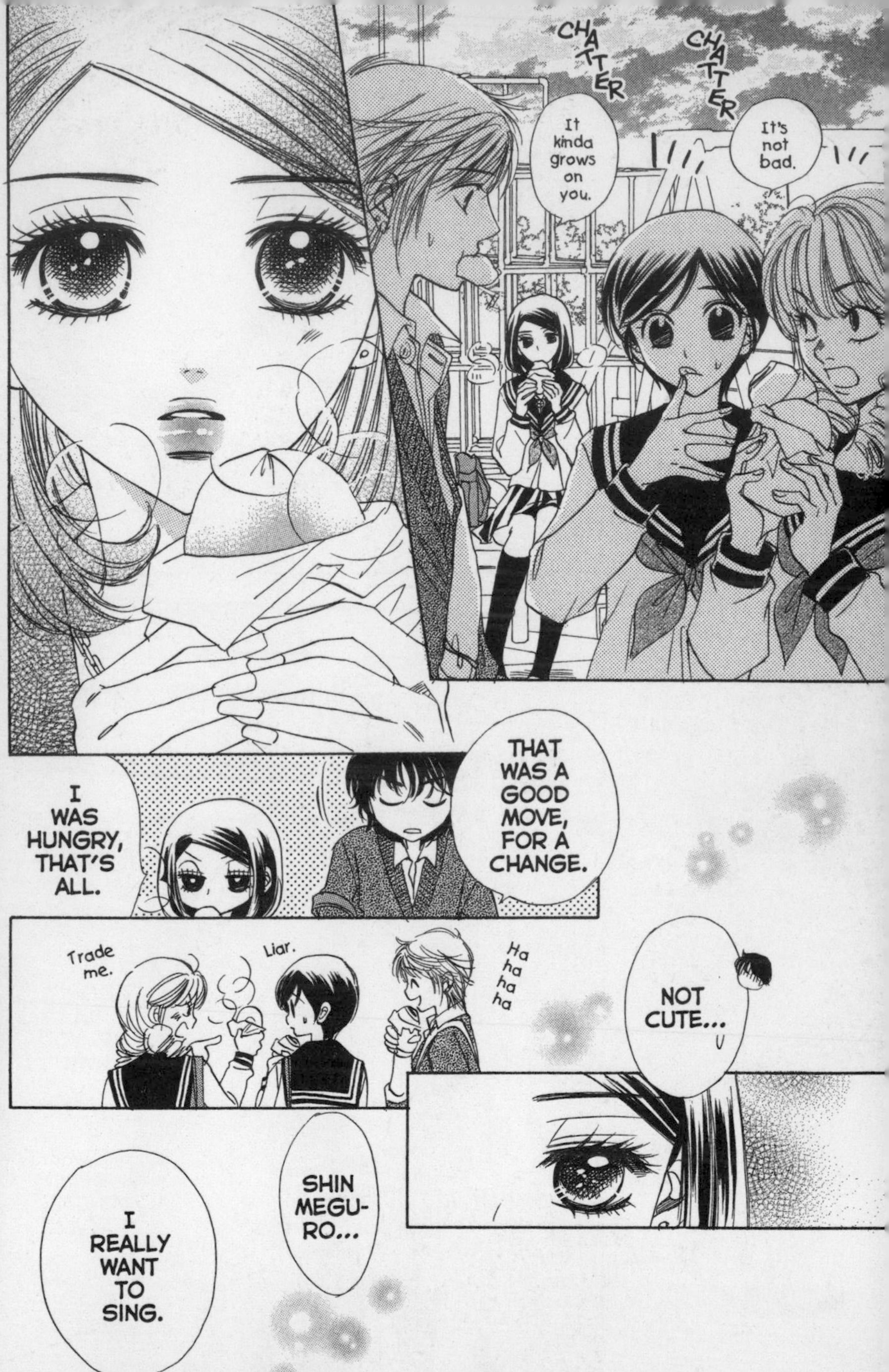
CHATTER
CHATTER
It's not bad.
It kinda grows on you.
THAT WAS A GOOD MOVE, FOR A CHANGE.
I WAS HUNGRY, THAT'S ALL.
NOT CUTE...
Ha ha ha ha
Liar.
Trade me.
SHIN MEGURO...
I REALLY WANT TO SING.

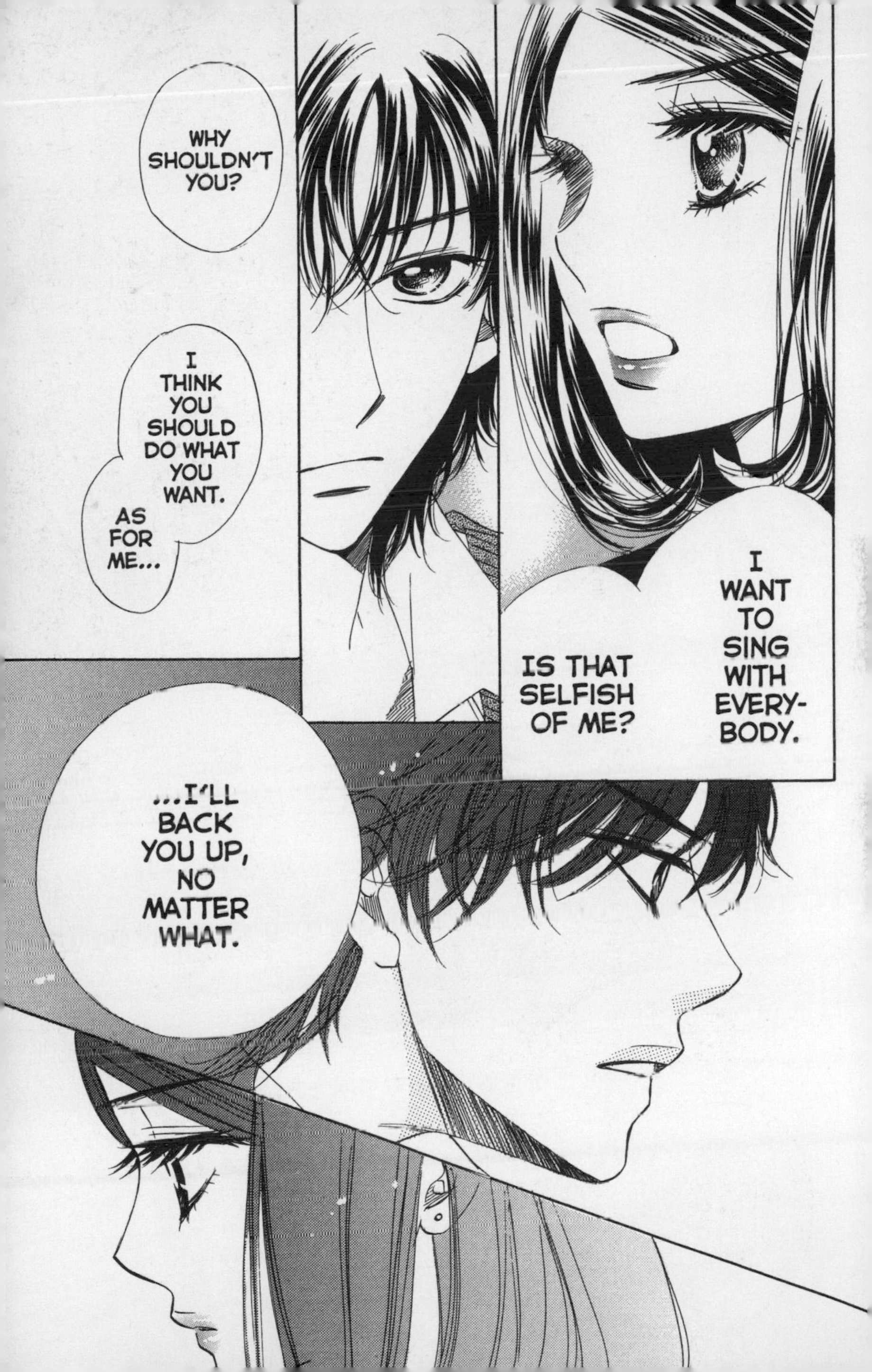
I WANT TO SING WITH EVERY-BODY.
IS THAT SELFISH OF ME?
WHY SHOULDN'T YOU?
I THINK YOU SHOULD DO WHAT YOU WANT.
AS FOR ME...
...I'LL BACK YOU UP, NO MATTER WHAT.

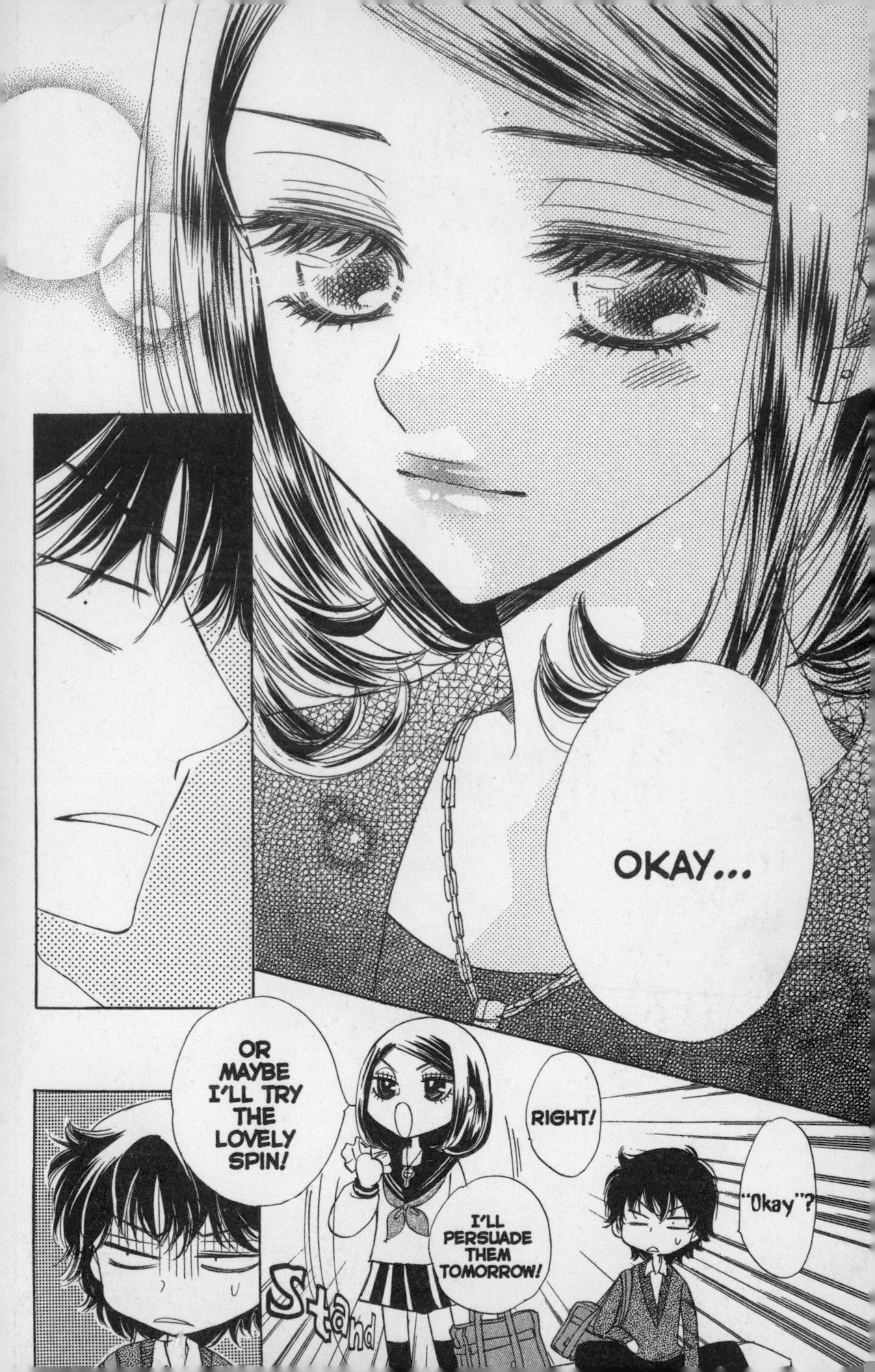
OKAY...
"Okay"?
RIGHT!
I'LL PERSUADE THEM TOMORROW!
OR MAYBE I'LL TRY THE LOVELY SPIN!
Stand

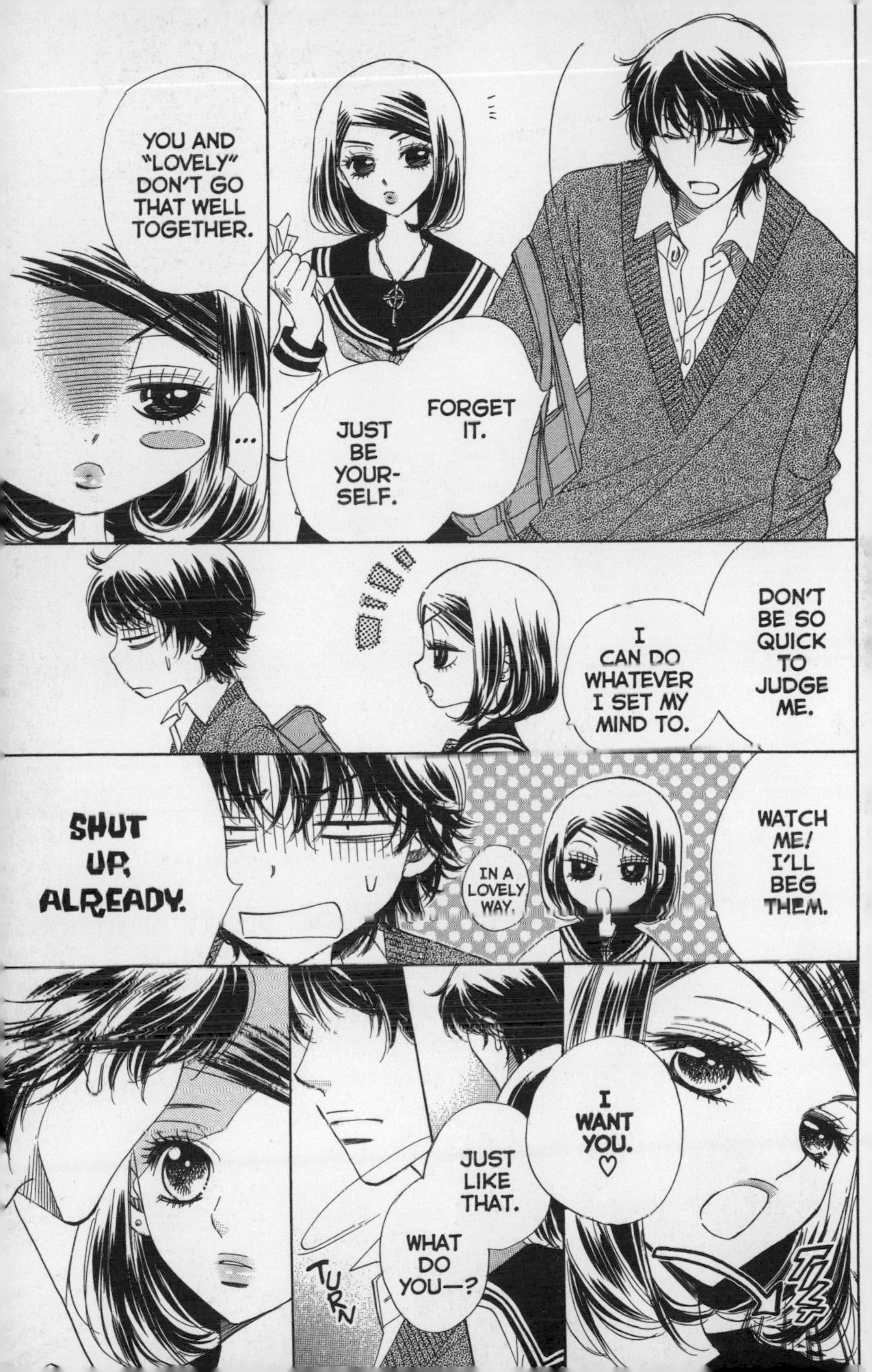
YOU AND "LOVELY" DON'T GO THAT WELL TOGETHER.
...
FORGET IT. JUST BE YOURSELF.
DON'T BE SO QUICK TO JUDGE ME.
I CAN DO WHATEVER I SET MY MIND TO.
WATCH ME! I'LL BEG THEM.
IN A LOVELY WAY.
SHUT UP, ALREADY.
I WANT YOU. ♡
TILT
JUST LIKE THAT.
WHAT DO YOU—?
TURN

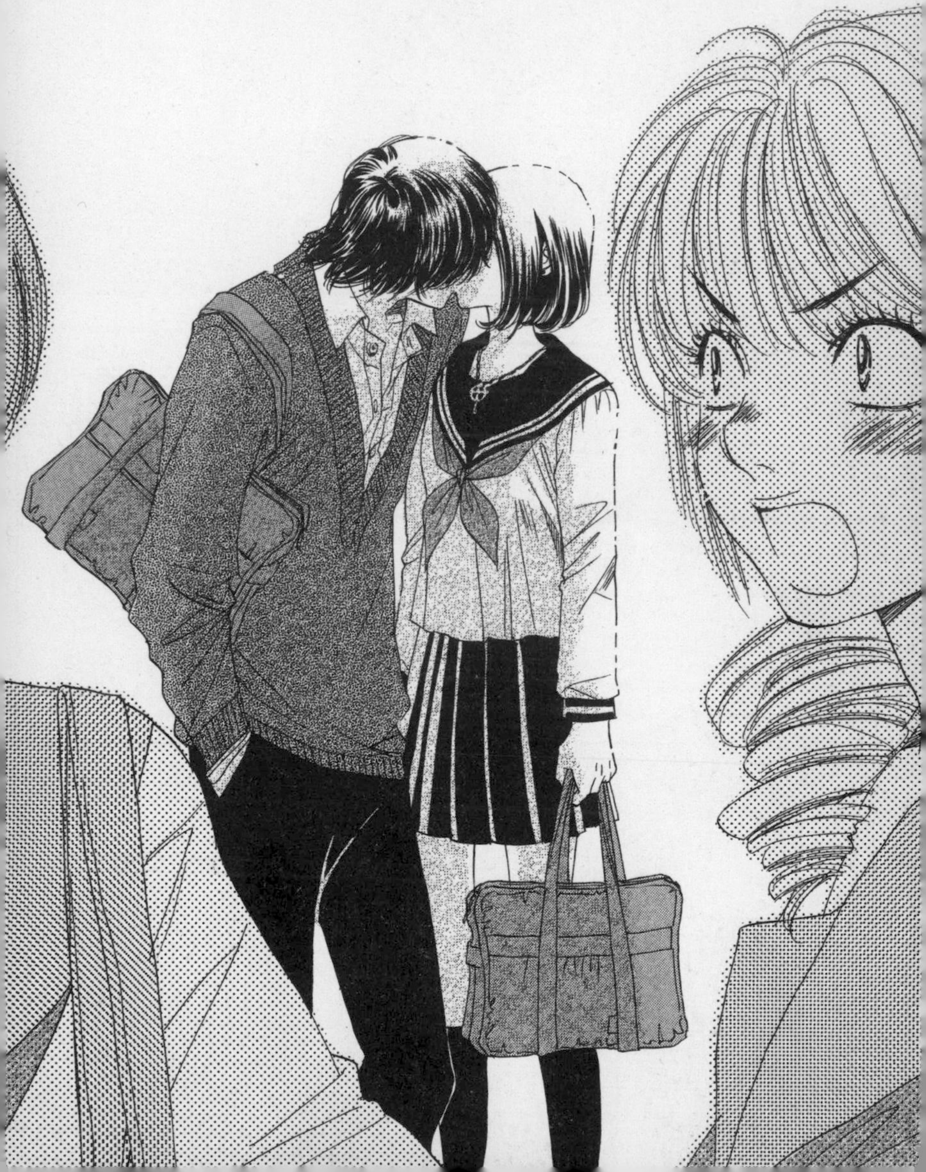

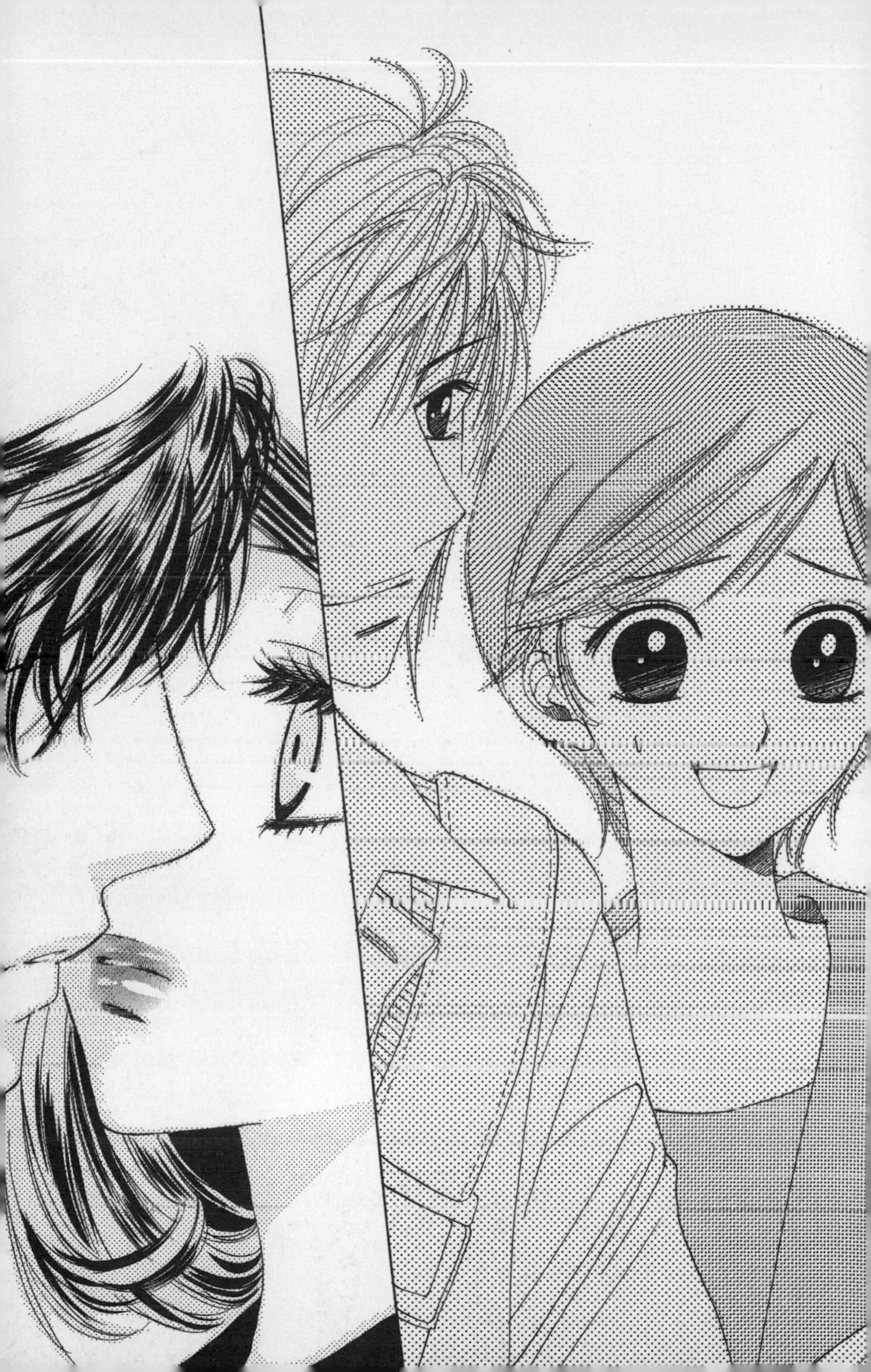

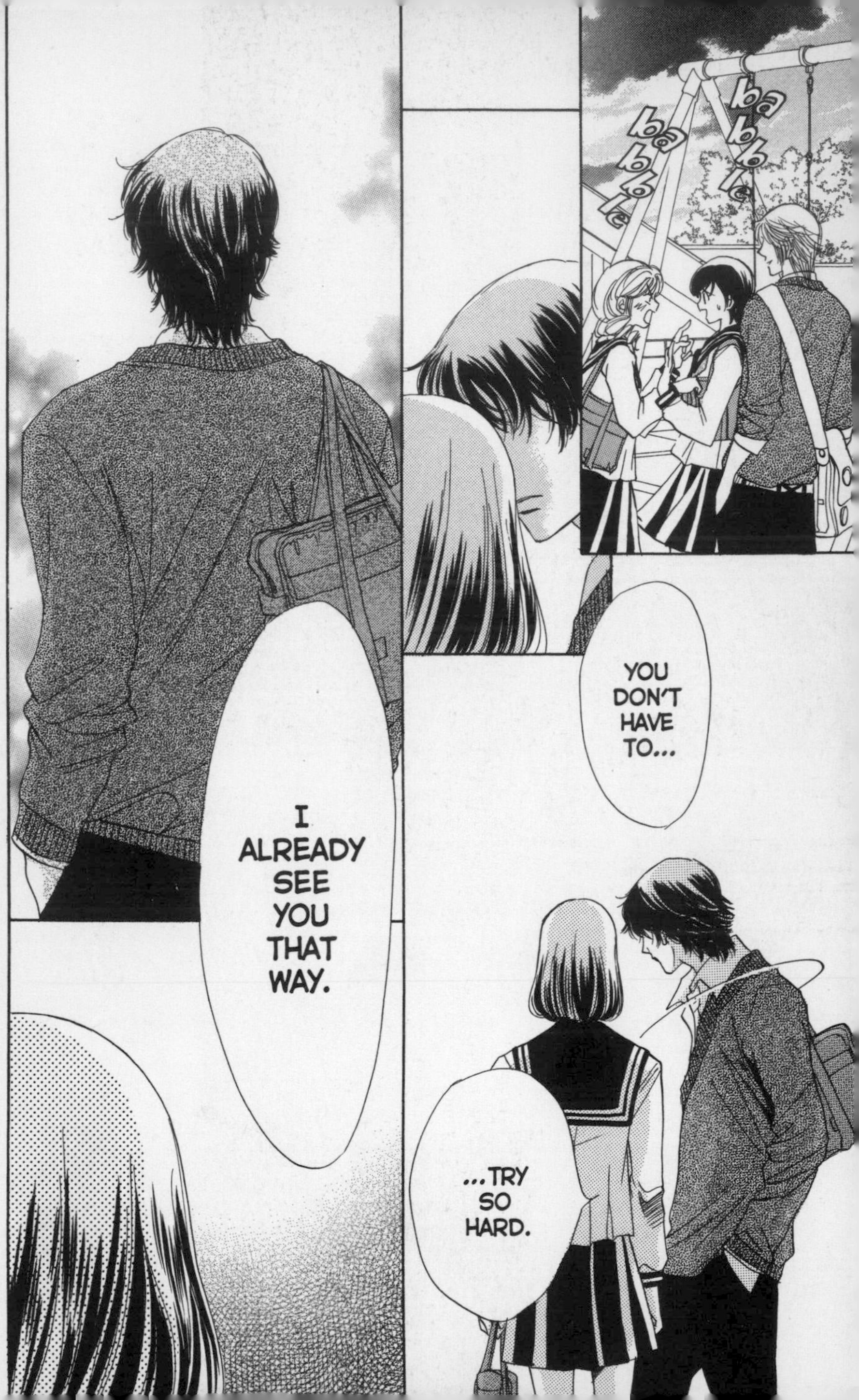
babble
babble
YOU DON'T HAVE TO...
...TRY SO HARD.
I ALREADY SEE YOU THAT WAY.

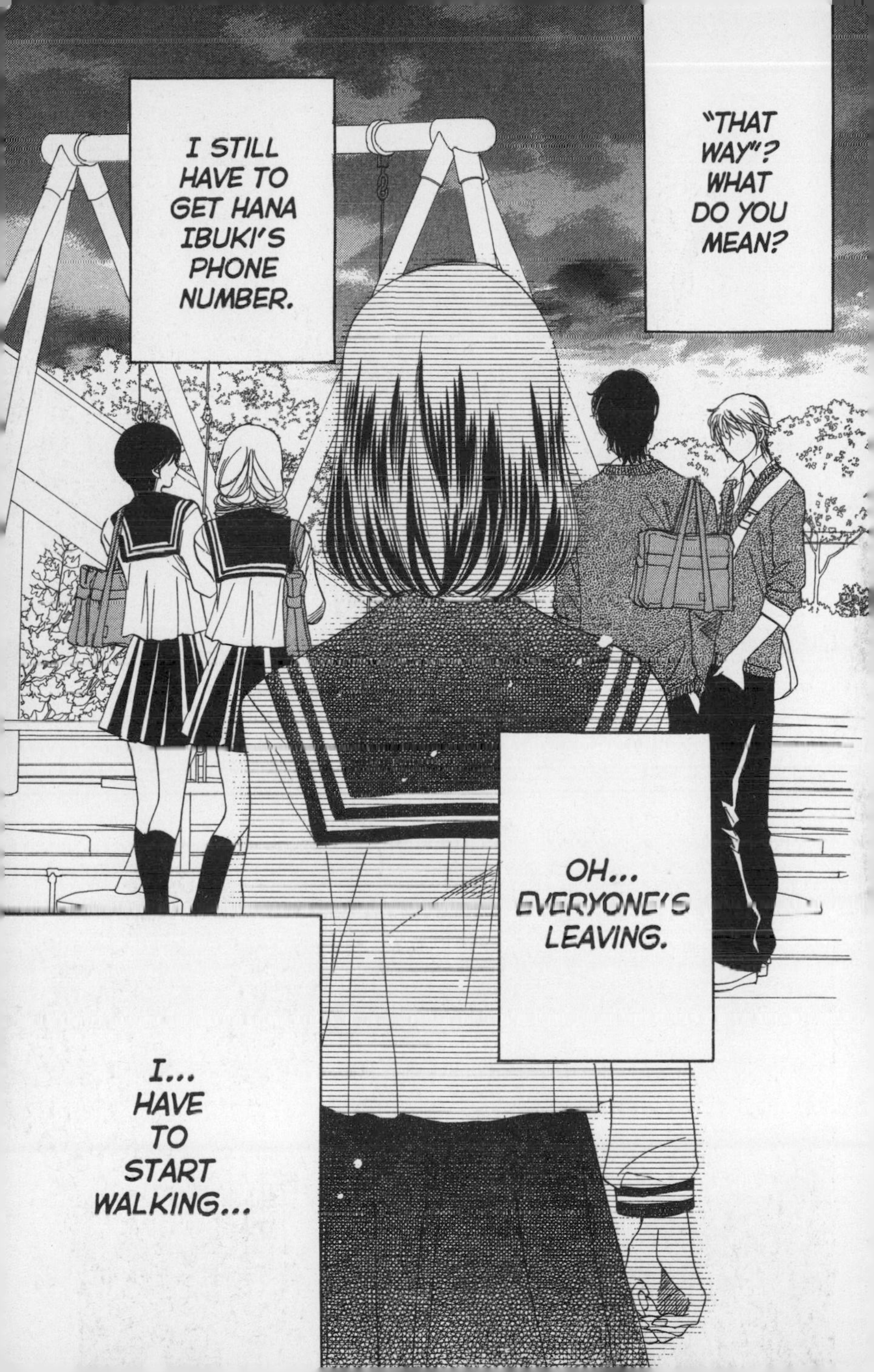
"THAT WAY"? WHAT DO YOU MEAN?
I STILL HAVE TO GET HANA IBUKI'S PHONE NUMBER.
OH... EVERYONE'S LEAVING.
I... HAVE TO START WALKING...

A Devil and
Her Love Song

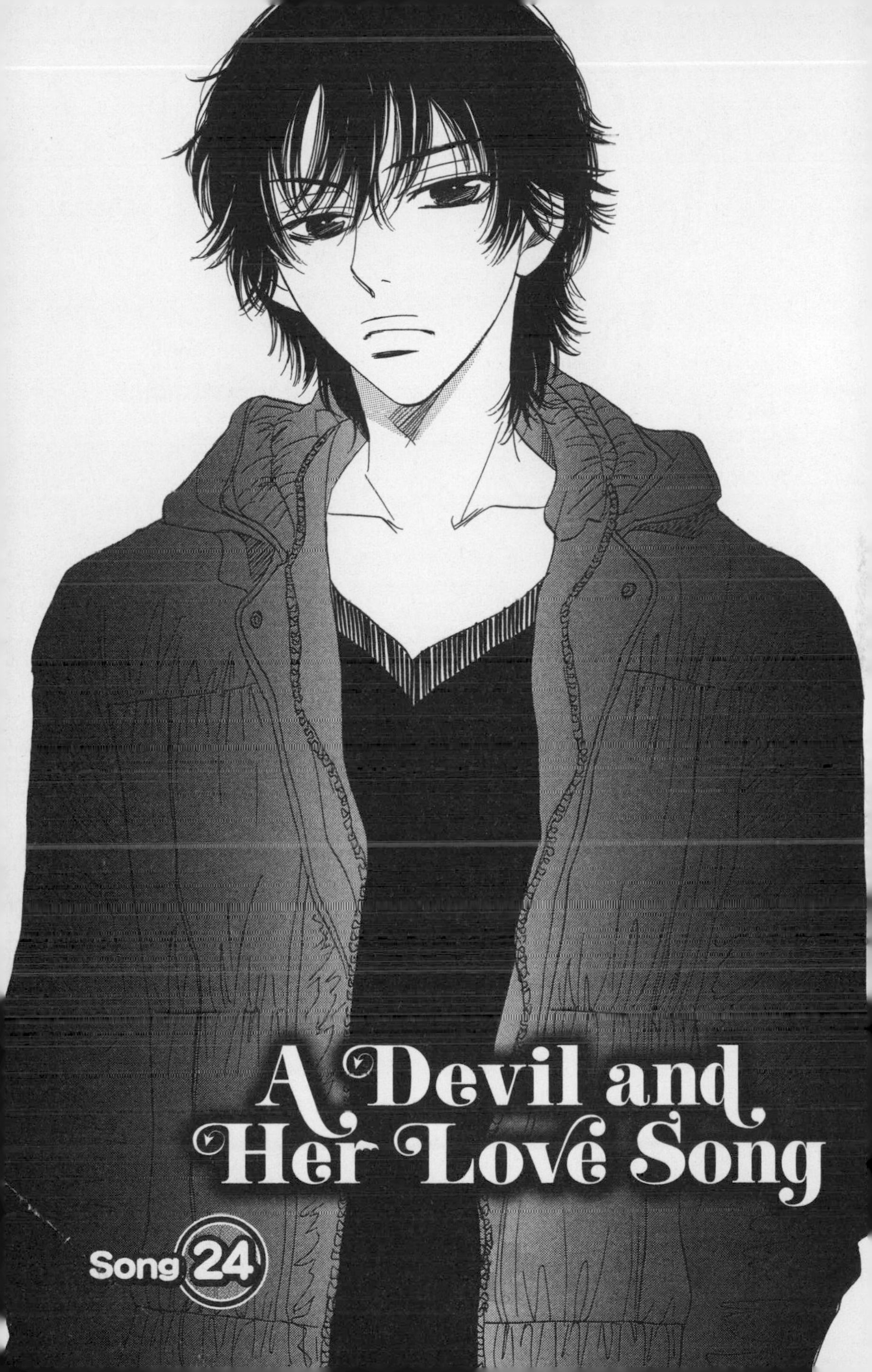
A Devil and Her Love Song
Song 24

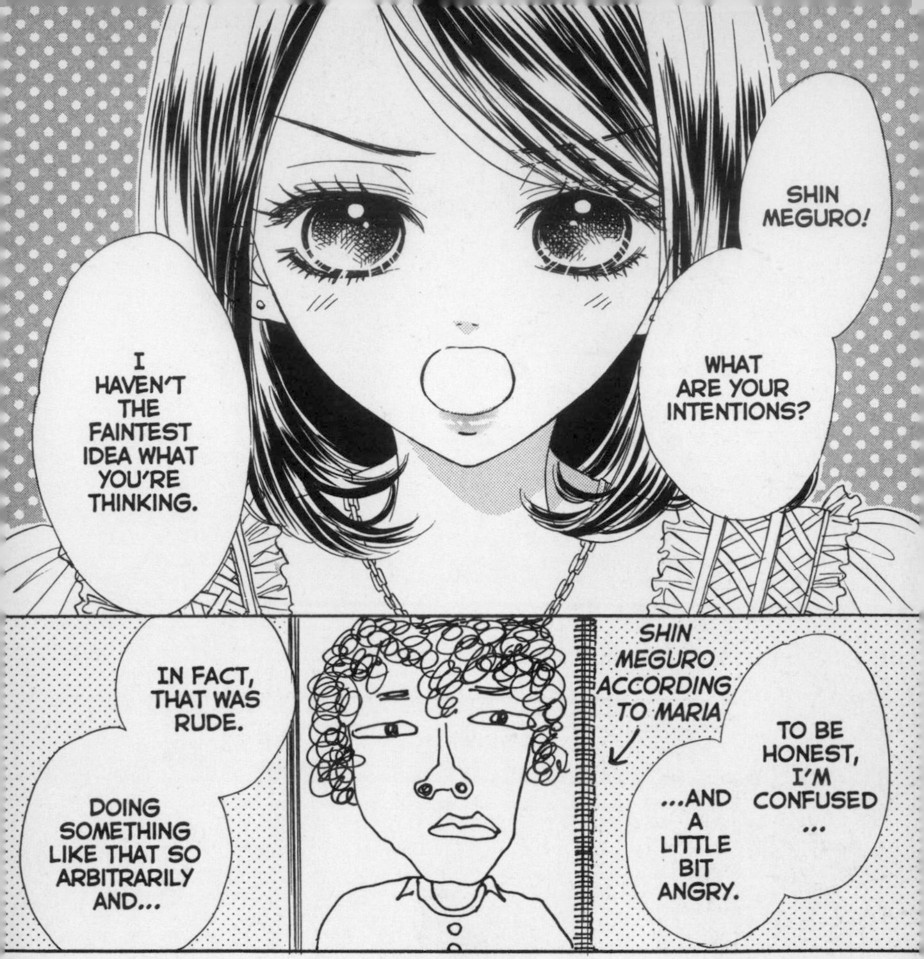
SHIN MEGURO!
WHAT ARE YOUR INTENTIONS?
I HAVEN'T THE FAINTEST IDEA WHAT YOU'RE THINKING.
TO BE HONEST, I'M CONFUSED...
...AND A LITTLE BIT ANGRY.
SHIN MEGURO ACCORDING TO MARIA
IN FACT, THAT WAS RUDE.
DOING SOMETHING LIKE THAT SO ARBITRARILY AND...

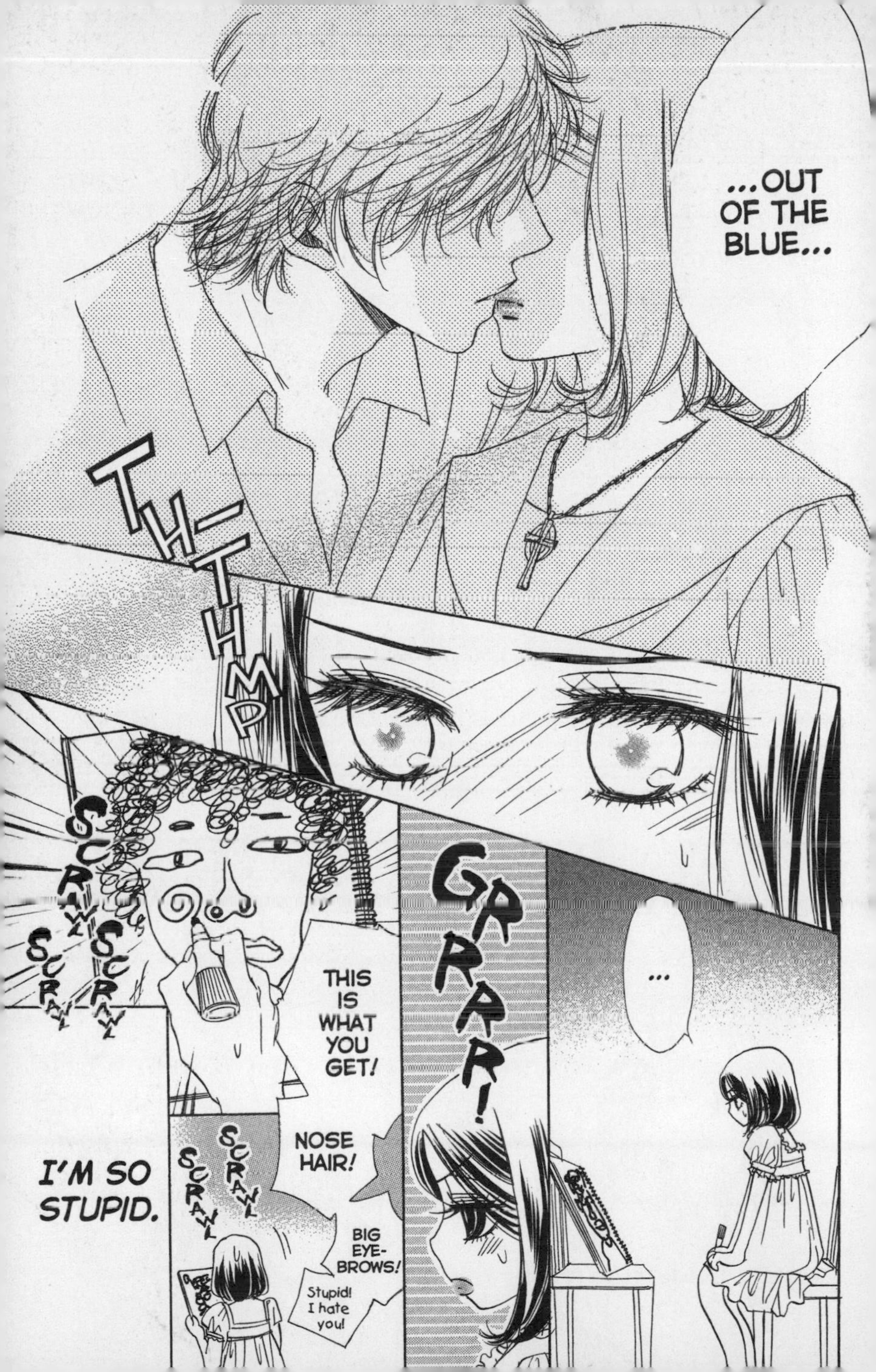
...OUT OF THE BLUE...
TH-THMP
...
GRRR!
SCRAWL SCRAWL SCRAWL
THIS IS WHAT YOU GET!
SCRAWL SCRAWL
NOSE HAIR!
BIG EYE-BROWS!
Stupid! I hate you!
I'M SO STUPID.

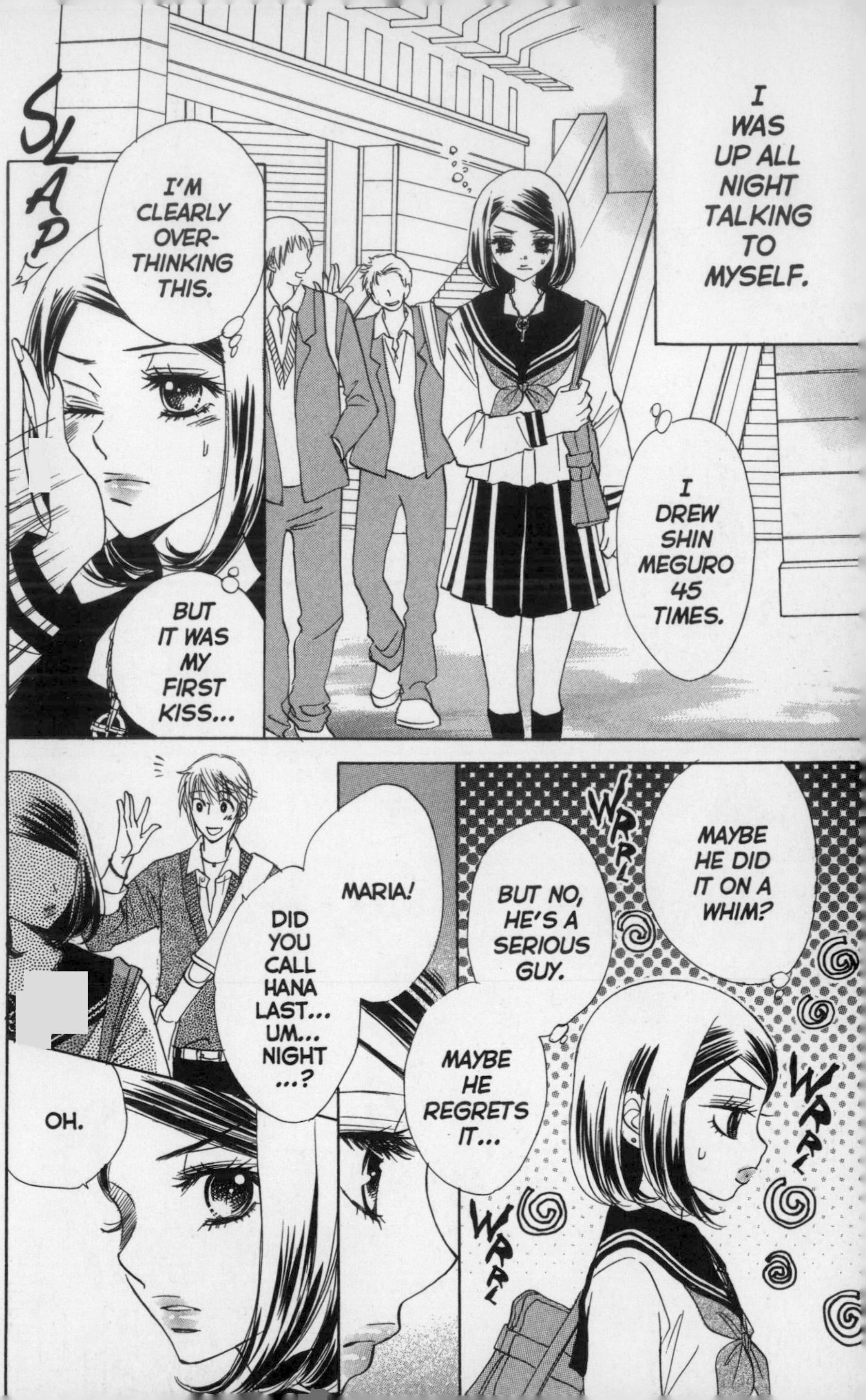
I WAS UP ALL NIGHT TALKING TO MYSELF.
I DREW SHIN MEGURO 45 TIMES.
SLAP
I'M CLEARLY OVER-THINKING THIS.
BUT IT WAS MY FIRST KISS...
MAYBE HE DID IT ON A WHIM?
WRRL
BUT NO, HE'S A SERIOUS GUY.
MAYBE HE REGRETS IT...
WRRL
WRRL
MARIA!
DID YOU CALL HANA LAST... UM... NIGHT...?
OH.

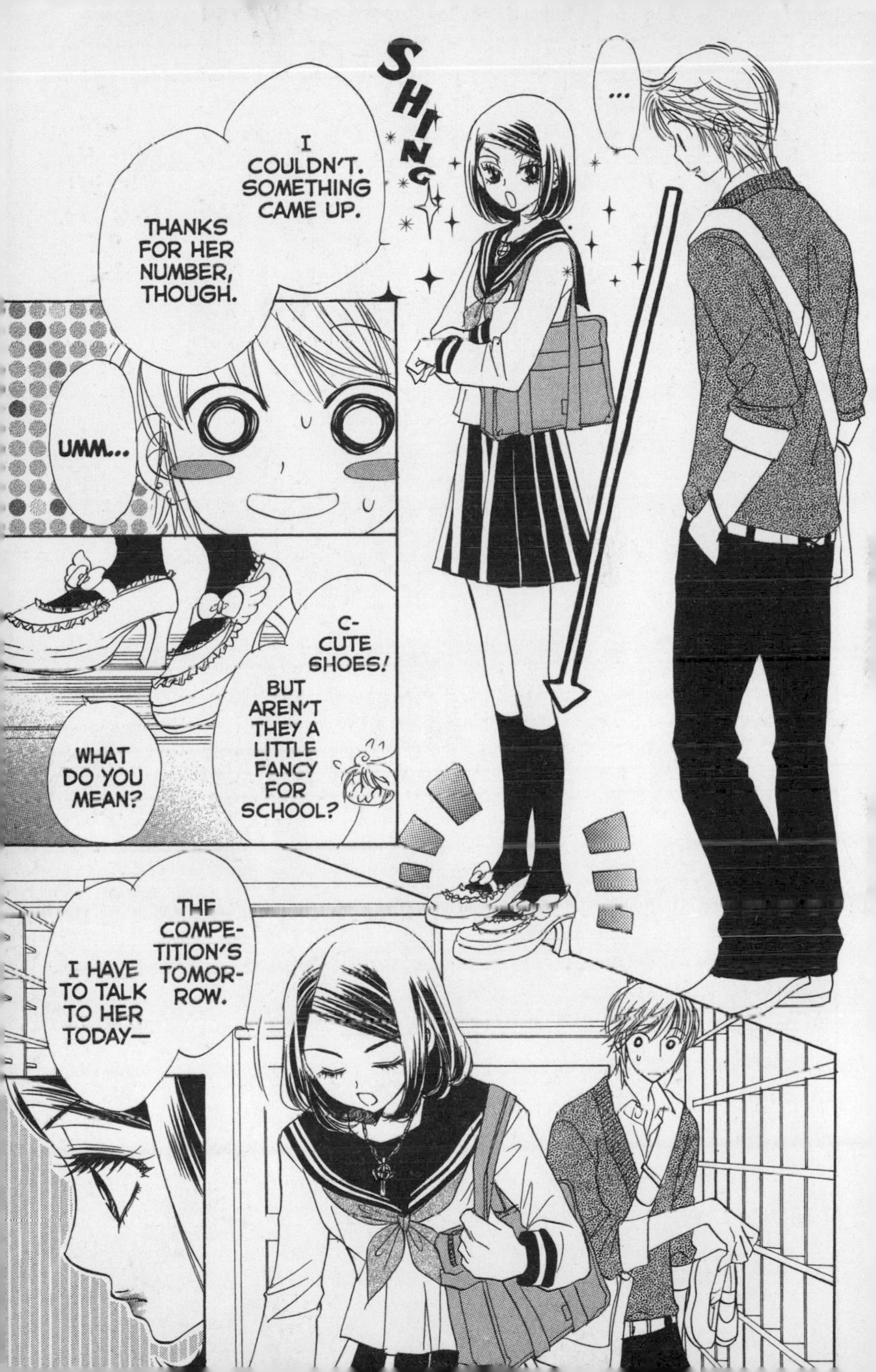
...
SHING
I COULDN'T. SOMETHING CAME UP.
THANKS FOR HER NUMBER, THOUGH.
UMM...
C-CUTE SHOES!
BUT AREN'T THEY A LITTLE FANCY FOR SCHOOL?
WHAT DO YOU MEAN?
THF COMPETITION'S TOMORROW.
I HAVE TO TALK TO HER TODAY—

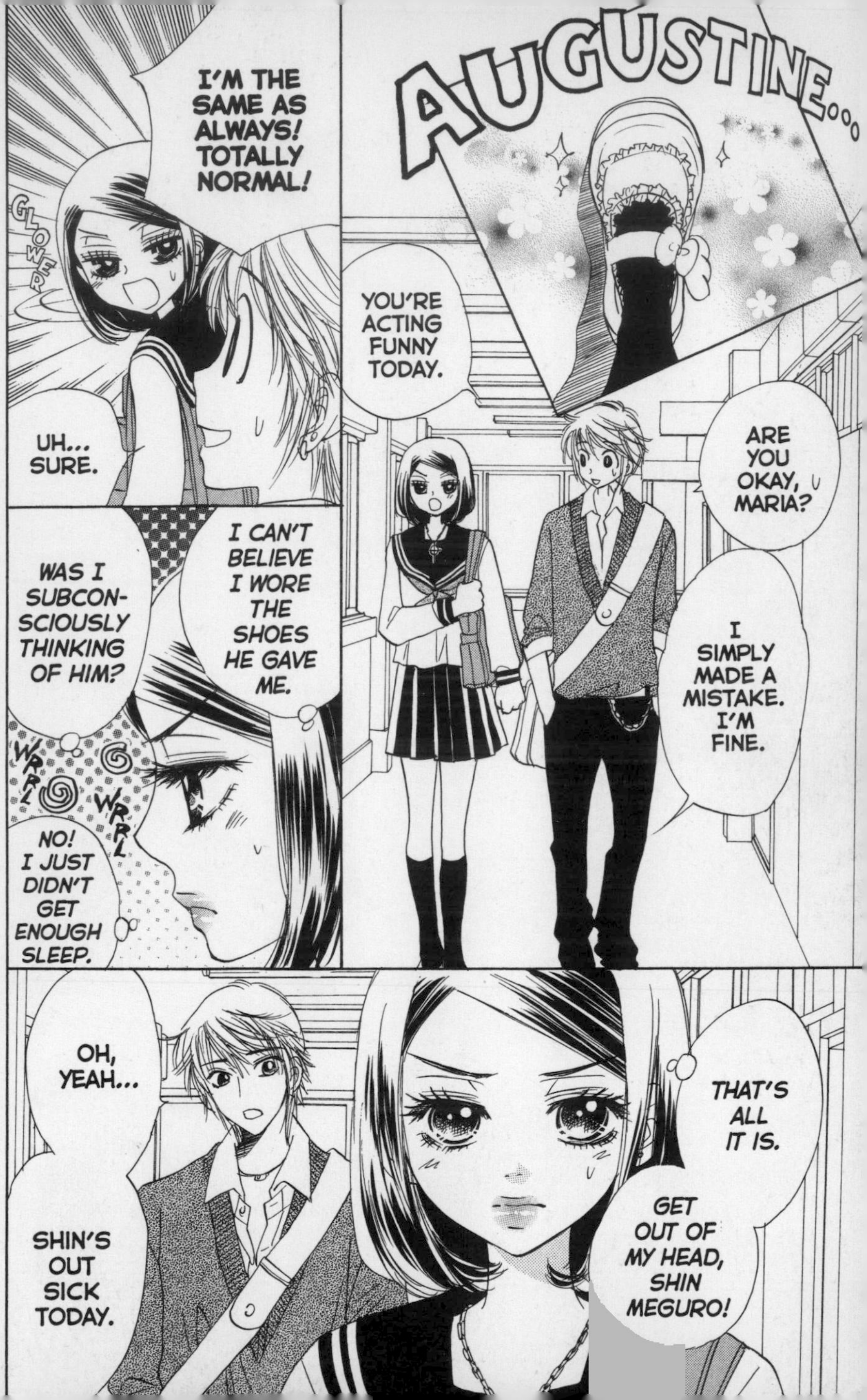
AUGUSTINE...
YOU'RE ACTING FUNNY TODAY.
ARE YOU OKAY, MARIA?
I SIMPLY MADE A MISTAKE. I'M FINE.
I'M THE SAME AS ALWAYS! TOTALLY NORMAL!
GLOWER
UH... SURE.
I CAN'T BELIEVE I WORE THE SHOES HE GAVE ME.
WAS I SUBCON-SCIOUSLY THINKING OF HIM?
WRRL
WRRL
NO! I JUST DIDN'T GET ENOUGH SLEEP.
THAT'S ALL IT IS.
GET OUT OF MY HEAD, SHIN MEGURO!
OH, YEAH...
SHIN'S OUT SICK TODAY.

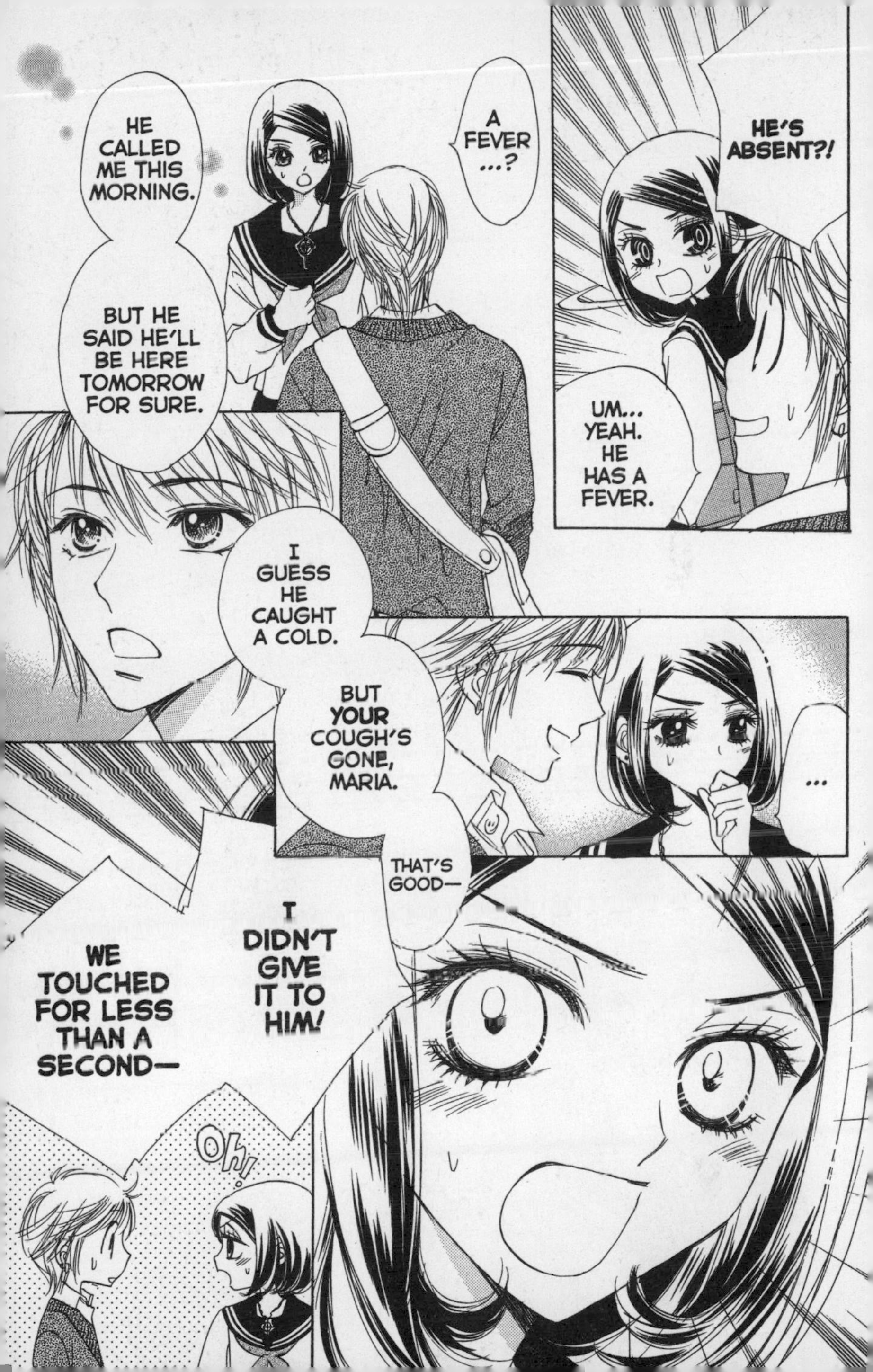
HE'S ABSENT?!
UM... YEAH. HE HAS A FEVER.
A FEVER ...?
HE CALLED ME THIS MORNING.
BUT HE SAID HE'LL BE HERE TOMORROW FOR SURE.
I GUESS HE CAUGHT A COLD.
BUT YOUR COUGH'S GONE, MARIA.
...
THAT'S GOOD—
I DIDN'T GIVE IT TO HIM!
WE TOUCHED FOR LESS THAN A SECOND—
Oh!

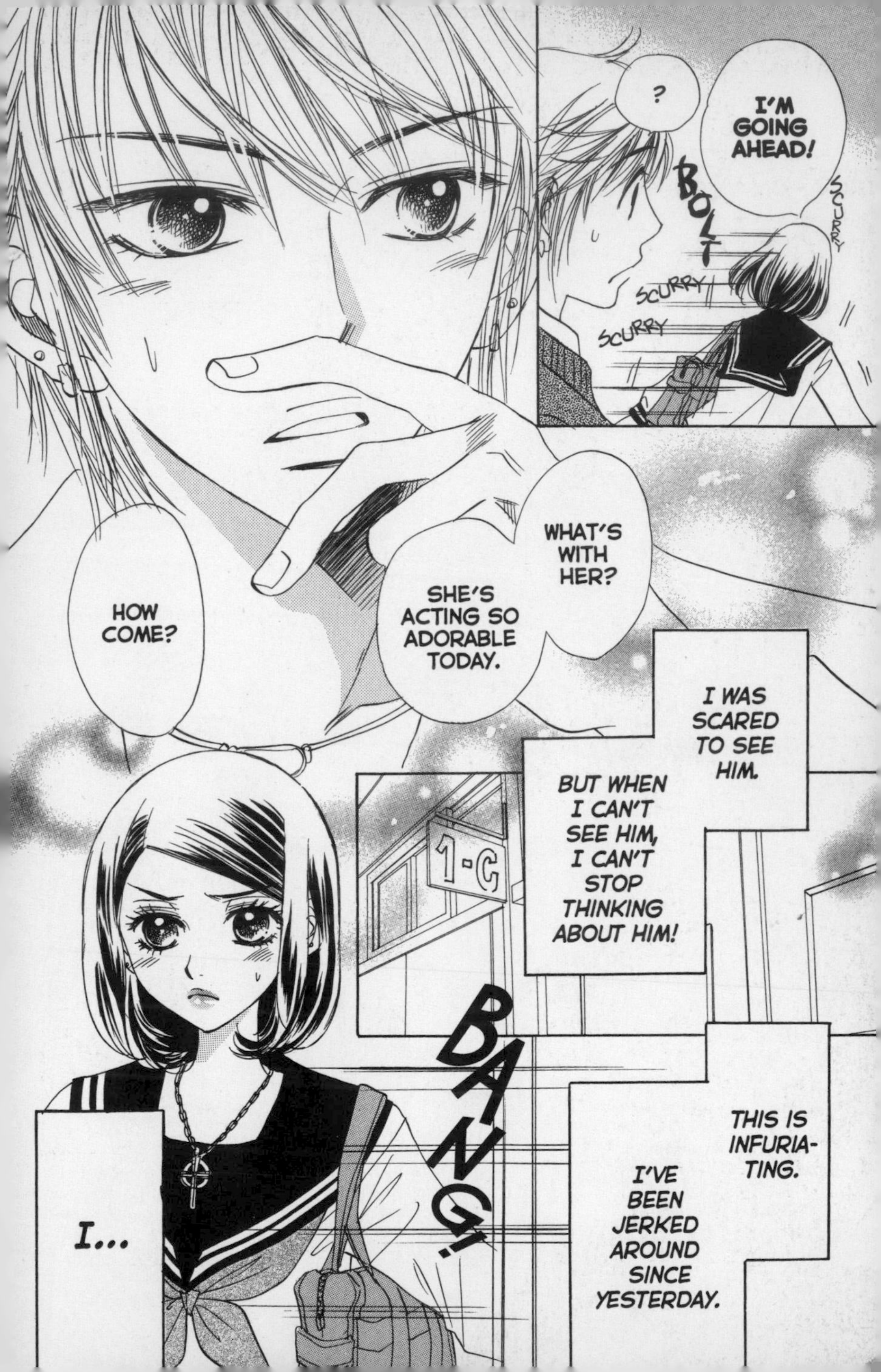
I'M GOING AHEAD!
SCURRY
?
BOLT
SCURRY
SCURRY
WHAT'S WITH HER?
SHE'S ACTING SO ADORABLE TODAY.
HOW COME?
I WAS SCARED TO SEE HIM.
BUT WHEN I CAN'T SEE HIM, I CAN'T STOP THINKING ABOUT HIM!
1-C
BANG!
THIS IS INFURIA-TING.
I'VE BEEN JERKED AROUND SINCE YESTERDAY.
I...

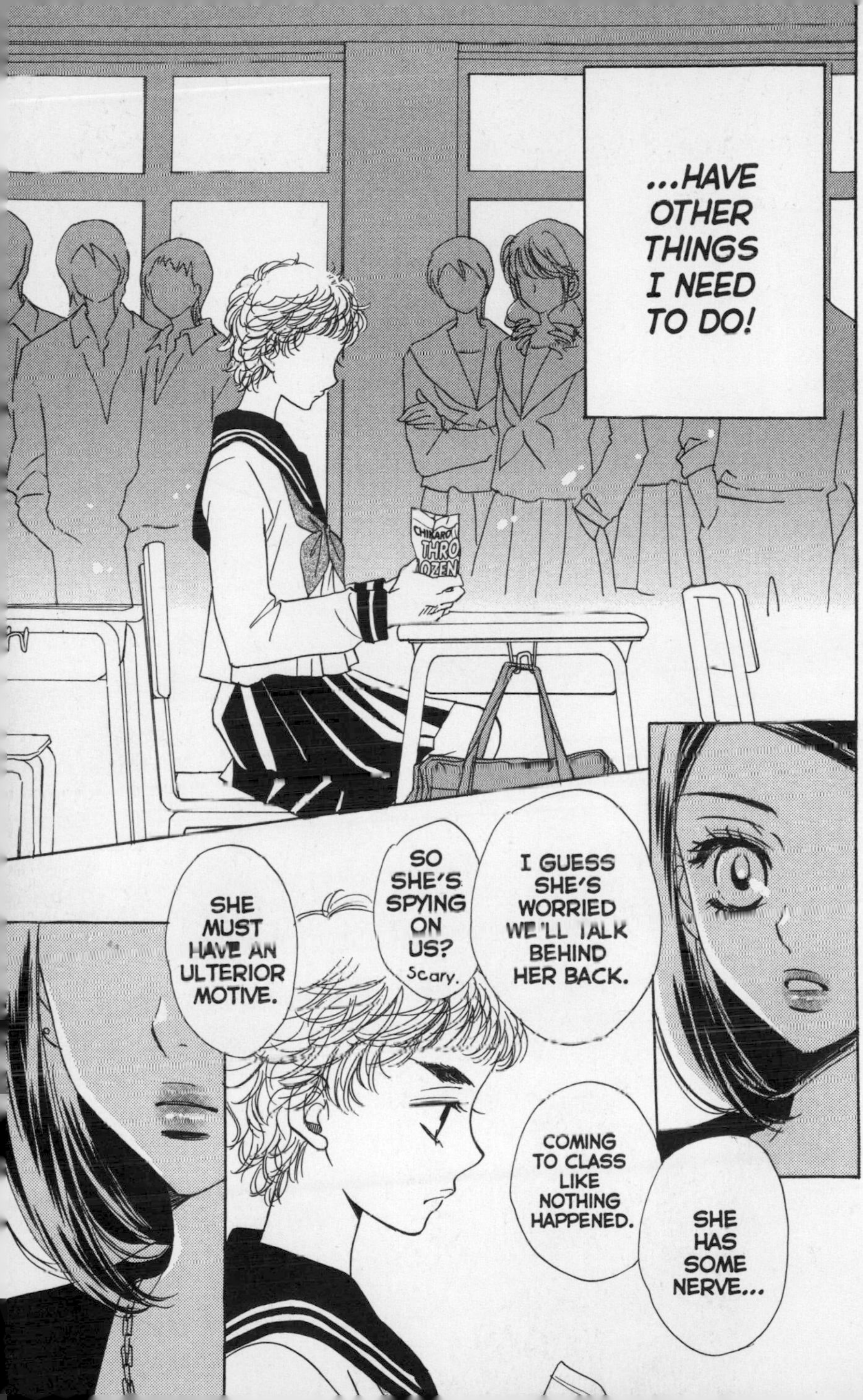
...HAVE OTHER THINGS I NEED TO DO!
CHIKARO THRO OZEN
I GUESS SHE'S WORRIED WE'LL TALK BEHIND HER BACK.
SO SHE'S SPYING ON US? Scary.
SHE MUST HAVE AN ULTERIOR MOTIVE.
COMING TO CLASS LIKE NOTHING HAPPENED.
SHE HAS SOME NERVE...

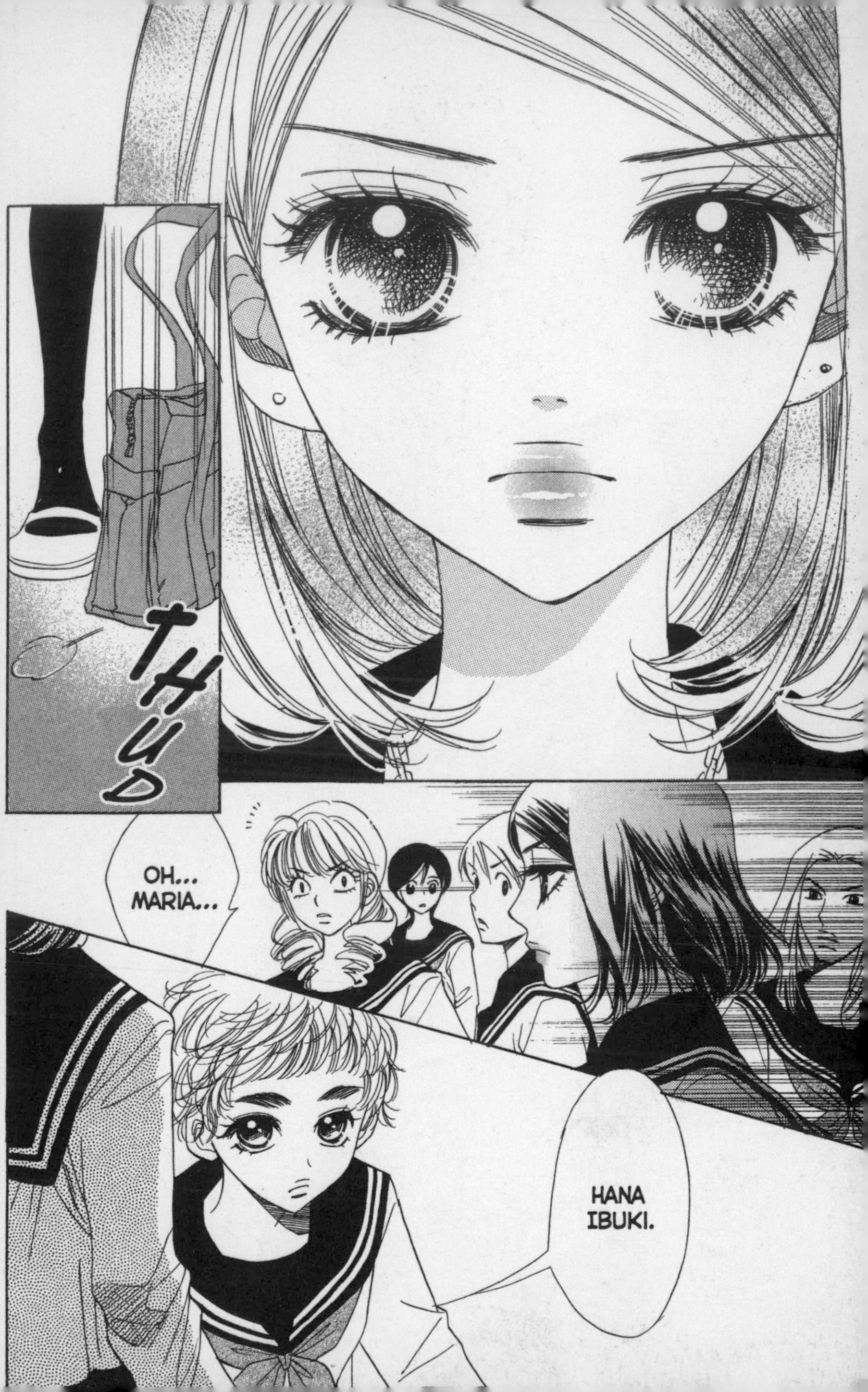
THUD
OH... MARIA...
HANA IBUKI.

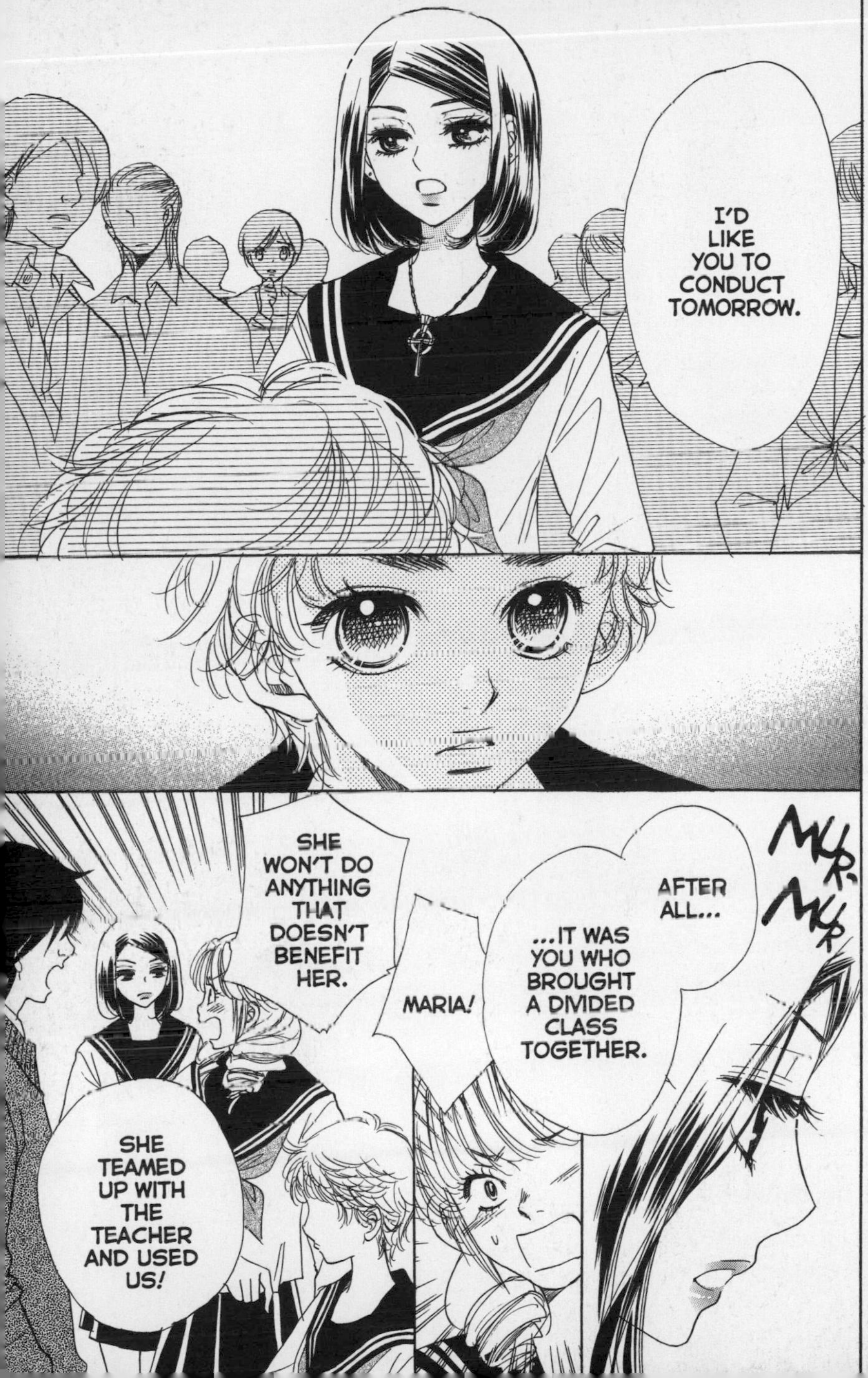
I'D LIKE YOU TO CONDUCT TOMORROW.
MUR-MUR
AFTER ALL...
...IT WAS YOU WHO BROUGHT A DIVIDED CLASS TOGETHER.
MARIA!
SHE WON'T DO ANYTHING THAT DOESN'T BENEFIT HER.
SHE TEAMED UP WITH THE TEACHER AND USED US!

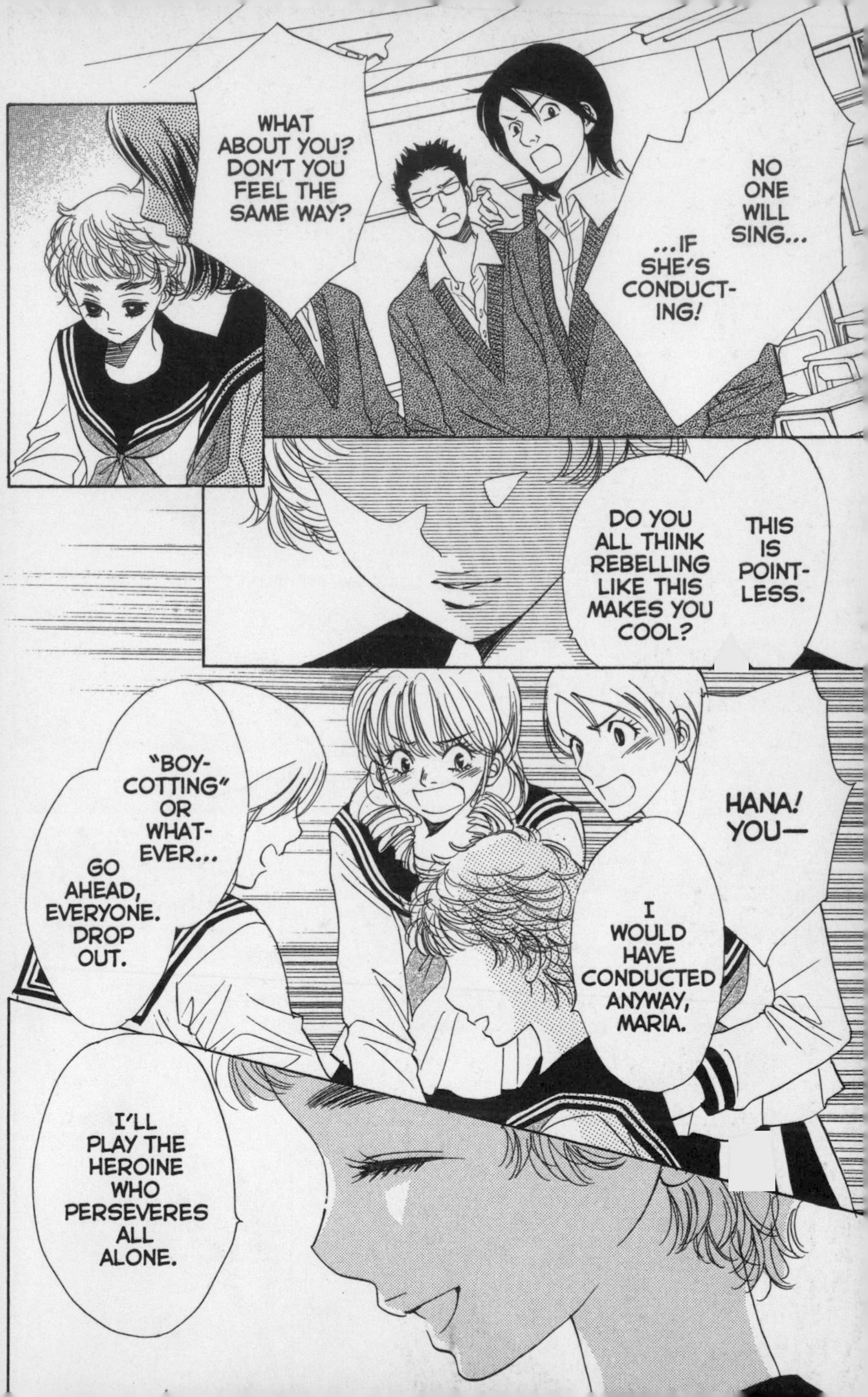
NO ONE WILL SING...
...IF SHE'S CONDUCTING!
WHAT ABOUT YOU? DON'T YOU FEEL THE SAME WAY?
THIS IS POINTLESS.
DO YOU ALL THINK REBELLING LIKE THIS MAKES YOU COOL?
HANA! YOU—
I WOULD HAVE CONDUCTED ANYWAY, MARIA.
"BOYCOTTING" OR WHATEVER...
GO AHEAD, EVERYONE. DROP OUT.
I'LL PLAY THE HEROINE WHO PERSEVERES ALL ALONE.

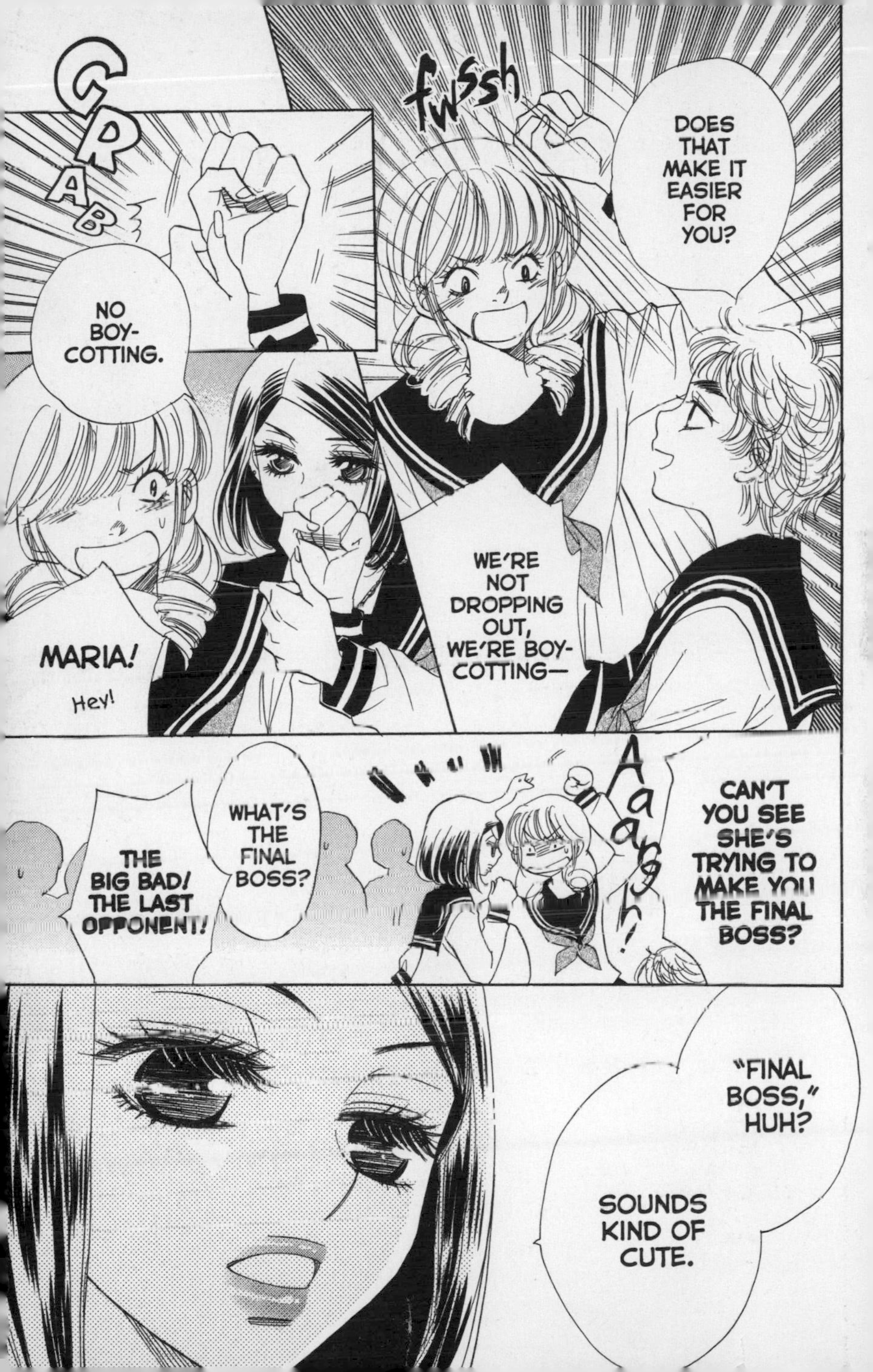
fwssh
DOES THAT MAKE IT EASIER FOR YOU?
GRAB
NO BOY-COTTING.
WE'RE NOT DROPPING OUT, WE'RE BOY-COTTING—
MARIA!
Hey!
CAN'T YOU SEE SHE'S TRYING TO MAKE YOU THE FINAL BOSS?
Aaagh!
WHAT'S THE FINAL BOSS?
THE BIG BAD! THE LAST OPPONENT!
"FINAL BOSS," HUH?
SOUNDS KIND OF CUTE.

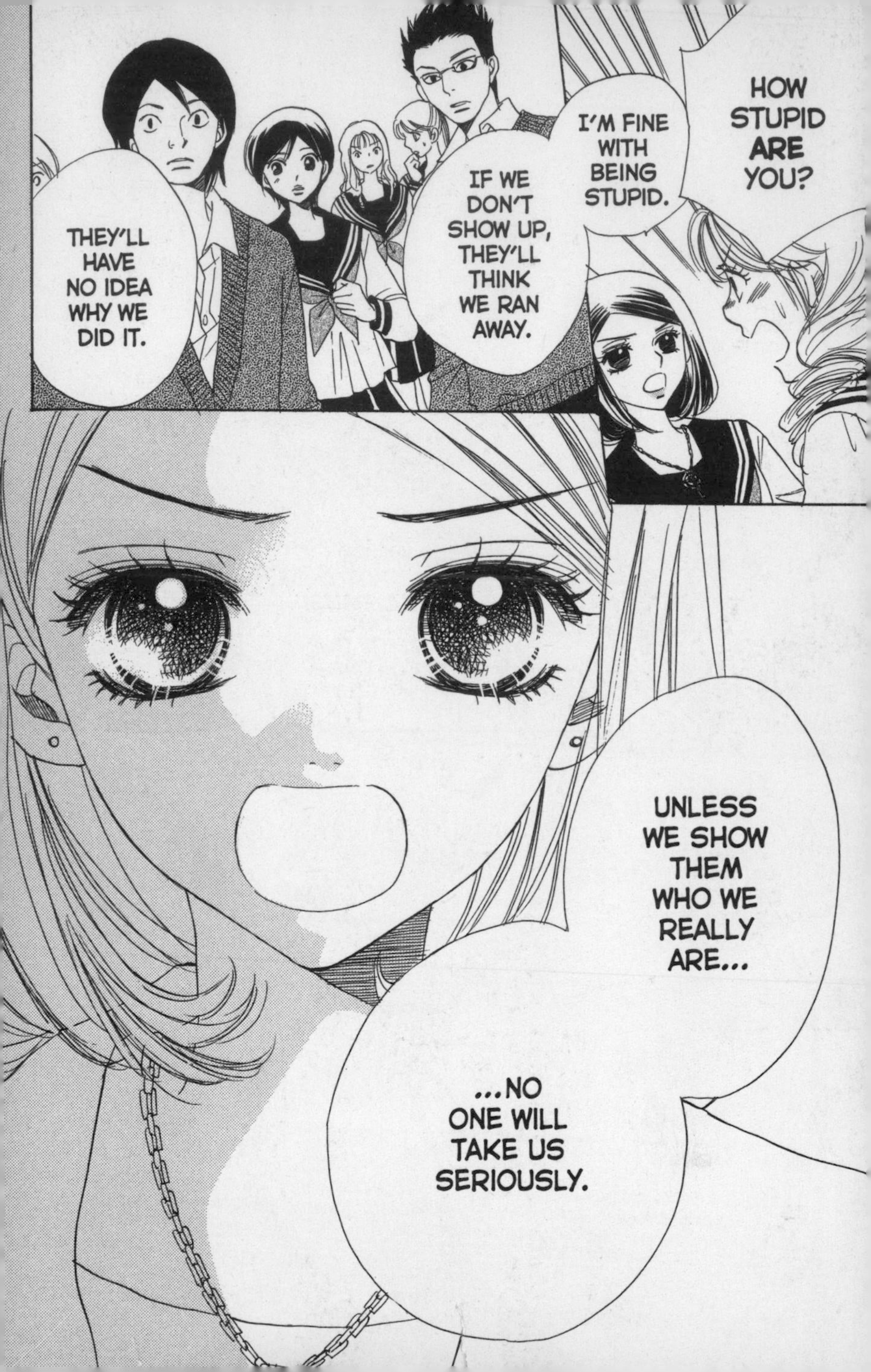
HOW STUPID ARE YOU?
I'M FINE WITH BEING STUPID.
IF WE DON'T SHOW UP, THEY'LL THINK WE RAN AWAY.
THEY'LL HAVE NO IDEA WHY WE DID IT.
UNLESS WE SHOW THEM WHO WE REALLY ARE...
...NO ONE WILL TAKE US SERIOUSLY.

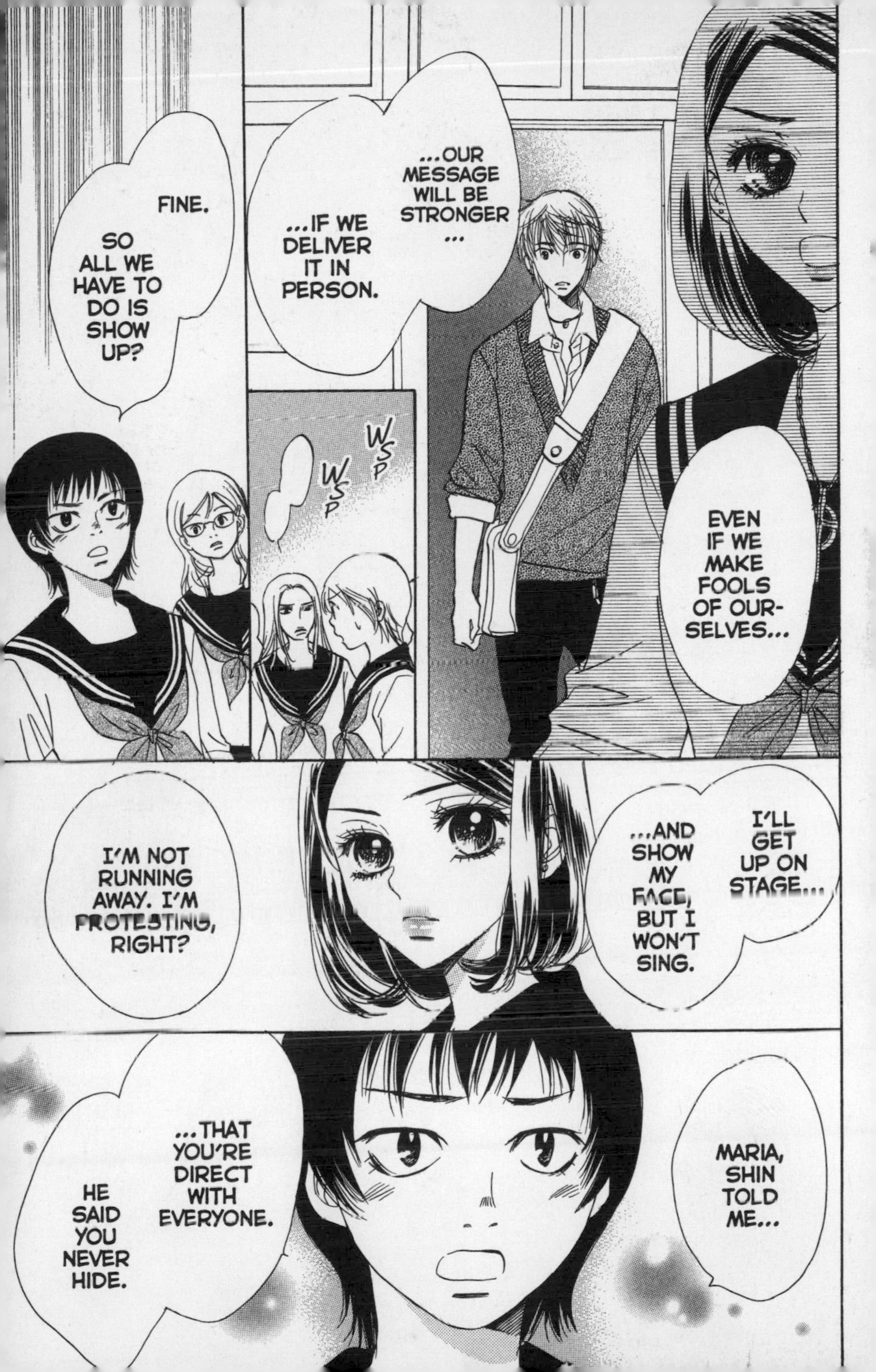
EVEN IF WE MAKE FOOLS OF OUR-SELVES...
...OUR MESSAGE WILL BE STRONGER...
...IF WE DELIVER IT IN PERSON.
WSP WSP
FINE.
SO ALL WE HAVE TO DO IS SHOW UP?
I'LL GET UP ON STAGE...
...AND SHOW MY FACE, BUT I WON'T SING.
I'M NOT RUNNING AWAY. I'M PROTESTING, RIGHT?
MARIA, SHIN TOLD ME...
...THAT YOU'RE DIRECT WITH EVERYONE.
HE SAID YOU NEVER HIDE.

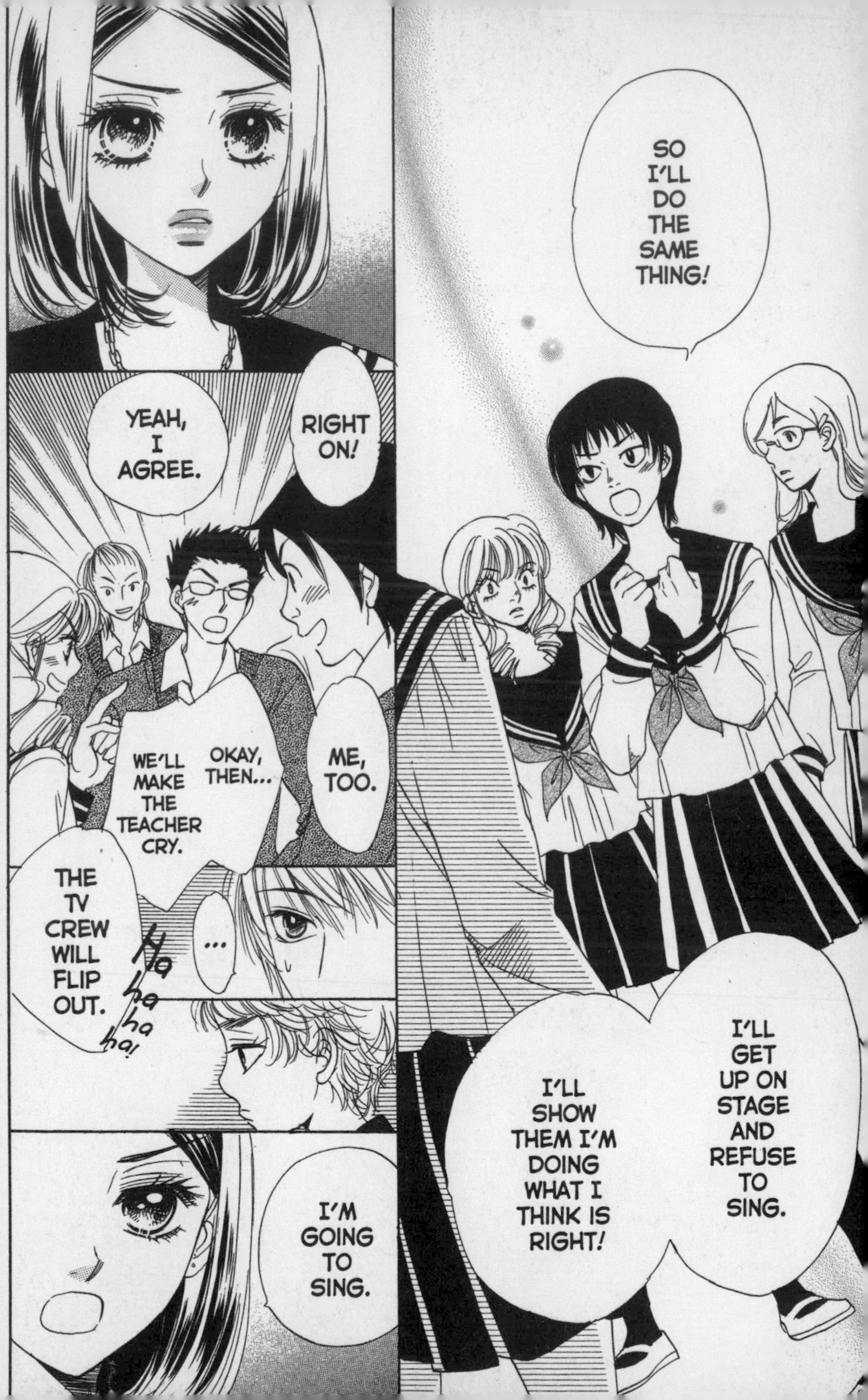
SO I'LL DO THE SAME THING!
I'LL GET UP ON STAGE AND REFUSE TO SING.
I'LL SHOW THEM I'M DOING WHAT I THINK IS RIGHT!
RIGHT ON!
YEAH, I AGREE.
ME, TOO.
OKAY, THEN... WE'LL MAKE THE TEACHER CRY.
...
THE TV CREW WILL FLIP OUT.
Ha ha ha ha!
I'M GOING TO SING.

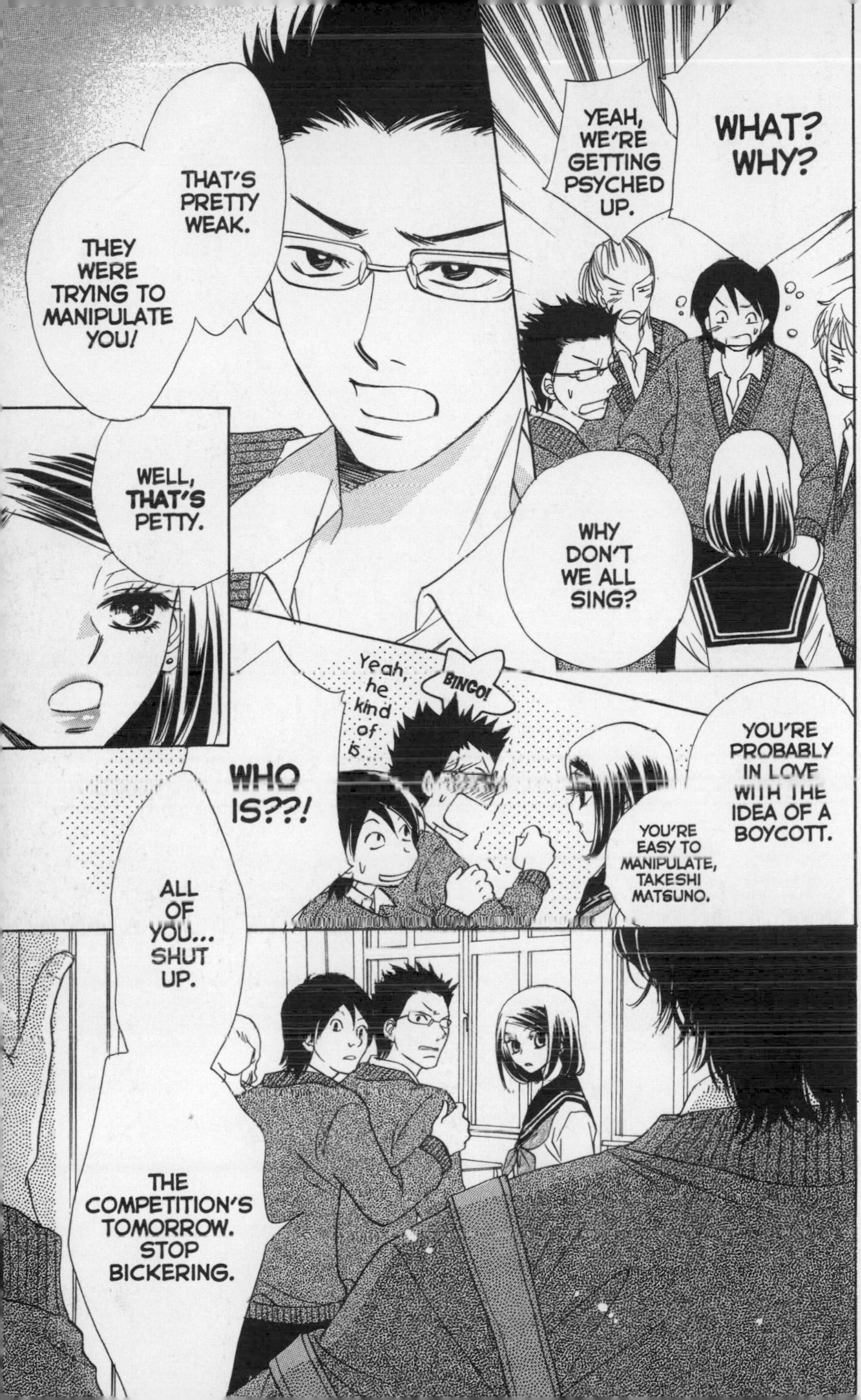
WHAT? WHY?
YEAH, WE'RE GETTING PSYCHED UP.
WHY DON'T WE ALL SING?
THAT'S PRETTY WEAK.
THEY WERE TRYING TO MANIPULATE YOU!
WELL, THAT'S PETTY.
YOU'RE PROBABLY IN LOVE WITH THE IDEA OF A BOYCOTT.
YOU'RE EASY TO MANIPULATE, TAKESHI MATSUNO.
BINGO!
Yeah, he kind of is...
WHO IS??!
ALL OF YOU... SHUT UP.
THE COMPETITION'S TOMORROW. STOP BICKERING.

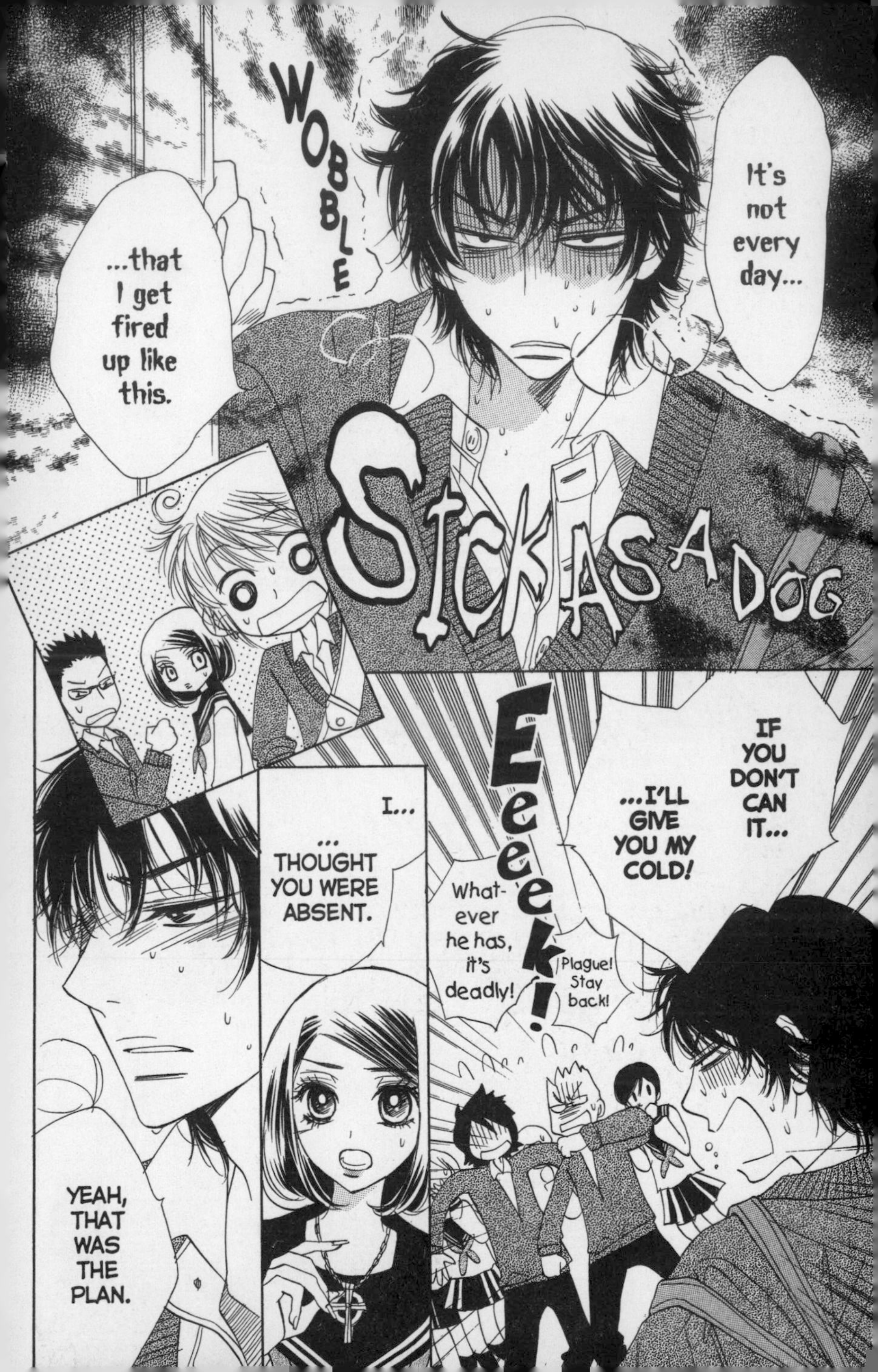
It's not every day...
WOBBLE
...that I get fired up like this.
SICK AS A DOG
IF YOU DON'T CAN IT...
...I'LL GIVE YOU MY COLD!
Eeeek!
Plague! Stay back!
What-ever he has, it's deadly!
I...
...THOUGHT YOU WERE ABSENT.
YEAH, THAT WAS THE PLAN.

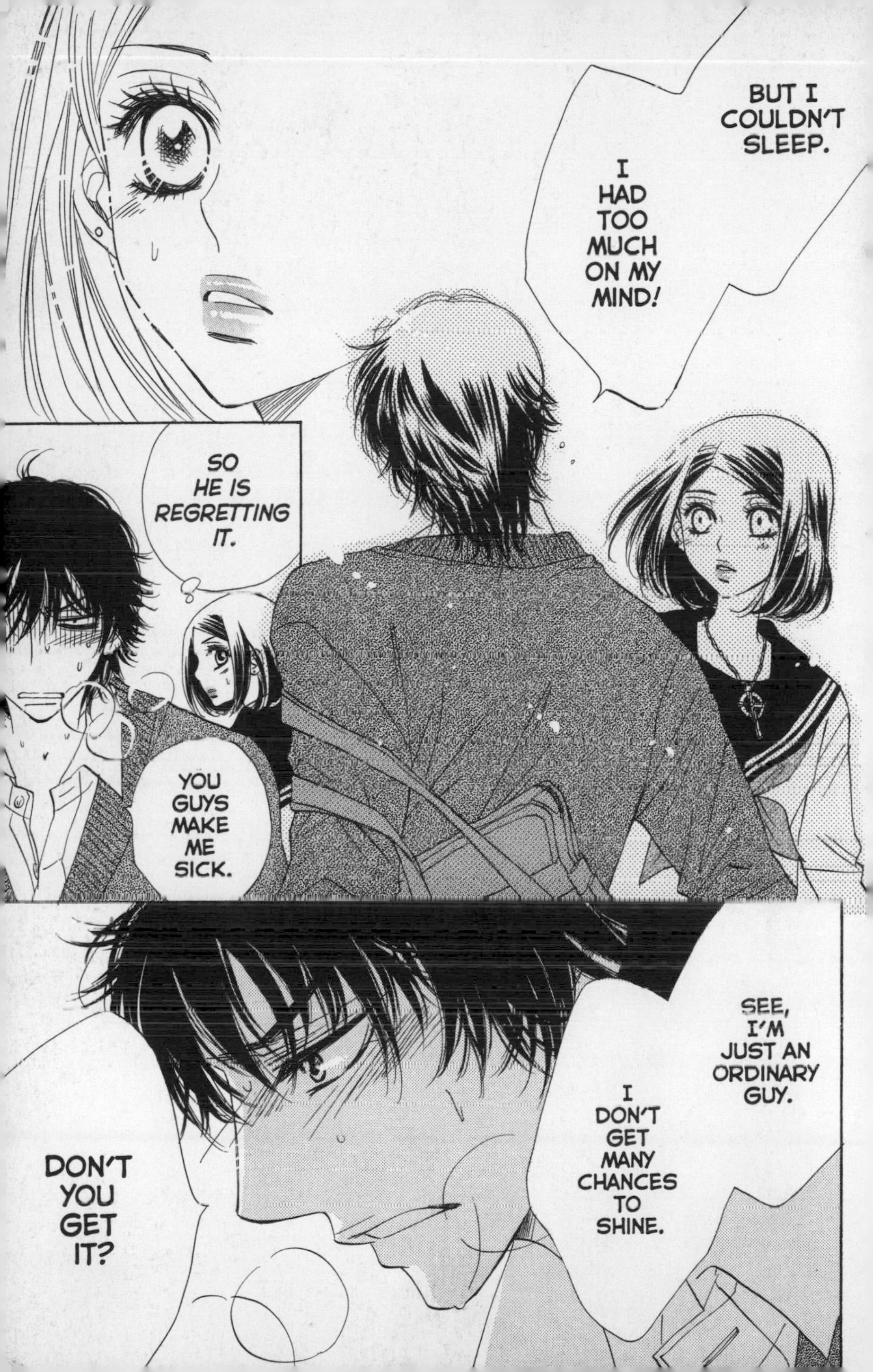
BUT I COULDN'T SLEEP.
I HAD TOO MUCH ON MY MIND!
SO HE IS REGRETTING IT.
YOU GUYS MAKE ME SICK.
SEE, I'M JUST AN ORDINARY GUY.
I DON'T GET MANY CHANCES TO SHINE.
DON'T YOU GET IT?

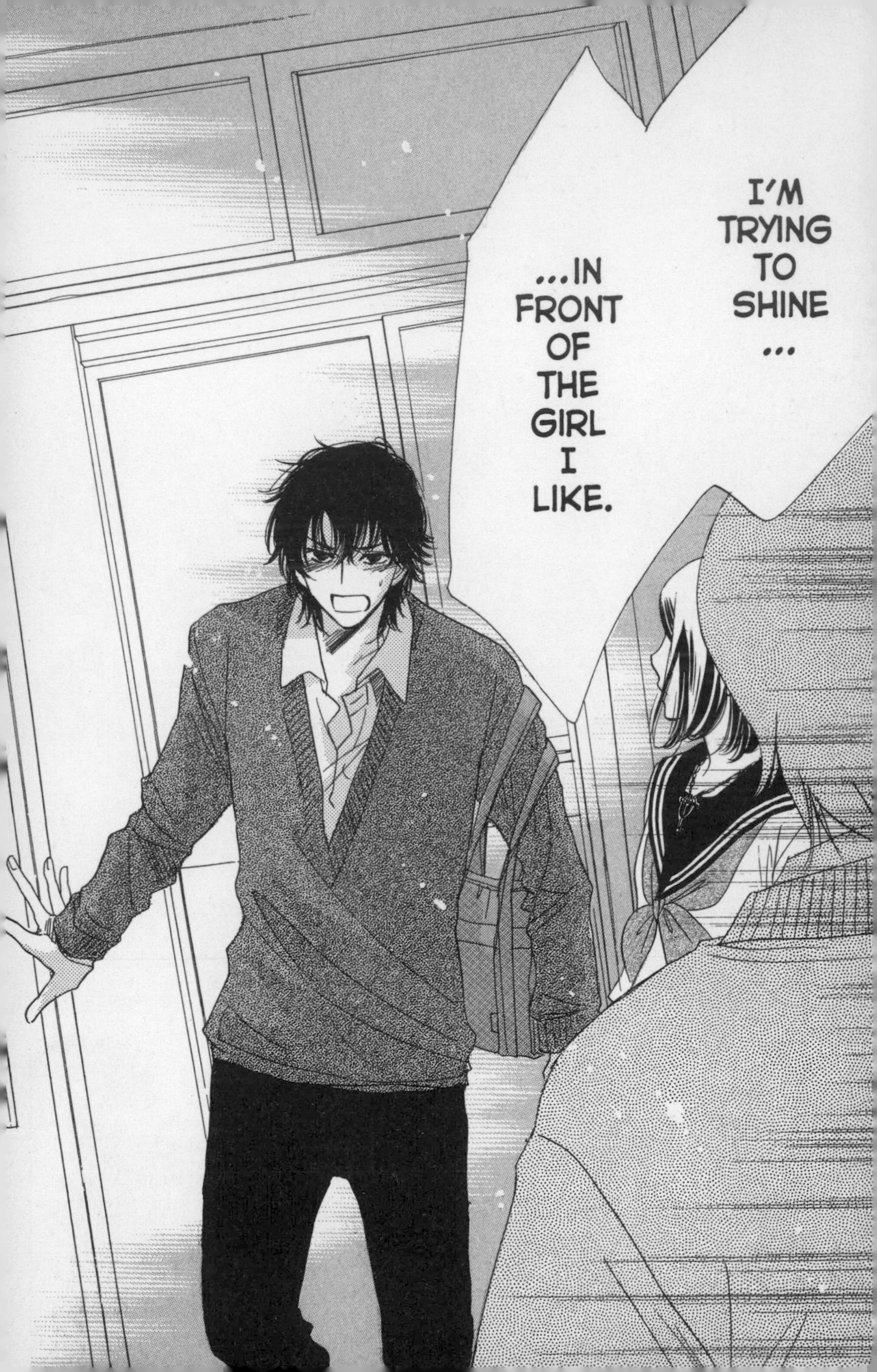

I'M TRYING TO SHINE ...
...IN FRONT OF THE GIRL I LIKE.

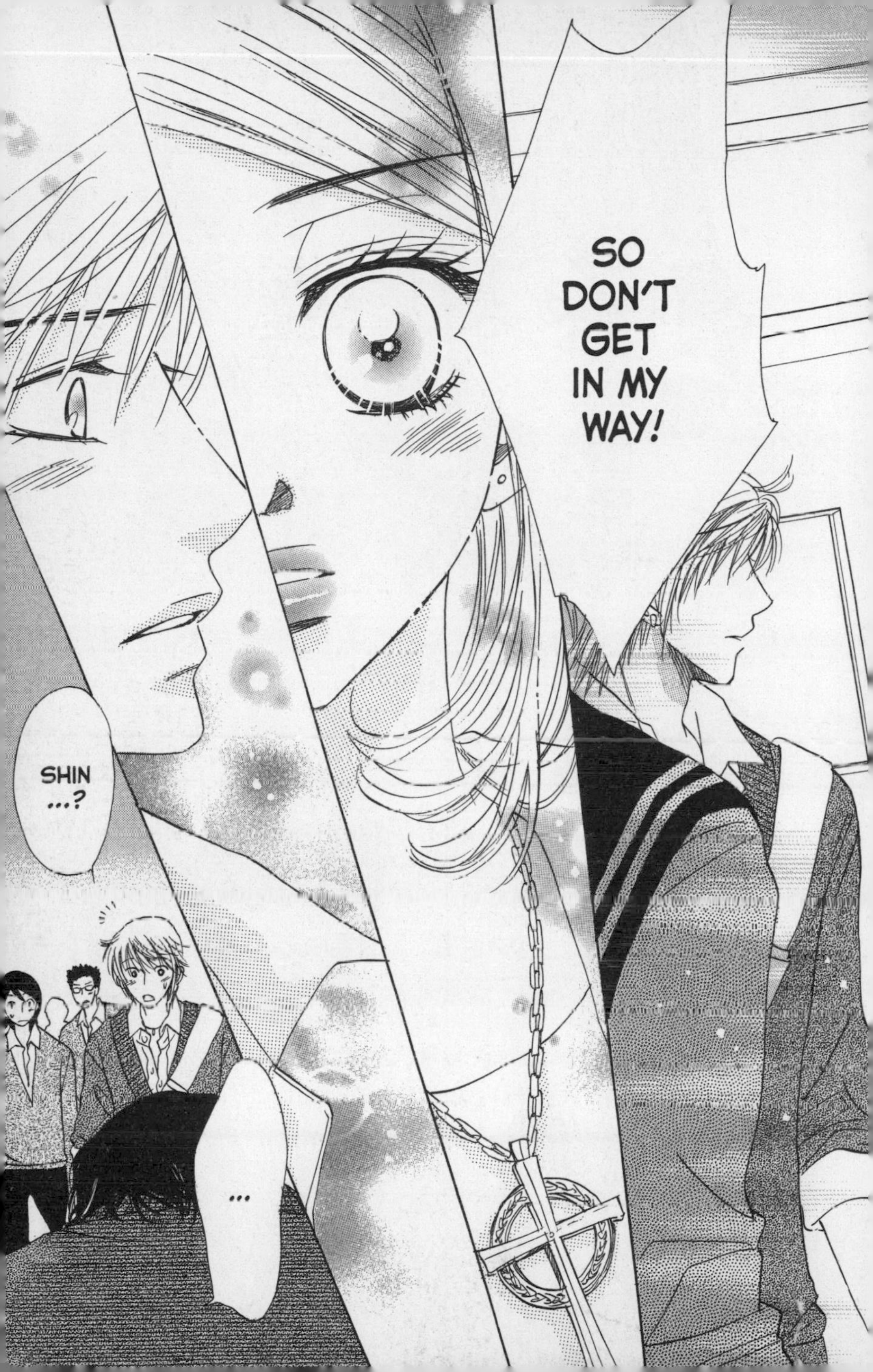
SO DON'T GET IN MY WAY!
SHIN ...?
...

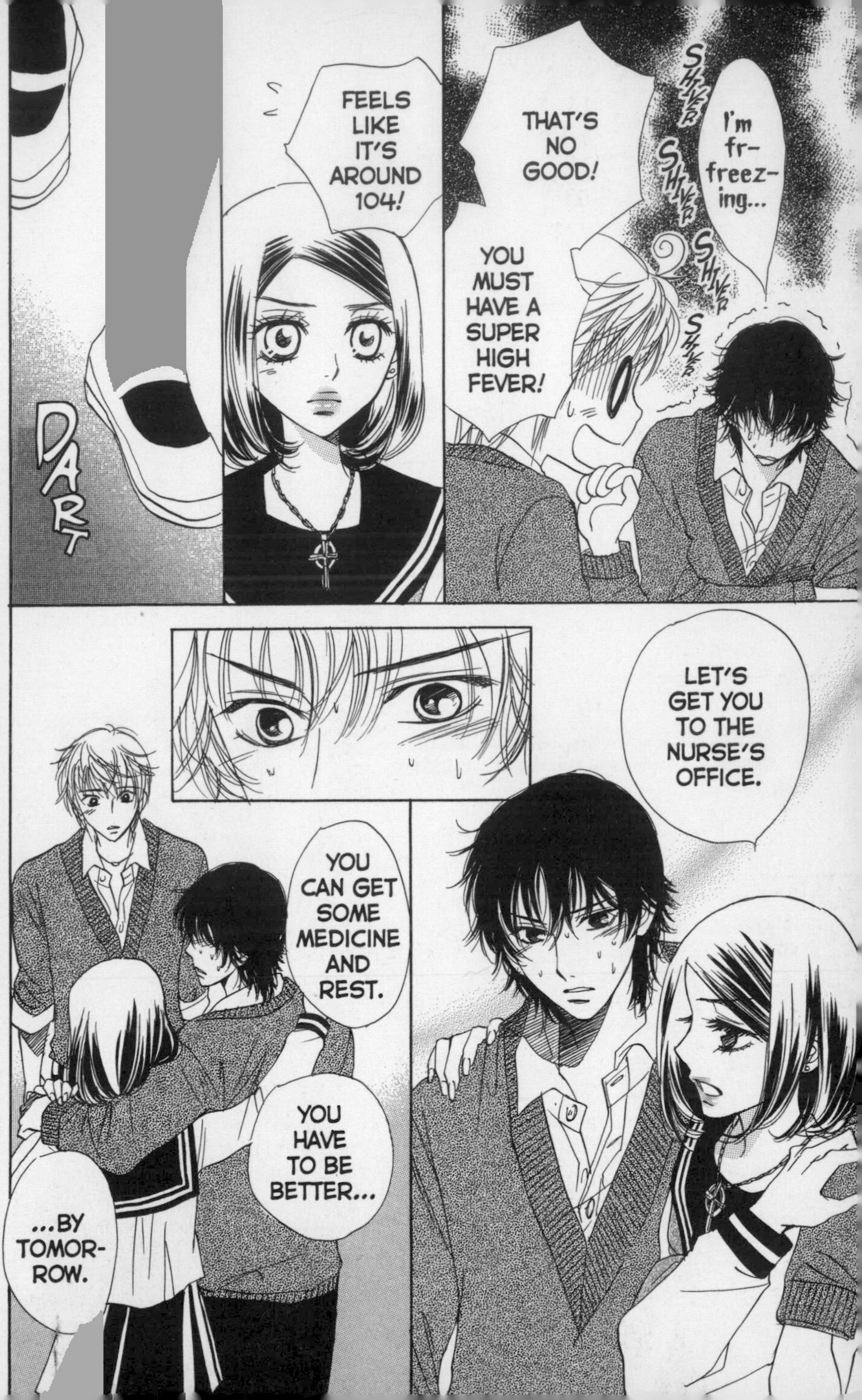
SHIVER SHIVER SHIVER SHIVER
I'm fr-freezing...
THAT'S NO GOOD!
YOU MUST HAVE A SUPER HIGH FEVER!
FEELS LIKE IT'S AROUND 104!
DART
LET'S GET YOU TO THE NURSE'S OFFICE.
YOU CAN GET SOME MEDICINE AND REST.
YOU HAVE TO BE BETTER...
...BY TOMORROW.

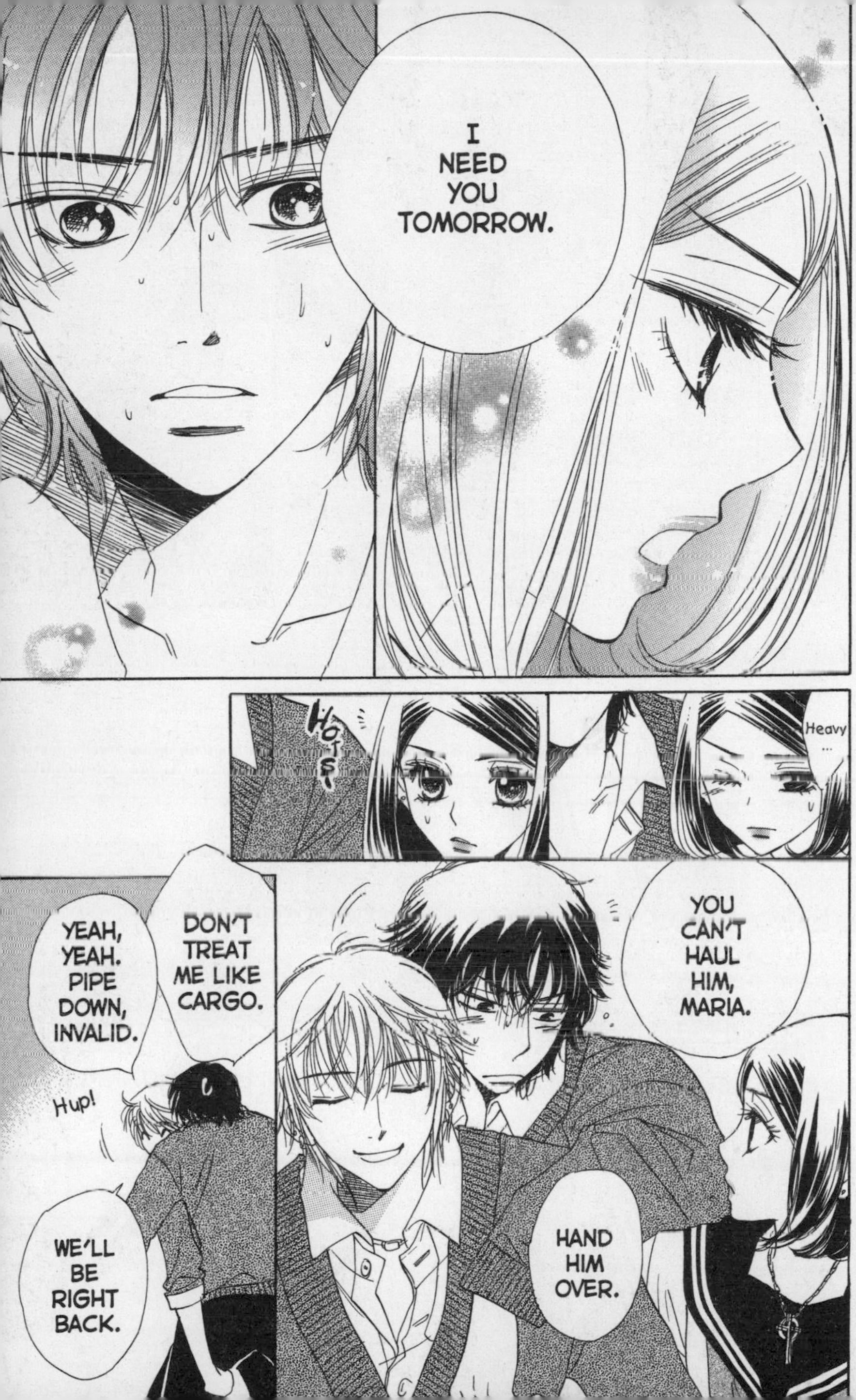

I NEED YOU TOMORROW.
Heavy ...
HOIST
YOU CAN'T HAUL HIM, MARIA.
HAND HIM OVER.
DON'T TREAT ME LIKE CARGO.
YEAH, YEAH. PIPE DOWN, INVALID.
Hup!
WE'LL BE RIGHT BACK.

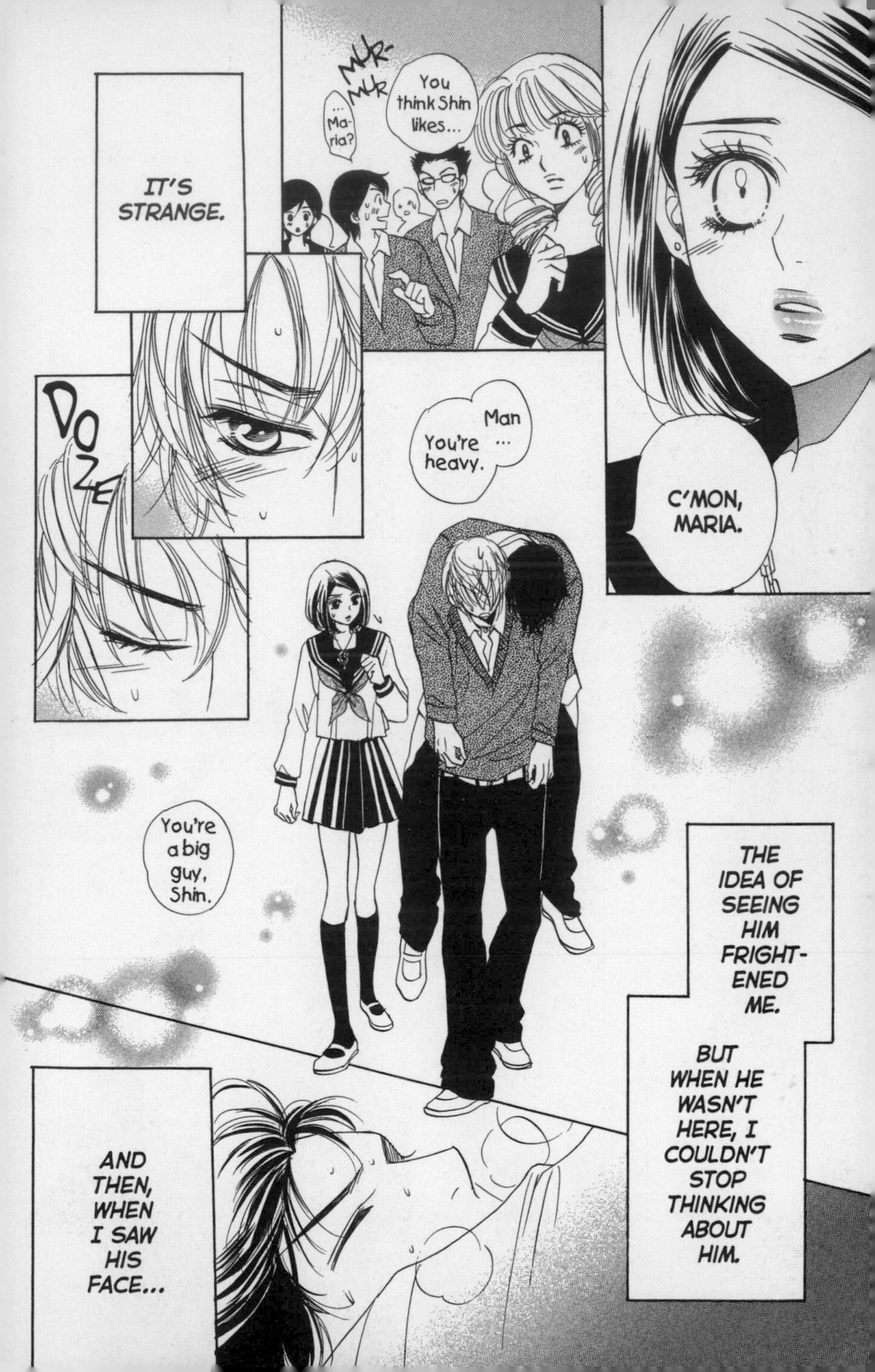
C'MON, MARIA.
MUR-MUR
You think Shin likes...
...Maria?
IT'S STRANGE.
Man... You're heavy.
DOZE
THE IDEA OF SEEING HIM FRIGHTENED ME.
BUT WHEN HE WASN'T HERE, I COULDN'T STOP THINKING ABOUT HIM.
You're a big guy, Shin.
AND THEN, WHEN I SAW HIS FACE...

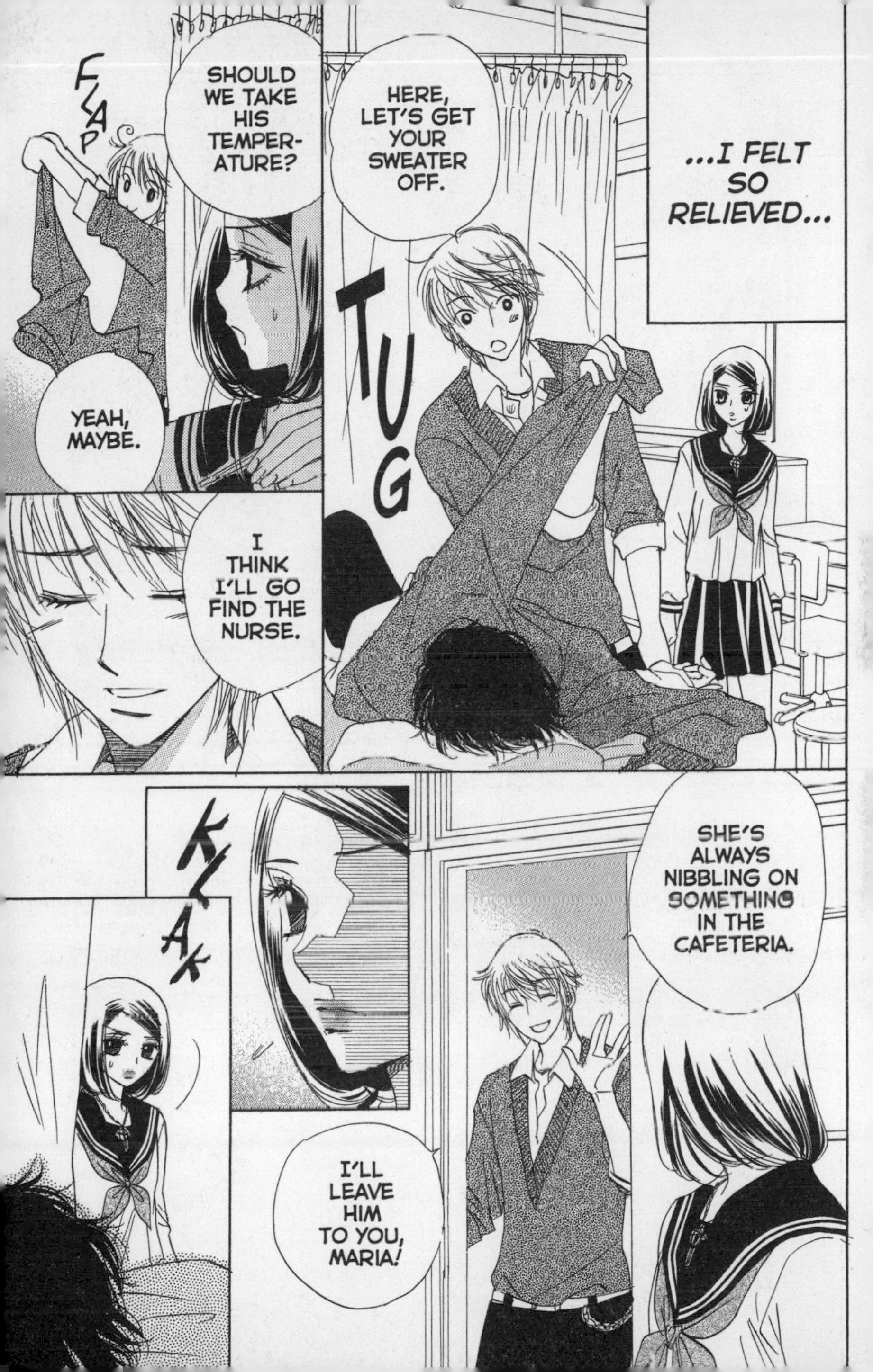

...I FELT SO RELIEVED...
HERE, LET'S GET YOUR SWEATER OFF.
TUG
SHOULD WE TAKE HIS TEMPER-ATURE?
FLAP
YEAH, MAYBE.
I THINK I'LL GO FIND THE NURSE.
SHE'S ALWAYS NIBBLING ON SOMETHING IN THE CAFETERIA.
I'LL LEAVE HIM TO YOU, MARIA!
KLAK

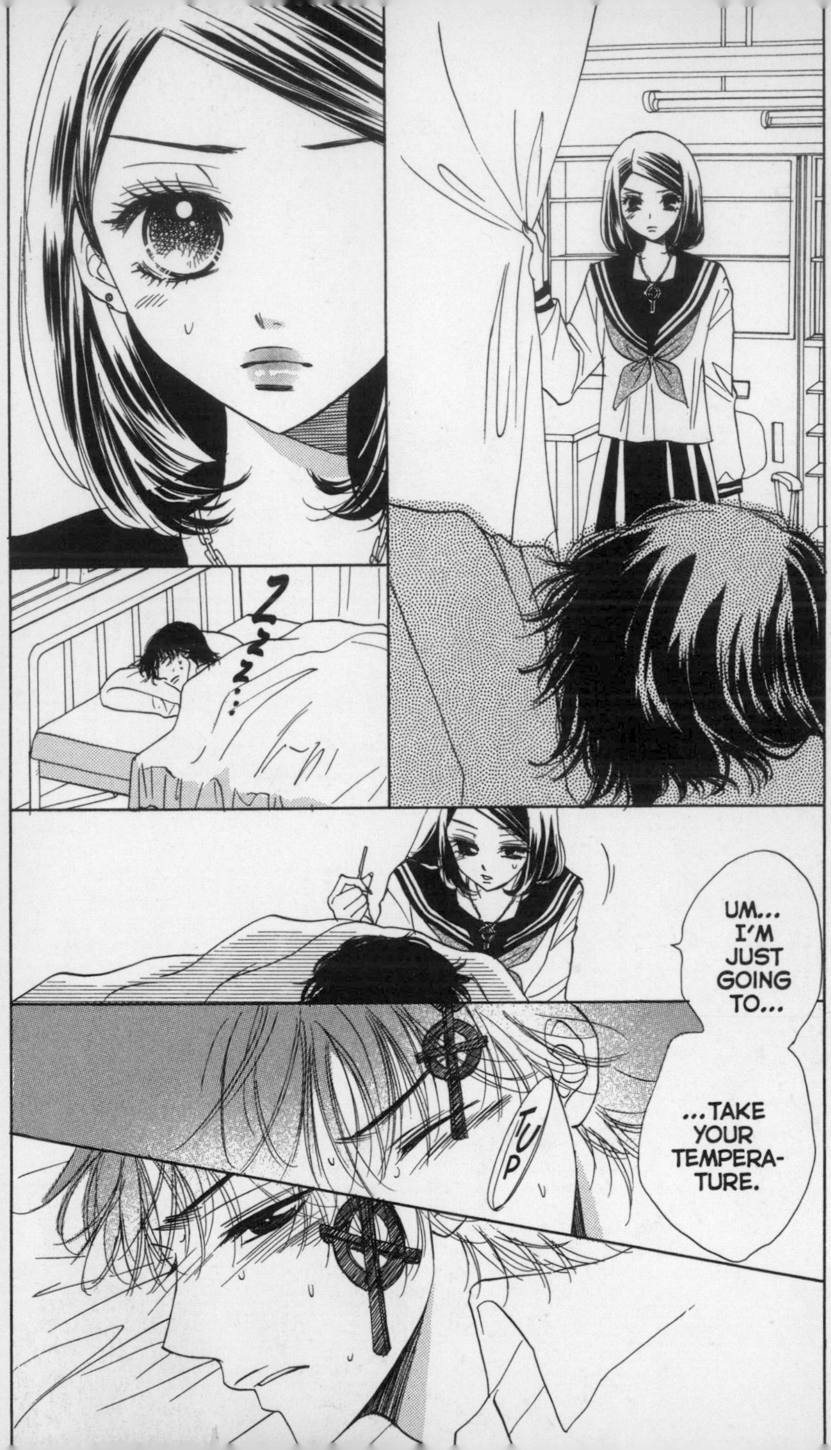
Zzzz...
UM... I'M JUST GOING TO...
...TAKE YOUR TEMPERA-TURE.
TUP

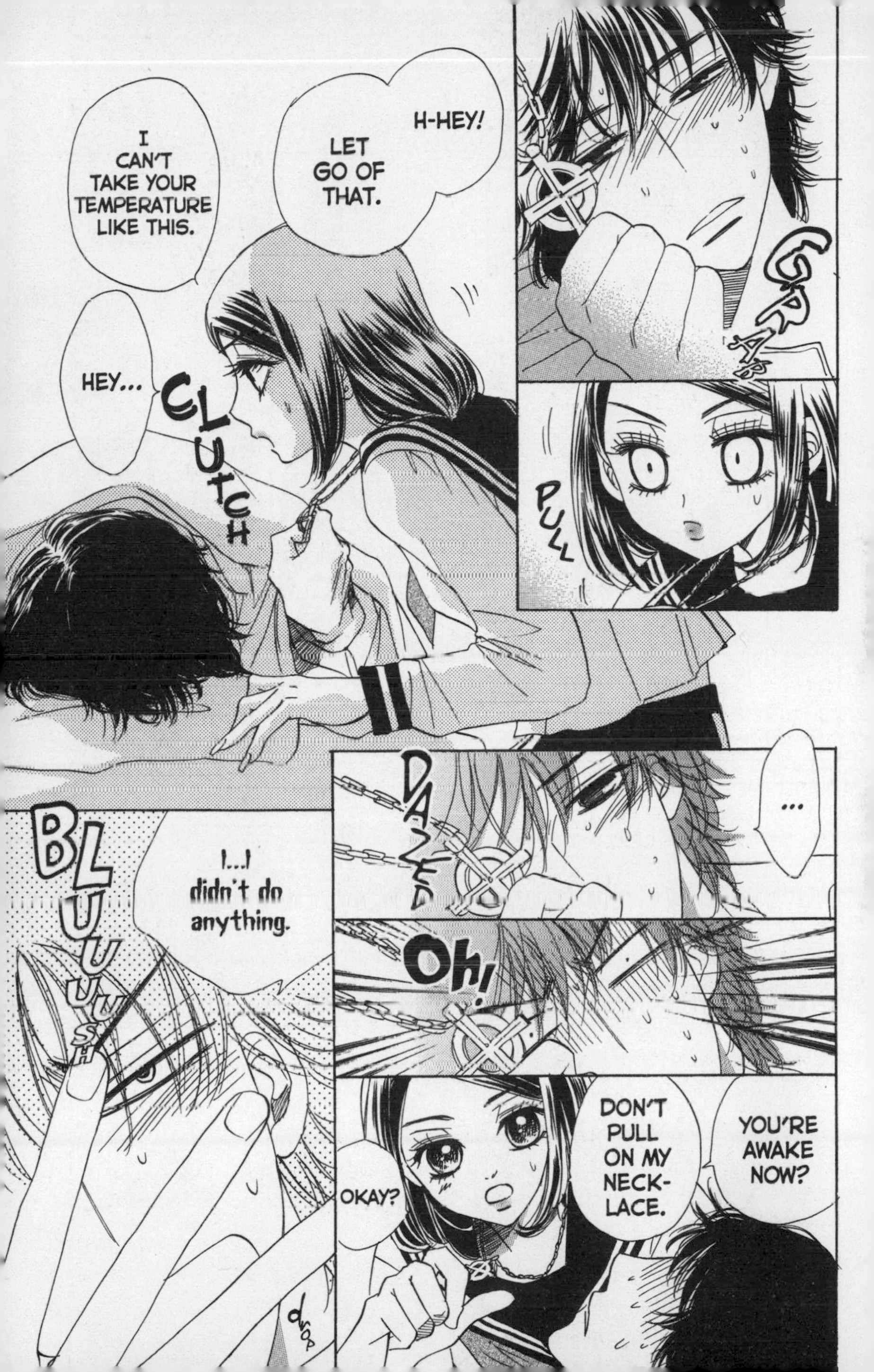
GRAB
PULL
H-HEY!
LET GO OF THAT.
I CAN'T TAKE YOUR TEMPERATURE LIKE THIS.
HEY...
CLUTCH
...
DAZED
Oh!
YOU'RE AWAKE NOW?
DON'T PULL ON MY NECK-LACE.
OKAY?
drop
BLUUUUSH
I...I didn't do anything.

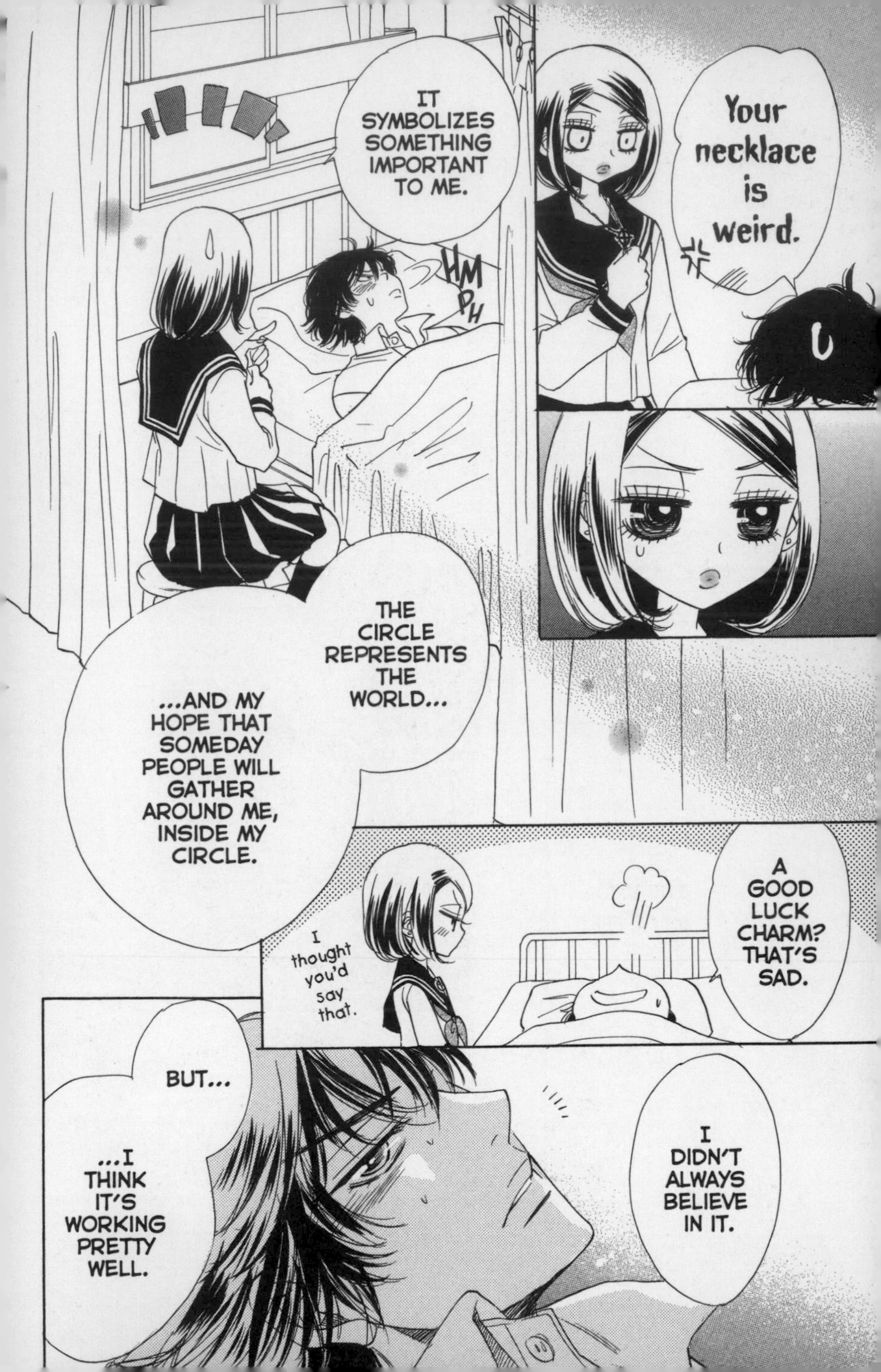
Your necklace is weird.
IT SYMBOLIZES SOMETHING IMPORTANT TO ME.
HMPH
THE CIRCLE REPRESENTS THE WORLD...
...AND MY HOPE THAT SOMEDAY PEOPLE WILL GATHER AROUND ME, INSIDE MY CIRCLE.
A GOOD LUCK CHARM? THAT'S SAD.
I thought you'd say that.
I DIDN'T ALWAYS BELIEVE IN IT.
BUT...
...I THINK IT'S WORKING PRETTY WELL.

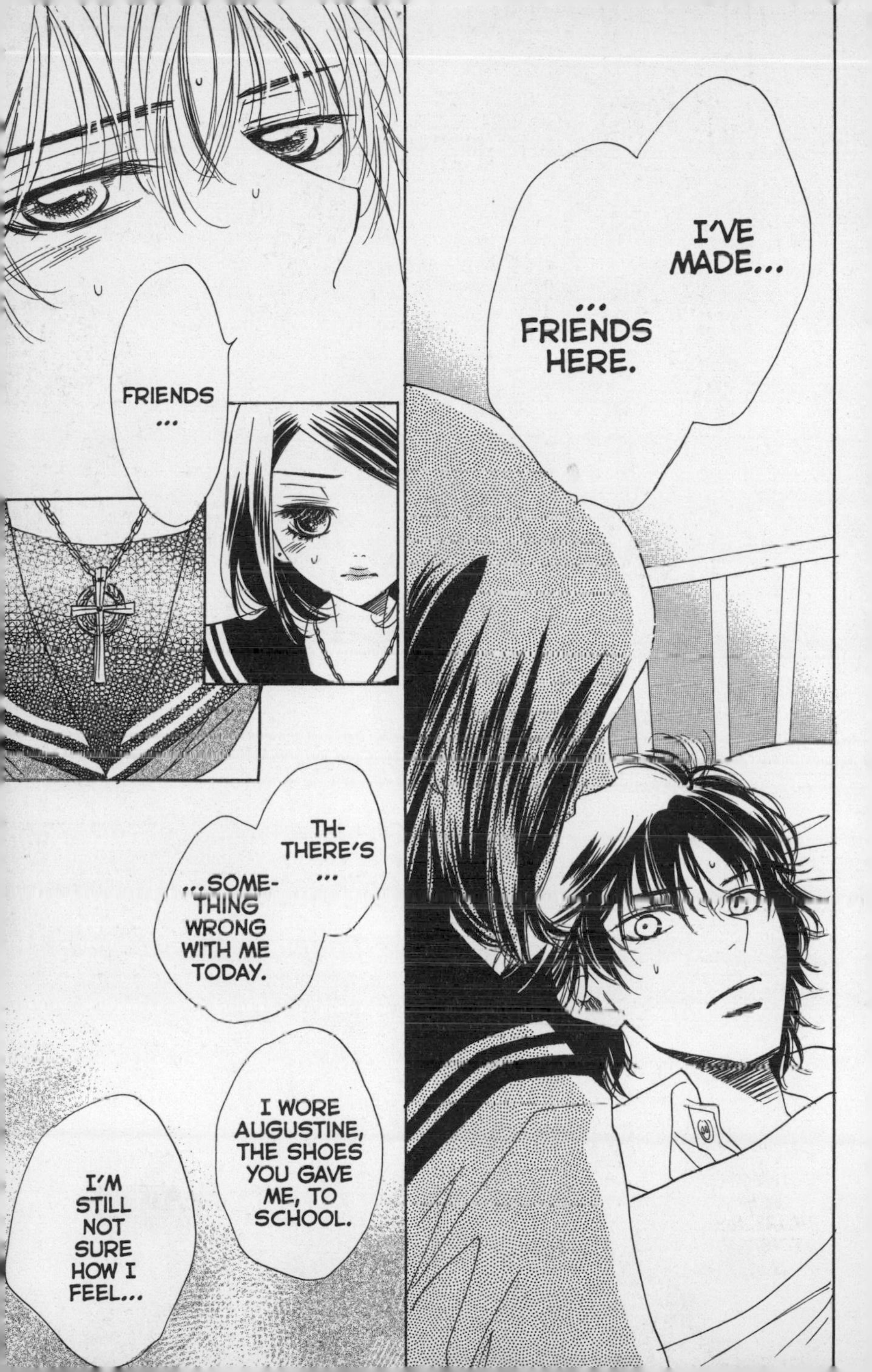
I'VE MADE...
...FRIENDS HERE.
FRIENDS ...
TH- THERE'S ...
...SOME-THING WRONG WITH ME TODAY.
I WORE AUGUSTINE, THE SHOES YOU GAVE ME, TO SCHOOL.
I'M STILL NOT SURE HOW I FEEL...

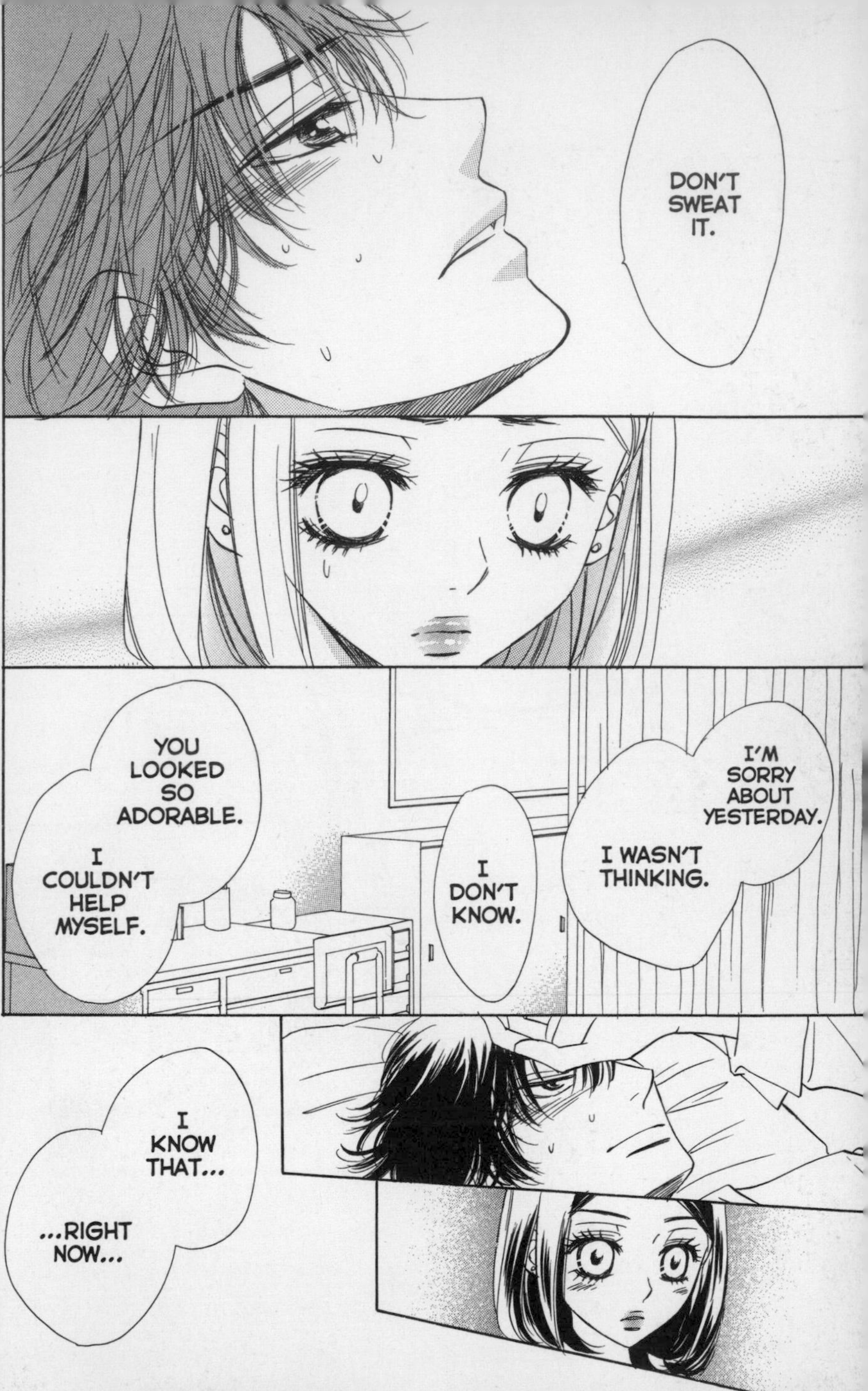
DON'T SWEAT IT.
I'M SORRY ABOUT YESTERDAY.
I WASN'T THINKING.
I DON'T KNOW.
YOU LOOKED SO ADORABLE.
I COULDN'T HELP MYSELF.
I KNOW THAT...
...RIGHT NOW...

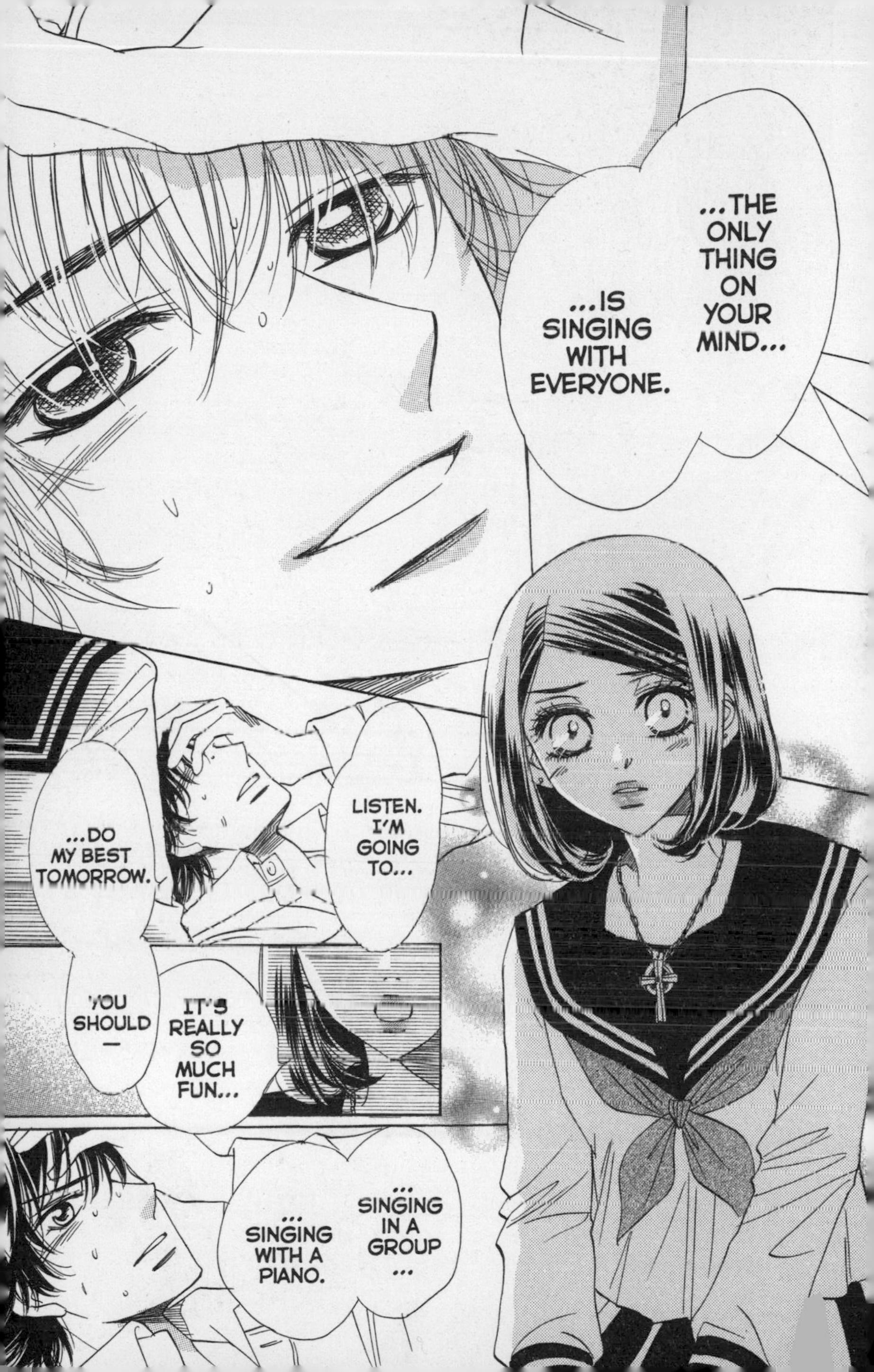
...THE ONLY THING ON YOUR MIND...
...IS SINGING WITH EVERYONE.
LISTEN. I'M GOING TO...
...DO MY BEST TOMORROW.
IT'S REALLY SO MUCH FUN...
YOU SHOULD—
...SINGING IN A GROUP...
...SINGING WITH A PIANO.

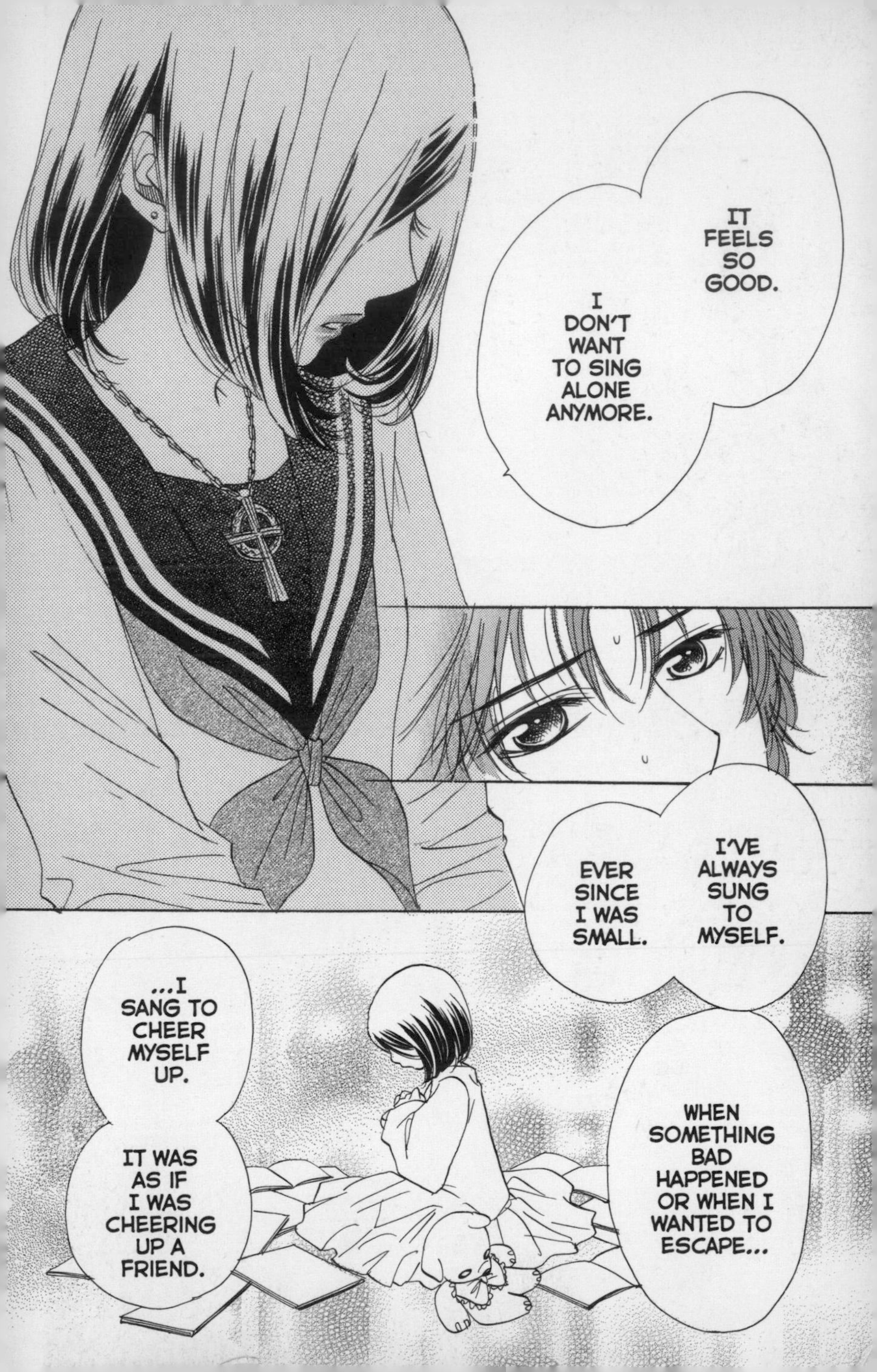
IT FEELS SO GOOD.
I DON'T WANT TO SING ALONE ANYMORE.
I'VE ALWAYS SUNG TO MYSELF.
EVER SINCE I WAS SMALL.
WHEN SOMETHING BAD HAPPENED OR WHEN I WANTED TO ESCAPE...
...I SANG TO CHEER MYSELF UP.
IT WAS AS IF I WAS CHEERING UP A FRIEND.

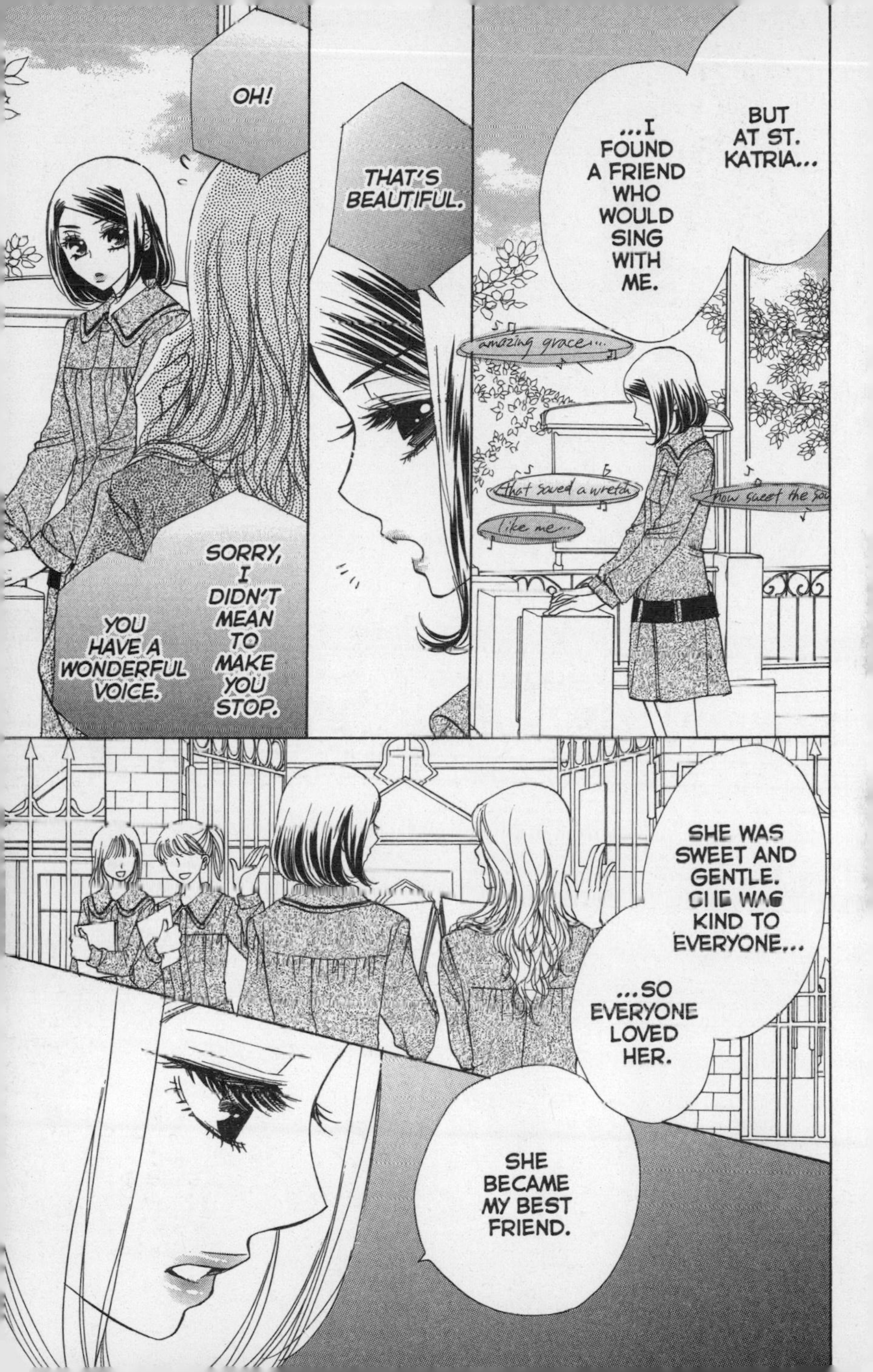
BUT AT ST. KATRIA...
...I FOUND A FRIEND WHO WOULD SING WITH ME.
amazing grace...
how sweet the sou
that saved a wretch
like me...
THAT'S BEAUTIFUL.
OH!
SORRY, I DIDN'T MEAN TO MAKE YOU STOP.
YOU HAVE A WONDERFUL VOICE.
SHE WAS SWEET AND GENTLE. SHE WAS KIND TO EVERYONE...
...SO EVERYONE LOVED HER.
SHE BECAME MY BEST FRIEND.

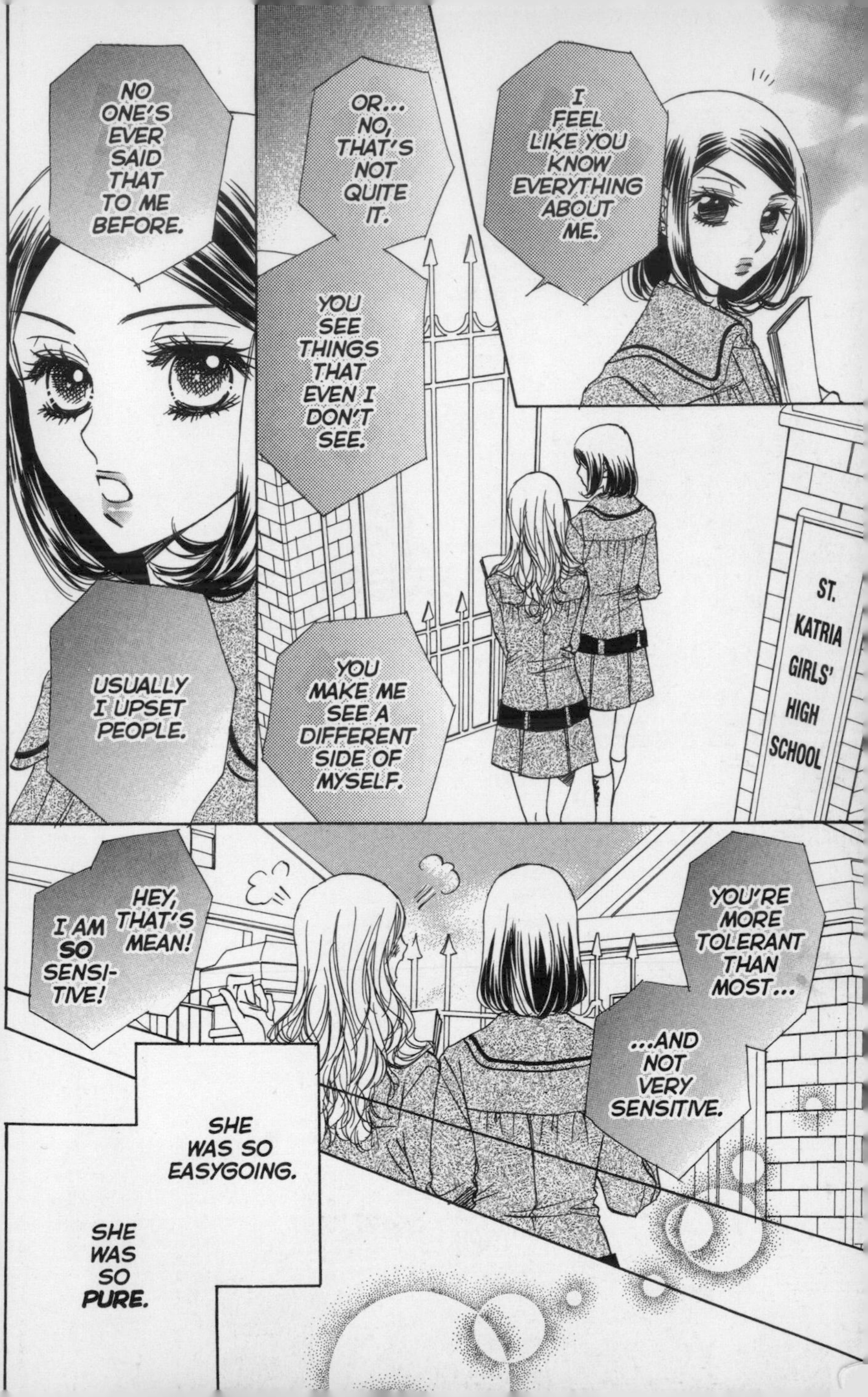
I FEEL LIKE YOU KNOW EVERYTHING ABOUT ME.
OR... NO, THAT'S NOT QUITE IT.
YOU SEE THINGS THAT EVEN I DON'T SEE.
ST. KATRIA GIRLS' HIGH SCHOOL
YOU MAKE ME SEE A DIFFERENT SIDE OF MYSELF.
NO ONE'S EVER SAID THAT TO ME BEFORE.
USUALLY I UPSET PEOPLE.
YOU'RE MORE TOLERANT THAN MOST...
...AND NOT VERY SENSITIVE.
HEY, THAT'S MEAN!
I AM SO SENSI-TIVE!
SHE WAS SO EASYGOING.
SHE WAS SO PURE.

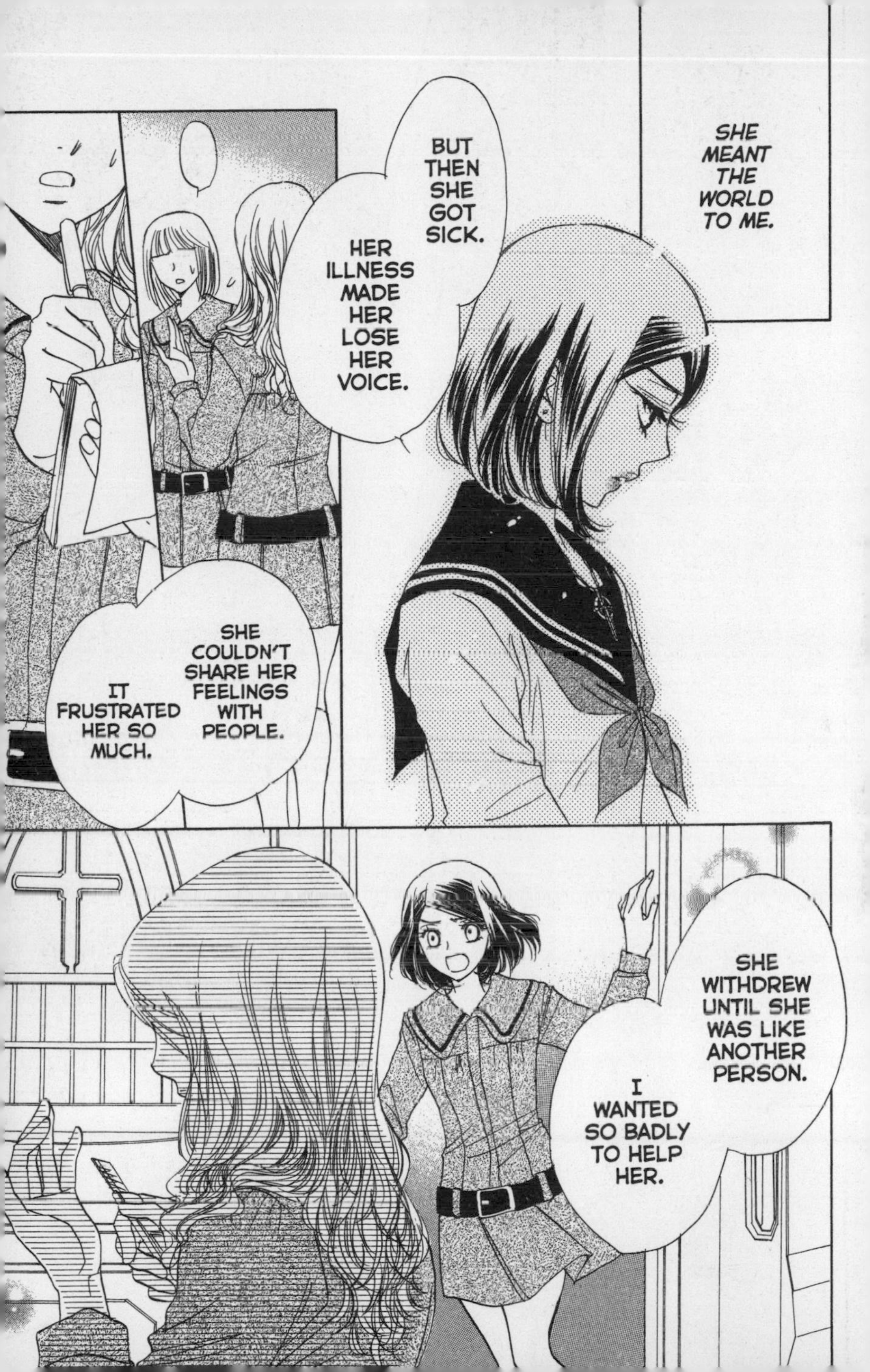
SHE MEANT THE WORLD TO ME.
BUT THEN SHE GOT SICK.
HER ILLNESS MADE HER LOSE HER VOICE.
SHE COULDN'T SHARE HER FEELINGS WITH PEOPLE.
IT FRUSTRATED HER SO MUCH.
SHE WITHDREW UNTIL SHE WAS LIKE ANOTHER PERSON.
I WANTED SO BADLY TO HELP HER.

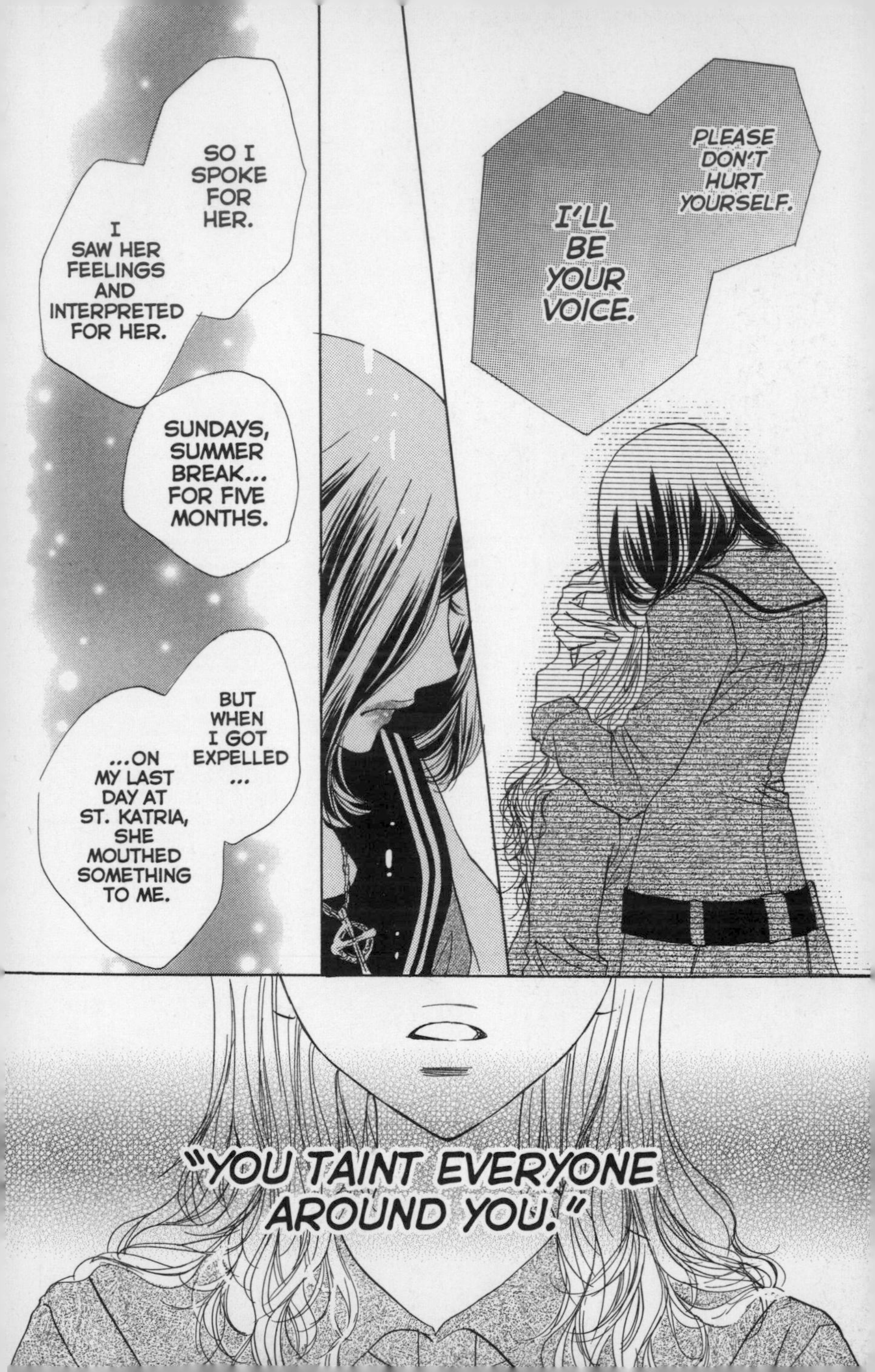
PLEASE DON'T HURT YOURSELF.
I'LL BE YOUR VOICE.
SO I SPOKE FOR HER.
I SAW HER FEELINGS AND INTERPRETED FOR HER.
SUNDAYS, SUMMER BREAK... FOR FIVE MONTHS.
BUT WHEN I GOT EXPELLED...
...ON MY LAST DAY AT ST. KATRIA, SHE MOUTHED SOMETHING TO ME.
"YOU TAINT EVERYONE AROUND YOU."

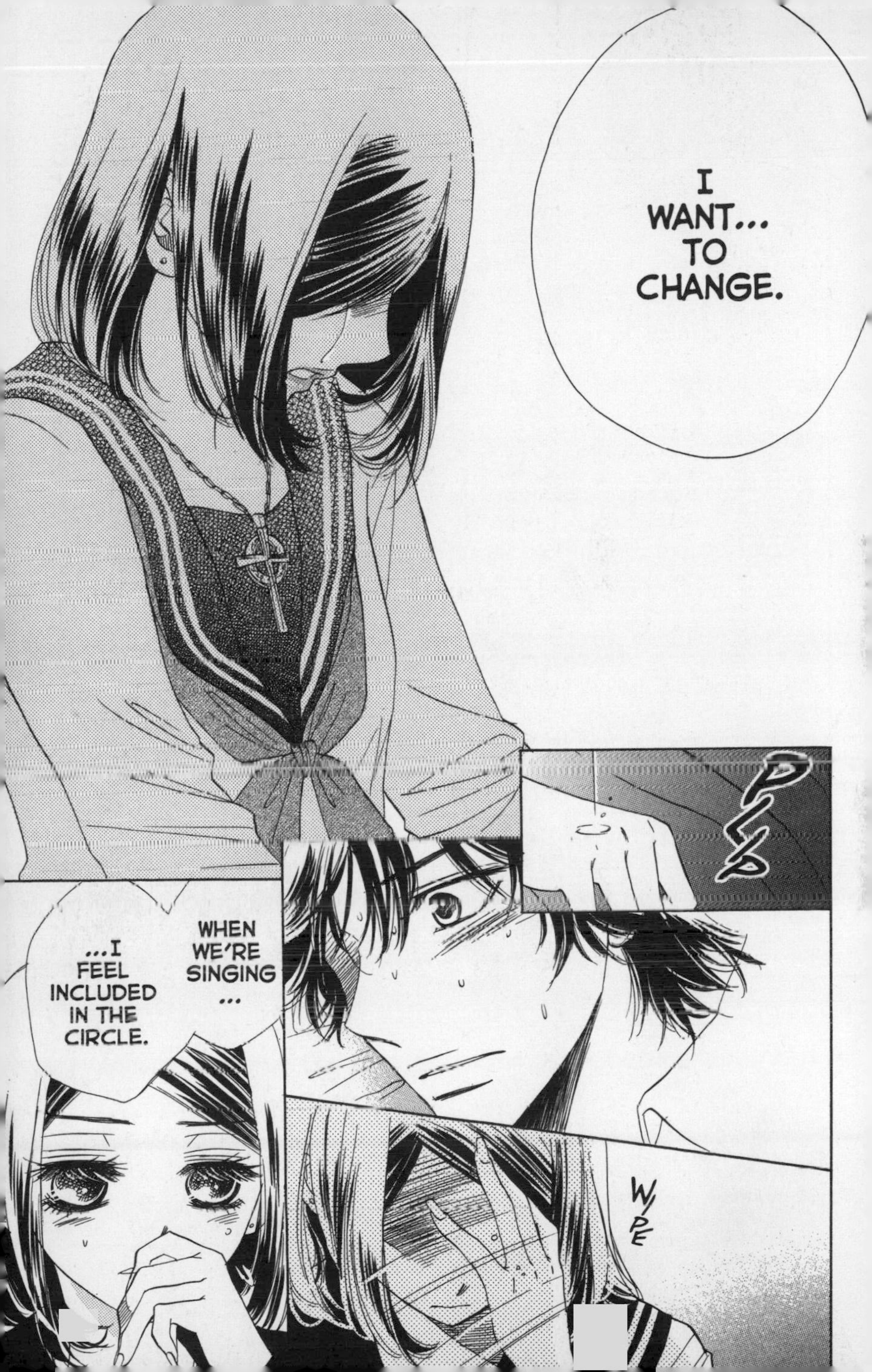
I WANT... TO CHANGE.
WHEN WE'RE SINGING...
...I FEEL INCLUDED IN THE CIRCLE.
WIPE

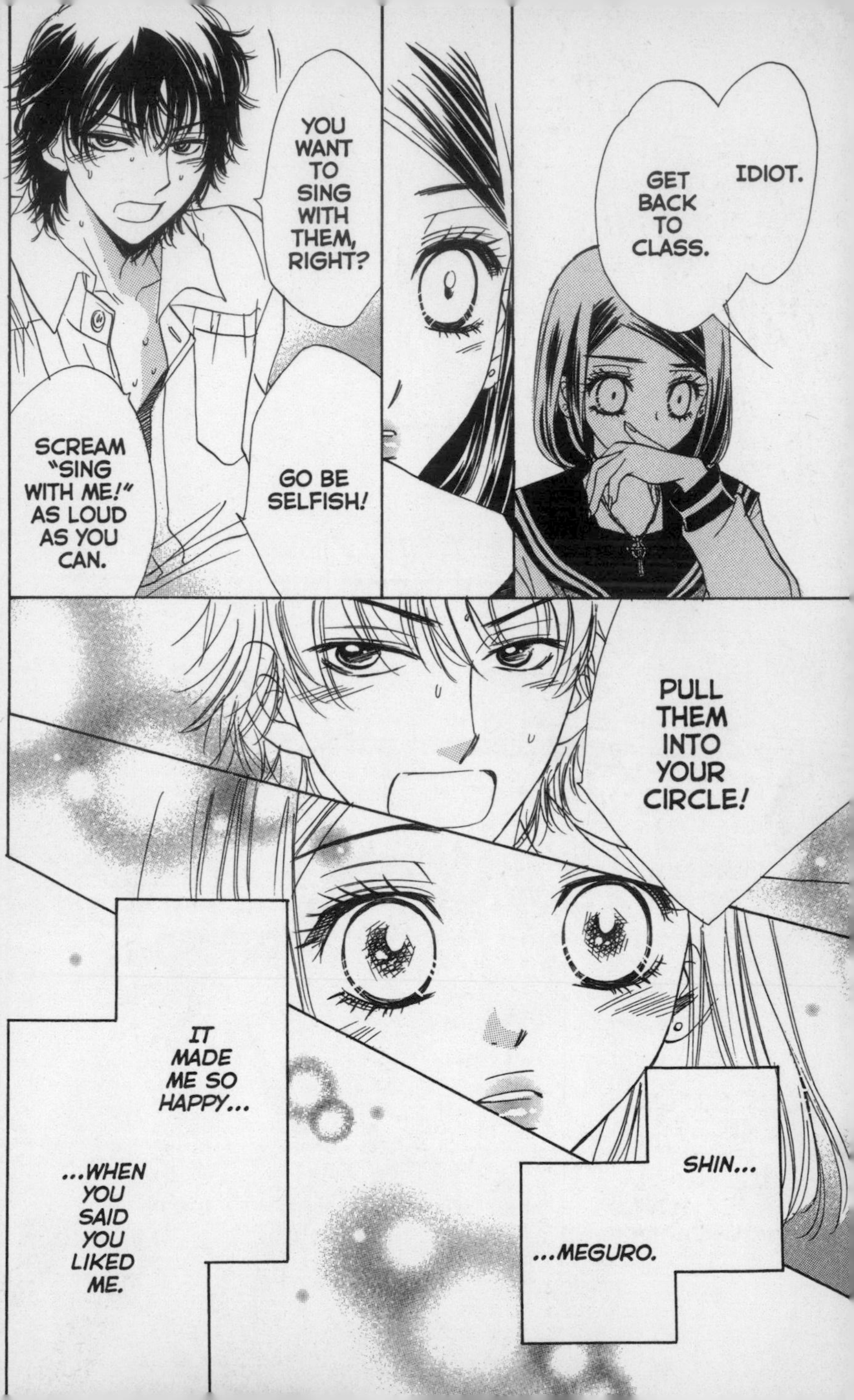
IDIOT.
GET BACK TO CLASS.
YOU WANT TO SING WITH THEM, RIGHT?
GO BE SELFISH!
SCREAM "SING WITH ME!" AS LOUD AS YOU CAN.
PULL THEM INTO YOUR CIRCLE!
SHIN...
...MEGURO.
IT MADE ME SO HAPPY...
...WHEN YOU SAID YOU LIKED ME.

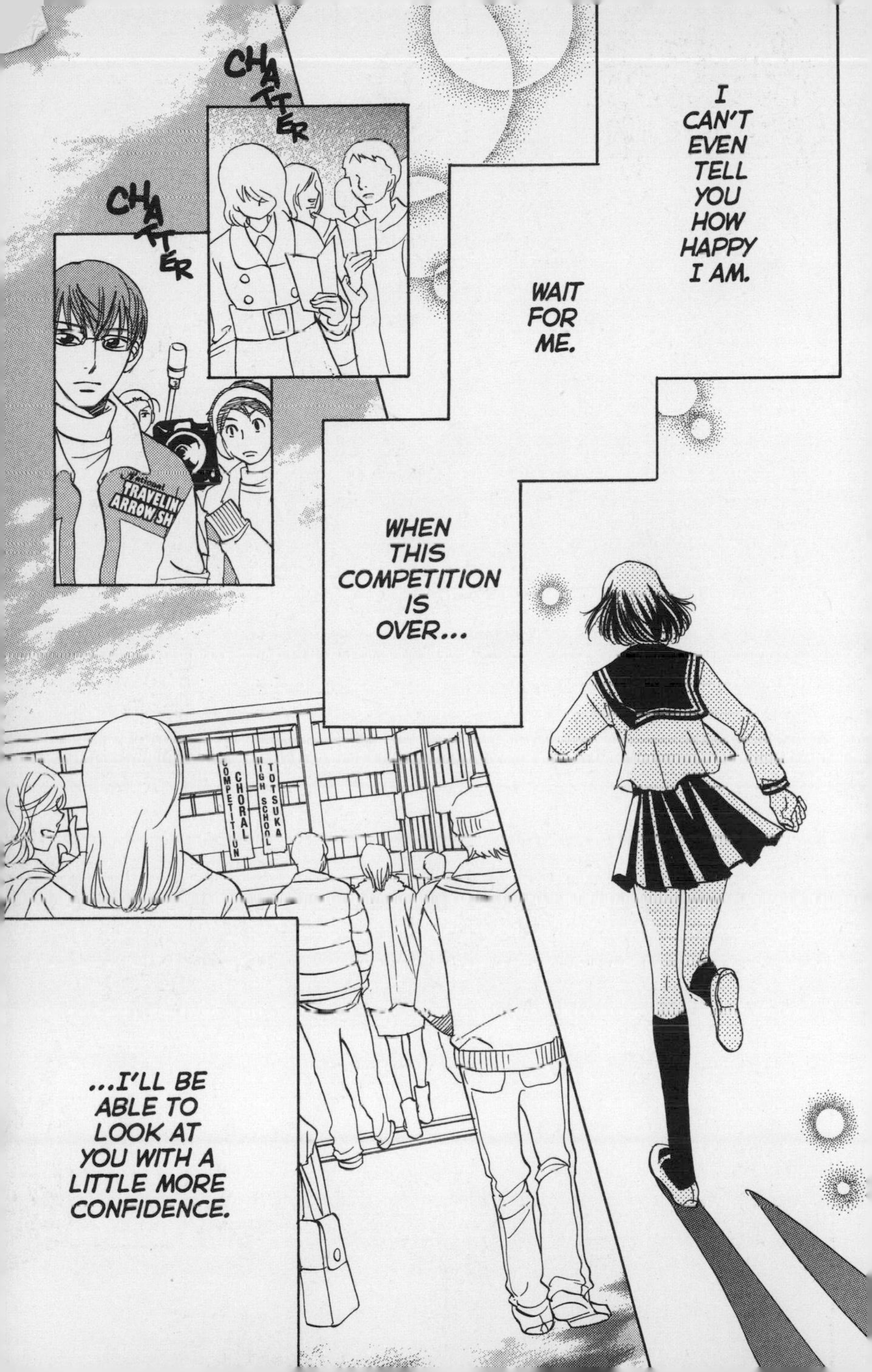
I CAN'T EVEN TELL YOU HOW HAPPY I AM.
WAIT FOR ME.
CHATTER
CHATTER
TRAVELIN
ARROW SH
WHEN THIS COMPETITION IS OVER...
TOTSUKA HIGH SCHOOL
CHORAL COMPETITION
...I'LL BE ABLE TO LOOK AT YOU WITH A LITTLE MORE CONFIDENCE.

A Devil and
Her Love Song

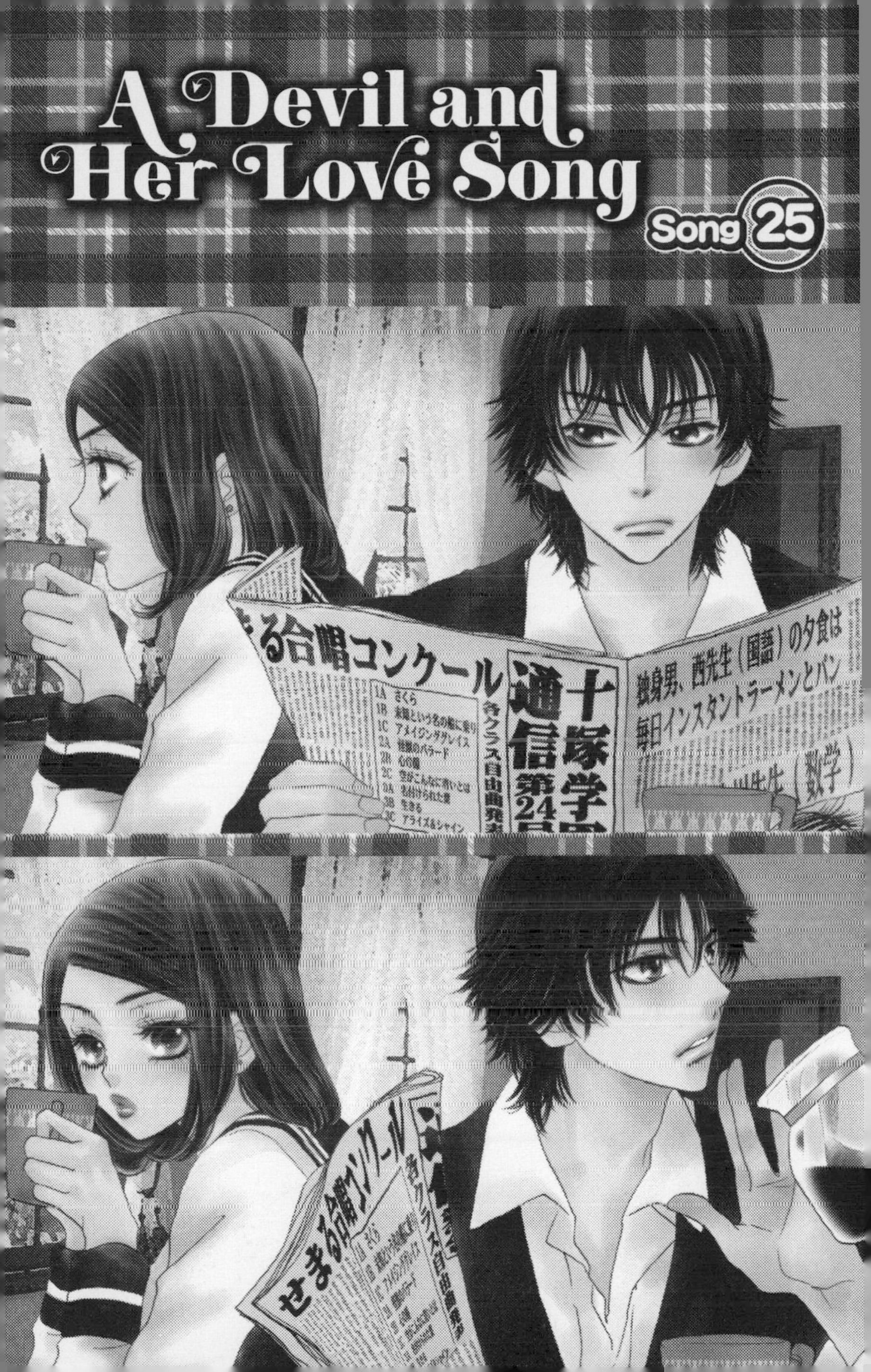
A Devil and Her Love Song
Song 25
る合唱コンクール
十塚学
通信第24
独身男、西先生（国語）の夕食は毎日インスタントラーメンとパン
数学
1A さくら
1C アメイジンググレイス
3B 生きる
3C アライズ&シャイン

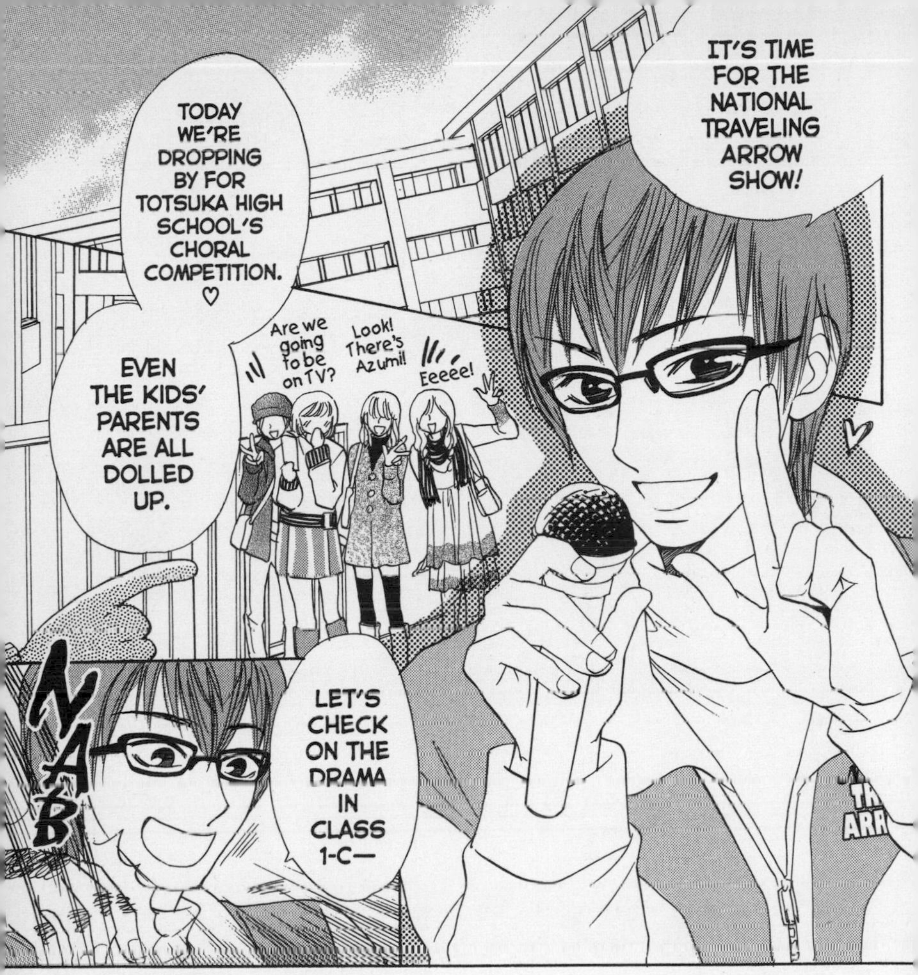
IT'S TIME FOR THE NATIONAL TRAVELING ARROW SHOW!
TODAY WE'RE DROPPING BY FOR TOTSUKA HIGH SCHOOL'S CHORAL COMPETITION. ♡
EVEN THE KIDS' PARENTS ARE ALL DOLLED UP.
Eeeee!
Look! There's Azumi!
Are we going to be on TV?
LET'S CHECK ON THE DRAMA IN CLASS 1-C—
NAB

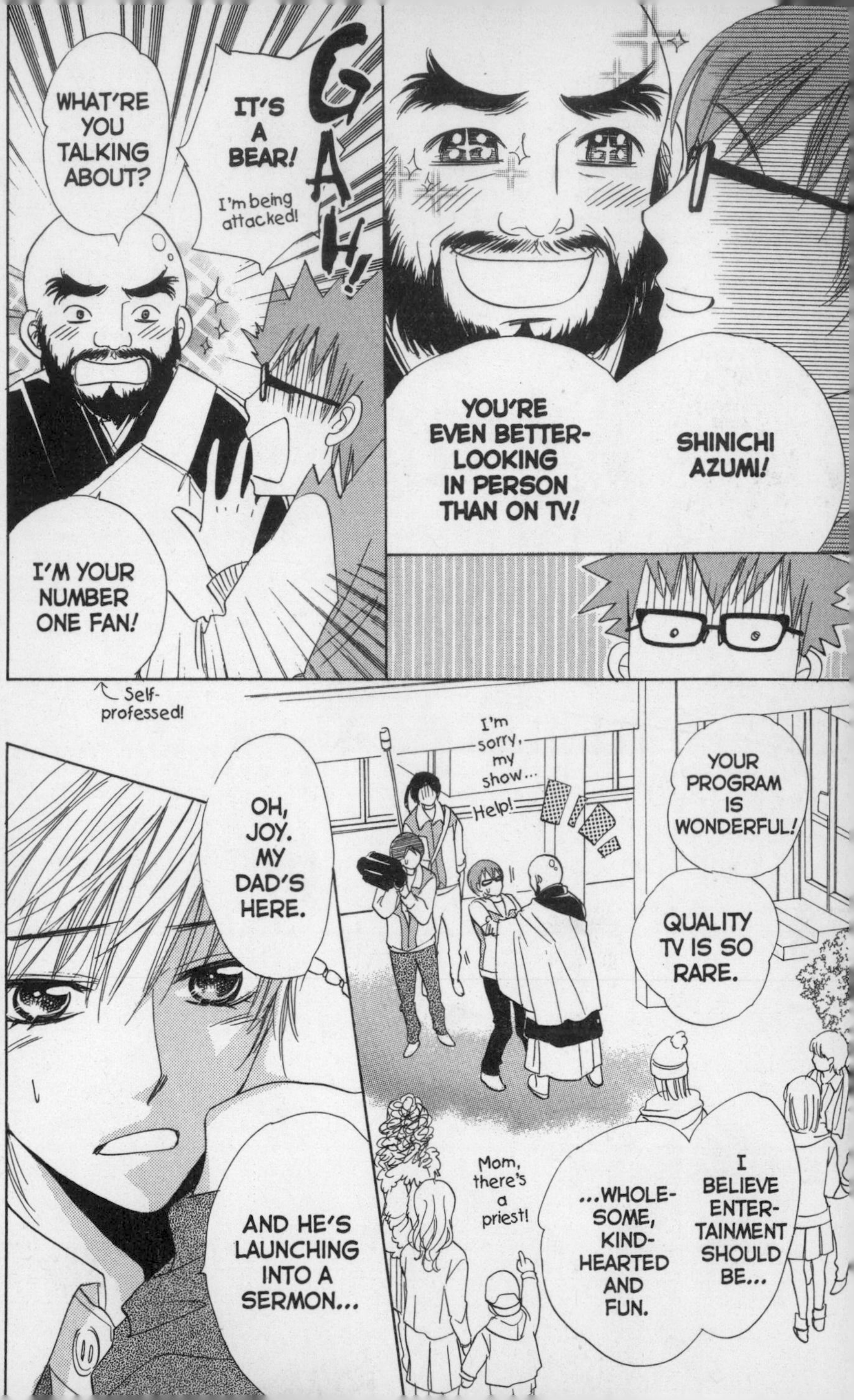
SHINICHI AZUMI!
YOU'RE EVEN BETTER-LOOKING IN PERSON THAN ON TV!
IT'S A BEAR!
GAH!
I'm being attacked!
WHAT'RE YOU TALKING ABOUT?
I'M YOUR NUMBER ONE FAN!
Self-professed!
YOUR PROGRAM IS WONDERFUL!
QUALITY TV IS SO RARE.
I BELIEVE ENTERTAINMENT SHOULD BE...
...WHOLESOME, KIND-HEARTED AND FUN.
Mom, there's a priest!
I'm sorry, my show...
Help!
OH, JOY. MY DAD'S HERE.
AND HE'S LAUNCHING INTO A SERMON...

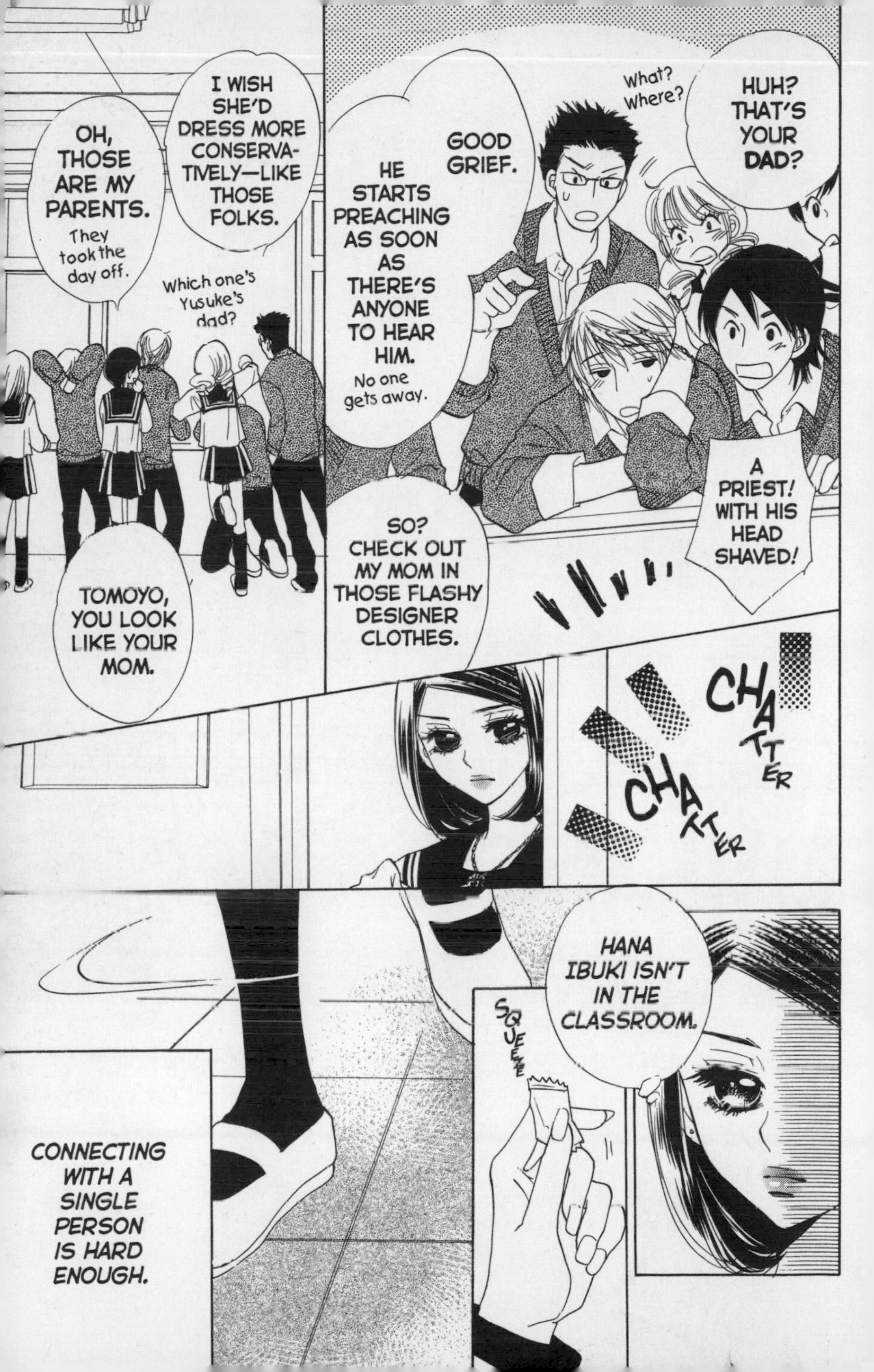
HUH? THAT'S YOUR DAD?
What? Where?
A PRIEST! WITH HIS HEAD SHAVED!
GOOD GRIEF.
HE STARTS PREACHING AS SOON AS THERE'S ANYONE TO HEAR HIM.
No one gets away.
SO? CHECK OUT MY MOM IN THOSE FLASHY DESIGNER CLOTHES.
I WISH SHE'D DRESS MORE CONSERVA-TIVELY—LIKE THOSE FOLKS.
OH, THOSE ARE MY PARENTS.
They took the day off.
Which one's Yusuke's dad?
TOMOYO, YOU LOOK LIKE YOUR MOM.
CHATTER
CHATTER
SQUEEZE
HANA IBUKI ISN'T IN THE CLASSROOM.
CONNECTING WITH A SINGLE PERSON IS HARD ENOUGH.

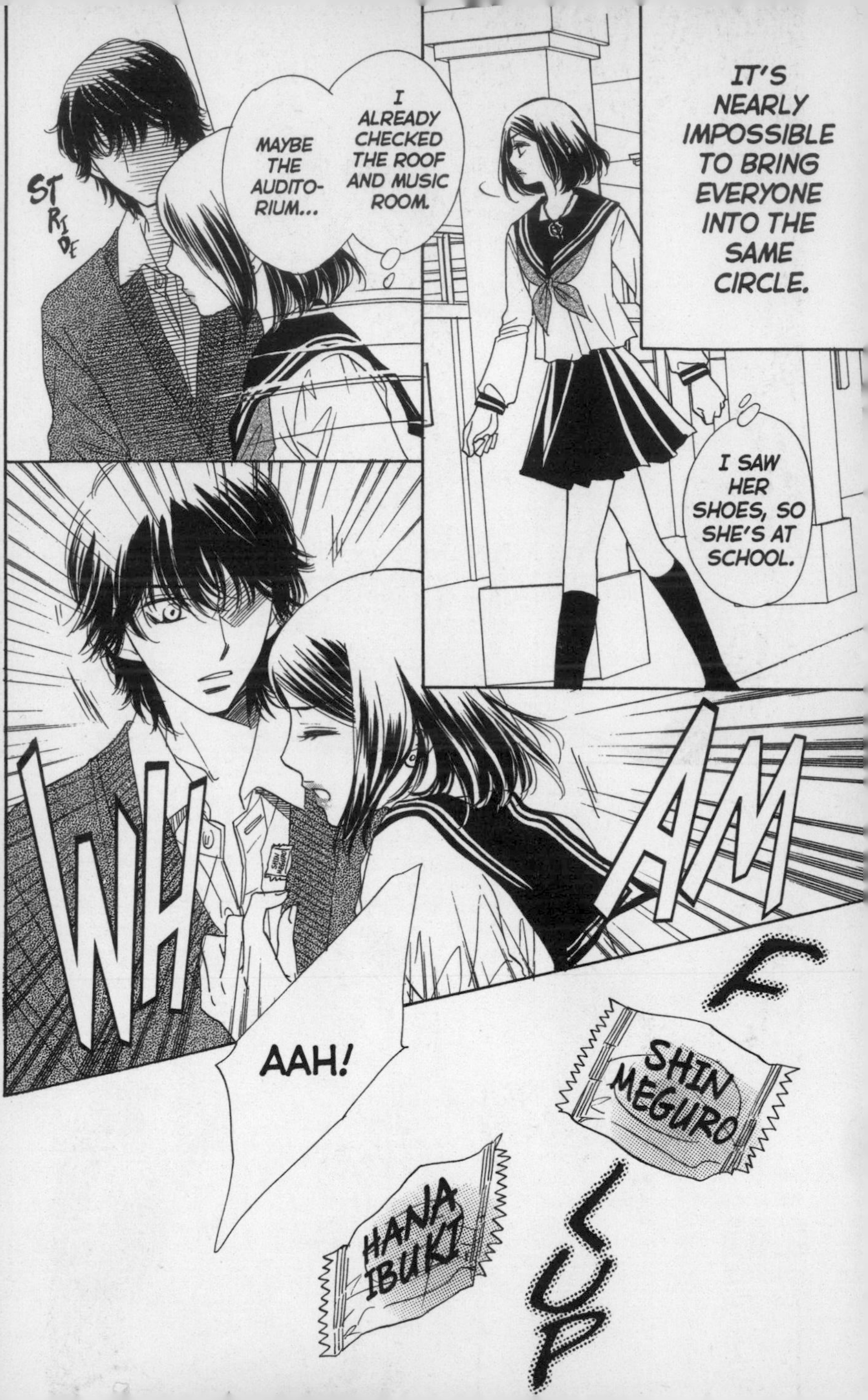
IT'S NEARLY IMPOSSIBLE TO BRING EVERYONE INTO THE SAME CIRCLE.
I SAW HER SHOES, SO SHE'S AT SCHOOL.
I ALREADY CHECKED THE ROOF AND MUSIC ROOM.
MAYBE THE AUDITORIUM...
STRIDE
WHAM
AAH!
FLUP
SHIN MEGURO
HANA IBUKI

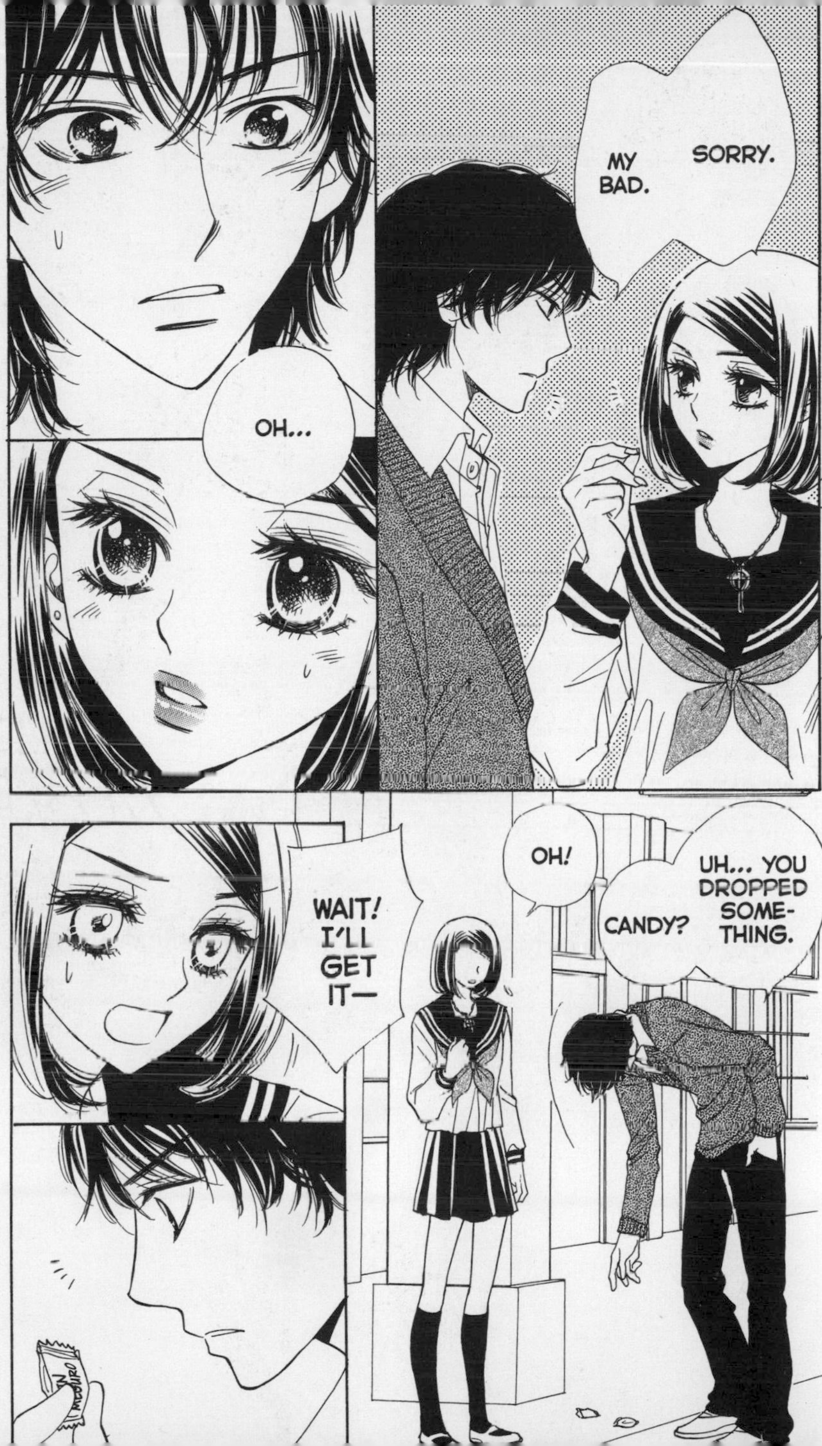
SORRY.
MY BAD.
OH...
UH... YOU DROPPED SOME-THING.
OH!
CANDY?
WAIT! I'LL GET IT—

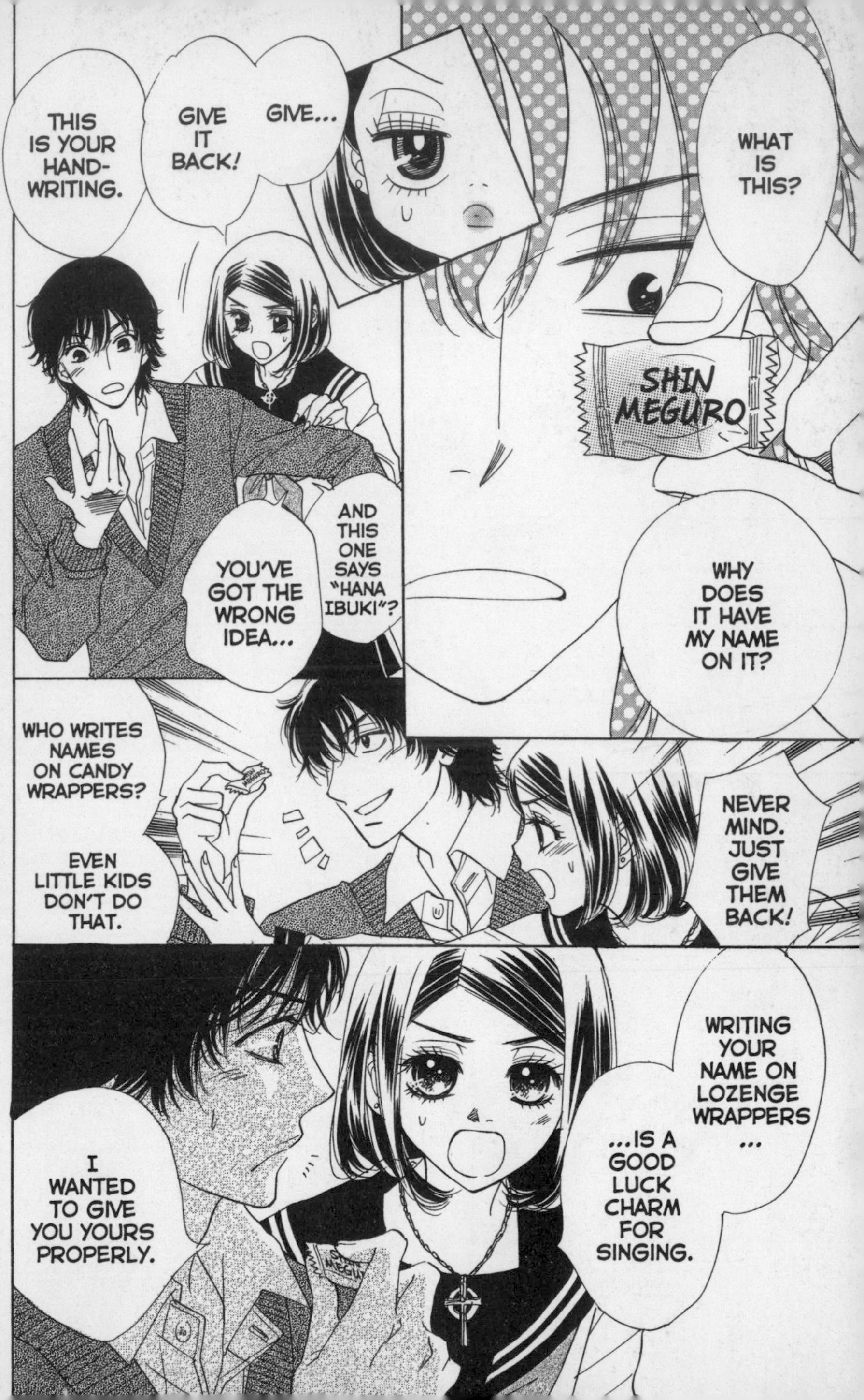
WHAT IS THIS?
SHIN MEGURO
WHY DOES IT HAVE MY NAME ON IT?
GIVE...
GIVE IT BACK!
THIS IS YOUR HANDWRITING.
AND THIS ONE SAYS "HANA IBUKI"?
YOU'VE GOT THE WRONG IDEA...
NEVER MIND. JUST GIVE THEM BACK!
WHO WRITES NAMES ON CANDY WRAPPERS?
EVEN LITTLE KIDS DON'T DO THAT.
WRITING YOUR NAME ON LOZENGE WRAPPERS ...
...IS A GOOD LUCK CHARM FOR SINGING.
I WANTED TO GIVE YOU YOURS PROPERLY.

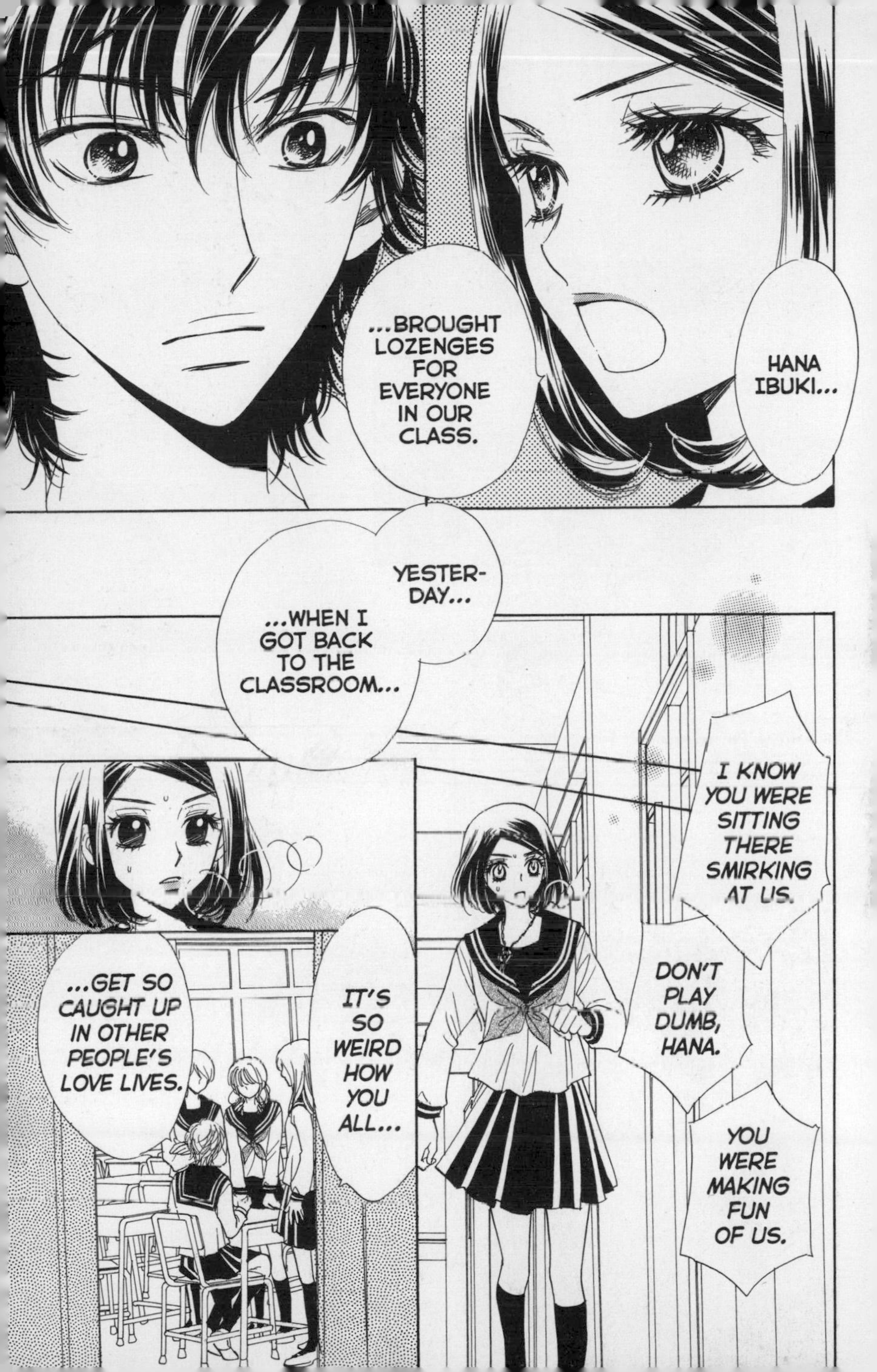
HANA IBUKI...
...BROUGHT LOZENGES FOR EVERYONE IN OUR CLASS.
YESTER-DAY...
...WHEN I GOT BACK TO THE CLASSROOM...
I KNOW YOU WERE SITTING THERE SMIRKING AT US.
DON'T PLAY DUMB, HANA.
YOU WERE MAKING FUN OF US.
IT'S SO WEIRD HOW YOU ALL...
...GET SO CAUGHT UP IN OTHER PEOPLE'S LOVE LIVES.

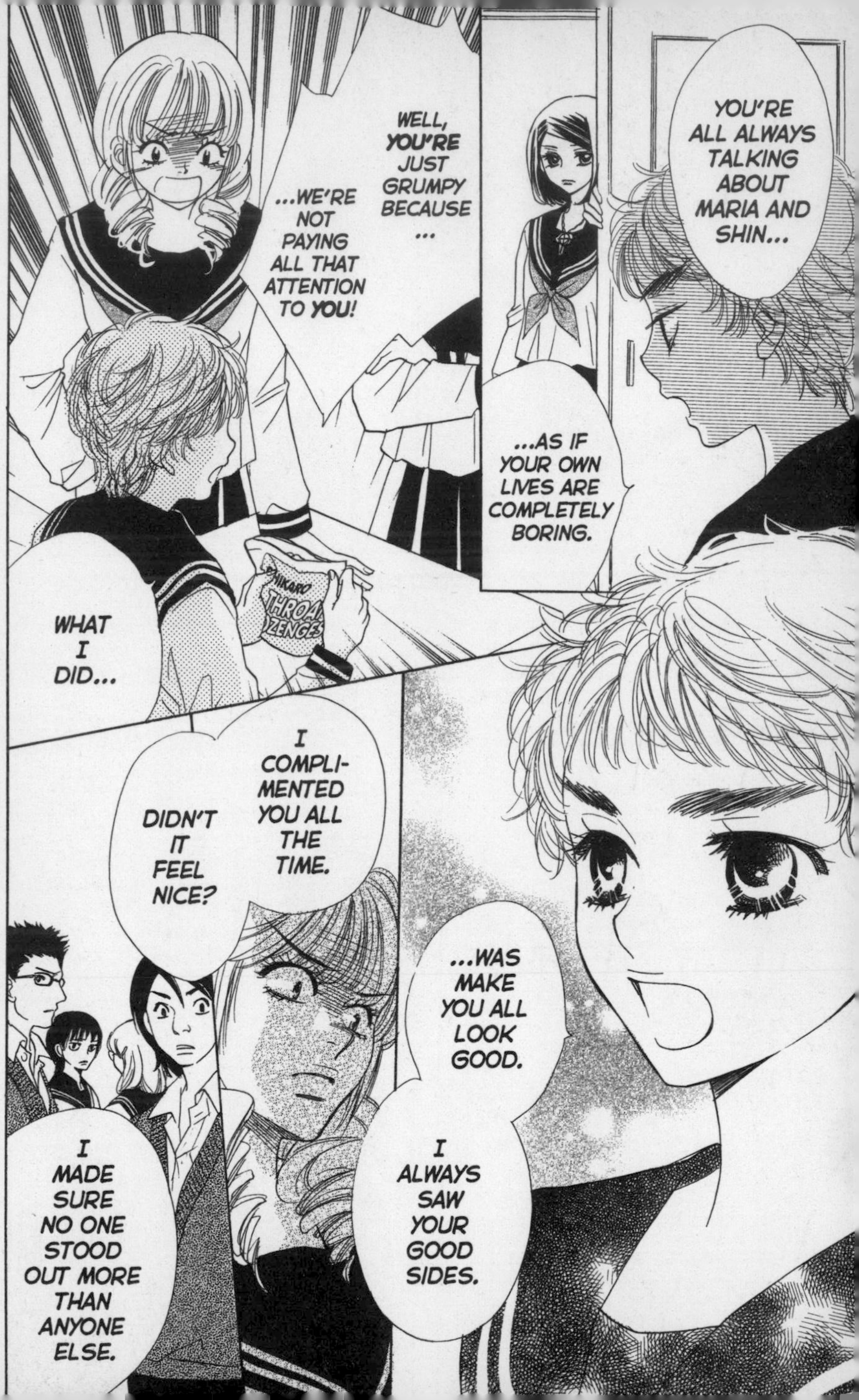
YOU'RE ALL ALWAYS TALKING ABOUT MARIA AND SHIN...
...AS IF YOUR OWN LIVES ARE COMPLETELY BORING.
WELL, YOU'RE JUST GRUMPY BECAUSE...
...WE'RE NOT PAYING ALL THAT ATTENTION TO YOU!
WHAT I DID...
...WAS MAKE YOU ALL LOOK GOOD.
I ALWAYS SAW YOUR GOOD SIDES.
I COMPLIMENTED YOU ALL THE TIME.
DIDN'T IT FEEL NICE?
I MADE SURE NO ONE STOOD OUT MORE THAN ANYONE ELSE.

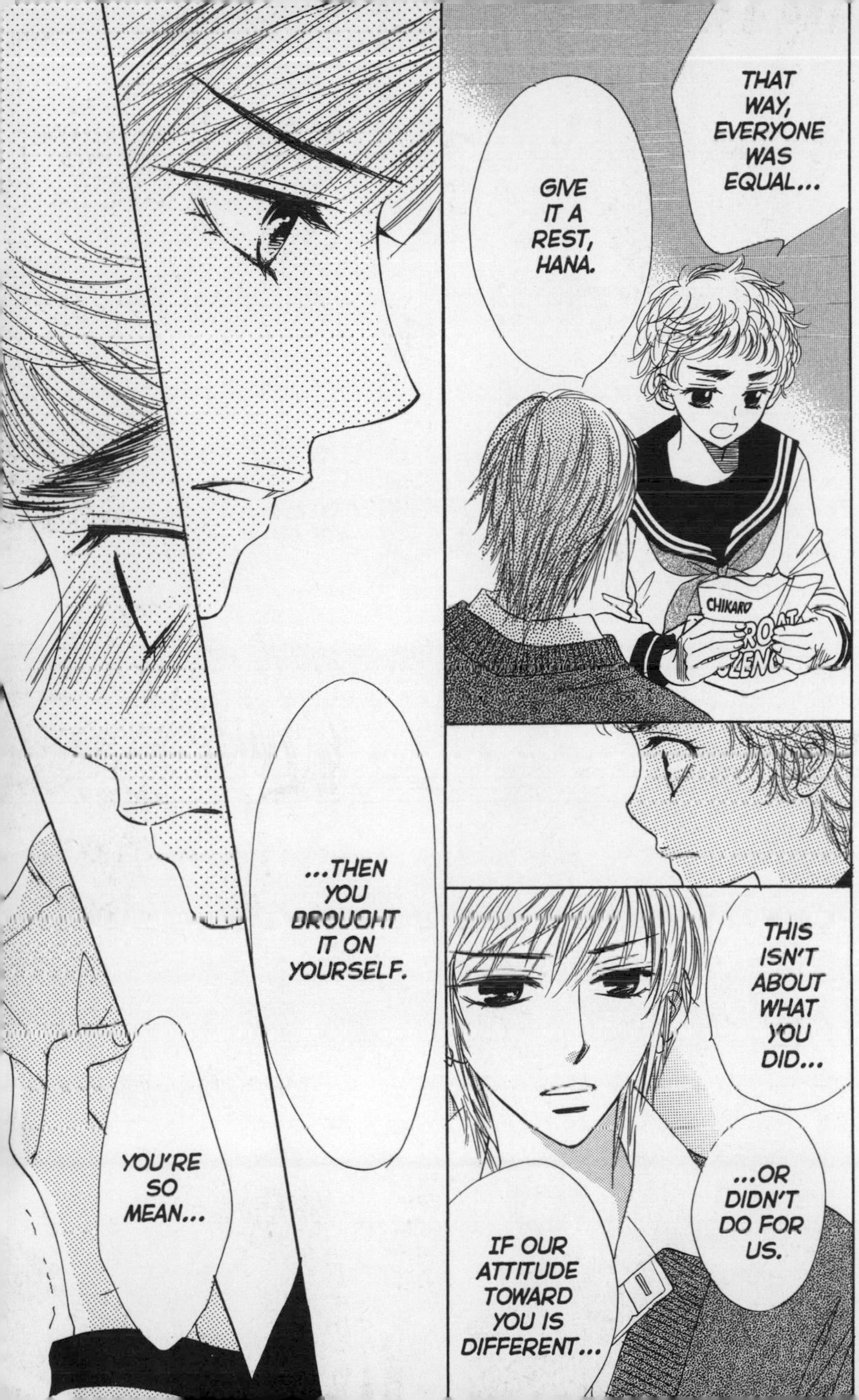
THAT WAY, EVERYONE WAS EQUAL...
GIVE IT A REST, HANA.
CHIKARU
THIS ISN'T ABOUT WHAT YOU DID...
...OR DIDN'T DO FOR US.
IF OUR ATTITUDE TOWARD YOU IS DIFFERENT...
...THEN YOU BROUGHT IT ON YOURSELF.
YOU'RE SO MEAN...

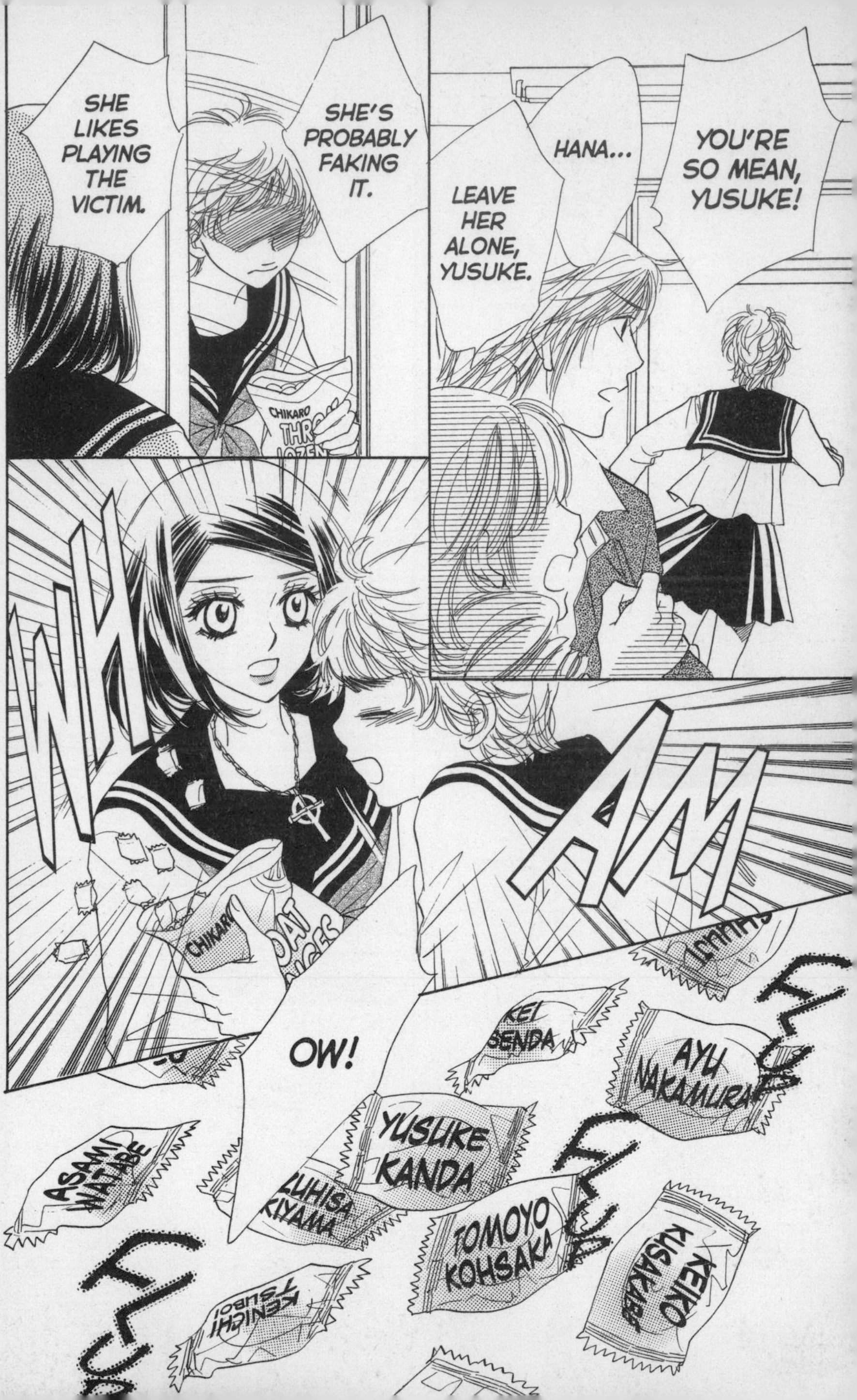
YOU'RE SO MEAN, YUSUKE!
HANA...
LEAVE HER ALONE, YUSUKE.
SHE'S PROBABLY FAKING IT.
CHIKARO
SHE LIKES PLAYING THE VICTIM.
WHAM
CHIKARO
OW!
KEI SENDA
AYU NAKAMURA
YUSUKE KANDA
ASAMI WATABE
KIYAMA
TOMOYO KOHSAKA
KEIKO KUSAKABE
KENICHI TSUBOI

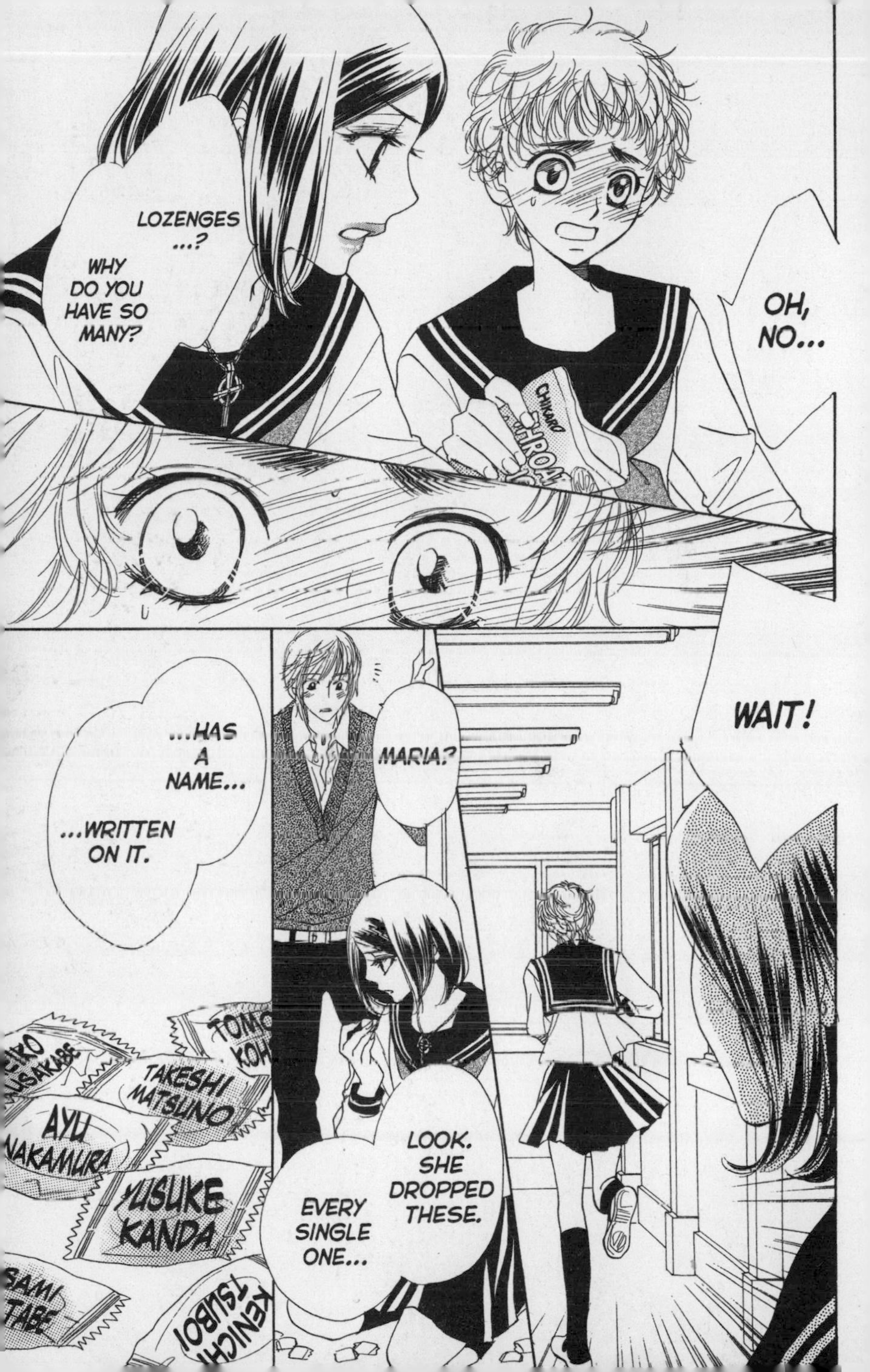
LOZENGES ...?
WHY DO YOU HAVE SO MANY?
OH, NO...
WAIT!
MARIA?
LOOK. SHE DROPPED THESE.
EVERY SINGLE ONE...
...HAS A NAME...
...WRITTEN ON IT.
TAKESHI MATSUNO
AYU NAKAMURA
YUSUKE KANDA

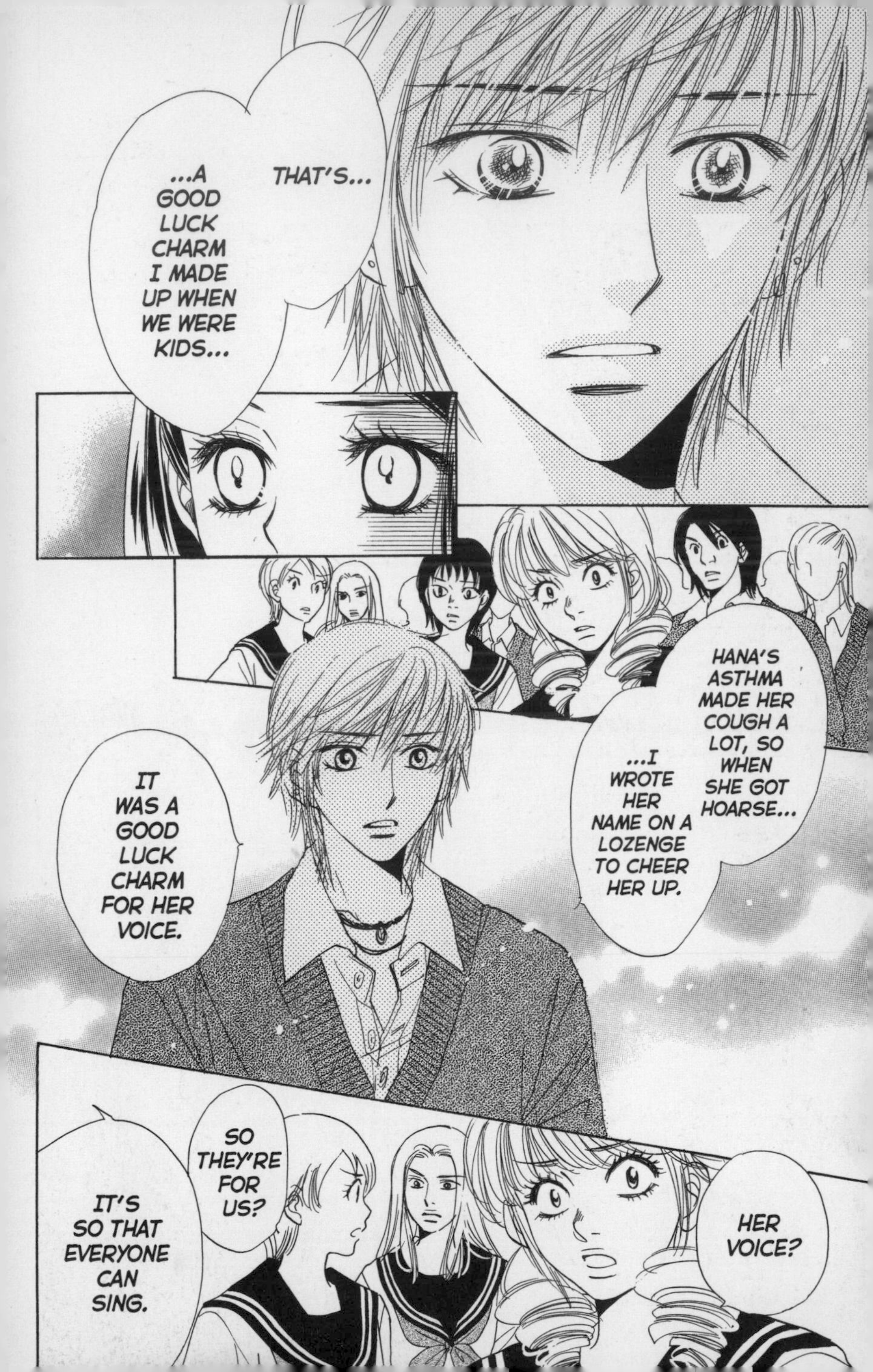
THAT'S...
...A GOOD LUCK CHARM I MADE UP WHEN WE WERE KIDS...
HANA'S ASTHMA MADE HER COUGH A LOT, SO WHEN SHE GOT HOARSE...
...I WROTE HER NAME ON A LOZENGE TO CHEER HER UP.
IT WAS A GOOD LUCK CHARM FOR HER VOICE.
HER VOICE?
SO THEY'RE FOR US?
IT'S SO THAT EVERYONE CAN SING.

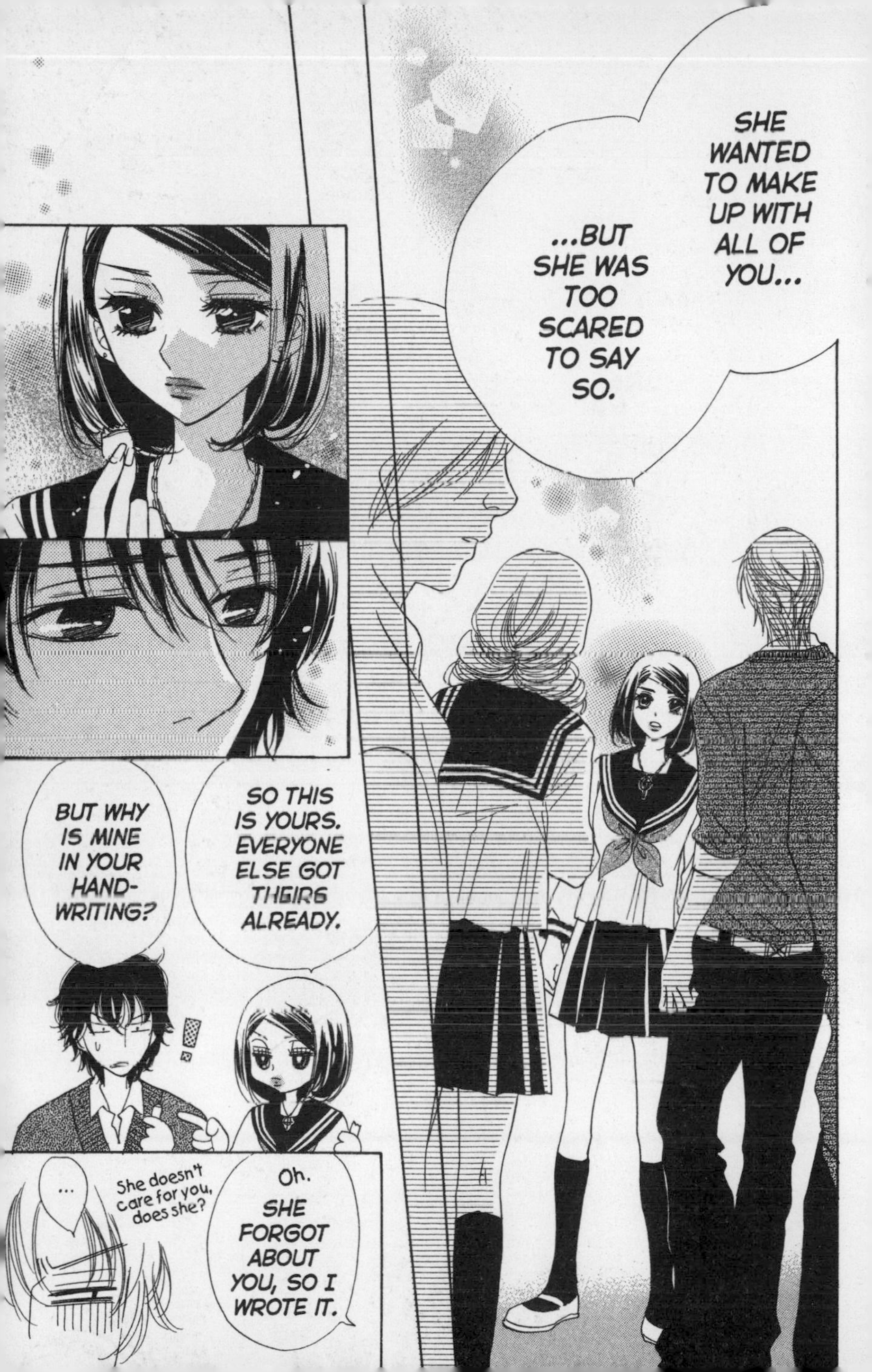
SHE WANTED TO MAKE UP WITH ALL OF YOU...
...BUT SHE WAS TOO SCARED TO SAY SO.
SO THIS IS YOURS. EVERYONE ELSE GOT THEIRS ALREADY.
BUT WHY IS MINE IN YOUR HAND-WRITING?
!
Oh.
SHE FORGOT ABOUT YOU, SO I WROTE IT.
She doesn't care for you, does she?
...

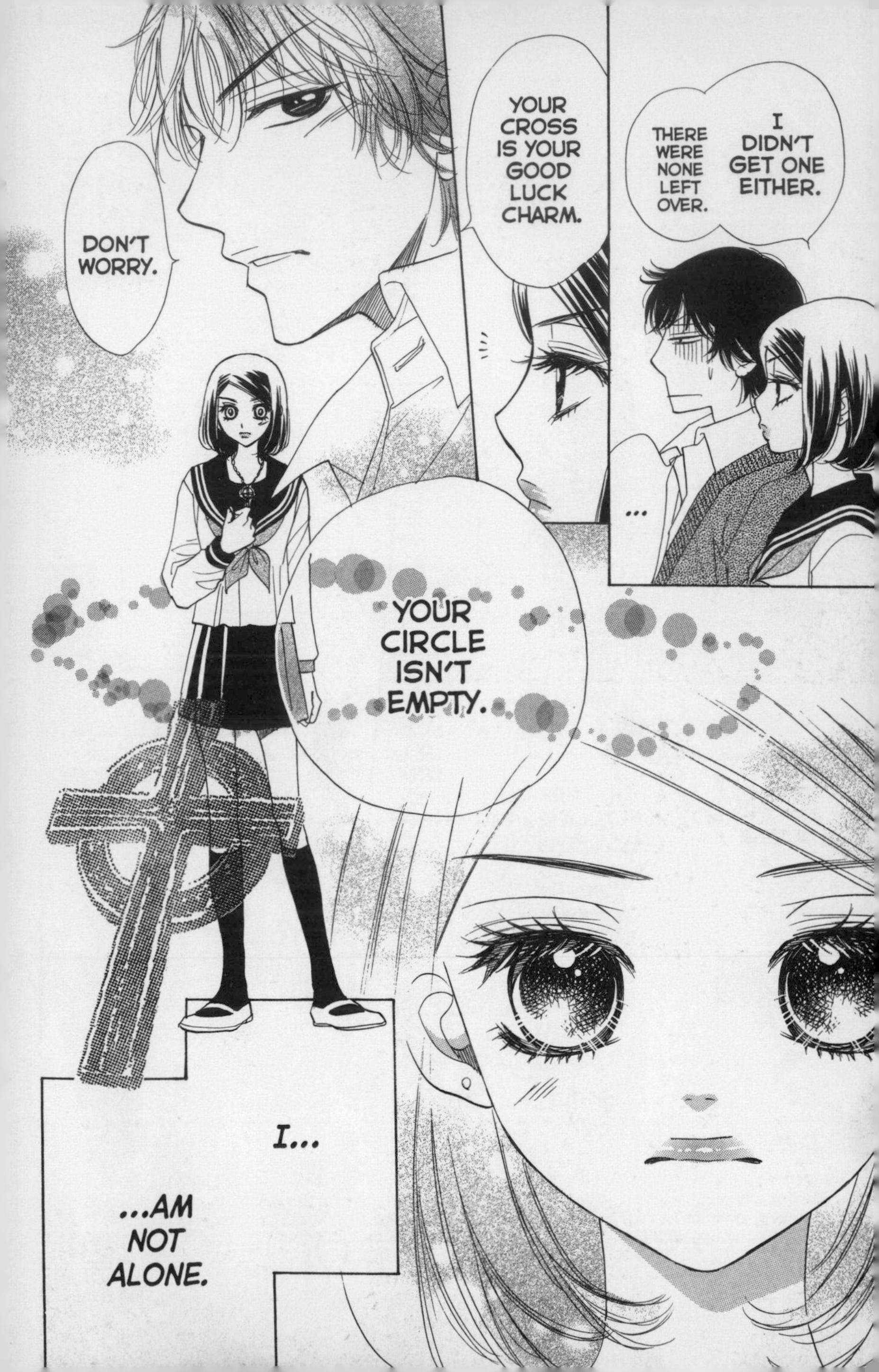
I DIDN'T GET ONE EITHER.
THERE WERE NONE LEFT OVER.
...
YOUR CROSS IS YOUR GOOD LUCK CHARM.
DON'T WORRY.
YOUR CIRCLE ISN'T EMPTY.
I...
...AM NOT ALONE.

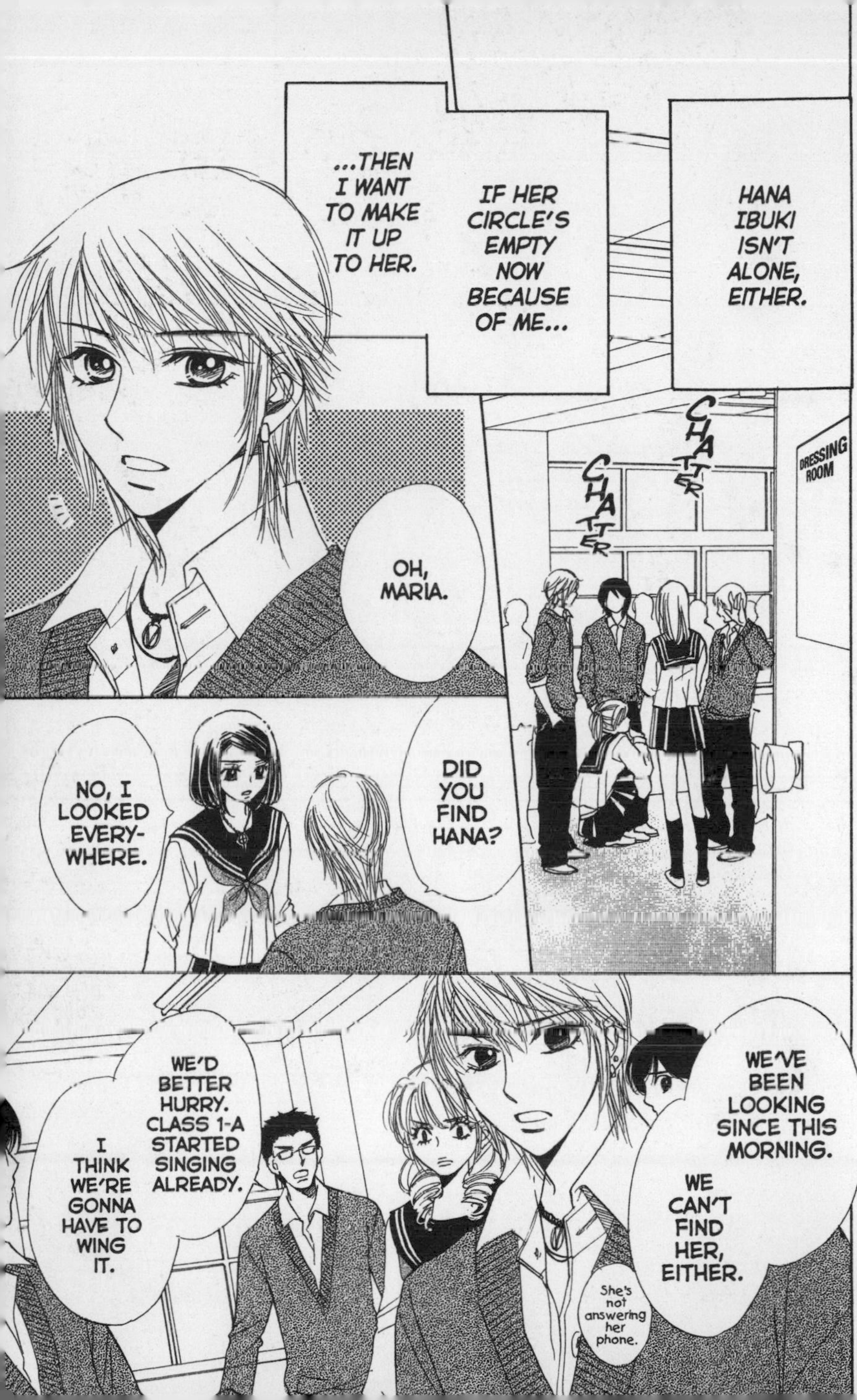
HANA IBUKI ISN'T ALONE, EITHER.
IF HER CIRCLE'S EMPTY NOW BECAUSE OF ME...
...THEN I WANT TO MAKE IT UP TO HER.
CHATTER
CHATTER
DRESSING ROOM
OH, MARIA.
DID YOU FIND HANA?
NO, I LOOKED EVERY-WHERE.
WE'VE BEEN LOOKING SINCE THIS MORNING.
WE CAN'T FIND HER, EITHER.
She's not answering her phone.
WE'D BETTER HURRY. CLASS 1-A STARTED SINGING ALREADY.
I THINK WE'RE GONNA HAVE TO WING IT.

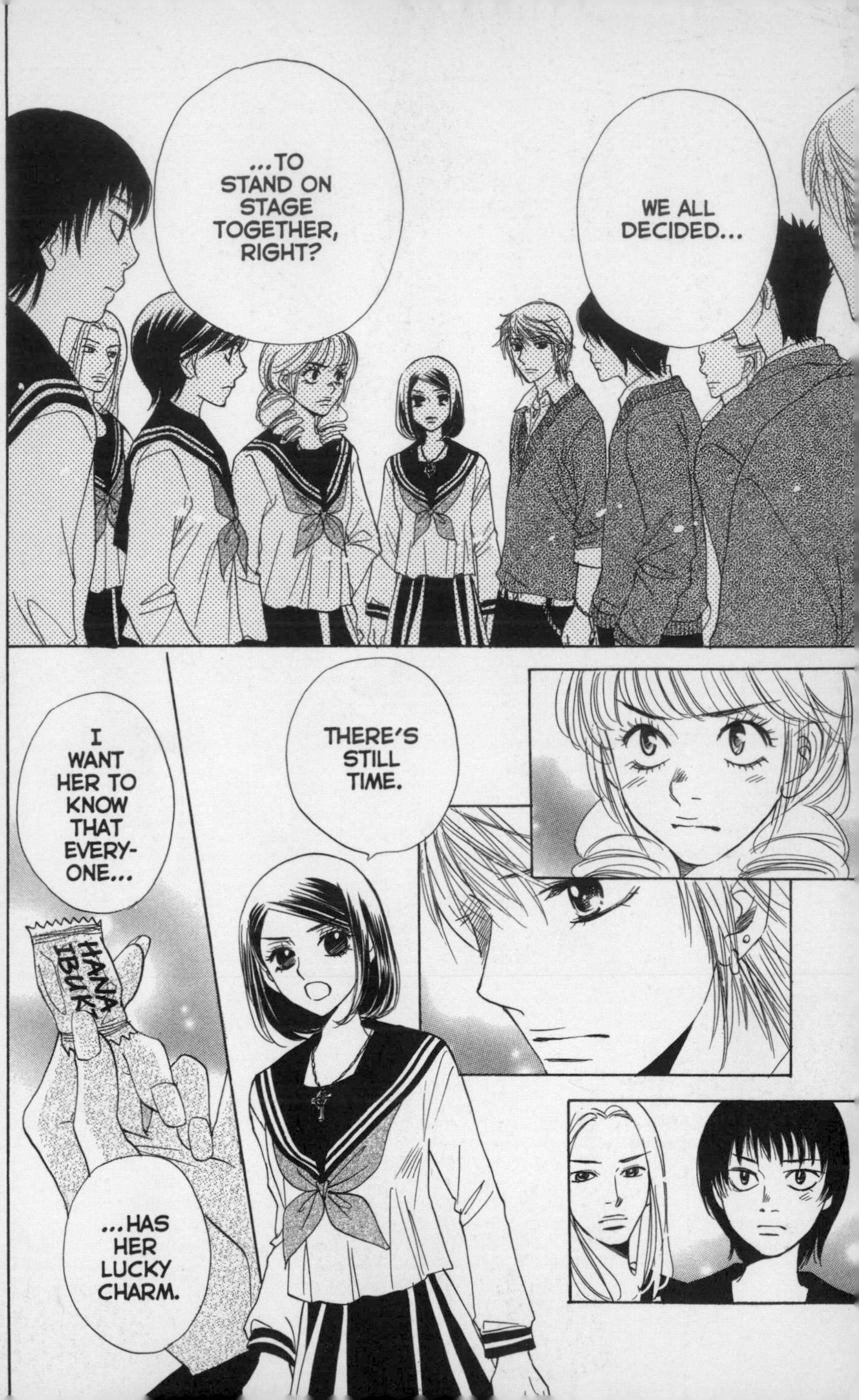
WE ALL DECIDED...
...TO STAND ON STAGE TOGETHER, RIGHT?
THERE'S STILL TIME.
I WANT HER TO KNOW THAT EVERY-ONE...
HANA IBUKI
...HAS HER LUCKY CHARM.

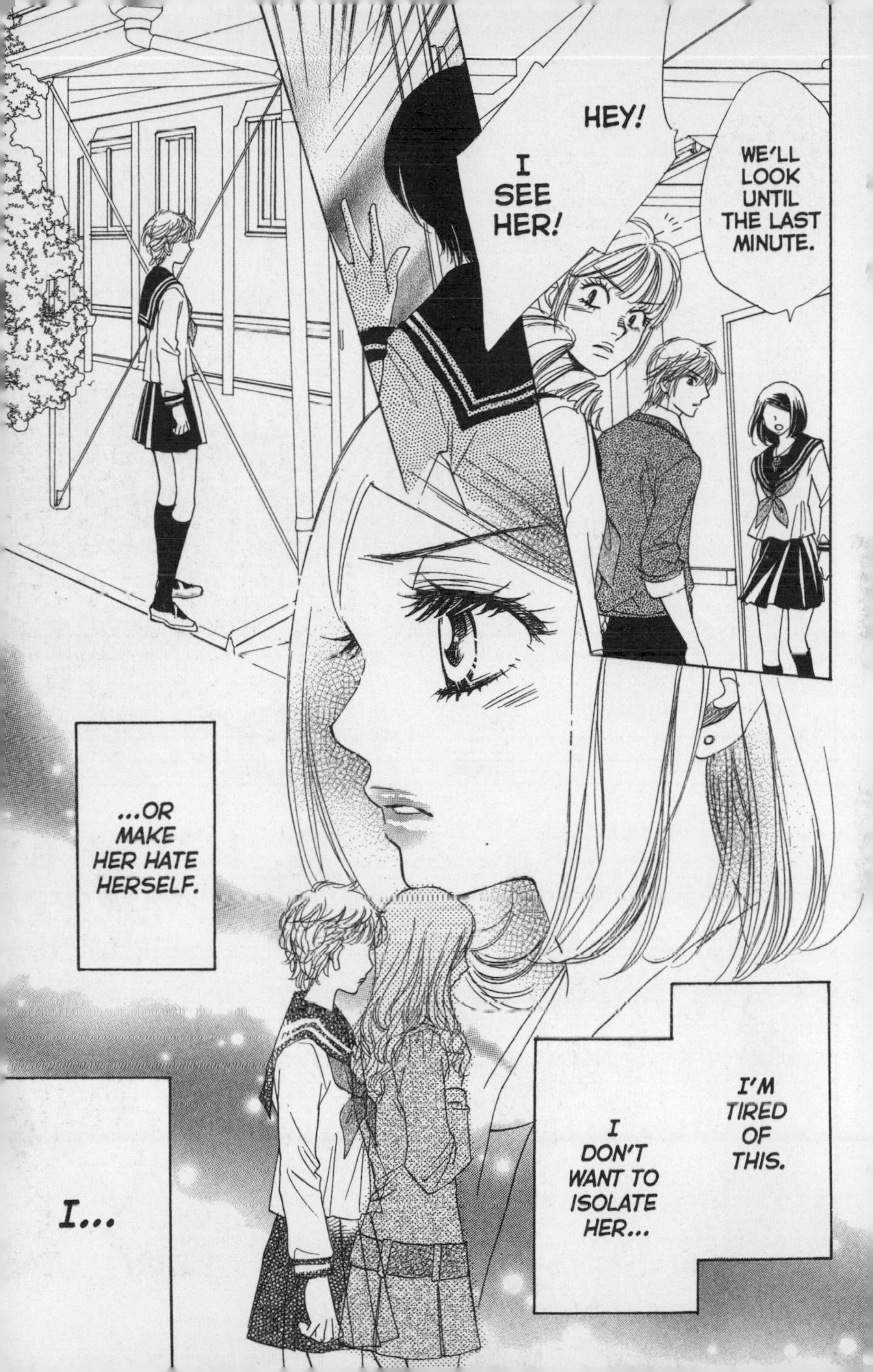
WE'LL LOOK UNTIL THE LAST MINUTE.
HEY!
I SEE HER!
I'M TIRED OF THIS.
I DON'T WANT TO ISOLATE HER...
...OR MAKE HER HATE HERSELF.
I...

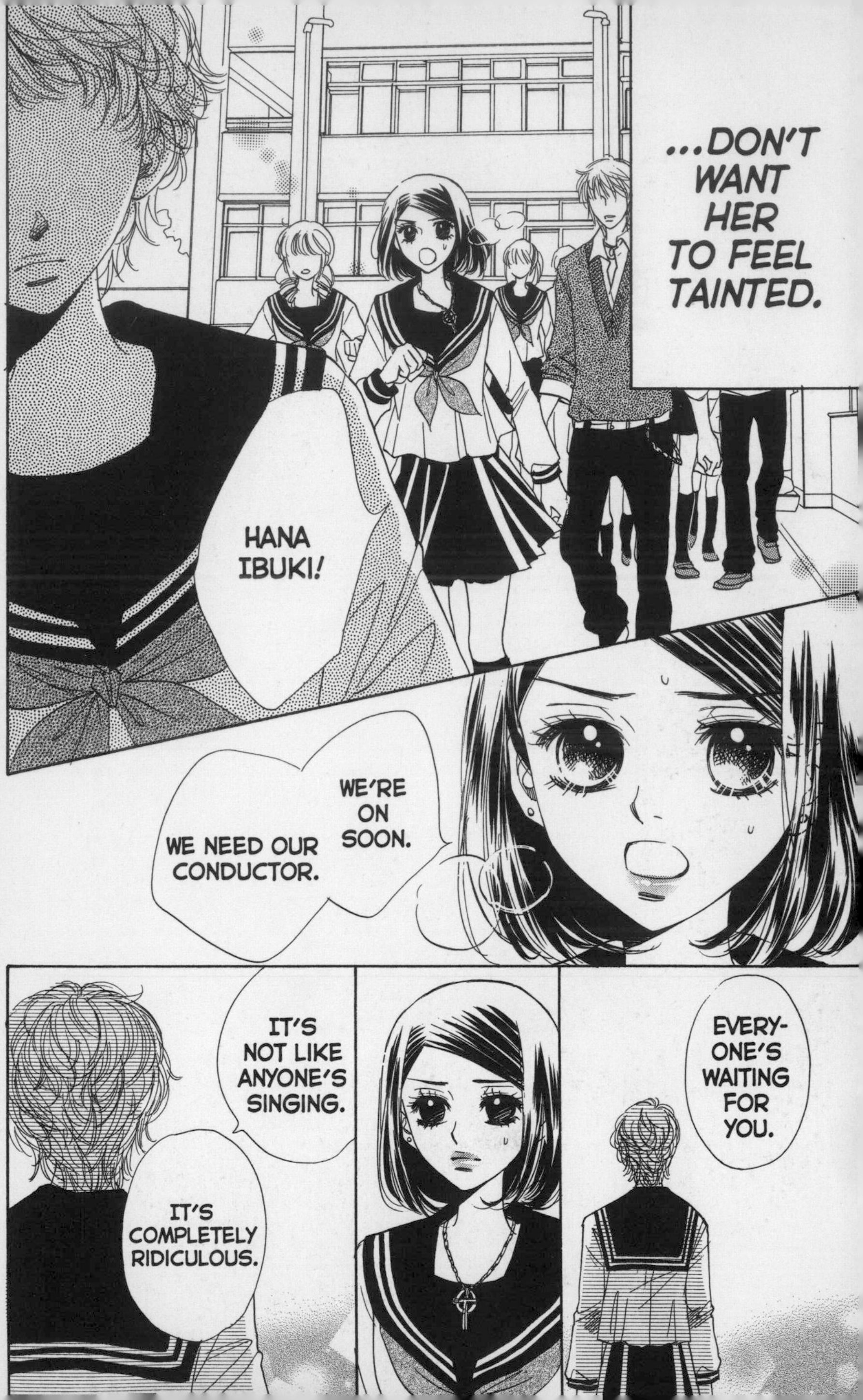
...DON'T WANT HER TO FEEL TAINTED.
HANA IBUKI!
WE'RE ON SOON.
WE NEED OUR CONDUCTOR.
EVERY-ONE'S WAITING FOR YOU.
IT'S NOT LIKE ANYONE'S SINGING.
IT'S COMPLETELY RIDICULOUS.

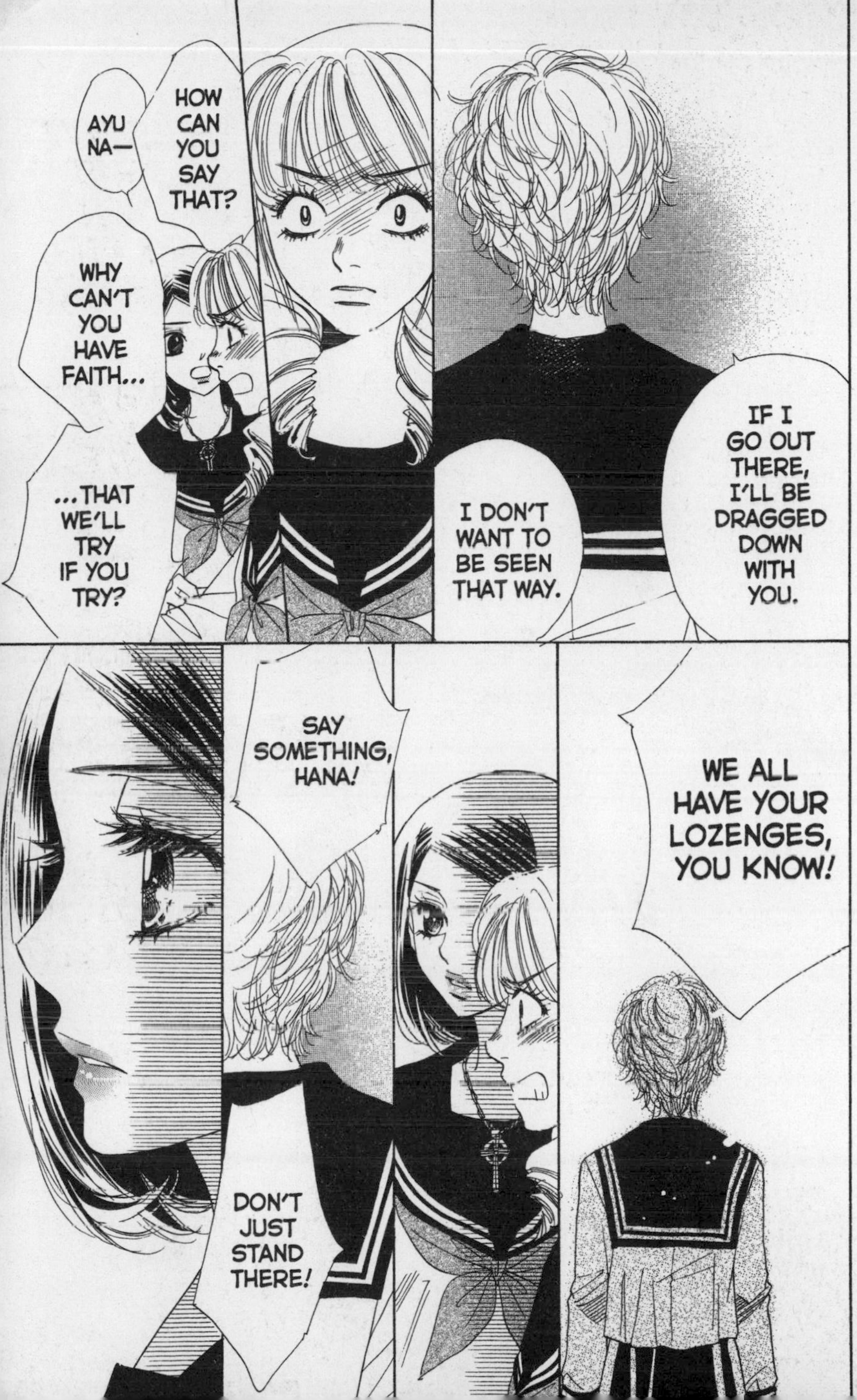
IF I GO OUT THERE, I'LL BE DRAGGED DOWN WITH YOU.
I DON'T WANT TO BE SEEN THAT WAY.
HOW CAN YOU SAY THAT?
AYU NA—
WHY CAN'T YOU HAVE FAITH...
...THAT WE'LL TRY IF YOU TRY?
WE ALL HAVE YOUR LOZENGES, YOU KNOW!
SAY SOMETHING, HANA!
DON'T JUST STAND THERE!

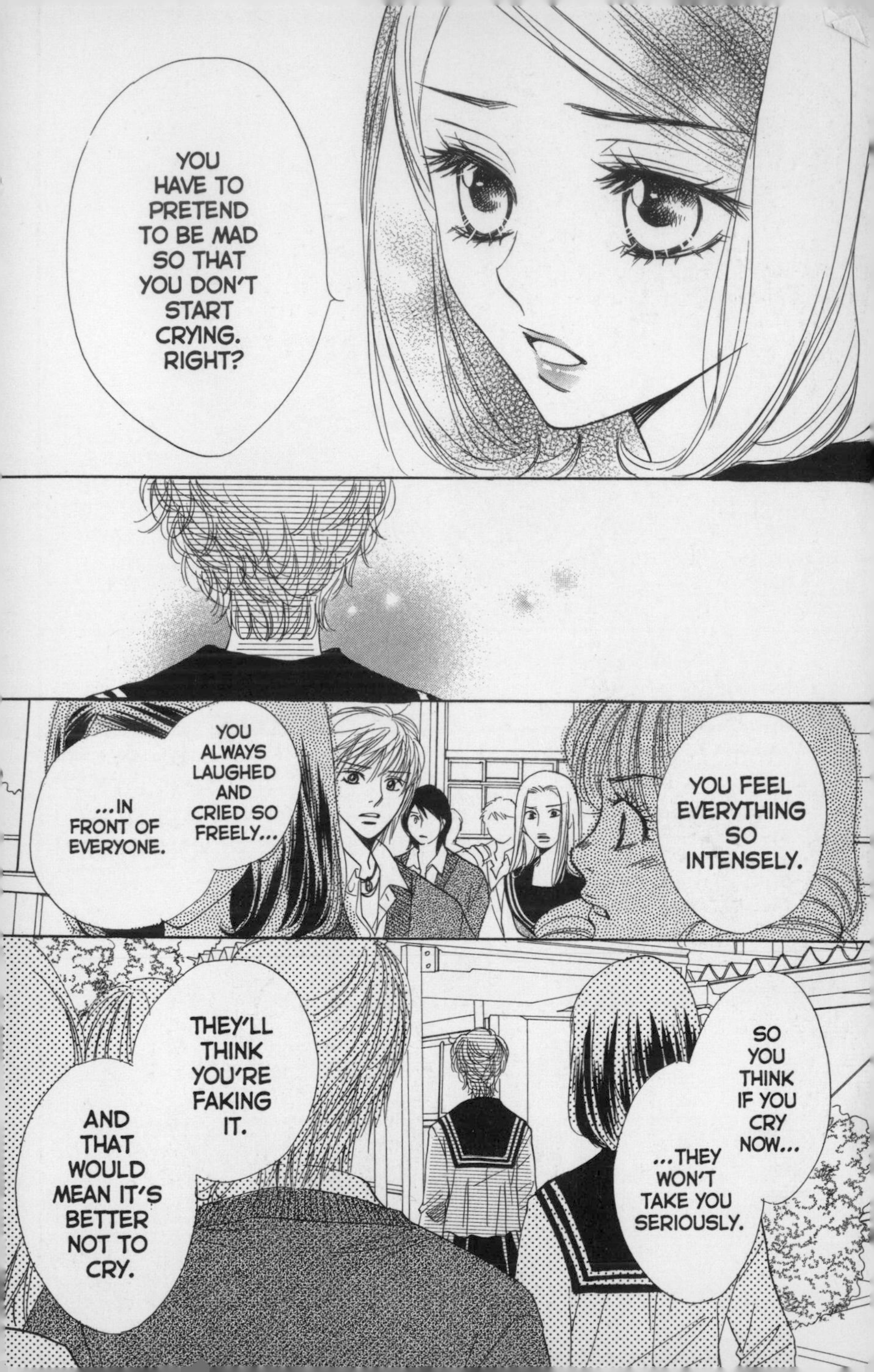
YOU HAVE TO PRETEND TO BE MAD SO THAT YOU DON'T START CRYING. RIGHT?
YOU FEEL EVERYTHING SO INTENSELY.
YOU ALWAYS LAUGHED AND CRIED SO FREELY...
...IN FRONT OF EVERYONE.
SO YOU THINK IF YOU CRY NOW...
...THEY WON'T TAKE YOU SERIOUSLY.
THEY'LL THINK YOU'RE FAKING IT.
AND THAT WOULD MEAN IT'S BETTER NOT TO CRY.

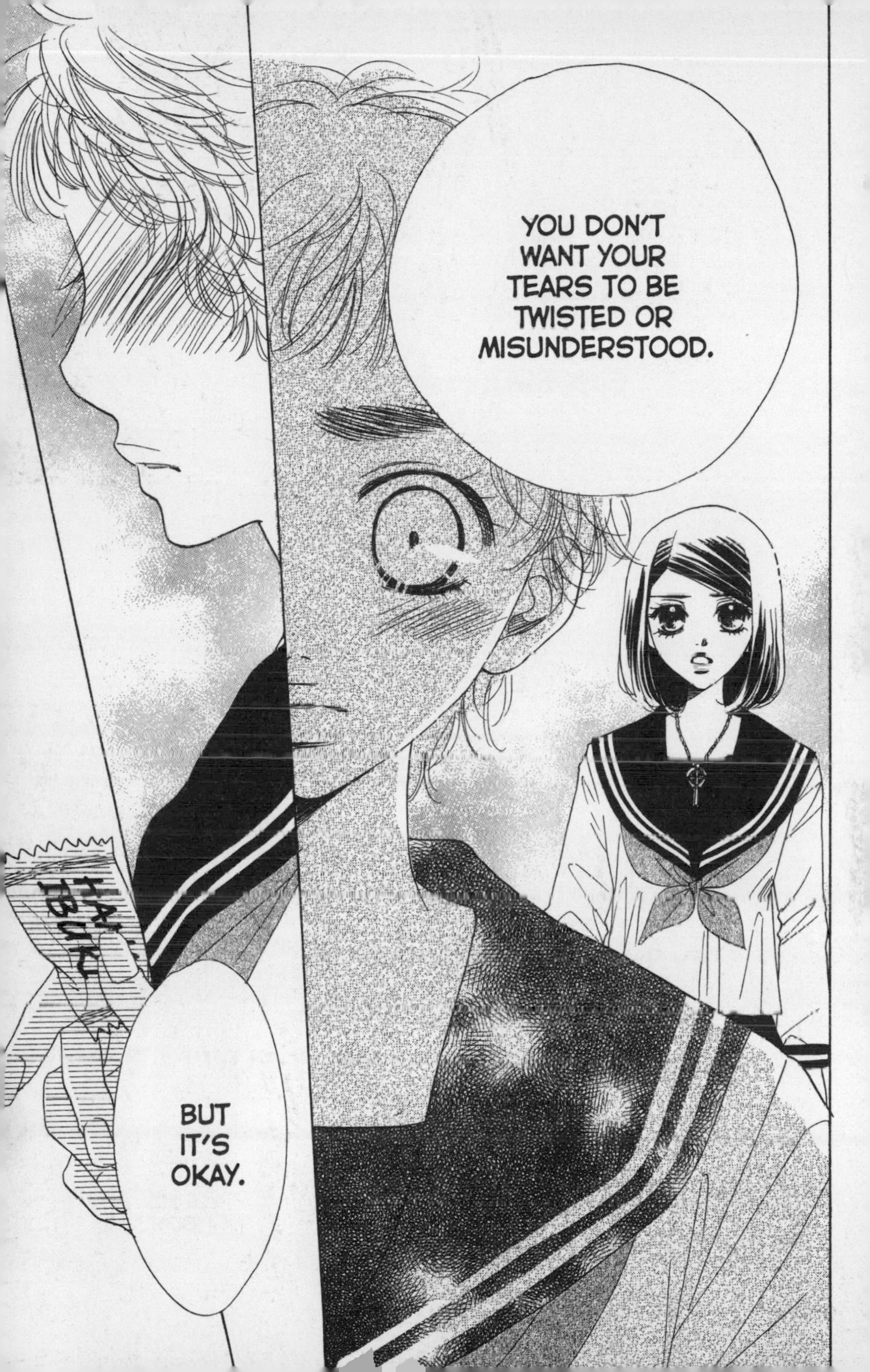
YOU DON'T WANT YOUR TEARS TO BE TWISTED OR MISUNDERSTOOD.
BUT IT'S OKAY.

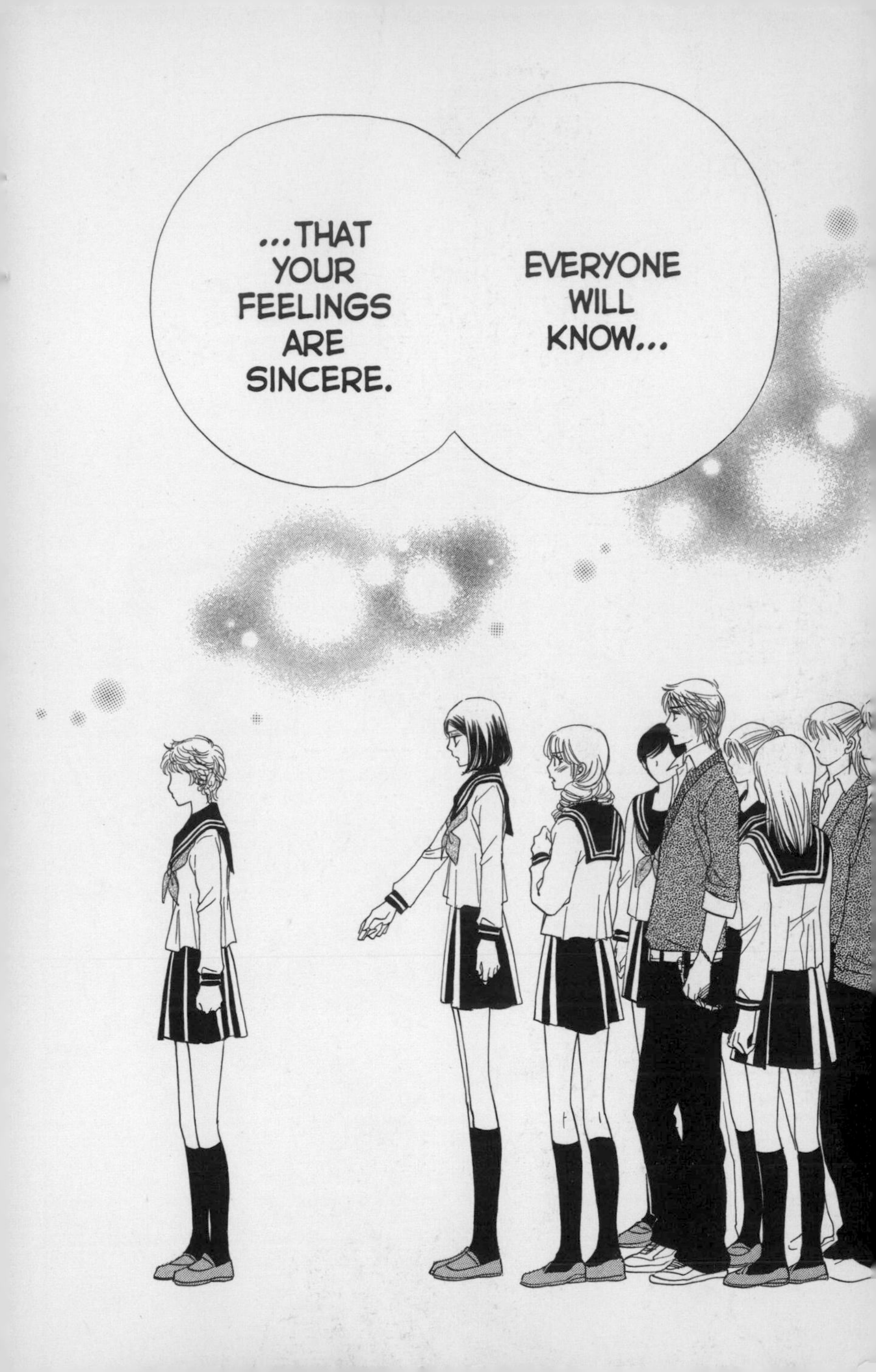
EVERYONE WILL KNOW...
...THAT YOUR FEELINGS ARE SINCERE.

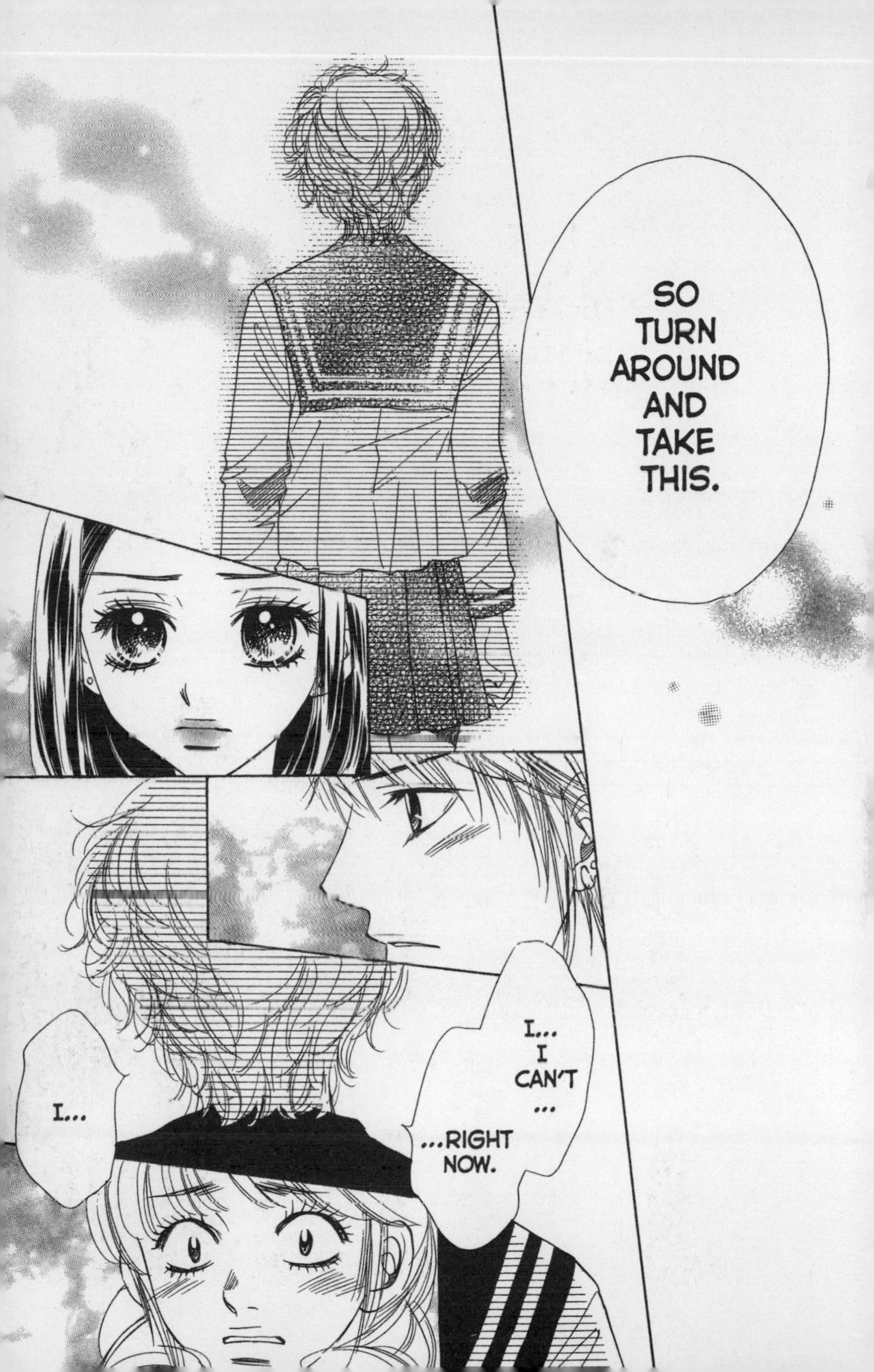
SO TURN AROUND AND TAKE THIS.
I... I CAN'T ...
...RIGHT NOW.
I...

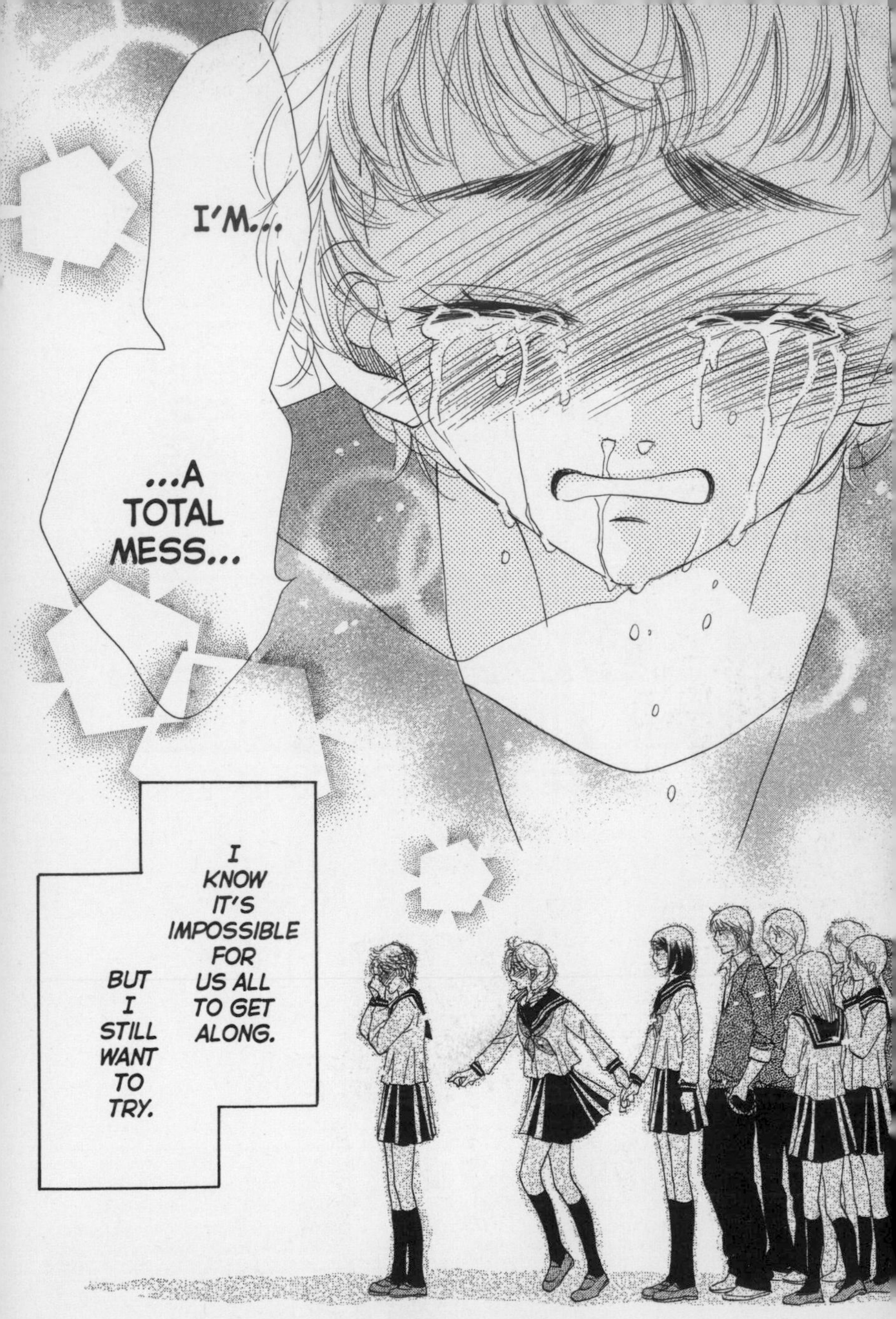
I'M...
...A TOTAL MESS...
I KNOW IT'S IMPOSSIBLE FOR US ALL TO GET ALONG.
BUT I STILL WANT TO TRY.

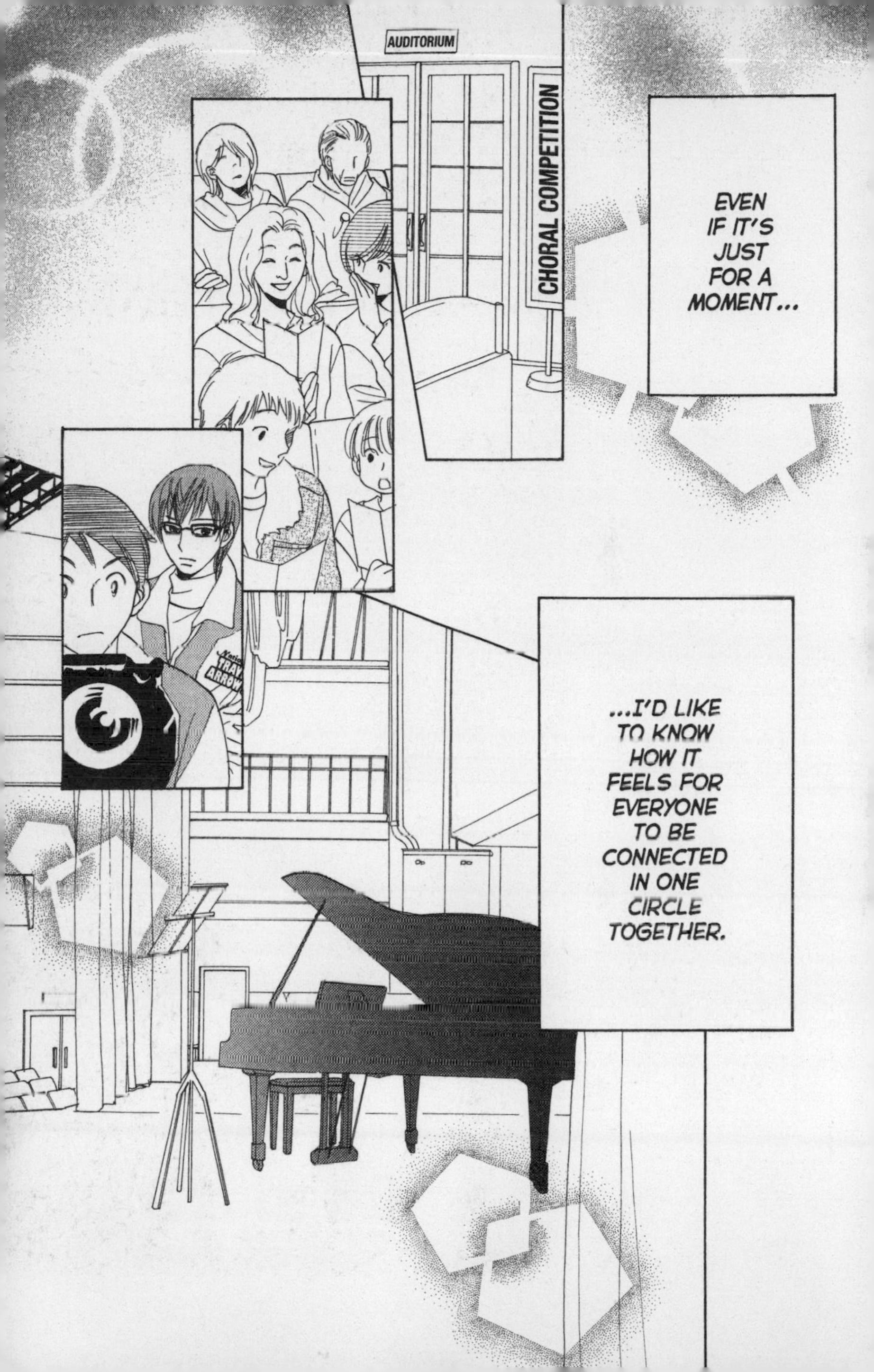
AUDITORIUM
CHORAL COMPETITION
EVEN IF IT'S JUST FOR A MOMENT...
...I'D LIKE TO KNOW HOW IT FEELS FOR EVERYONE TO BE CONNECTED IN ONE CIRCLE TOGETHER.

A Devil and Her Love Song

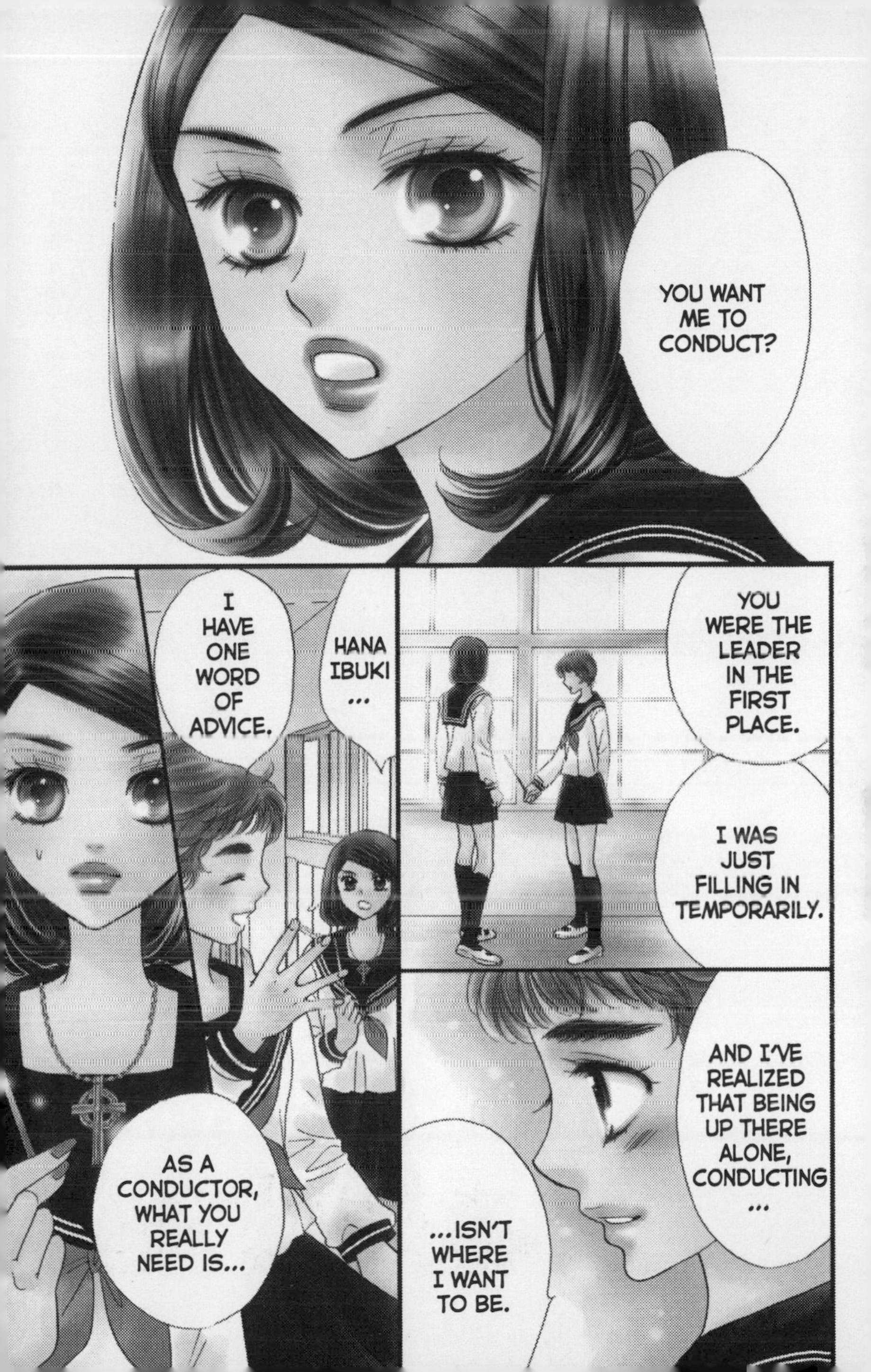
YOU WANT ME TO CONDUCT?
YOU WERE THE LEADER IN THE FIRST PLACE.
I WAS JUST FILLING IN TEMPORARILY.
AND I'VE REALIZED THAT BEING UP THERE ALONE, CONDUCTING...
...ISN'T WHERE I WANT TO BE.
HANA IBUKI...
I HAVE ONE WORD OF ADVICE.
AS A CONDUCTOR, WHAT YOU REALLY NEED IS...

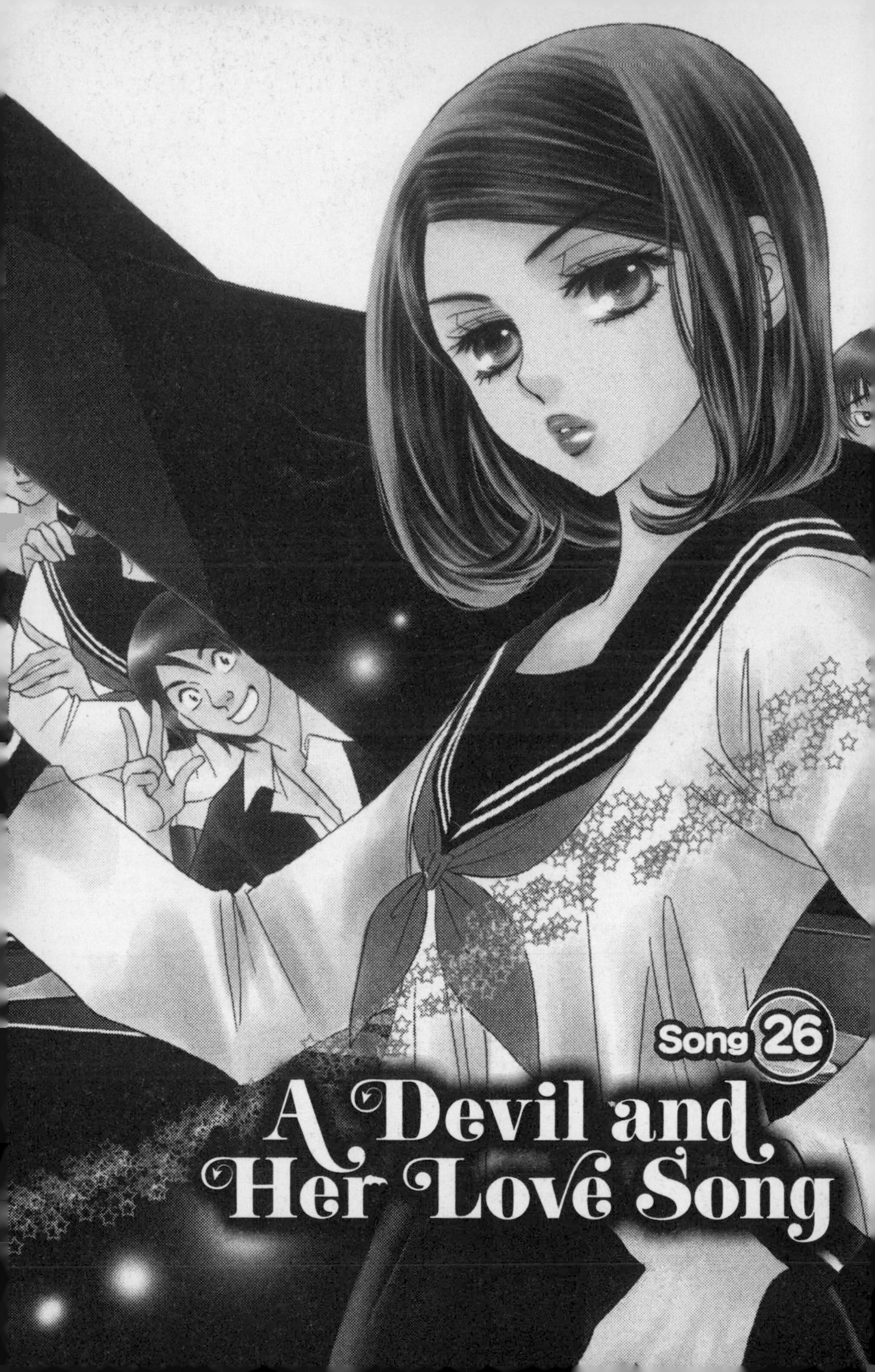
Song 26
A Devil and Her Love Song

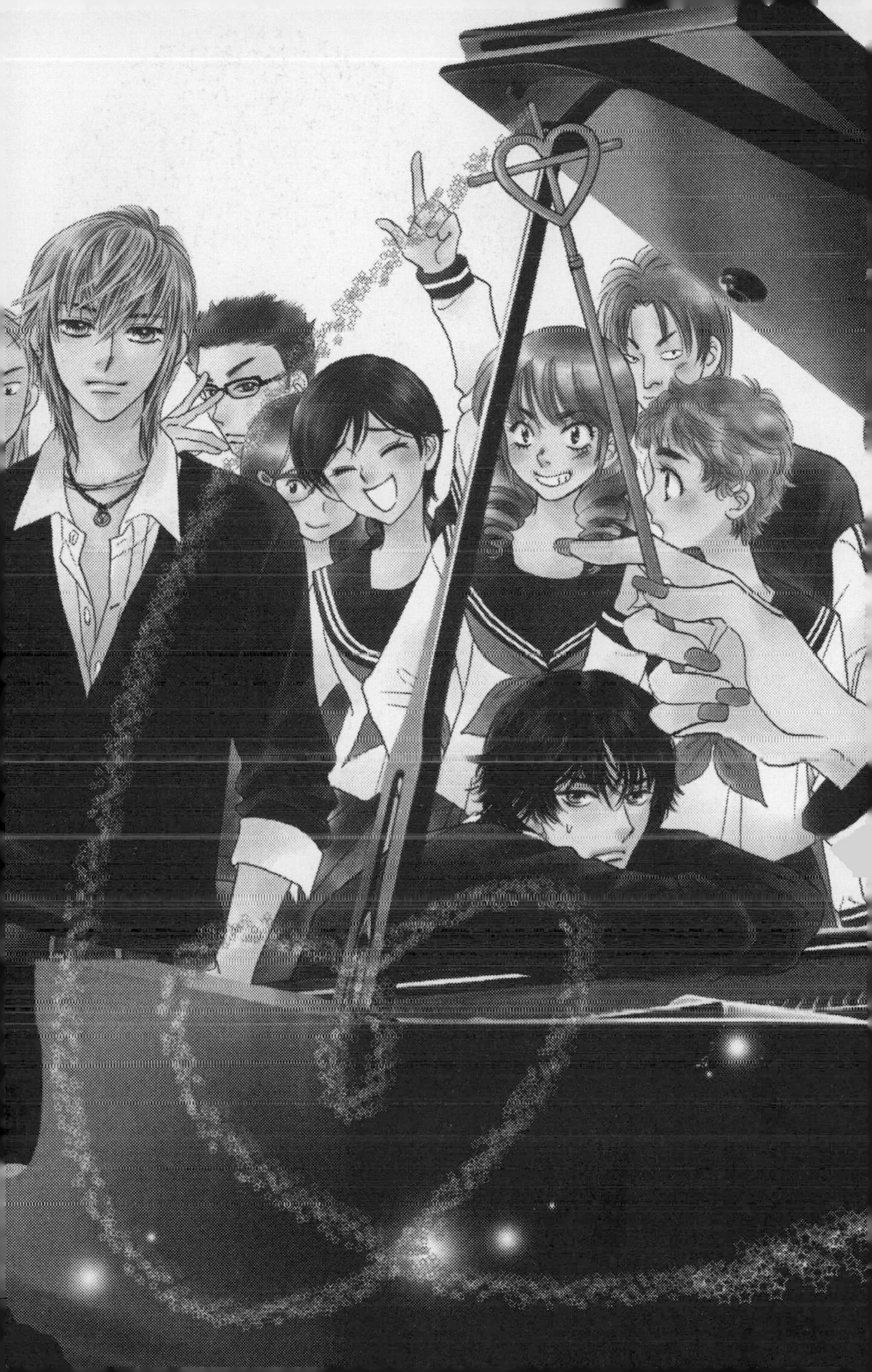

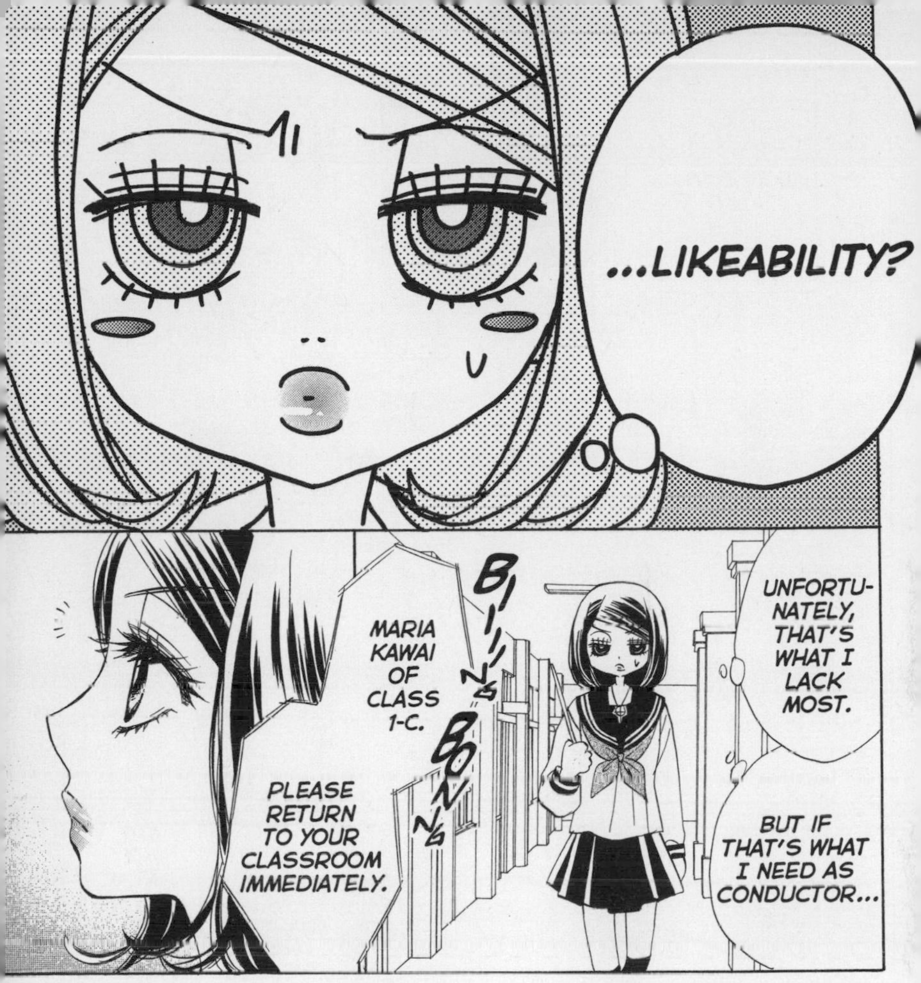
...LIKEABILITY?
UNFORTUNATELY, THAT'S WHAT I LACK MOST.
BUT IF THAT'S WHAT I NEED AS CONDUCTOR...
BIIING BONNG
MARIA KAWAI OF CLASS 1-C.
PLEASE RETURN TO YOUR CLASSROOM IMMEDIATELY.

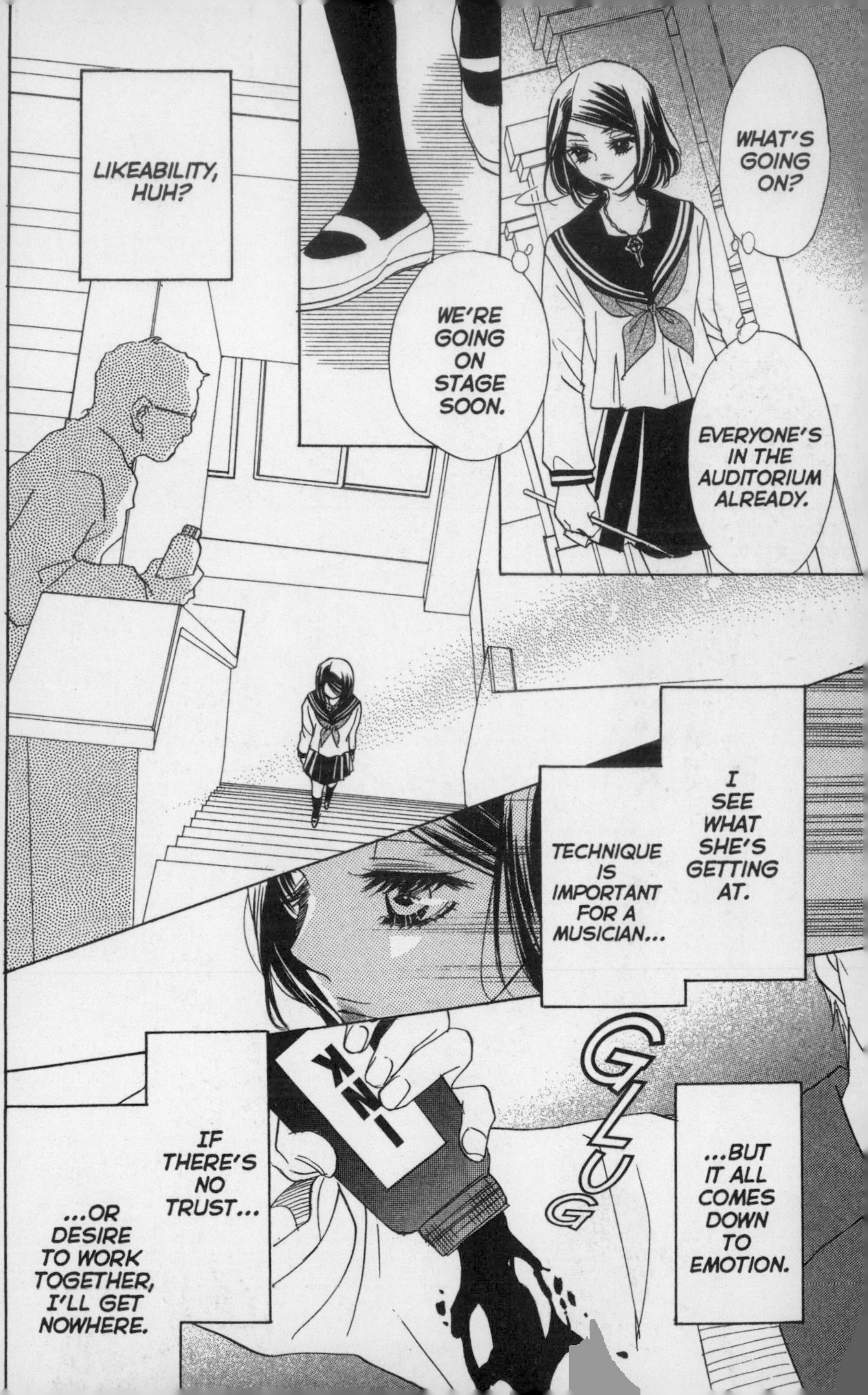
WHAT'S GOING ON?
EVERYONE'S IN THE AUDITORIUM ALREADY.
WE'RE GOING ON STAGE SOON.
LIKEABILITY, HUH?
I SEE WHAT SHE'S GETTING AT.
TECHNIQUE IS IMPORTANT FOR A MUSICIAN...
...BUT IT ALL COMES DOWN TO EMOTION.
GLUG
IF THERE'S NO TRUST...
...OR DESIRE TO WORK TOGETHER, I'LL GET NOWHERE.

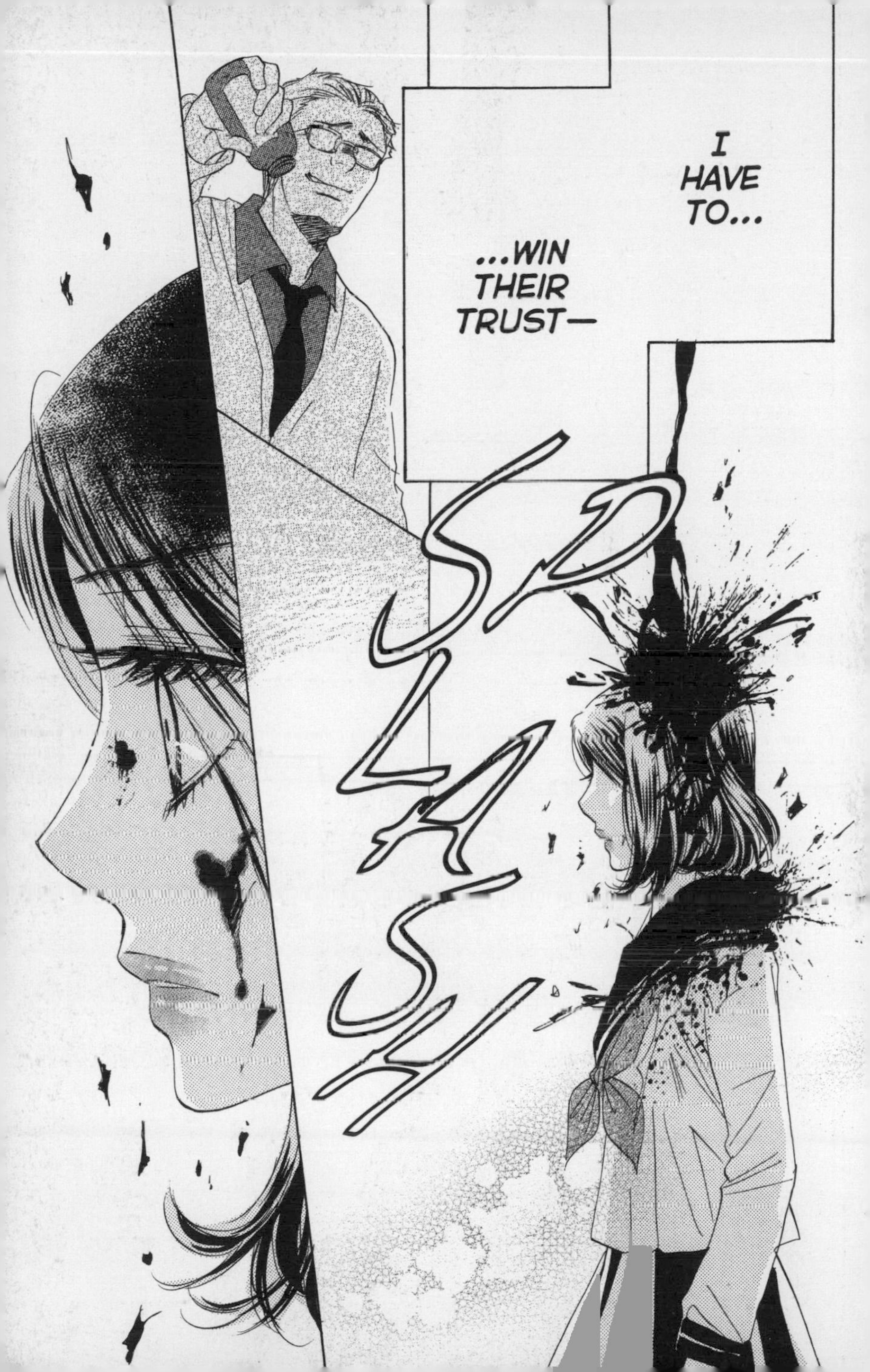

I HAVE TO...
...WIN THEIR TRUST—
SPLASH

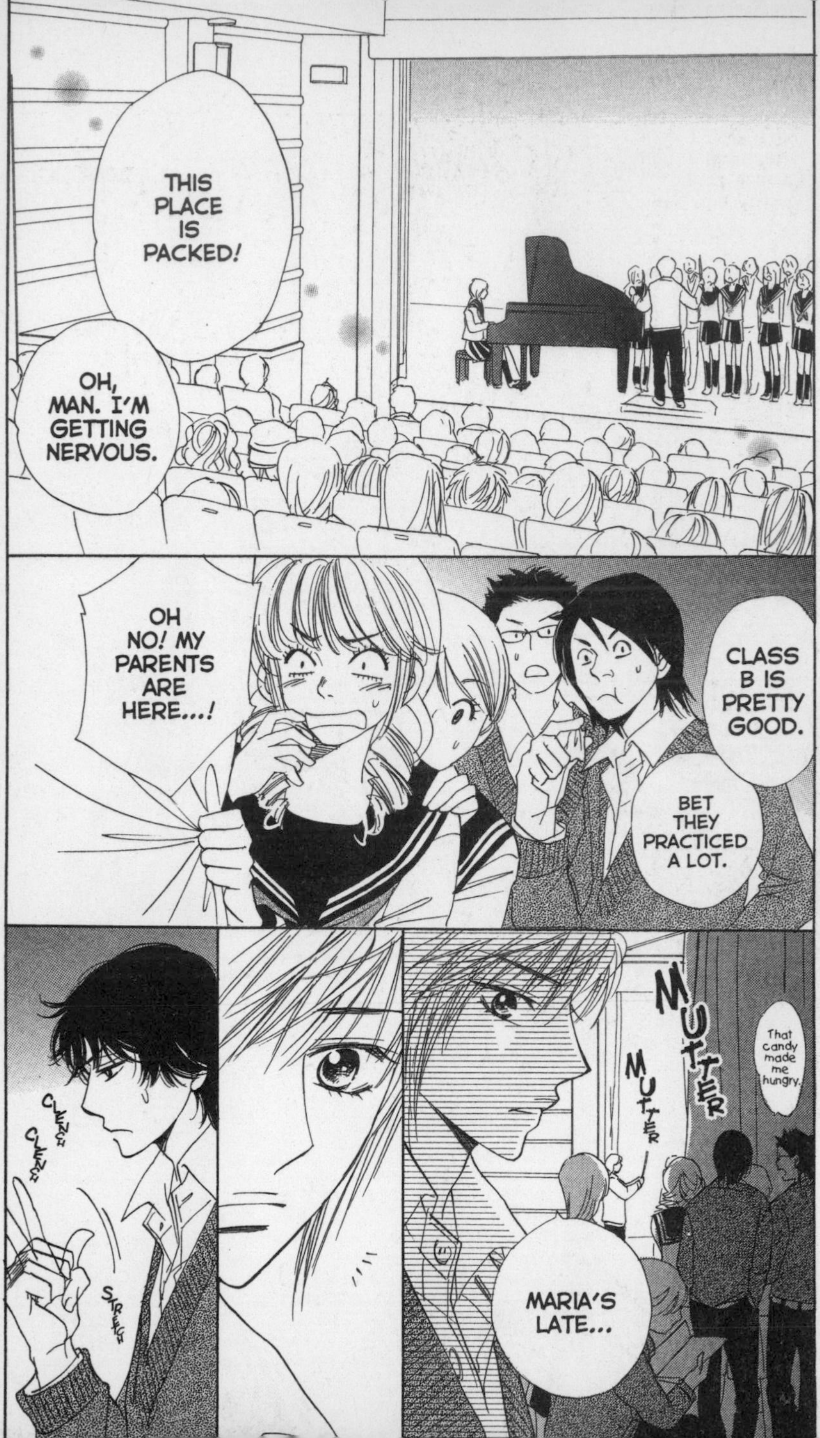
THIS PLACE IS PACKED!
OH, MAN. I'M GETTING NERVOUS.
CLASS B IS PRETTY GOOD.
BET THEY PRACTICED A LOT.
OH NO! MY PARENTS ARE HERE...!
MUTTER
MUTTER
That candy made me hungry.
MARIA'S LATE...
CLENCH
CLENCH
STRETCH

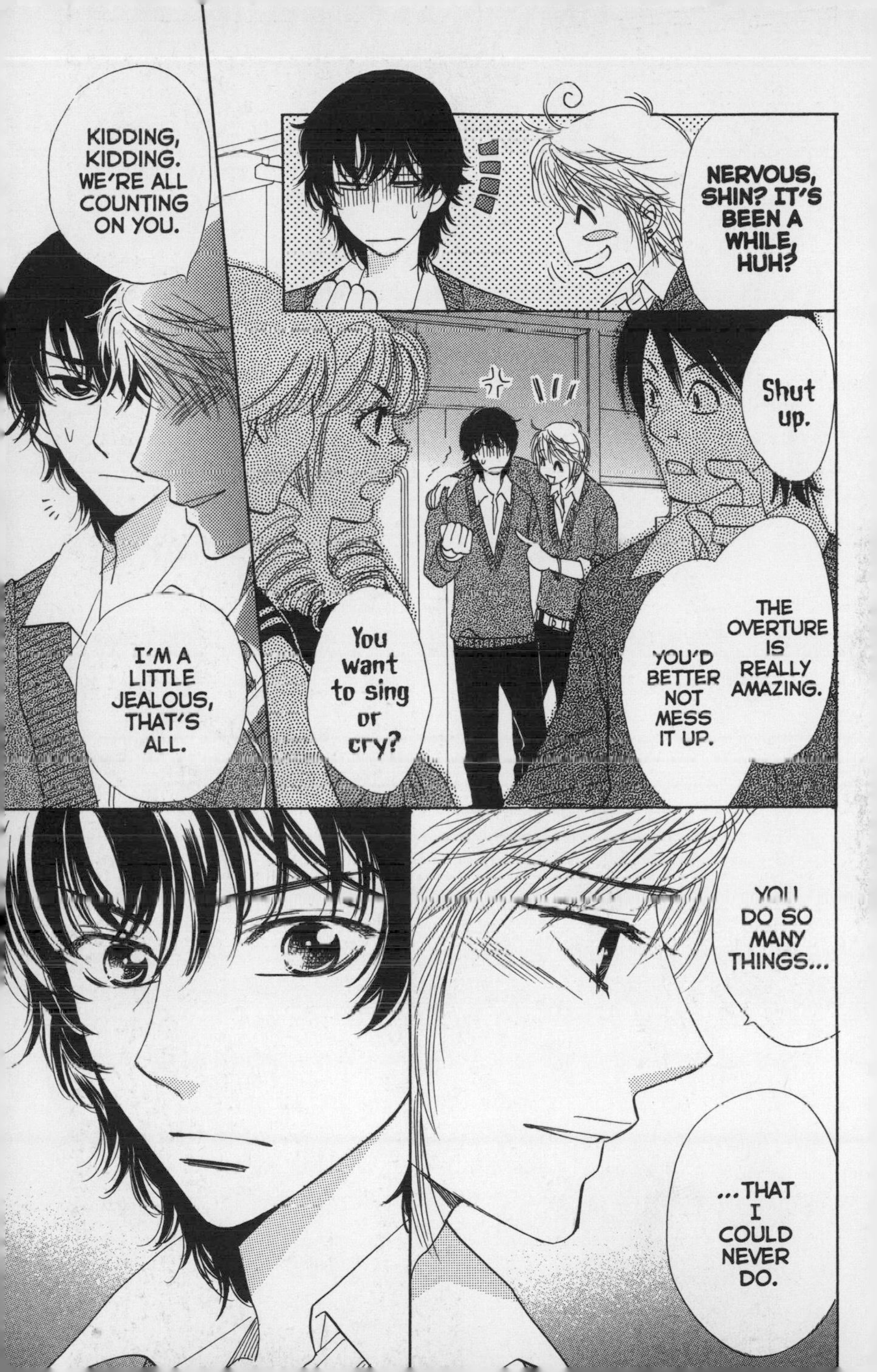
NERVOUS, SHIN? IT'S BEEN A WHILE, HUH?
Shut up.
THE OVERTURE IS REALLY AMAZING.
YOU'D BETTER NOT MESS IT UP.
You want to sing or cry?
KIDDING, KIDDING. WE'RE ALL COUNTING ON YOU.
I'M A LITTLE JEALOUS, THAT'S ALL.
YOU DO SO MANY THINGS...
...THAT I COULD NEVER DO.

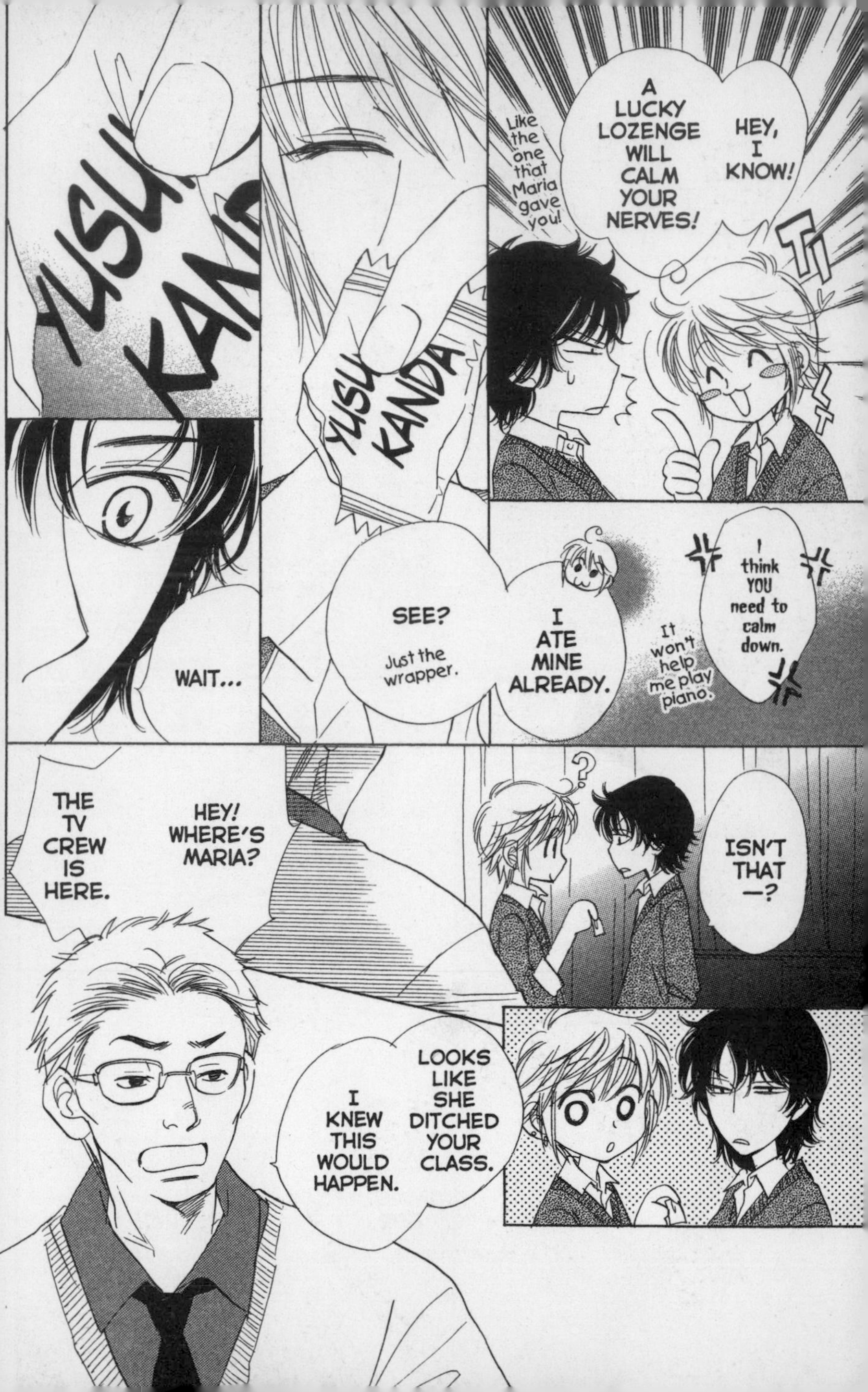

HEY, I KNOW!
A LUCKY LOZENGE WILL CALM YOUR NERVES!
Like the one that Maria gave you!
I think YOU need to calm down.
It won't help me play piano.
I ATE MINE ALREADY.
SEE?
Just the wrapper.
YUSU KANDA
YUSU KAND
WAIT...
ISN'T THAT —?
HEY! WHERE'S MARIA?
THE TV CREW IS HERE.
LOOKS LIKE SHE DITCHED YOUR CLASS.
I KNEW THIS WOULD HAPPEN.

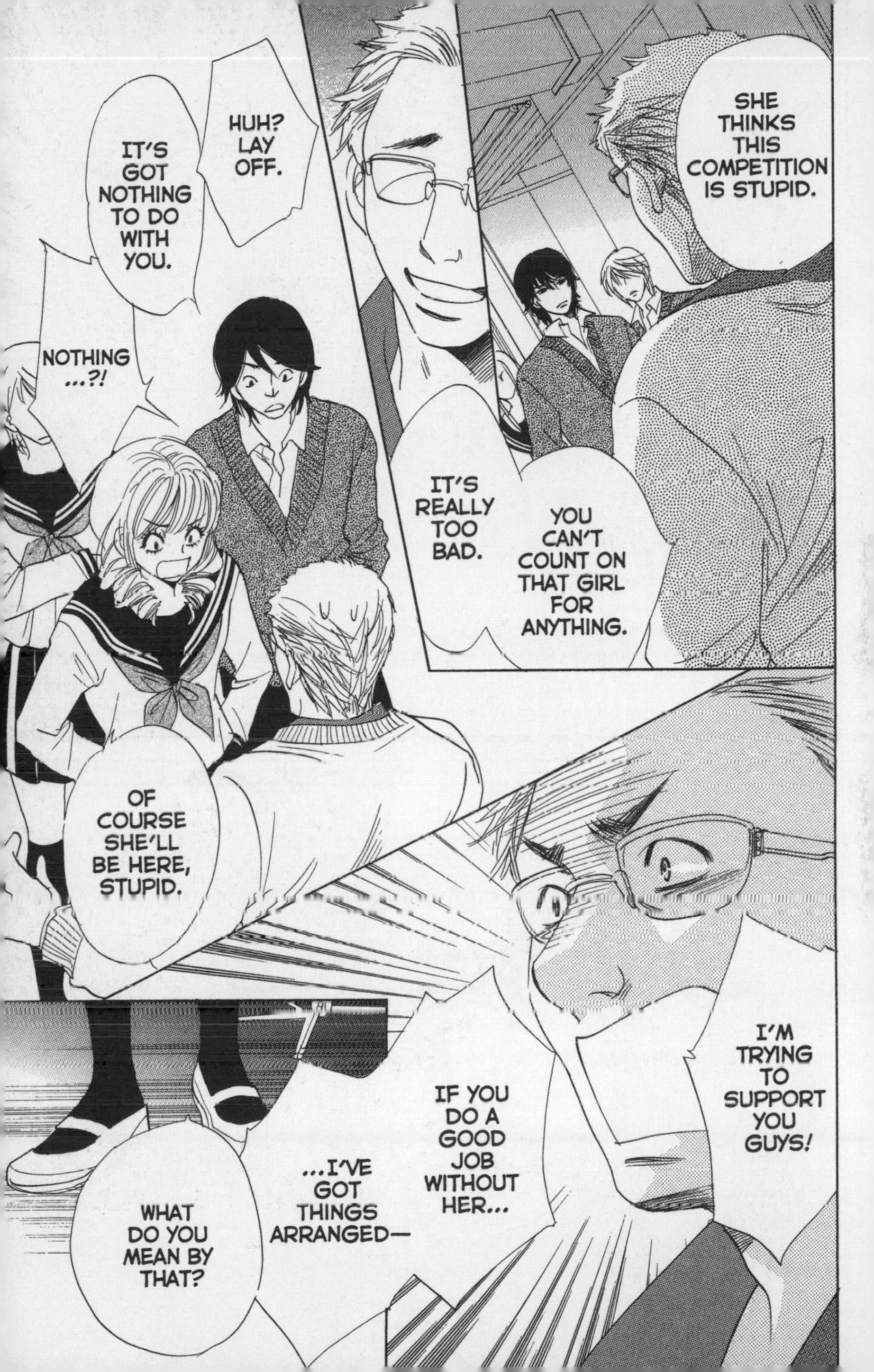
SHE THINKS THIS COMPETITION IS STUPID.
IT'S REALLY TOO BAD.
YOU CAN'T COUNT ON THAT GIRL FOR ANYTHING.
HUH? LAY OFF.
IT'S GOT NOTHING TO DO WITH YOU.
NOTHING ...?!
OF COURSE SHE'LL BE HERE, STUPID.
I'M TRYING TO SUPPORT YOU GUYS!
IF YOU DO A GOOD JOB WITHOUT HER...
...I'VE GOT THINGS ARRANGED—
WHAT DO YOU MEAN BY THAT?

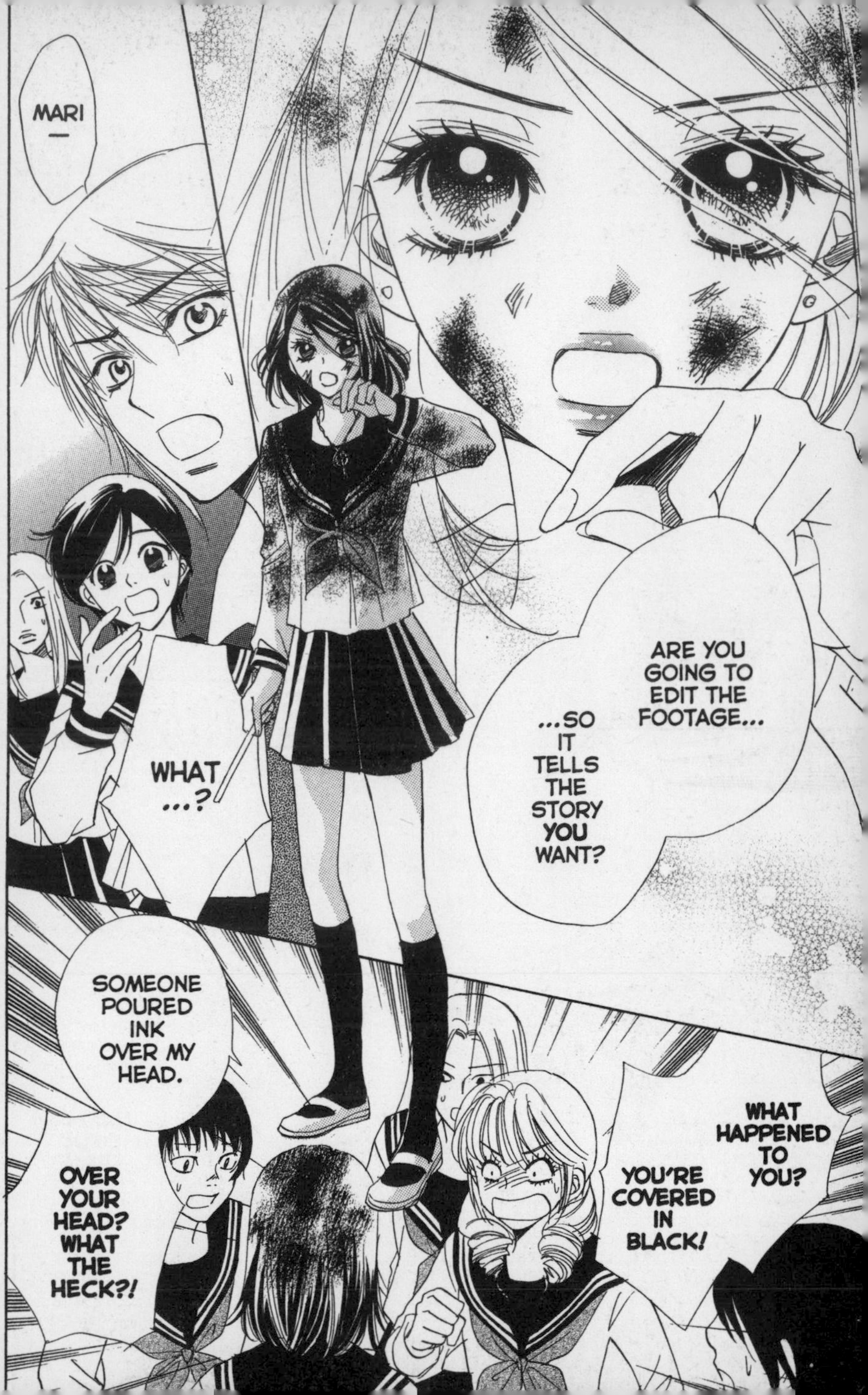
ARE YOU GOING TO EDIT THE FOOTAGE...
...SO IT TELLS THE STORY YOU WANT?
MARI —
WHAT ...?
WHAT HAPPENED TO YOU?
YOU'RE COVERED IN BLACK!
SOMEONE POURED INK OVER MY HEAD.
OVER YOUR HEAD? WHAT THE HECK?!

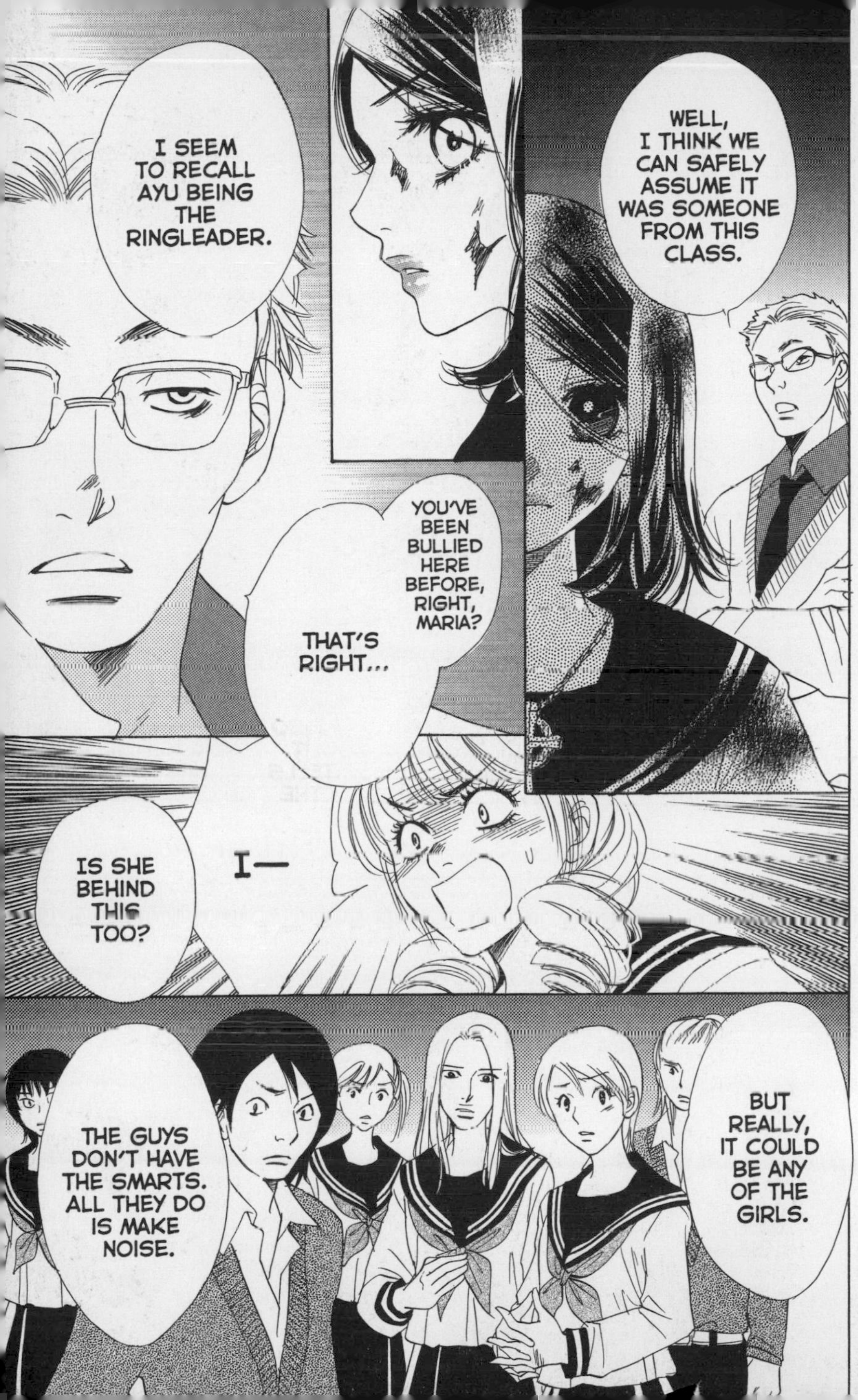
WELL, I THINK WE CAN SAFELY ASSUME IT WAS SOMEONE FROM THIS CLASS.
I SEEM TO RECALL AYU BEING THE RINGLEADER.
YOU'VE BEEN BULLIED HERE BEFORE, RIGHT, MARIA?
THAT'S RIGHT...
I—
IS SHE BEHIND THIS TOO?
BUT REALLY, IT COULD BE ANY OF THE GIRLS.
THE GUYS DON'T HAVE THE SMARTS. ALL THEY DO IS MAKE NOISE.

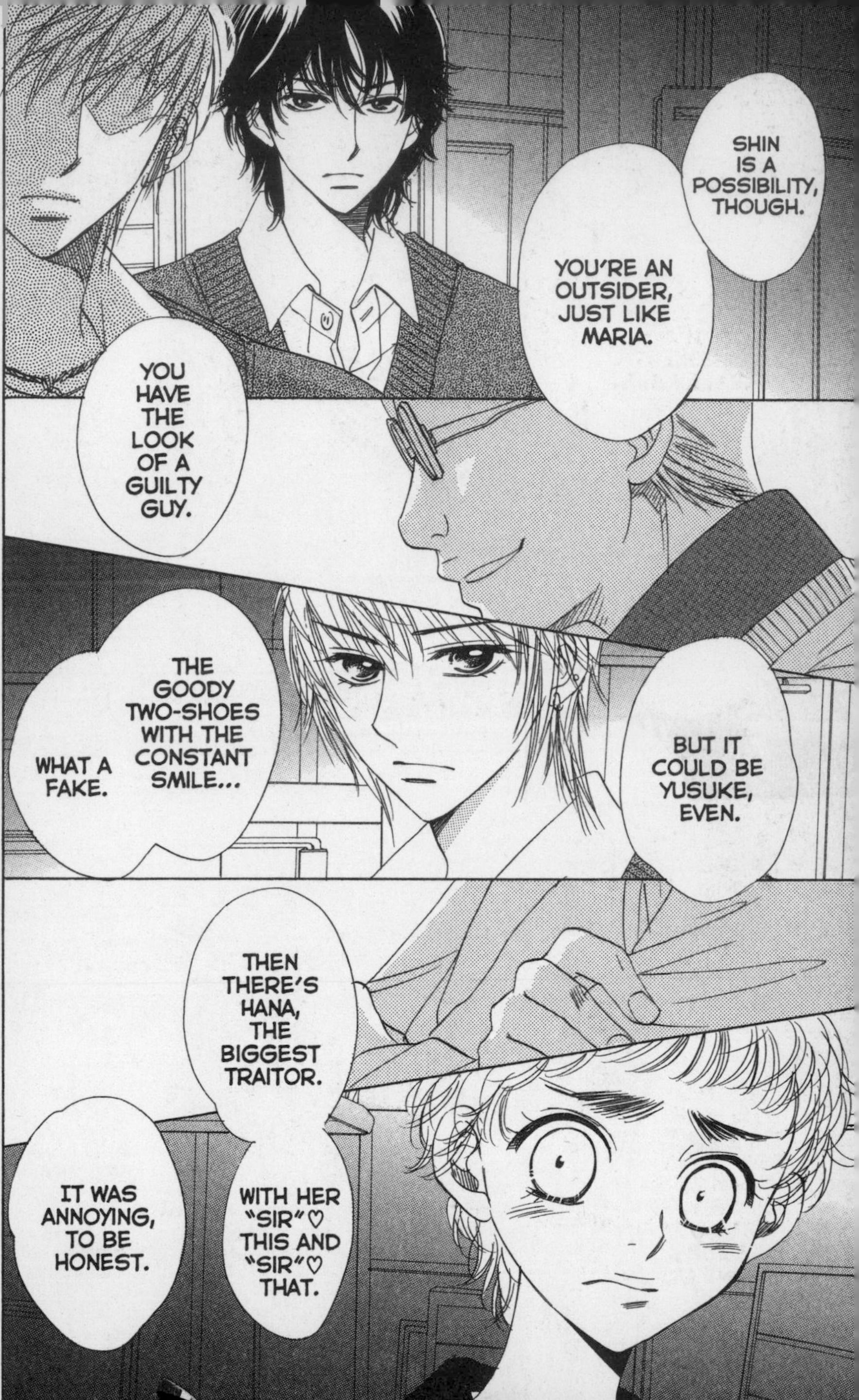
SHIN IS A POSSIBILITY, THOUGH.
YOU'RE AN OUTSIDER, JUST LIKE MARIA.
YOU HAVE THE LOOK OF A GUILTY GUY.
BUT IT COULD BE YUSUKE, EVEN.
THE GOODY TWO-SHOES WITH THE CONSTANT SMILE...
WHAT A FAKE.
THEN THERE'S HANA, THE BIGGEST TRAITOR.
WITH HER "SIR"♡ THIS AND "SIR"♡ THAT.
IT WAS ANNOYING, TO BE HONEST.

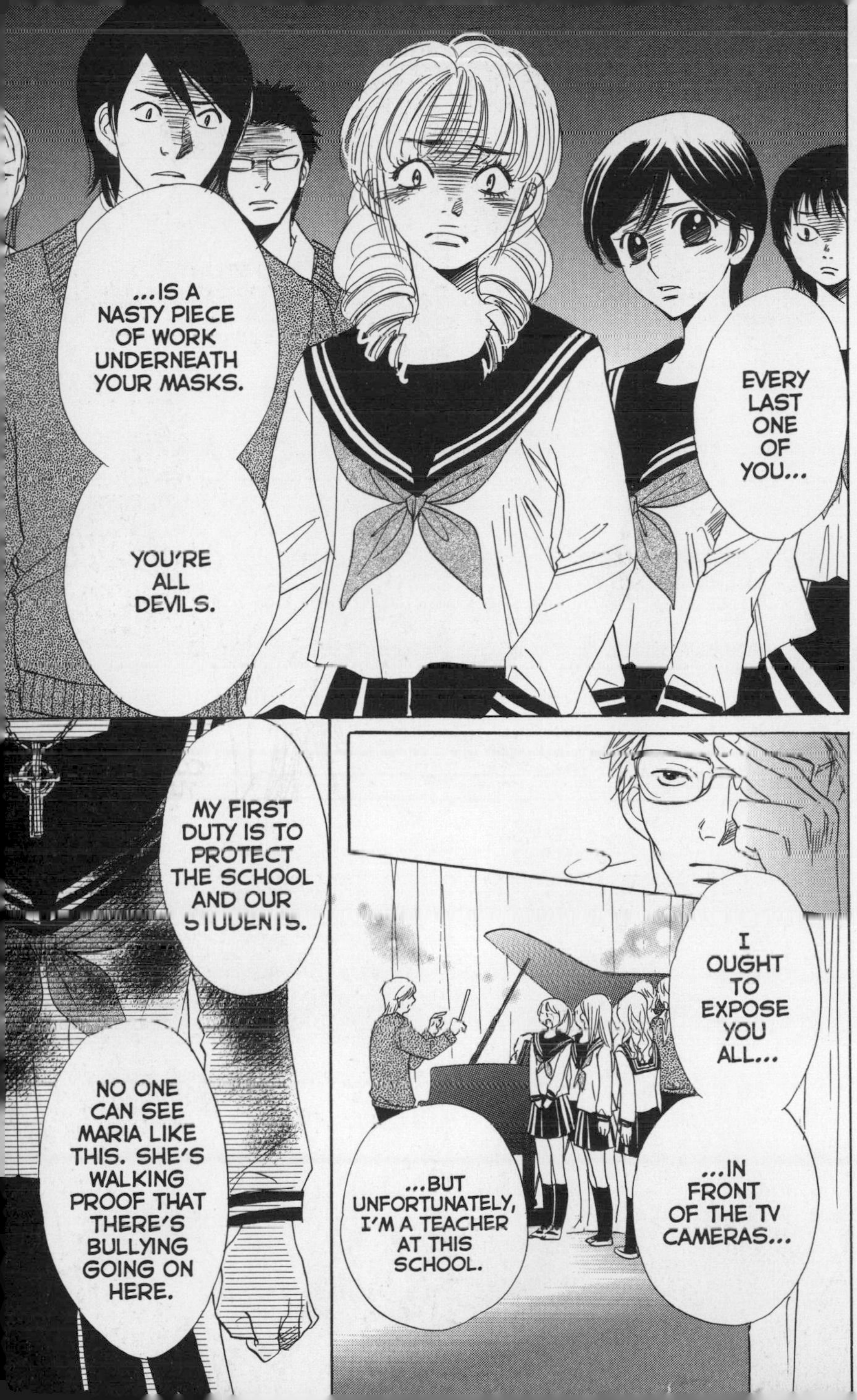
EVERY LAST ONE OF YOU...
...IS A NASTY PIECE OF WORK UNDERNEATH YOUR MASKS.
YOU'RE ALL DEVILS.
I OUGHT TO EXPOSE YOU ALL...
...IN FRONT OF THE TV CAMERAS...
...BUT UNFORTUNATELY, I'M A TEACHER AT THIS SCHOOL.
MY FIRST DUTY IS TO PROTECT THE SCHOOL AND OUR STUDENTS.
NO ONE CAN SEE MARIA LIKE THIS. SHE'S WALKING PROOF THAT THERE'S BULLYING GOING ON HERE.

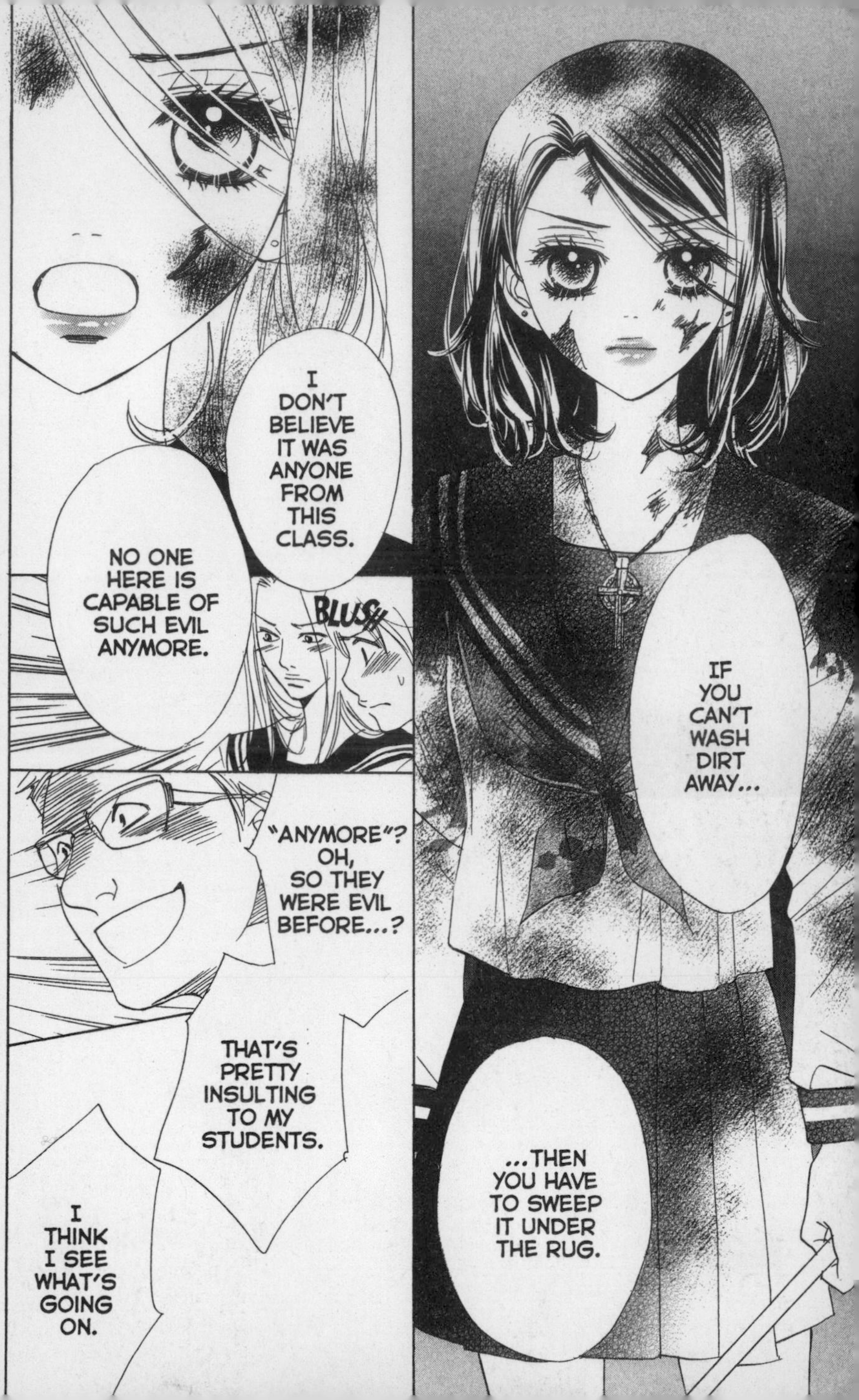
IF YOU CAN'T WASH DIRT AWAY...
...THEN YOU HAVE TO SWEEP IT UNDER THE RUG.
I DON'T BELIEVE IT WAS ANYONE FROM THIS CLASS.
NO ONE HERE IS CAPABLE OF SUCH EVIL ANYMORE.
BLUSH
"ANYMORE"? OH, SO THEY WERE EVIL BEFORE...?
THAT'S PRETTY INSULTING TO MY STUDENTS.
I THINK I SEE WHAT'S GOING ON.

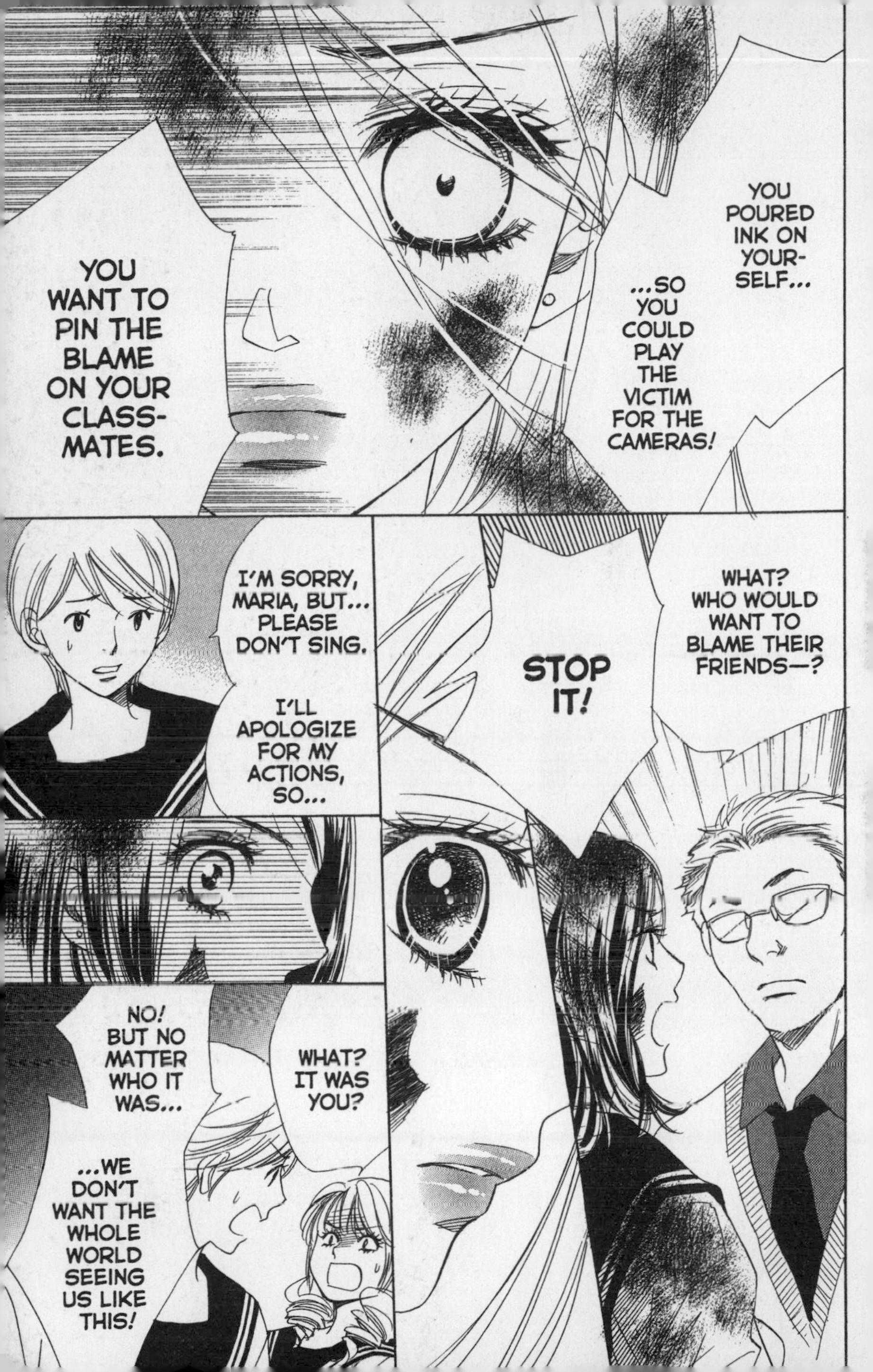
YOU POURED INK ON YOUR-SELF...
...SO YOU COULD PLAY THE VICTIM FOR THE CAMERAS!
YOU WANT TO PIN THE BLAME ON YOUR CLASSMATES.
WHAT? WHO WOULD WANT TO BLAME THEIR FRIENDS—?
STOP IT!
I'M SORRY, MARIA, BUT... PLEASE DON'T SING.
I'LL APOLOGIZE FOR MY ACTIONS, SO...
WHAT? IT WAS YOU?
NO! BUT NO MATTER WHO IT WAS...
...WE DON'T WANT THE WHOLE WORLD SEEING US LIKE THIS!

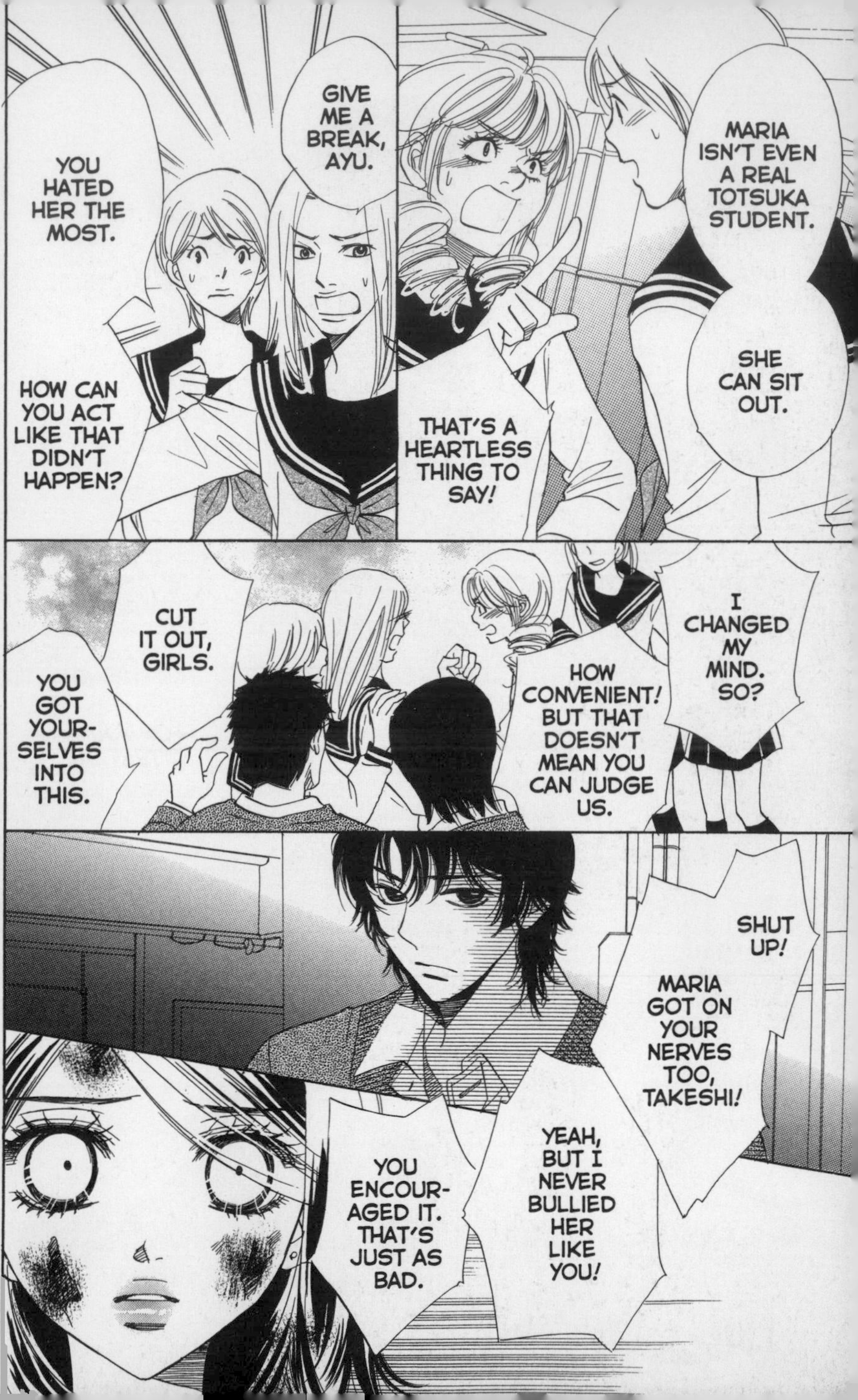
MARIA ISN'T EVEN A REAL TOTSUKA STUDENT.
SHE CAN SIT OUT.
THAT'S A HEARTLESS THING TO SAY!
GIVE ME A BREAK, AYU.
YOU HATED HER THE MOST.
HOW CAN YOU ACT LIKE THAT DIDN'T HAPPEN?
I CHANGED MY MIND. SO?
HOW CONVENIENT! BUT THAT DOESN'T MEAN YOU CAN JUDGE US.
CUT IT OUT, GIRLS.
YOU GOT YOURSELVES INTO THIS.
SHUT UP!
MARIA GOT ON YOUR NERVES TOO, TAKESHI!
YEAH, BUT I NEVER BULLIED HER LIKE YOU!
YOU ENCOURAGED IT. THAT'S JUST AS BAD.

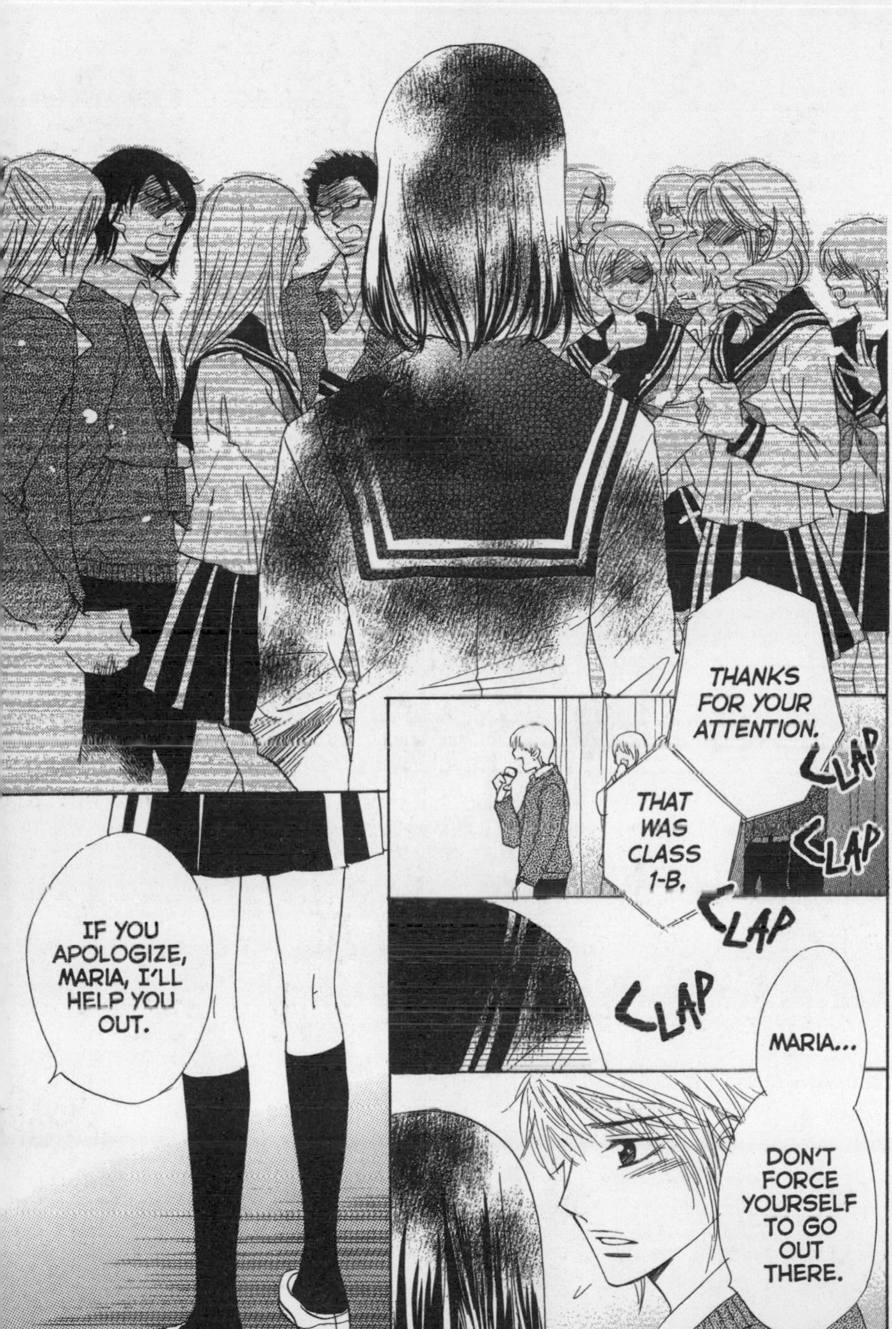
THANKS FOR YOUR ATTENTION.
CLAP
CLAP
THAT WAS CLASS 1-B.
CLAP
CLAP
MARIA...
DON'T FORCE YOURSELF TO GO OUT THERE.
IF YOU APOLOGIZE, MARIA, I'LL HELP YOU OUT.

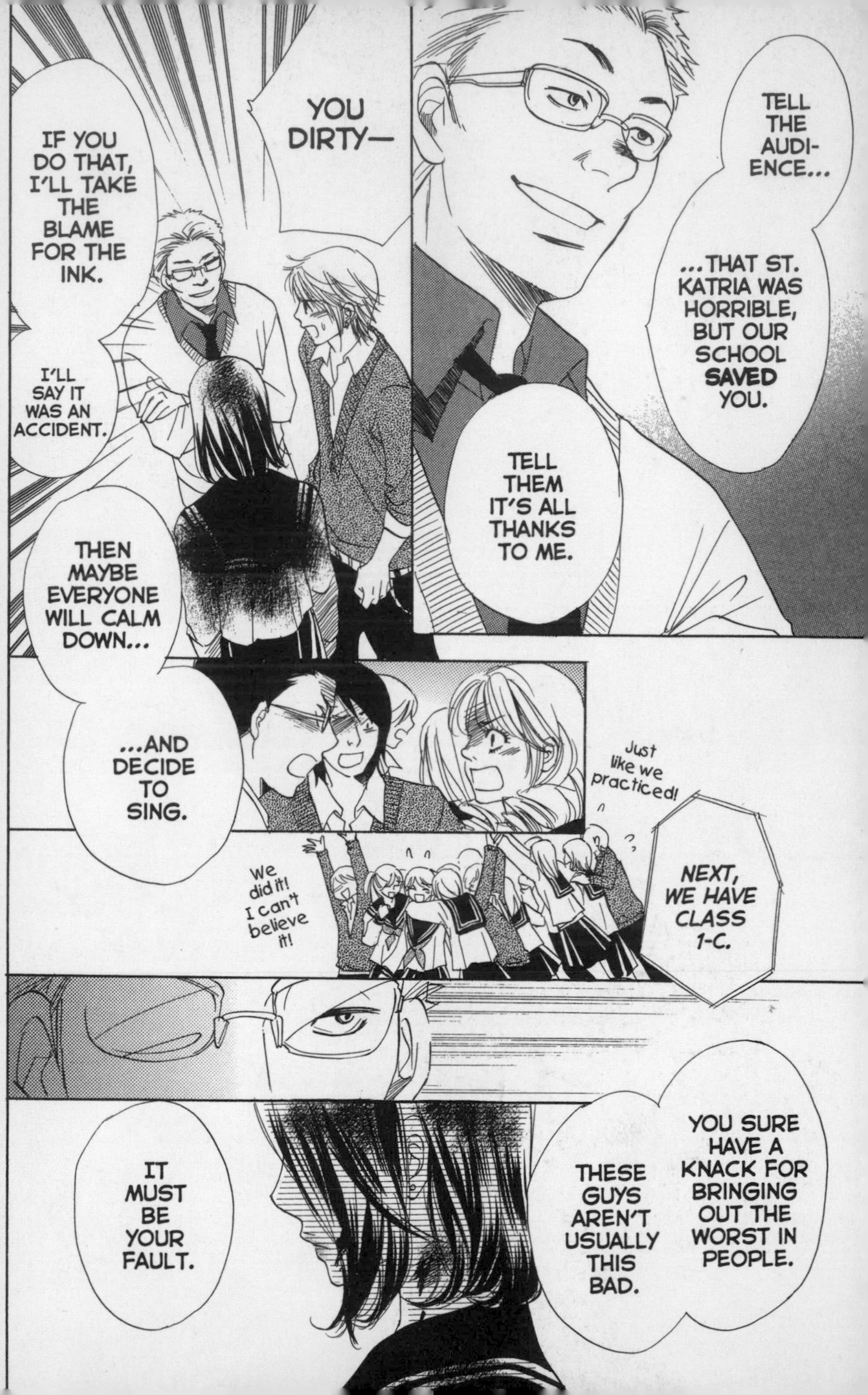
TELL THE AUDIENCE...
...THAT ST. KATRIA WAS HORRIBLE, BUT OUR SCHOOL **SAVED** YOU.
TELL THEM IT'S ALL THANKS TO ME.
YOU DIRTY—
IF YOU DO THAT, I'LL TAKE THE BLAME FOR THE INK.
I'LL SAY IT WAS AN ACCIDENT.
THEN MAYBE EVERYONE WILL CALM DOWN...
...AND DECIDE TO SING.
Just like we practiced!
NEXT, WE HAVE CLASS 1-C.
We did it! I can't believe it!
YOU SURE HAVE A KNACK FOR BRINGING OUT THE WORST IN PEOPLE.
THESE GUYS AREN'T USUALLY THIS BAD.
IT MUST BE YOUR FAULT.

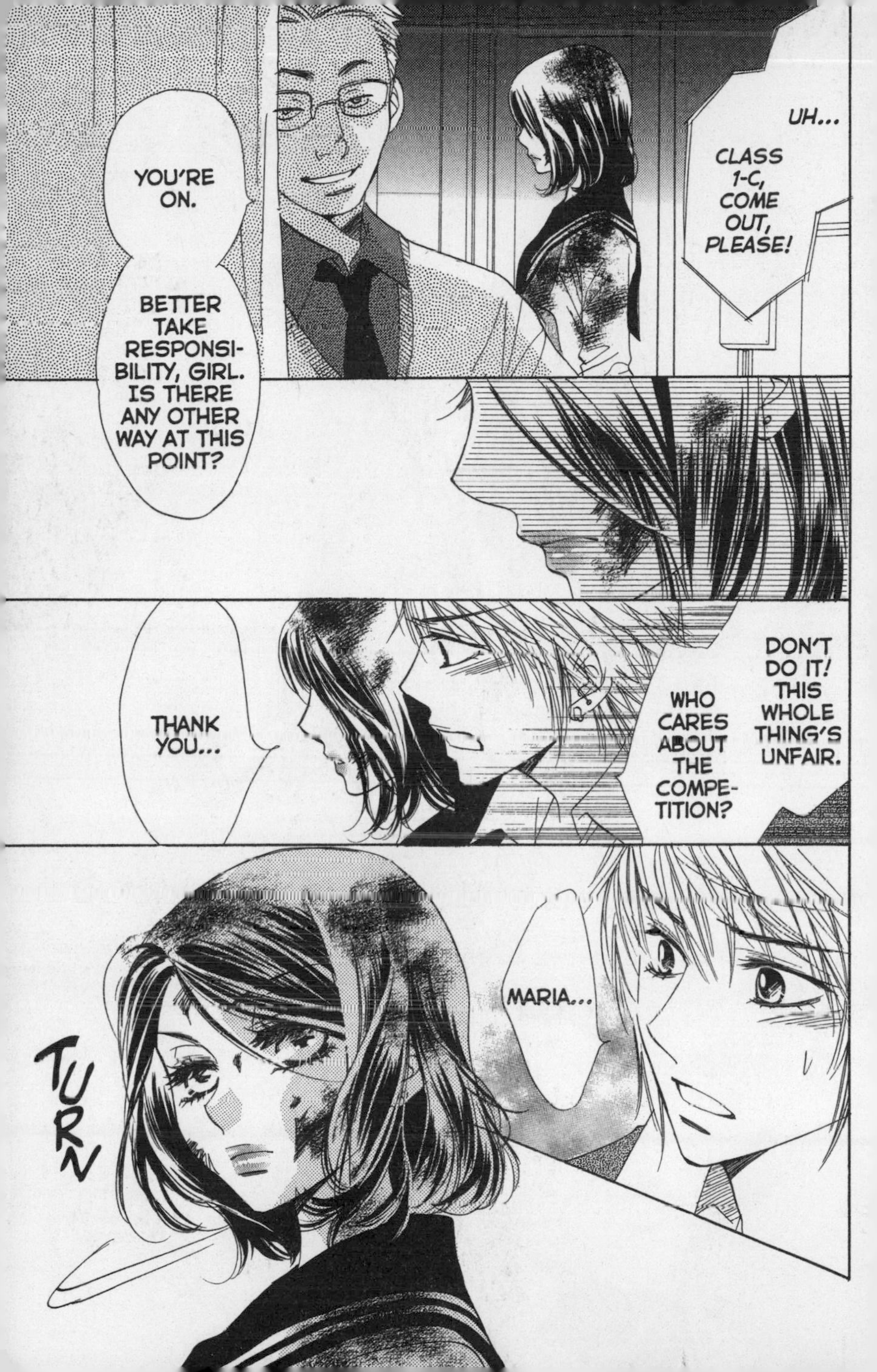
UH...
CLASS 1-C, COME OUT, PLEASE!
YOU'RE ON.
BETTER TAKE RESPONSIBILITY, GIRL. IS THERE ANY OTHER WAY AT THIS POINT?
DON'T DO IT! THIS WHOLE THING'S UNFAIR.
WHO CARES ABOUT THE COMPETITION?
THANK YOU...
MARIA...
TURN

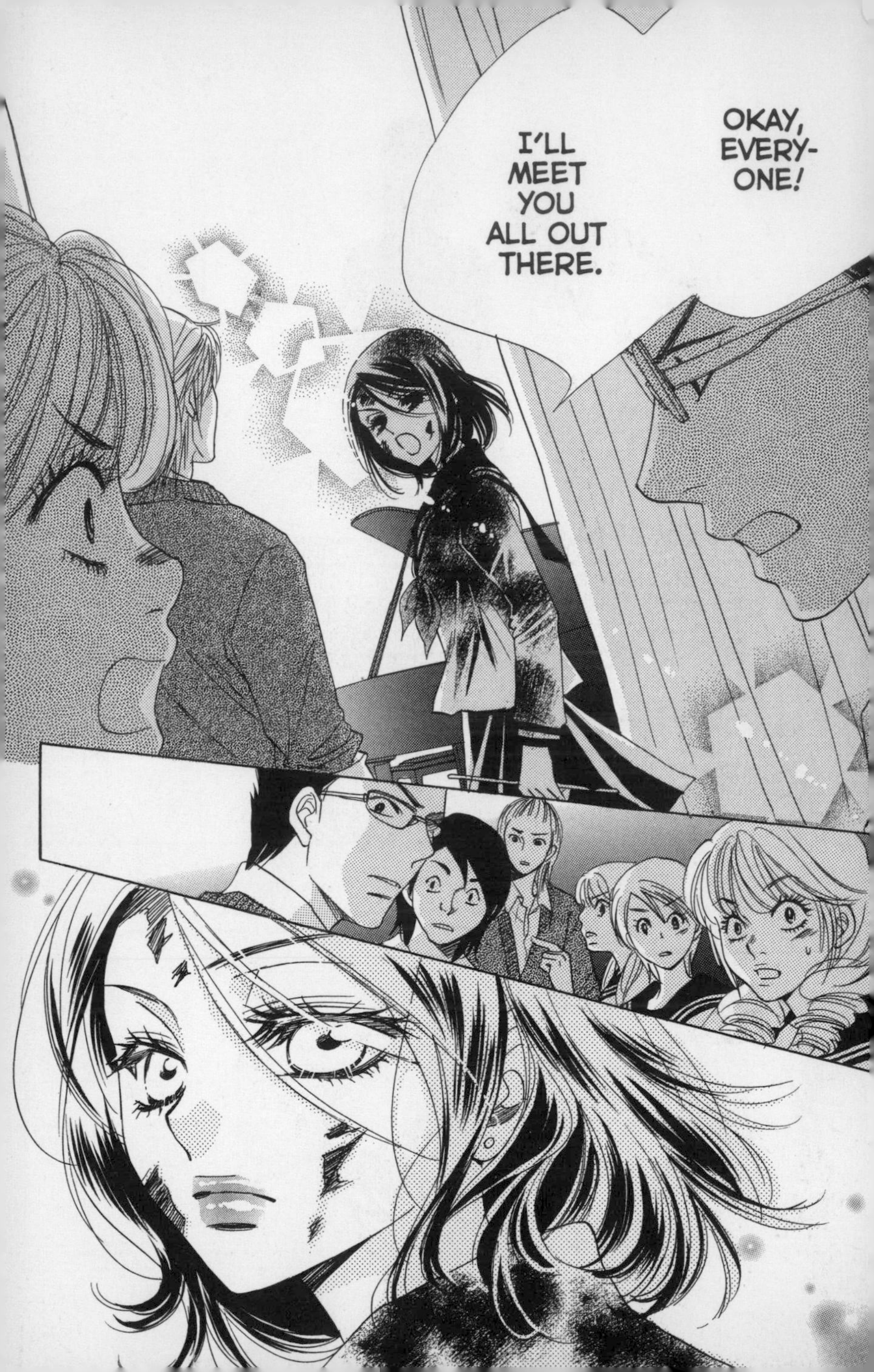
OKAY, EVERYONE!
I'LL MEET YOU ALL OUT THERE.

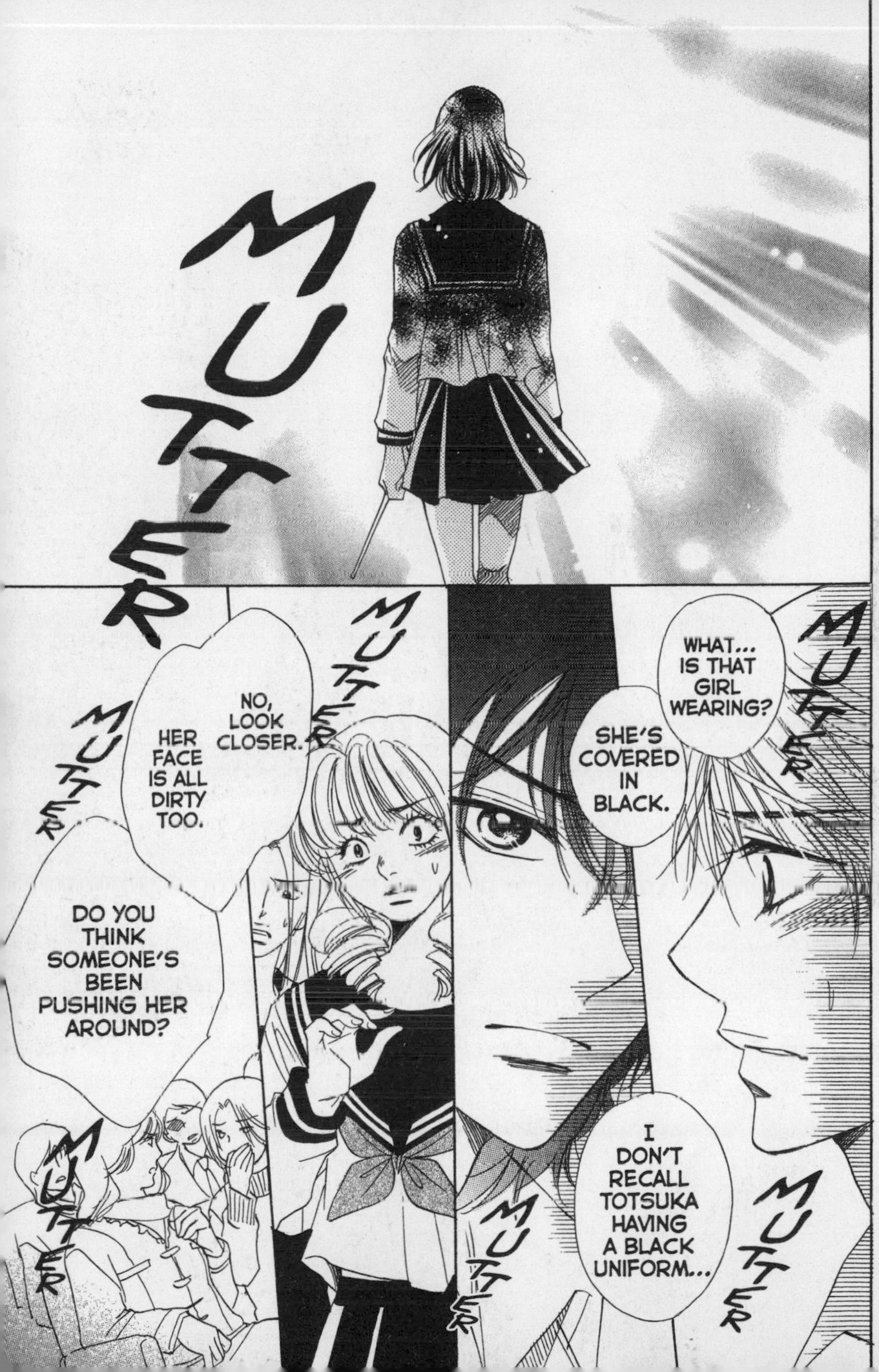
MUTTER
MUTTER
WHAT... IS THAT GIRL WEARING?
SHE'S COVERED IN BLACK.
I DON'T RECALL TOTSUKA HAVING A BLACK UNIFORM...
MUTTER
MUTTER
MUTTER
NO, LOOK CLOSER.
HER FACE IS ALL DIRTY TOO.
MUTTER
DO YOU THINK SOMEONE'S BEEN PUSHING HER AROUND?
MUTTER

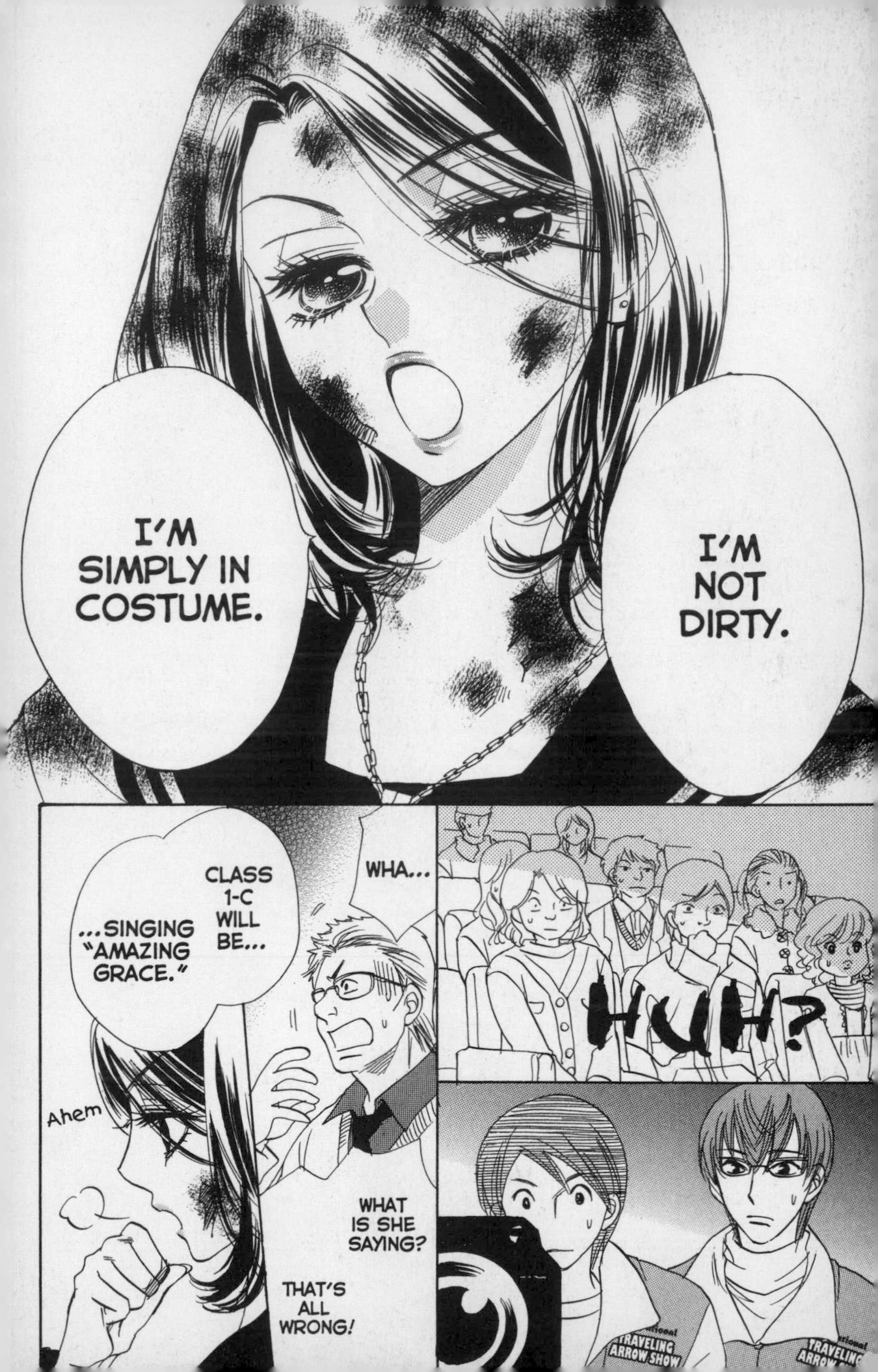
I'M NOT DIRTY.
I'M SIMPLY IN COSTUME.
HUH?
WHA...
CLASS 1-C WILL BE...
...SINGING "AMAZING GRACE."
Ahem
WHAT IS SHE SAYING?
THAT'S ALL WRONG!
TRAVELING ARROW SHOW
TRAVELING ARROW

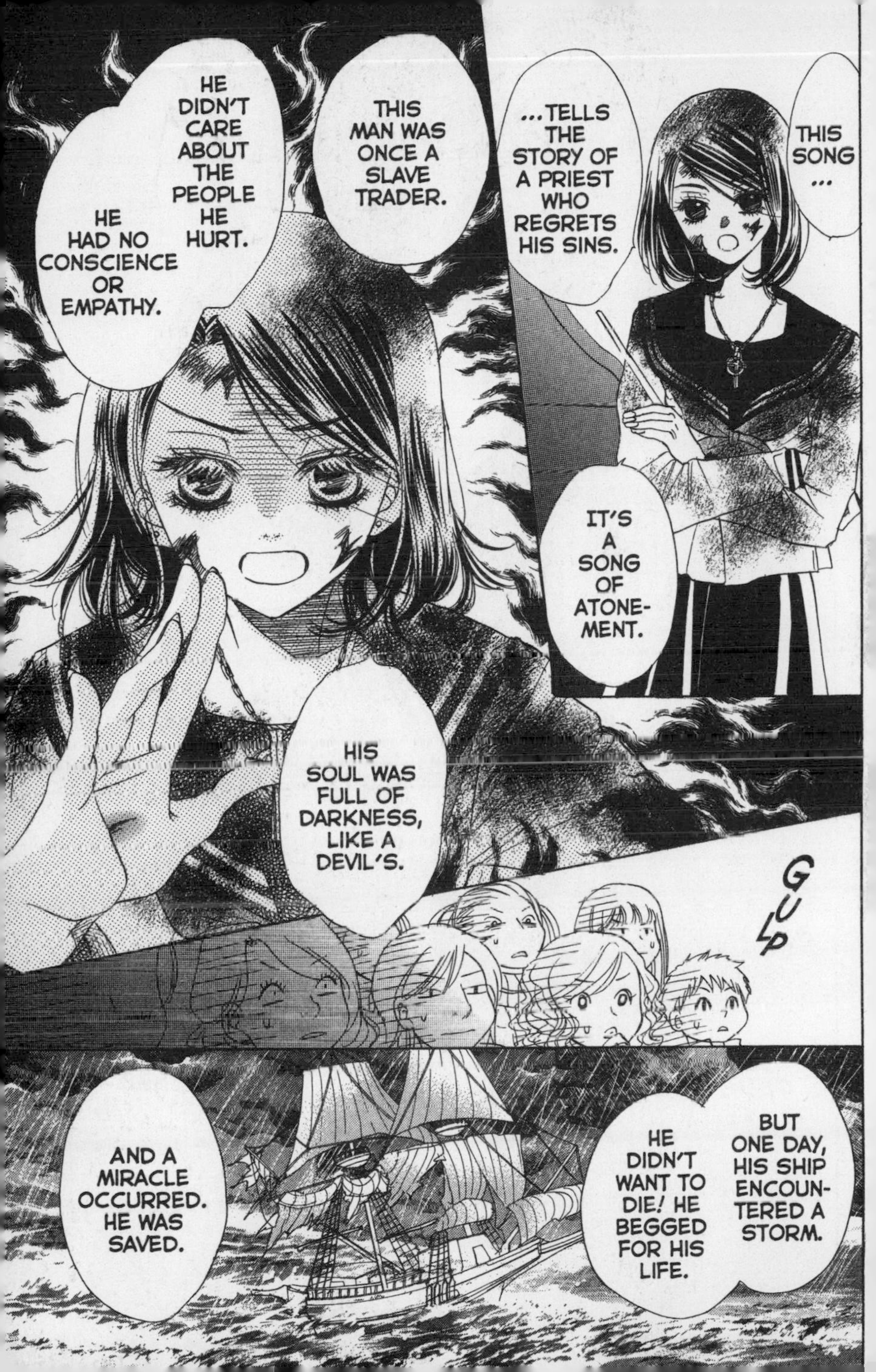
THIS SONG ...
...TELLS THE STORY OF A PRIEST WHO REGRETS HIS SINS.
IT'S A SONG OF ATONE-MENT.
THIS MAN WAS ONCE A SLAVE TRADER.
HE DIDN'T CARE ABOUT THE PEOPLE HE HURT.
HE HAD NO CONSCIENCE OR EMPATHY.
HIS SOUL WAS FULL OF DARKNESS, LIKE A DEVIL'S.
GULP
BUT ONE DAY, HIS SHIP ENCOUN-TERED A STORM.
HE DIDN'T WANT TO DIE! HE BEGGED FOR HIS LIFE.
AND A MIRACLE OCCURRED. HE WAS SAVED.

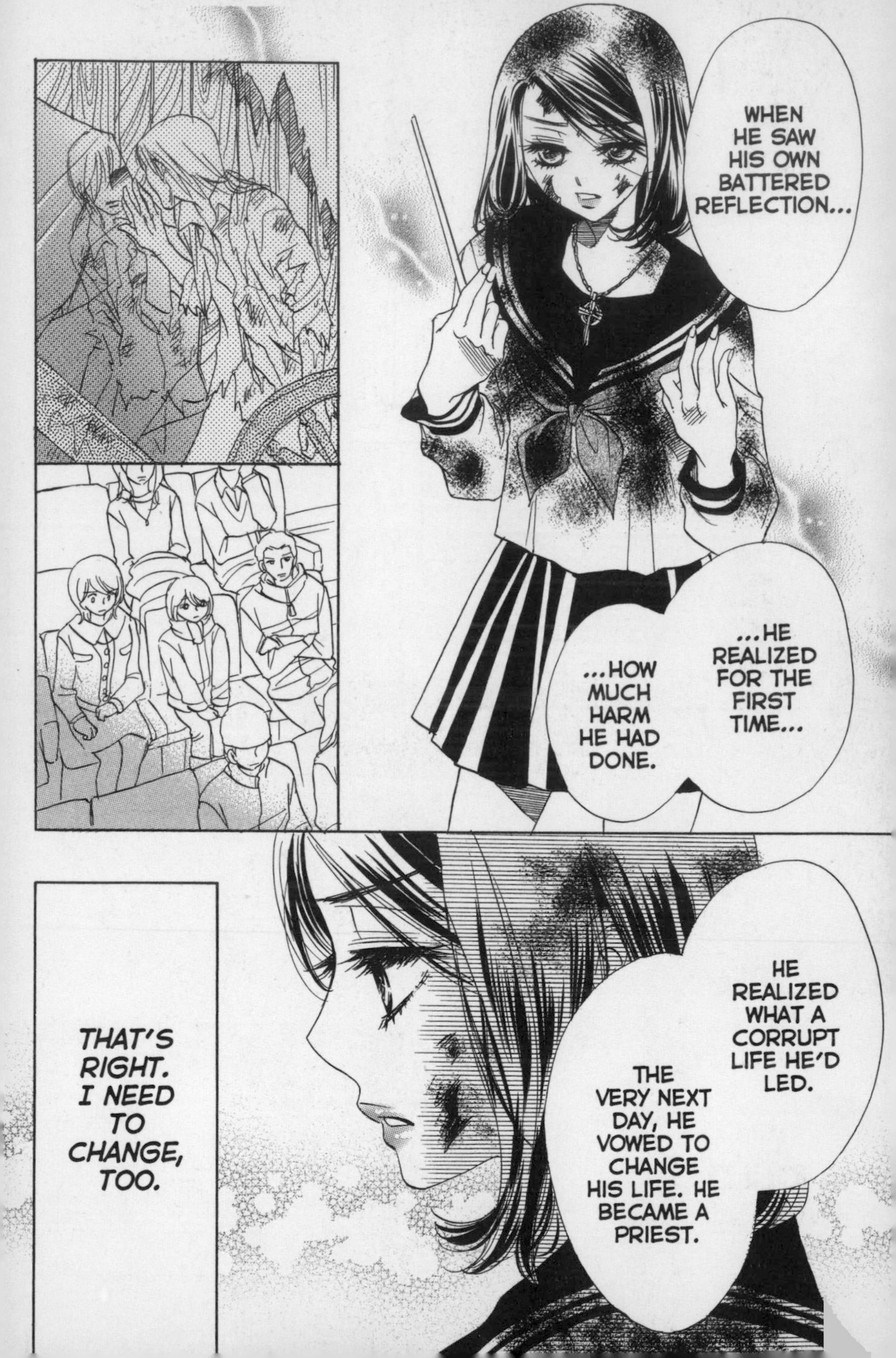
WHEN HE SAW HIS OWN BATTERED REFLECTION...
...HE REALIZED FOR THE FIRST TIME...
...HOW MUCH HARM HE HAD DONE.
HE REALIZED WHAT A CORRUPT LIFE HE'D LED.
THE VERY NEXT DAY, HE VOWED TO CHANGE HIS LIFE. HE BECAME A PRIEST.
THAT'S RIGHT. I NEED TO CHANGE, TOO.

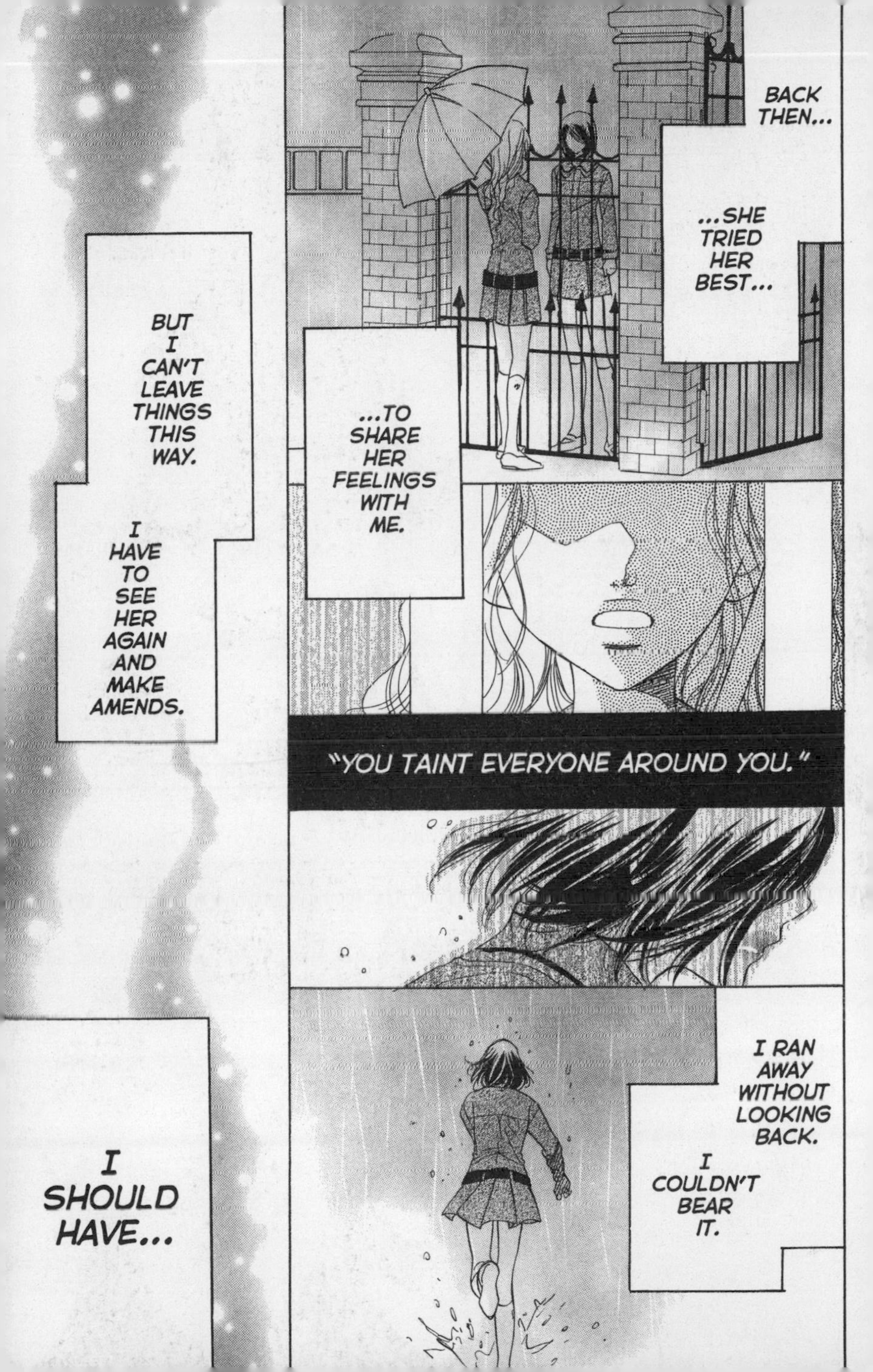
BACK THEN...
...SHE TRIED HER BEST...
...TO SHARE HER FEELINGS WITH ME.
"YOU TAINT EVERYONE AROUND YOU."
I RAN AWAY WITHOUT LOOKING BACK.
I COULDN'T BEAR IT.
BUT I CAN'T LEAVE THINGS THIS WAY.
I HAVE TO SEE HER AGAIN AND MAKE AMENDS.
I SHOULD HAVE...

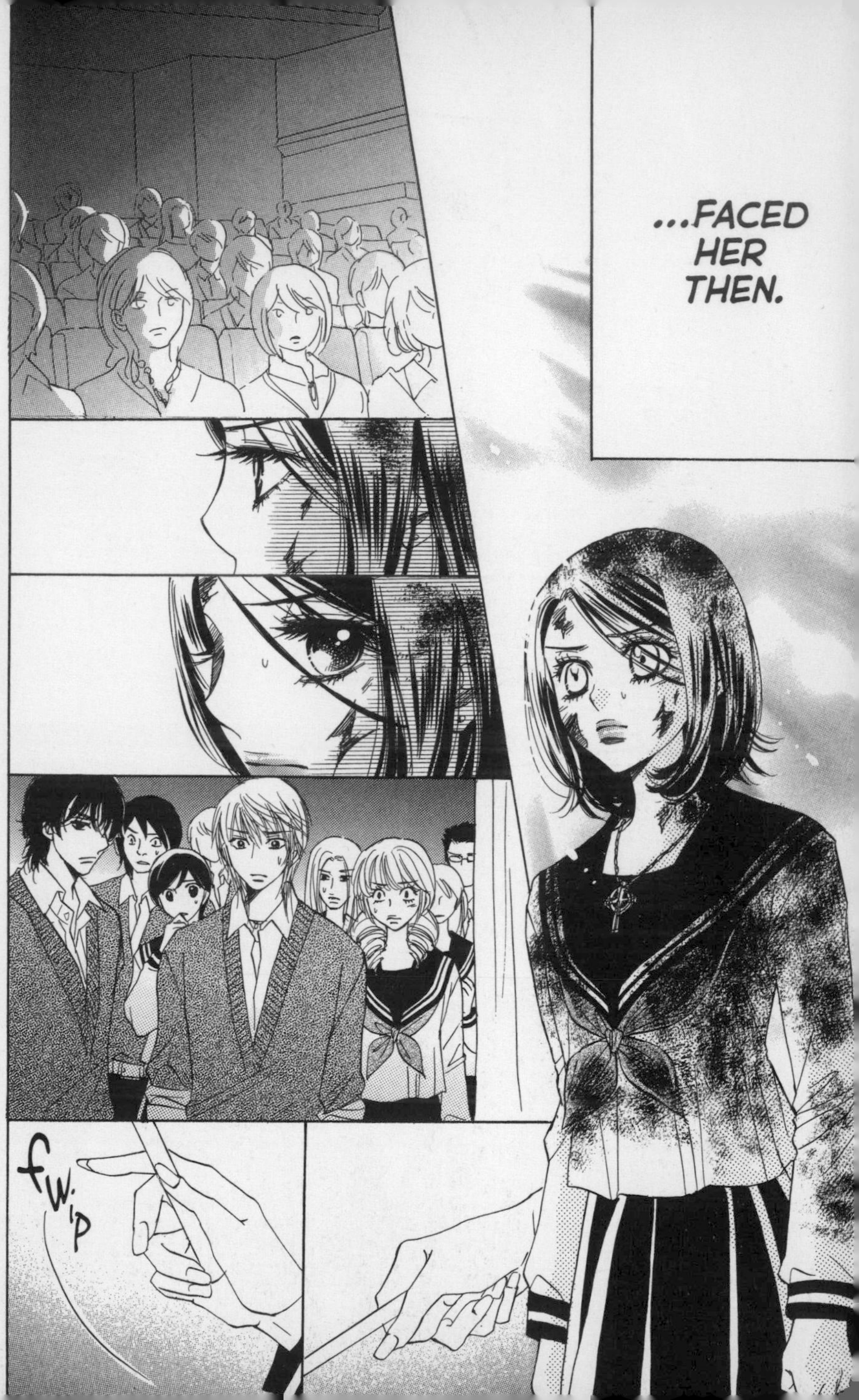
...FACED
HER
THEN.
FWIP

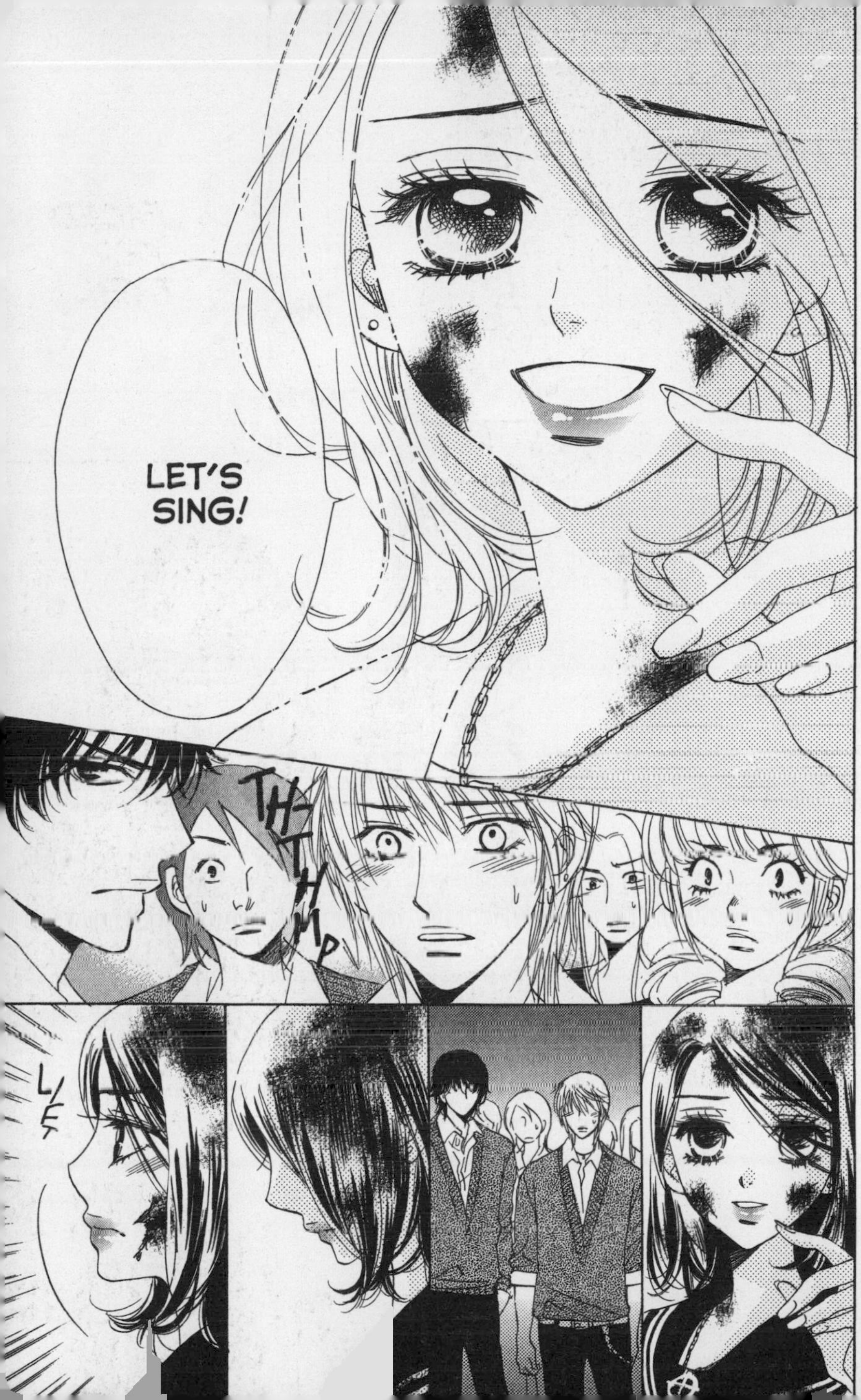
LET'S SING!
TH-THMP
LIFT

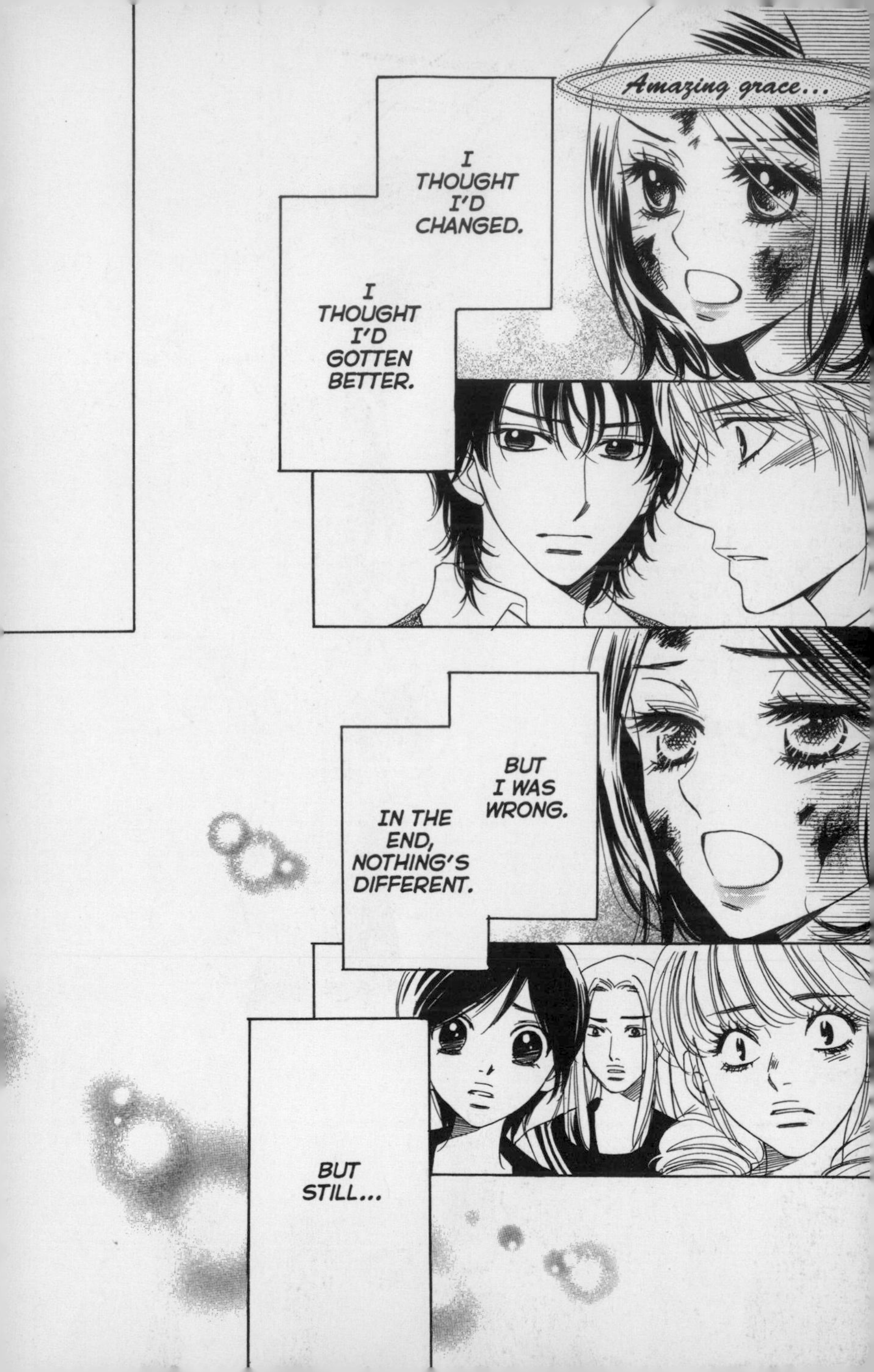
Amazing grace...
I THOUGHT I'D CHANGED.
I THOUGHT I'D GOTTEN BETTER.
BUT I WAS WRONG.
IN THE END, NOTHING'S DIFFERENT.
BUT STILL...

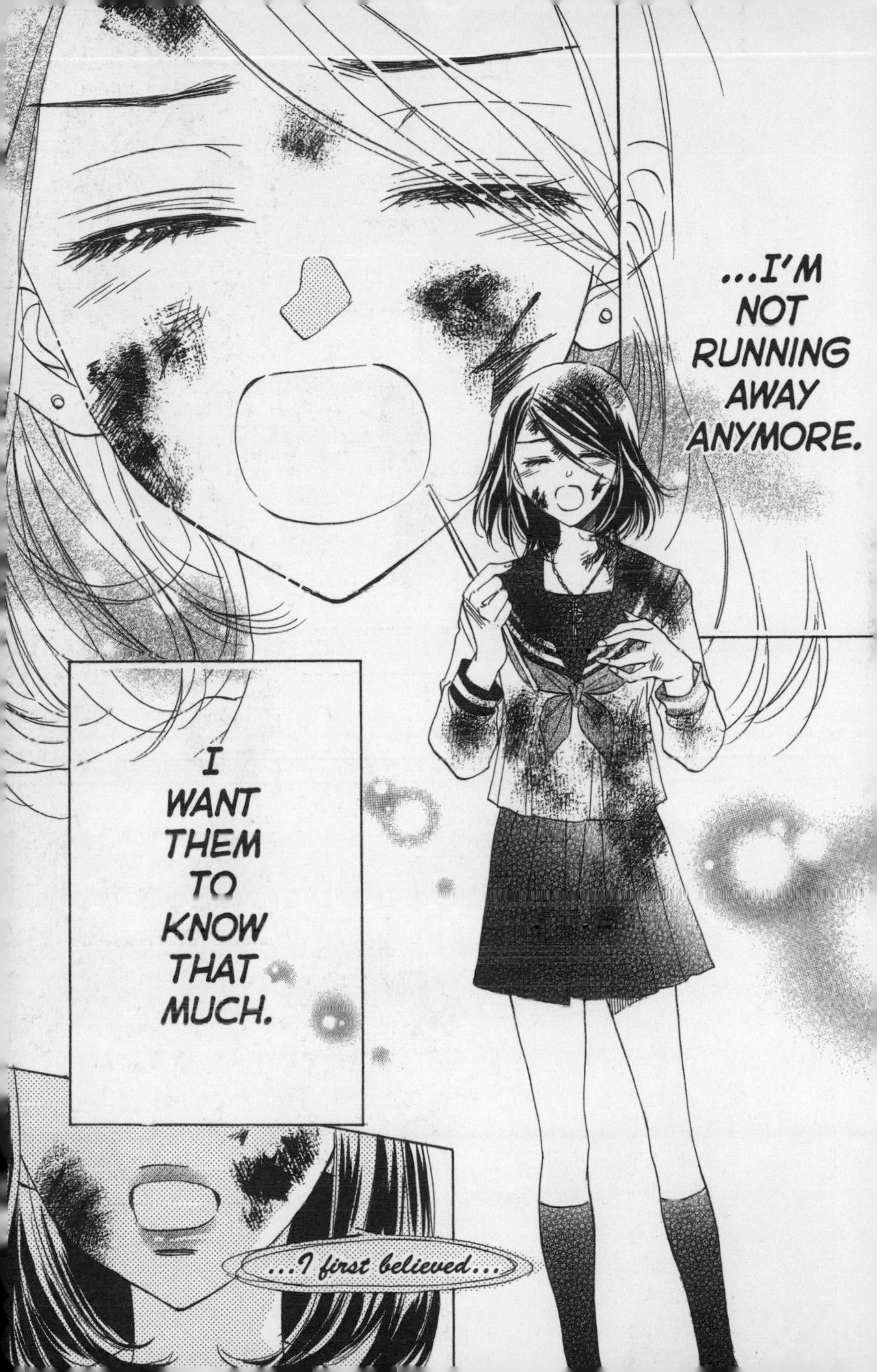
...I'M NOT RUNNING AWAY ANYMORE.
I WANT THEM TO KNOW THAT MUCH.
...I first believed...

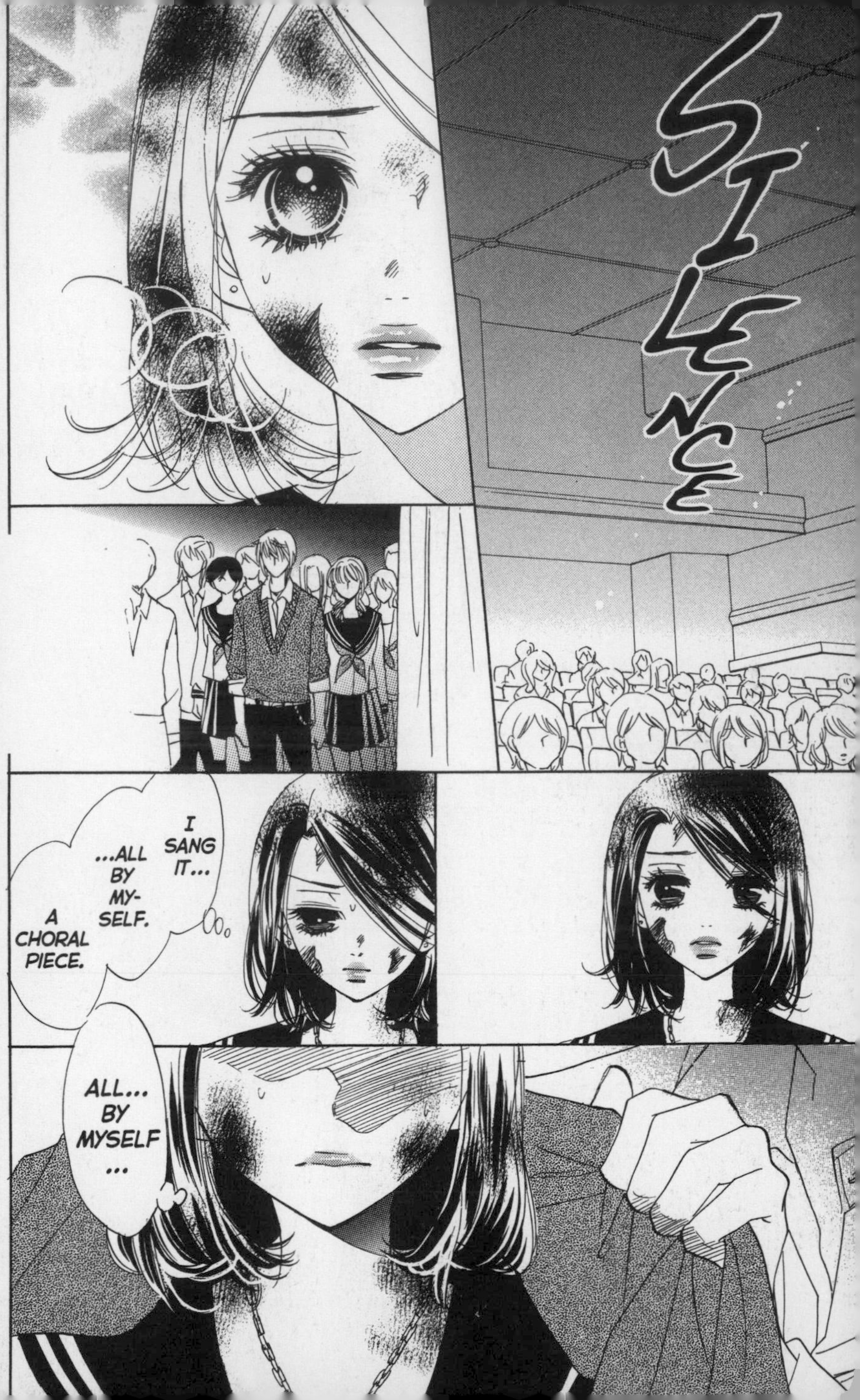
SILENCE
I SANG IT...
...ALL BY MYSELF.
A CHORAL PIECE.
ALL... BY MYSELF...

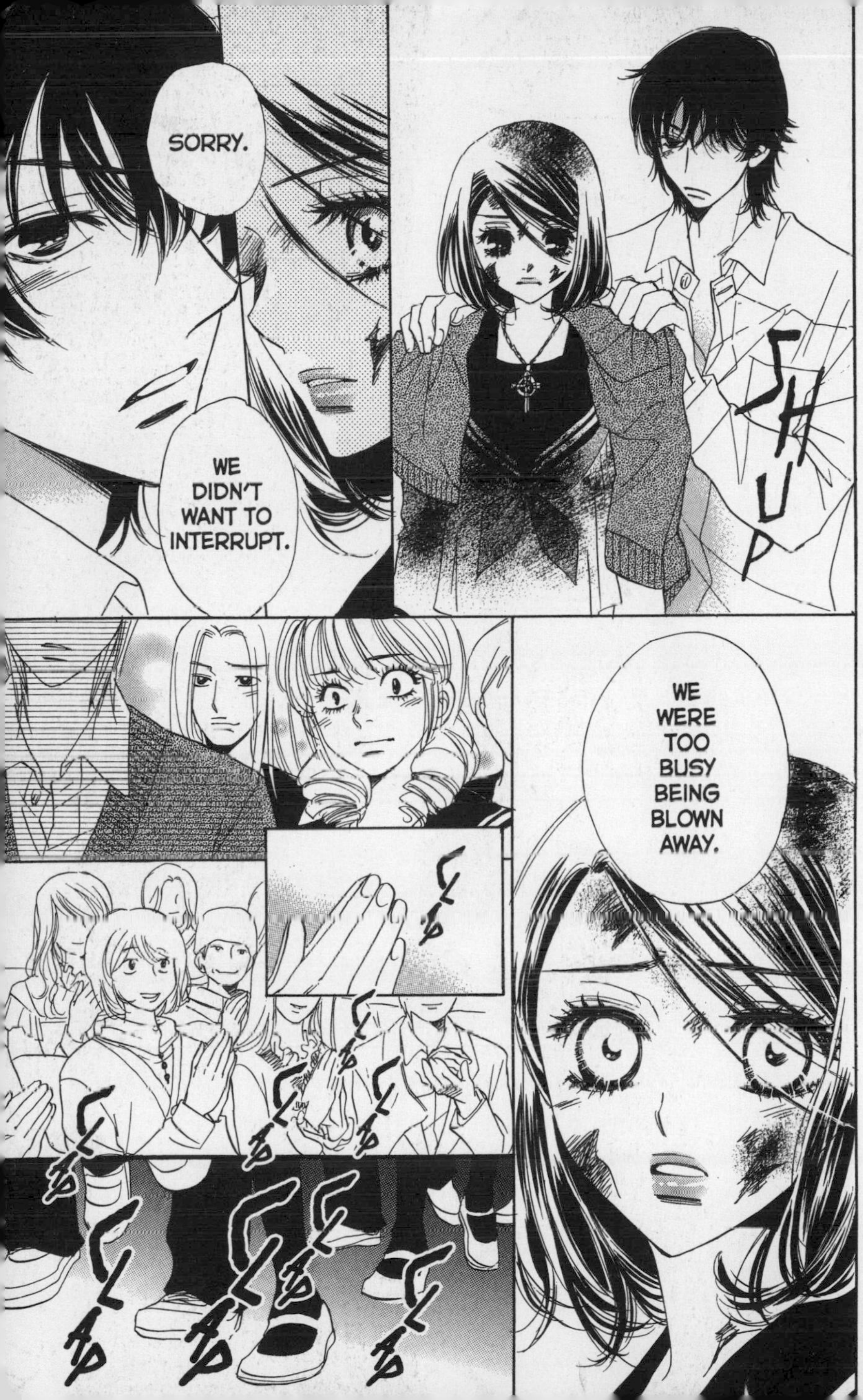
SHUP
SORRY.
WE DIDN'T WANT TO INTERRUPT.
WE WERE TOO BUSY BEING BLOWN AWAY.
CLAP
CLAP CLAP CLAP CLAP CLAP CLAP CLAP CLAP

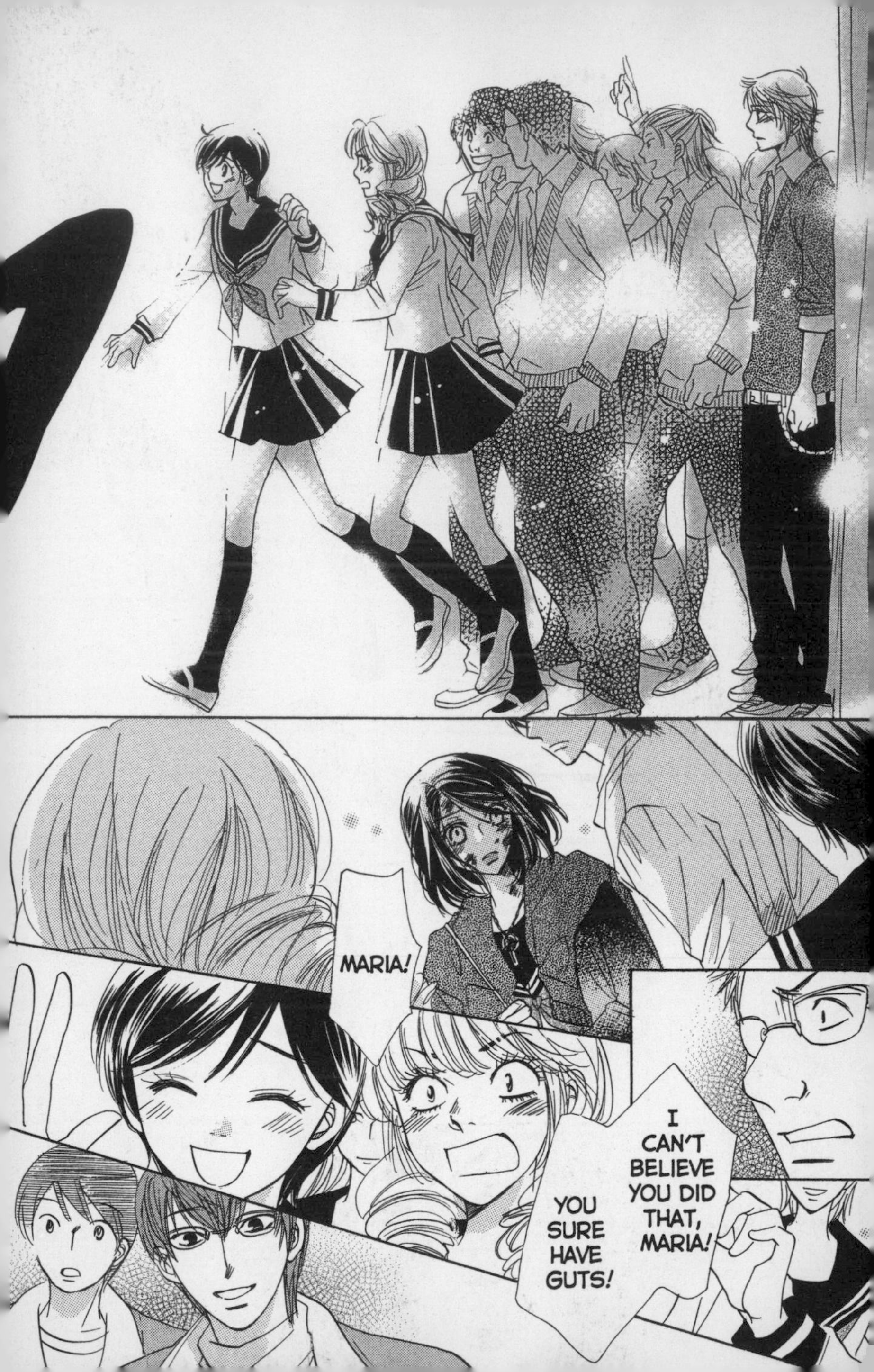
MARIA!
I CAN'T BELIEVE YOU DID THAT, MARIA!
YOU SURE HAVE GUTS!

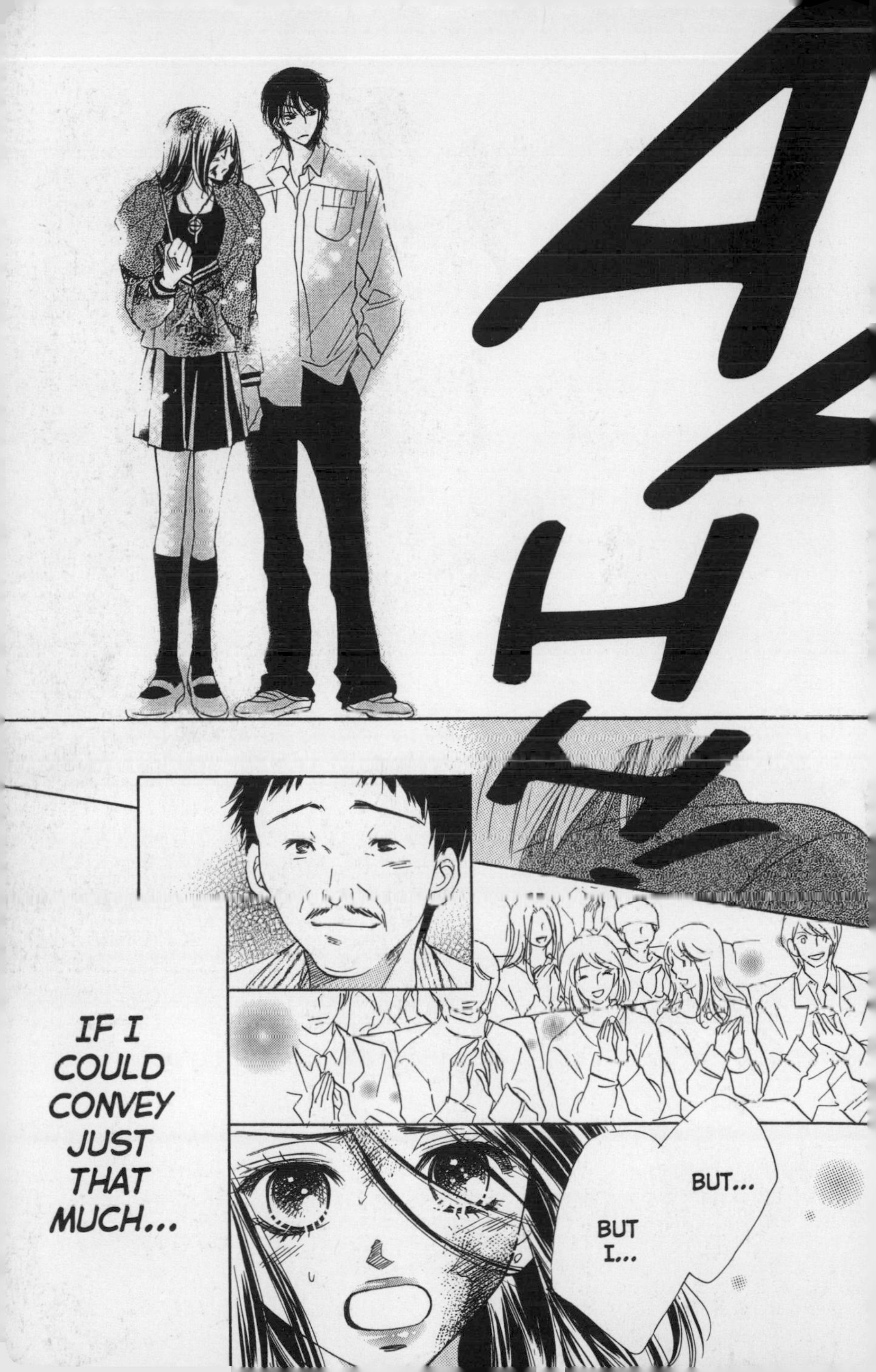

AAH!
BUT...
BUT I...
IF I COULD CONVEY JUST THAT MUCH...

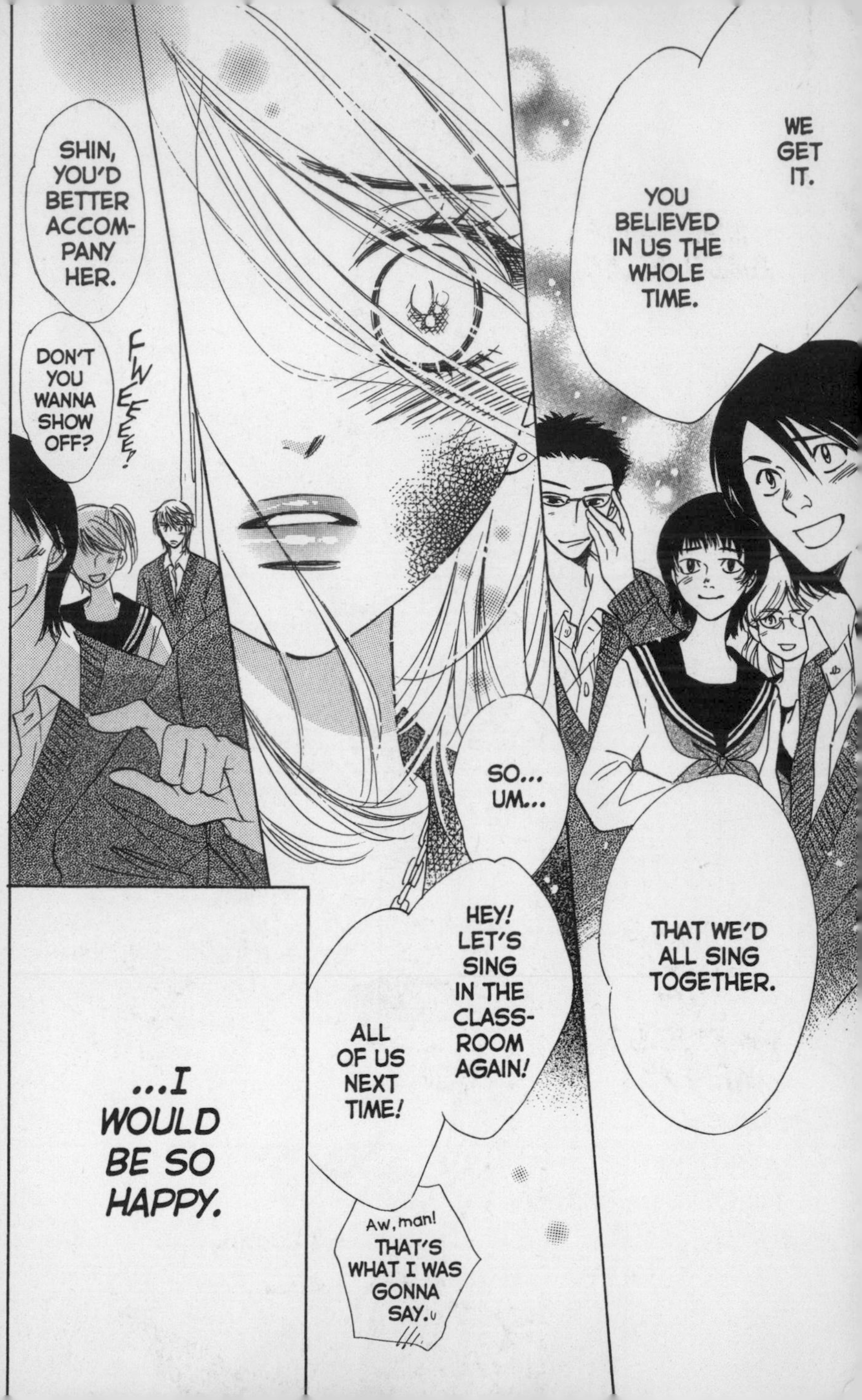
WE GET IT.
YOU BELIEVED IN US THE WHOLE TIME.
SO... UM...
THAT WE'D ALL SING TOGETHER.
HEY! LET'S SING IN THE CLASSROOM AGAIN!
ALL OF US NEXT TIME!
Aw, man! THAT'S WHAT I WAS GONNA SAY.
SHIN, YOU'D BETTER ACCOMPANY HER.
DON'T YOU WANNA SHOW OFF?
FWEEEE!
...I WOULD BE SO HAPPY.

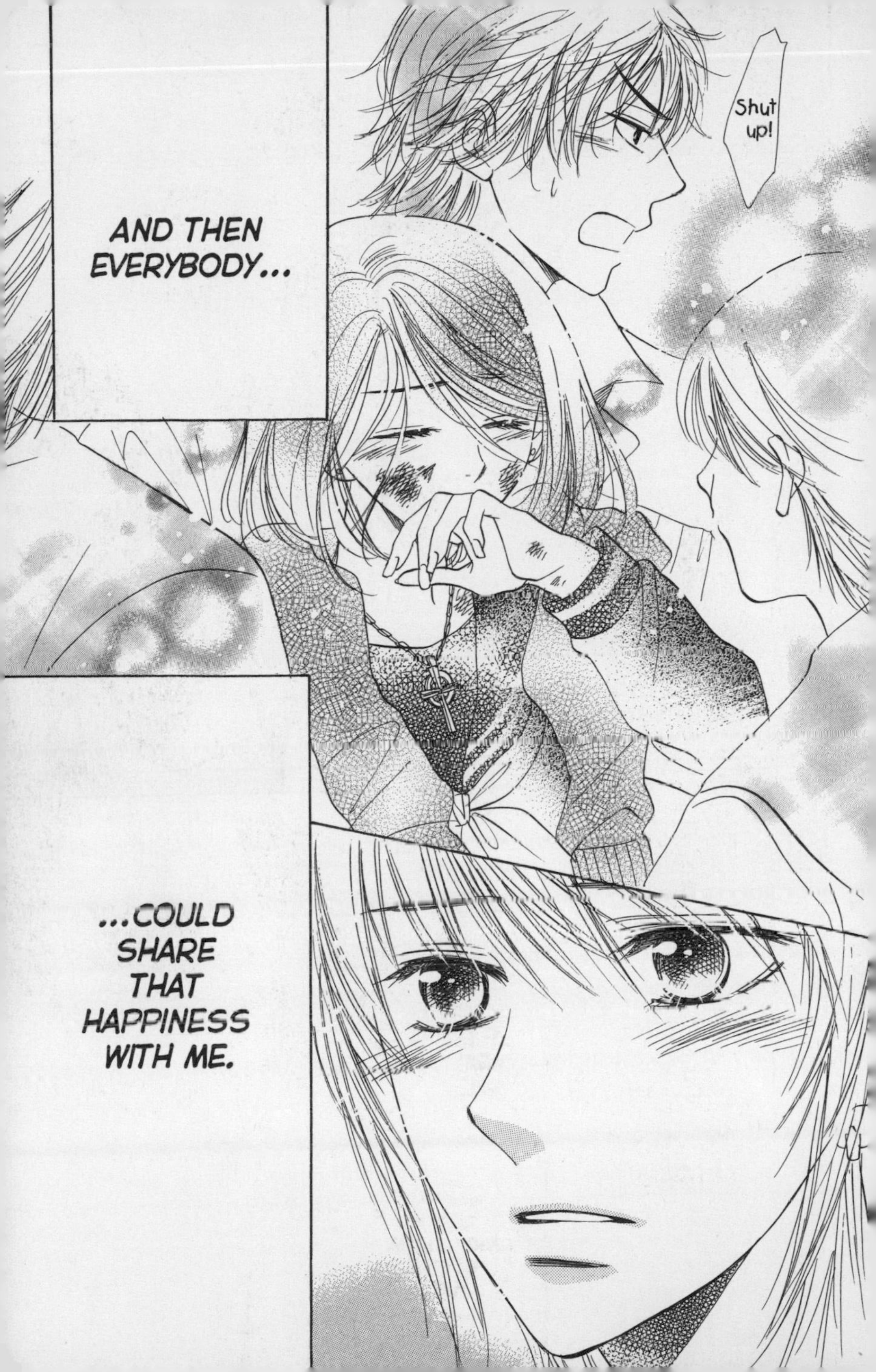
Shut up!
AND THEN EVERYBODY...
...COULD SHARE THAT HAPPINESS WITH ME.

Continued
in
volume 5

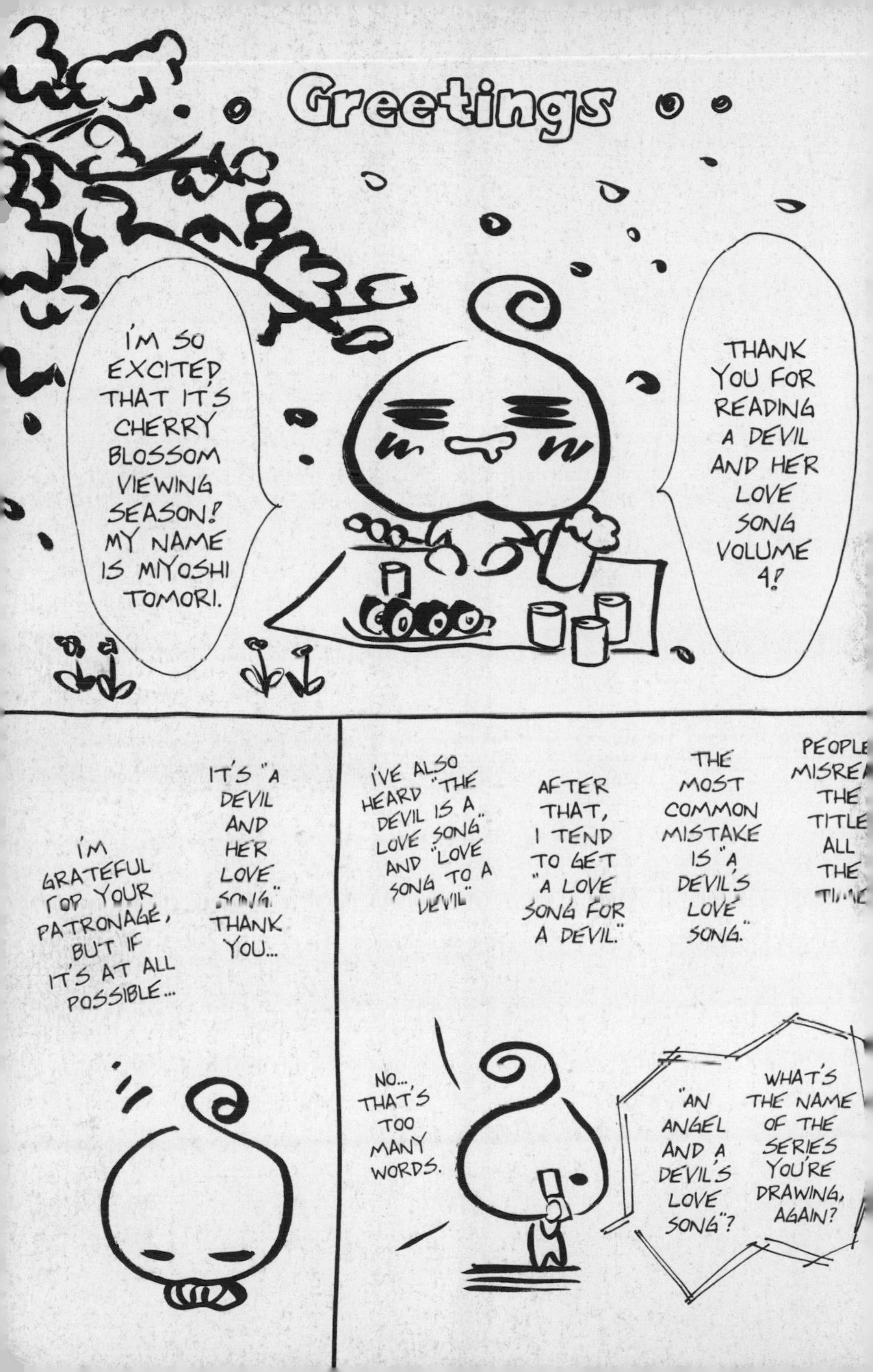
Greetings
THANK YOU FOR READING A DEVIL AND HER LOVE SONG VOLUME 4!
I'M SO EXCITED THAT IT'S CHERRY BLOSSOM VIEWING SEASON! MY NAME IS MIYOSHI TOMORI.
PEOPLE MISREA THE TITLE ALL THE
THE MOST COMMON MISTAKE IS "A DEVIL'S LOVE SONG."
AFTER THAT, I TEND TO GET "A LOVE SONG FOR A DEVIL."
I'VE ALSO HEARD "THE DEVIL IS A LOVE SONG" AND "LOVE SONG TO A DEVIL."
WHAT'S THE NAME OF THE SERIES YOU'RE DRAWING, AGAIN?
"AN ANGEL AND A DEVIL'S LOVE SONG"?
NO... THAT'S TOO MANY WORDS.
IT'S "A DEVIL AND HER LOVE SONG." THANK YOU...
I'M GRATEFUL FOR YOUR PATRONAGE, BUT IF IT'S AT ALL POSSIBLE...

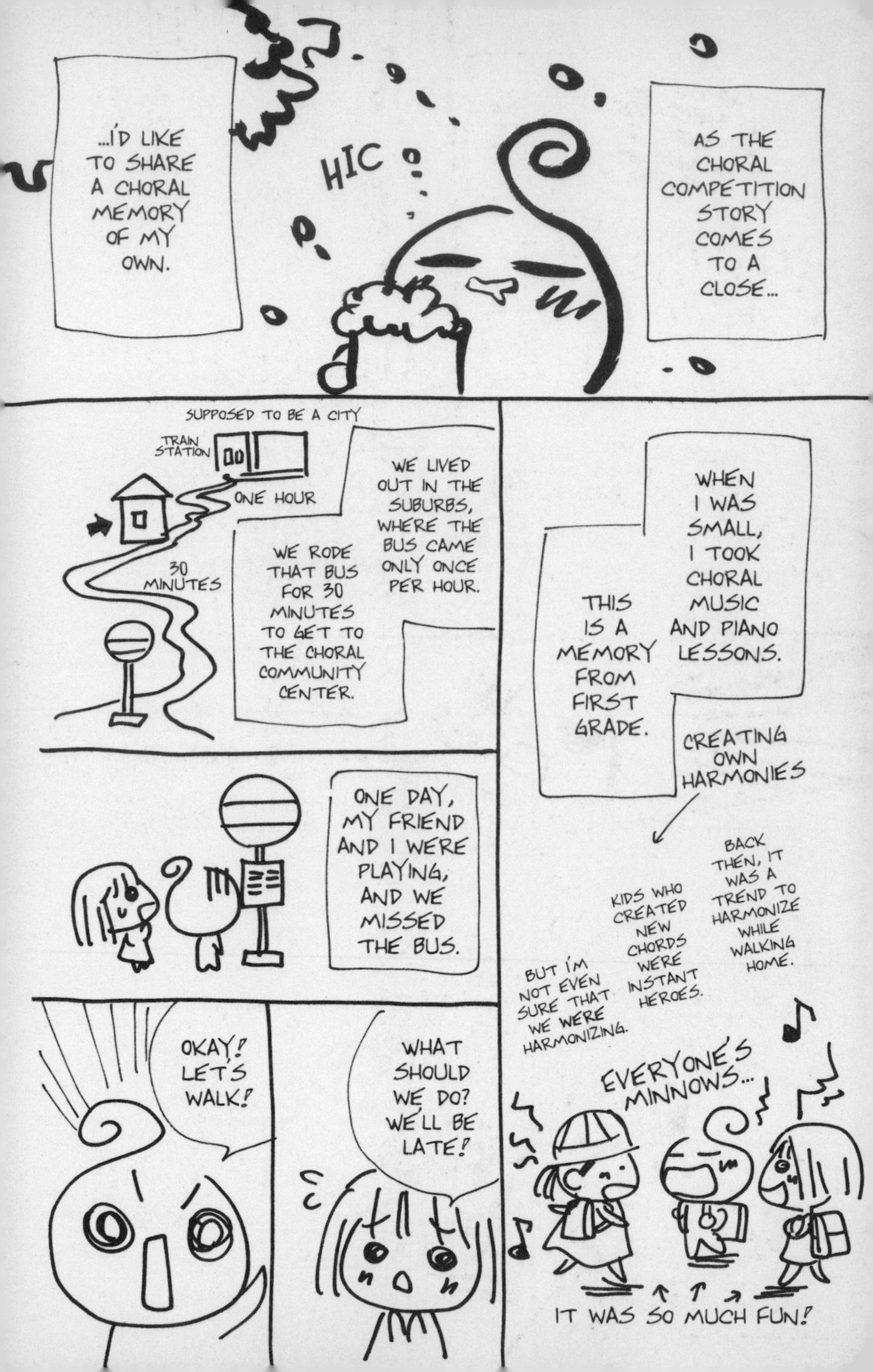

AS THE CHORAL COMPETITION STORY COMES TO A CLOSE...
HIC
...I'D LIKE TO SHARE A CHORAL MEMORY OF MY OWN.
WHEN I WAS SMALL, I TOOK CHORAL MUSIC AND PIANO LESSONS.
THIS IS A MEMORY FROM FIRST GRADE.
CREATING OWN HARMONIES
BACK THEN, IT WAS A TREND TO HARMONIZE WHILE WALKING HOME.
KIDS WHO CREATED NEW CHORDS WERE INSTANT HEROES.
BUT I'M NOT EVEN SURE THAT WE WERE HARMONIZING.
EVERYONE'S MINNOWS...
IT WAS SO MUCH FUN!
WE LIVED OUT IN THE SUBURBS, WHERE THE BUS CAME ONLY ONCE PER HOUR.
WE RODE THAT BUS FOR 30 MINUTES TO GET TO THE CHORAL COMMUNITY CENTER.
SUPPOSED TO BE A CITY
TRAIN STATION
ONE HOUR
30 MINUTES
ONE DAY, MY FRIEND AND I WERE PLAYING, AND WE MISSED THE BUS.
WHAT SHOULD WE DO? WE'LL BE LATE!
OKAY! LET'S WALK!

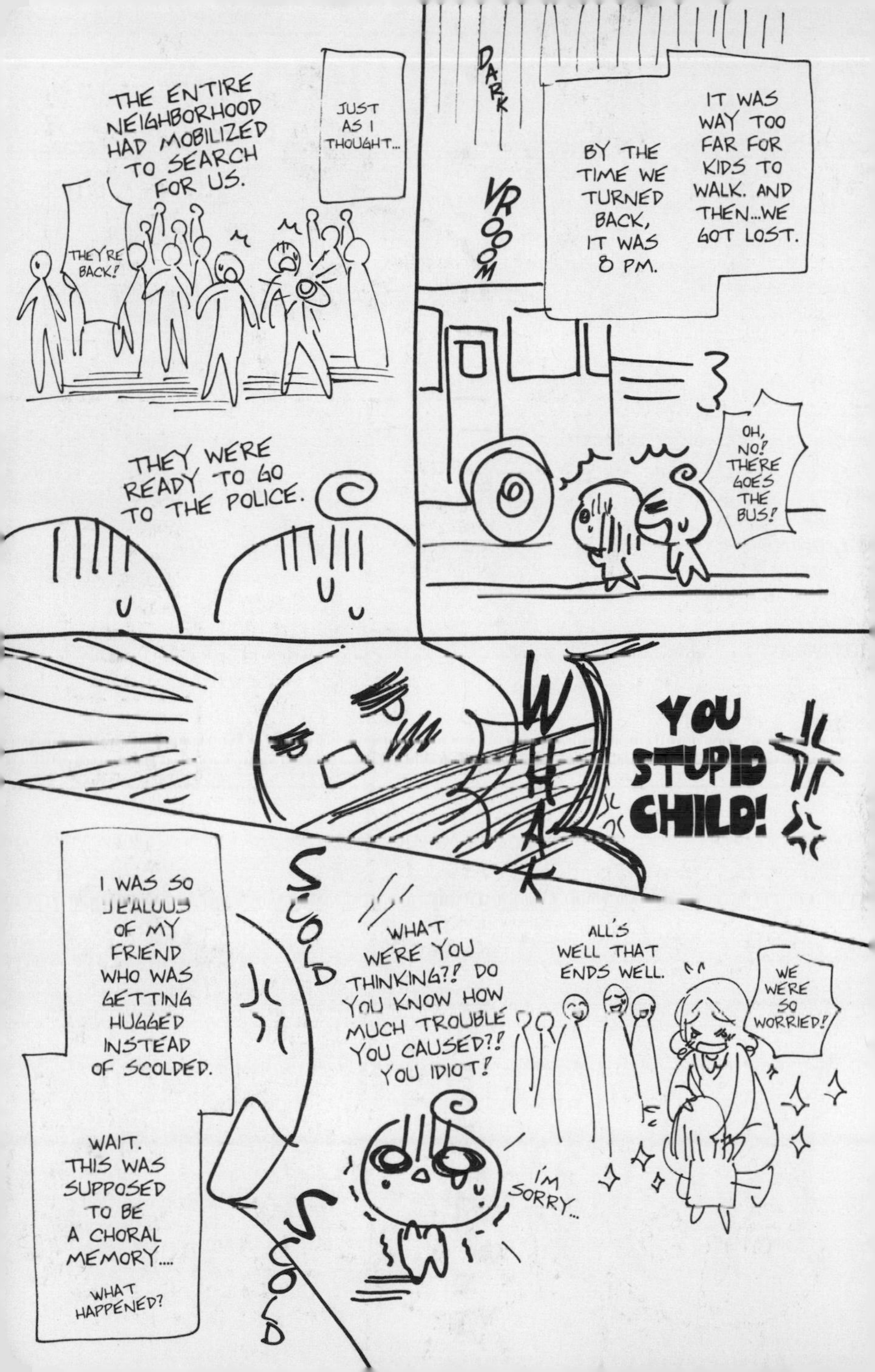
IT WAS WAY TOO FAR FOR KIDS TO WALK. AND THEN...WE GOT LOST.
BY THE TIME WE TURNED BACK, IT WAS 8 PM.
DARK
VROOOM
OH, NO! THERE GOES THE BUS!
JUST AS I THOUGHT...
THE ENTIRE NEIGHBORHOOD HAD MOBILIZED TO SEARCH FOR US.
THEY'RE BACK!
THEY WERE READY TO GO TO THE POLICE.
YOU STUPID CHILD!
WHAK
ALL'S WELL THAT ENDS WELL.
WE WERE SO WORRIED!
WHAT WERE YOU THINKING?! DO YOU KNOW HOW MUCH TROUBLE YOU CAUSED?! YOU IDIOT!
SCOLD
SCOLD
I'M SORRY...
I WAS SO JEALOUS OF MY FRIEND WHO WAS GETTING HUGGED INSTEAD OF SCOLDED.
WAIT. THIS WAS SUPPOSED TO BE A CHORAL MEMORY....
WHAT HAPPENED?

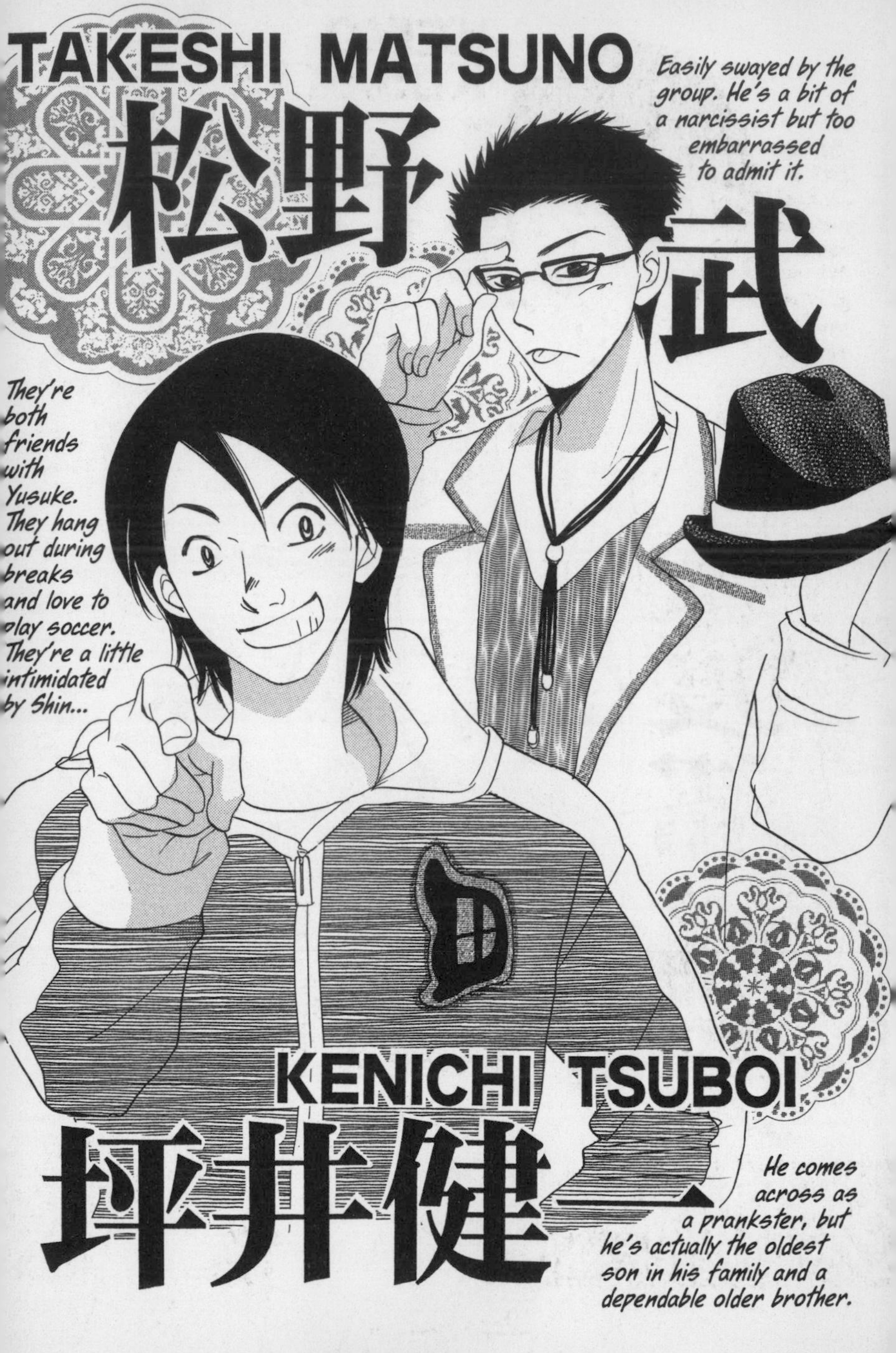
TAKESHI MATSUNO
松野武
Easily swayed by the group. He's a bit of a narcissist but too embarrassed to admit it.
They're both friends with Yusuke. They hang out during breaks and love to play soccer. They're a little intimidated by Shin...
KENICHI TSUBOI
坪井健一
He comes across as a prankster, but he's actually the oldest son in his family and a dependable older brother.

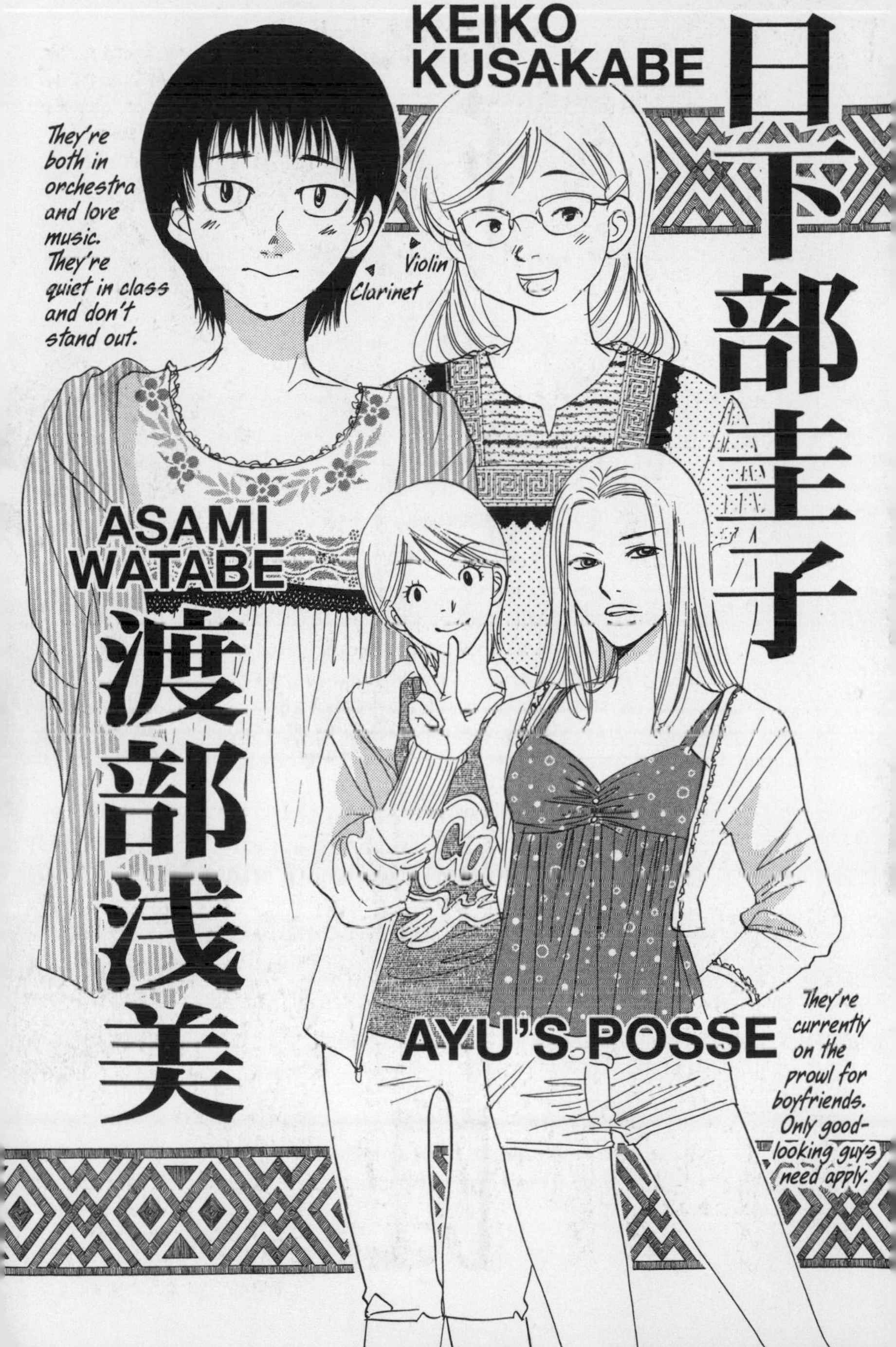
KEIKO KUSAKABE
日下部圭子
Violin
Clarinet
They're both in orchestra and love music. They're quiet in class and don't stand out.
ASAMI WATABE
渡部浅美
AYU'S POSSE
They're currently on the prowl for boyfriends. Only good-looking guys need apply.

I have a dilemma every year: Cherry blossom-viewing season and allergy season arrive at about the same time. Up until now, my allergies weren't bad enough to stop me from drinking sake under the lovely cherry blossoms, but this year, I was tearing up and sneezing so badly, I could hardly breathe... Has my body finally succumbed to hay fever? But I'm still not ready to give up my annual ritual of drinking under the cherry blossom trees...

-Miyoshi Tomori

Miyoshi Tomori made her debut as a manga creator in 2001, and her previous titles include *Hatsukare* (First Boyfriend), *Tongari Root* (Square Root), and *Brass Love!!* In her spare time she likes listening to music in the bath and playing musical instruments.

A DEVIL AND HER LOVE SONG

Volume 4

Shojo Beat Edition

STORY AND ART BY
MIYOSHI TOMORI

English Adaptation/Ysabet MacFarlane
Translation/JN Productions
Touch-up Art & Lettering/Monalisa de Asis
Cover Design/Yukiko Whitley
Interior Design/Courtney Utt
Editor/Amy Yu

Printed in the U.S.A.

Published by VIZ Media, LLC
P.O. Box 77010
San Francisco, CA 94107

10 9 8 7 6 5 4 3 2 1
First printing, August 2012

viz media
www.viz.com
Shojo Beat
www.shojobeat.com

RATED T FOR TEEN

PARENTAL ADVISORY
A DEVIL AND HER LOVE SONG is rated T for Teen and is recommended for ages 13 and up. This volume contains suggestive themes.

ratings.viz.com